INTRODUCTION TO
WORLD RELIGIONS

INTRODUCTION TO
WORLD RELIGIONS

COMMUNITIES AND CULTURES

EDITED BY

JACOB NEUSNER

ABINGDON PRESS

Nashville

Library of Congress Cataloging-in-Publication Data

Introduction to world religions : communities and cultures / edited by Jacob Neusner.
   p. cm.
Includes bibliographical references.
ISBN 978-0-687-66000-1 (pbk. : alk. paper)
1. Religions. I. Neusner, Jacob, 1932–
BL80.3.I59 2010
200—dc22

2009053600

10 11 12 13 14 15 16 17 18 19—10 9 8 7 6 5 4 3 2 1

MANUFACTURED IN THE UNITED STATES OF AMERICA

CONTENTS

Introduction
A "Humanly Relevant" Cosmos: What We Study
When We Study Religion vii
William Scott Green

1. Judaism
• Judaism: Beginnings 1
  Baruch A. Levine
• The Formation 21
  Jacob Neusner
• Judaism in Modern Times: Reform, Orthodox, and
  Conservative Judaism; Zionism 37
  Jacob Neusner

2. Christianity
• Christianity: Beginnings 51
  Bruce Chilton
• Roman Catholicism 67
  Lawrence S. Cunningham
• Orthodox Christianity 85
  J. A. McGuckin
• Protestantism 101
  Martin E. Marty

3. Islam
• Islam: Beginnings 119
  Th. Emil Homerin
• The Shi'i Tradition 133
  Liyakat Takim
• The Sunni Tradition 149
  Th. Emil Homerin

CONTENTS

4. Hinduism 163
   Douglas Brooks

5. Buddhism
   • Buddhism: Beginnings 181
   Mario Poceski
   • The Theravada Tradition 197
   Kristin Scheible
   • The Mahayana Tradition 215
   Mark L. Blum

6. Daoism 233
   Mark Meulenbeld

7. Confucianism 251
   Mark A. Csikszentmihalyi

8. Shinto 265
   James L. Ford

9. Indigenous Religions
   • Indigenous Religious Tradition 283
   Jualynne E. Dodson and Sonya Maria Johnson
   • African Indigenous Religions 291
   Jacob Olupona

10. New Nineteenth-century American Religions 309
    Danny L. Jorgensen

11. New Twentieth-century American Religions 327
    Dell deChant

Contributors 345

Notes 347

INTRODUCTION
A "HUMANLY RELEVANT" COSMOS: WHAT WE STUDY WHEN WE STUDY RELIGION

William Scott Green

Religion is a powerful force in contemporary life. It both unites nations and divides peoples. It both teaches charity and generates suspicion. It both offers solace and causes anxiety. It provides hope and inspires fear. It promotes human rights and preserves social inequity. It advances social justice and obstructs social mobility. It calls for peace and causes war. It preaches love and breeds intolerance. Americans in particular think religion is a significant part of human experience. Because religion is so consequential, it also is controversial. Some see it as a destructive delusion,[1] and others as a mode of evolutionary adaptation.[2] We study religion to make sense of all this to understand what religions advocate, what religious people do, why they do it, and why it matters. In doing so, we use disciplined investigation to find the rationality—or irrationality—in what religions teach and how their adherents behave. We will look at these issues in the rest of this introduction.

Why Religion Matters

Religion matters for two reasons. First, globally, religion is an increasingly important part of contemporary life. Second, religion is a basic element in American politics, society, and culture. Let us take these up in turn.

Contemporary research shows that in the past thirty or forty years, religion has grown significantly in the world's cultures.[3] Consider the following data:

- "The world's largest religions have expanded at a rate that exceeds that of global population growth."[4]
- "A greater proportion of the world's population adhered to *each* of" the religious systems of Catholicism, Protestantism, Islam, and Hinduism "in 2000 than in 1900."[5]
- "The overwhelming preponderance of this growth occurred between... 1970 and 2000."[6]
- More people in the world hold "traditional religious beliefs" than ever before.[7]
- "Today religion is the most common source of civil wars currently raging.... Since 2000, fully 47 percent of civil wars have been religious."[8]
- "Religious ideology is the leading motivator for most translational terrorist attacks, particularly but not exclusively those committed by al Qaeda."[9]
- Religion's influence appears to increase with democracy and democratization.[10]
- "Far from stamping out religion, modernization has spawned a new generation of say, organizationally sophisticated, and technologically adept religious movements."[11]
- The new religious movements are "politically capable."[12]

These data show the expanding influence of religion in the world's population and emphasize its impact on world politics. The correlation of religion's growth with the "economic and political modernization"[13] of the past three or four decades suggests that religion will be significant in global life well into the future.

Why We Care about Religion

Even if religion were less important than it is in the contemporary world, it still would matter to Americans because the U.S. Constitution, in the First Amendment, mandates and privileges the category of religion. Indeed, religion may be the only field in the humanities whose subject matter is explicitly named and governed by the U.S. Constitution.

The First Amendment states: "Congress shall make no law respecting an establishment of religion, or prohibiting the free exercise thereof." It assumes that religion and government are different and distinct, and it sets religion apart as a particular kind or sphere of experience. In so doing, the First Amendment makes religion into a fundamental component of American life. Indeed, religion is so familiar in American discourse that it can be called a native category for Americans.[14] It is something we inherit as an assumed part of our national and personal lives. This does not mean that all Americans practice religion, but rather that religion is a culturally legitimate marker both of Americans' individual and national identities. Americans routinely define themselves in terms of being either religious or not religious. Because of the First Amendment, in America religion is—and historically has been—a matter of choice and therefore of fundamental freedom. American culture assumes that religion exists and that it matters enough to be protected from government imposition and government interference. The freedom of religion as expressed in the First Amendment shapes a distinctive context for the practice of religion, and this is one primary reason American colleges and universities teach and study religion as they do.

To say that religion is an American native category means that it is not a global one. Other nations, societies, or cultures do not necessarily have the term *religion* or use it as American culture does. But what we might call the American ethnocentrism of religion does not invalidate religion as a lens through which to make sense of human experience. So long as we remain aware that we use the term in a culturally specific way—that it is native to us but may be alien to others—we can draw analogies from our culture to others' to see which aspects of other cultures we might call "religion" in ours. In this way, the study of religion provides a mirror for American self-reflection and self-awareness.

What Religion Means

Now that we have an idea of why religion matters and why it is worthy of attention, we need to try to determine what it means. This introduction takes two approaches to this question. One is theoretical. It defines religion abstractly in terms of a set of intellectual suppositions. The second is more descriptive. It supplements the theoretical definition with, and assesses it against, some representative examples—ideas, practices, behaviors, and so on—drawn from well-known religions.

Our theoretical definition begins with some basic assumptions that are essential to studying religion rationally. First, the term *religion* refers to a human, this-worldly construction, something created and maintained by human beings. Second, the study of religion must be based on empirical evidence, on what we can see and observe. If we assume otherwise on these two points, then religion becomes by definition something uncanny and unseen, mysterious and indiscernible, and therefore unintelligible. Without putting religion into some kind of preliminary limiting framework, studying it risks becoming undisciplined, notional, and aimless. When we study religion we have to start somewhere, with the full awareness that, in accord with the process of reason, an initial definition is always provisional.

Religion Defined

Anthropologist Melford Spiro devised one established and particularly useful definition of religion. He defined *religion* as "an institution consisting of culturally patterned interaction with culturally postulated superhuman beings."[15] This scholarly and academic definition contains several important elements that help sketch out distinctive traits of religion.

First, it understands the distinguishing trait of religion to be "culturally postulated superhuman beings." This means that religion differs from politics or economics or philosophy because it has in it "superhuman beings." These are beings regarded as more powerful than humans. On their own, they are believed able to do things to and for humans that humans cannot do in return or unaided.

The variable of "superhuman beings"—in contrast to a religiously specific category like "faith," for instance—is primarily descriptive and reasonably neutral. Without imposing or presupposing too much of a Western or American system, we can observe empirically if a culture attributes greater than human powers to beings it regards as real. In this sense, the category "superhuman beings" usefully can be applied across cultures.

Second, the definition posits that the culture in which a religion exists shapes the kinds of superhuman beings a religion has and the way humans are to interact with those superhuman beings. Some cultures envision a pantheon, multiple superhuman beings with limited powers and spheres of action, while others suppose a single, unique superhuman being who is all-powerful. Superhuman beings might be deities, spirits, saints, deceased ancestors, or sages with extraordinary powers of discernment and understanding, to list a few more obvious examples.

Interaction with superhuman beings includes both behavior that reflects the "will or desire of the superhuman beings or powers" and behavior that "influence[s]" them to respond to humans' "needs."[16] It can take varied and nuanced forms: prayer, obedience, meditation, trances, veneration, imitation, consumption, textual study, healing, illness, fasting, asceticism, exorcism, pacifism, violence, and war, to name just a few. For some cultures—as in ancient Greece and Rome—it makes sense to think that humans can have sexual relations with superhuman beings; for others it does not. In some religions, humans interact by studying the teachings of superhuman beings; in others, the superhuman beings inhabit humans' bodies or speak directly to humans without mediation. Humans' interactions with superhuman beings are empirical. We can observe them in the ways human beings speak, dress, eat, do business, marry, and manage death, among other behaviors.

Third, the definition understands religion to be an institution, "an attribute of social groups, comprising part of their cultural heritage"; as such, "its beliefs are normative, its rituals collective, its values prescriptive."[17] On this account, religion is public rather than personal. Because religions are embedded in culture, institutional forms vary. Some religions are hierarchical, others more egalitarian. The social and cultural—in Spiro's terms, institutional—nature of religion means that religious speech and behavior are neither random nor arbitrary nor idiosyncratic. They have social meaning because they are pieces of a shared cluster of ideas and values. Thus, even intense individual religious experiences, such as trances and "speaking in tongues" (glossolalia), typically occur not in isolation but in community where they are recognized, understood, and validated.

Spiro's general definition provides an empirical framework for a disciplined comparison of multiple religions that can chart both similarity and difference. Although discrete cultures postulate superhuman beings, humans' patterned interaction with those beings can diverge—sometimes sharply—from culture to culture. Consider the example of men's head-covering in religious communities. In Judaism men are expected to cover their heads during prayer as a sign of respect to the deity. Many Jewish men wear a small skull-cap—called a *yarmulke* or *kippah*—throughout the day for the same purpose. Sikhism mandates that men cover their heads when they pray and when they engage with the Sikh scripture, the Guru Ganth. Many Sikh men also wear a turban in public as a mark of religious, cultural, or political identity.[18] In Islam, it is customary,[19] but not religiously mandated, that men wear headgear during worship, but some communities would be offended by a bareheaded male worshiper. In most forms of Christianity, however, men remove their hats as a sign of deference to the deity. The bareheadedness derives from the comments of the Apostle Paul in 1 Corinthians 11:4 that "a man who keeps his head covered when he prays or prophesies brings shame upon his head" (NEB).[20] To make matters a bit more complicated, some Roman Catholic clerics wear a skullcap, customarily called a *zucchetto,* as a sign of office—so the head-covering has institutional religious significance—but they remove it at various points during the Mass as a gesture of respect to God. Thus, men's head-covering in religious communities can have multiple meanings. Covering the head during worship can be a religious act. It also can be a gesture of humility or identity but not necessarily a religious practice. Covering the head during worship also can be an act of irreligion. Finally, both wearing and removing the head-covering can be religious acts. The framework of Spiro's definition helps us see difference despite similarity and illustrates how understanding specific religious practices requires knowledge of cultural patterns.

If we use Spiro's definition to study religions, we will pay attention to the concrete observable ways people relate to beings they regard as more powerful than themselves. We will ask how cultures construct their superhuman beings, how they instruct people to engage with them, and how that engagement is institutional.

Religion Described

Spiro's definition provides an analytical focus for understanding how religion works. The best way to use a definition, however, no matter how useful, is to read it together with empirical evidence to see both how well it distinguishes religion from other things and if and where it requires modification. To do that we can enrich the three foci of Spiro's definition—superhuman beings, interaction, and religion as an institution—with broadly conventional, mainstream, uncontroversial, and widely acknowledged examples of religion from Judaism, Christianity, Islam, Buddhism, and Hinduism.[21]

Superhuman Beings and the Normative Cosmos

In Spiro's definition, the difference between religion and other aspects of a culture is the postulation of superhuman beings, who are regarded as more powerful than human beings. This suggests that to understand a religion we will want to know how that religion conceives of the distribution of power between humans and superhumans. What does a religion claim are the limits of human activity in the world? Which capacities do humans not have that superhumans possess?

If we follow this line of questioning, then "superhuman beings" points to another characteristic. Religions certainly claim that there are superhuman beings, but they typically profess more than that. Judaism, Christianity, Islam, Hinduism, and Buddhism all aver that there is an order to existence—a reality, a set of life conditions and circumstances—that humans did not make and in principle cannot change. Superhuman beings normally play a role in bringing this order about or in discerning it, or both. This cosmic order constitutes the foundation and framework for human action in the world. Traditions in both the Hebrew Bible and the New Testament illustrate and capture the tone of the superhuman creation of the cosmic order. Consider the well-known first verses of the book of Genesis 1:1-5 (*TANAKH*):

> When God began to create heaven and earth—the earth being unformed and void, with darkness over the surface of the deep and a wind from God sweeping over the water—God said, "Let there be light"; and there was light. God saw that the light was good, and God separated the light from the darkness. God called the light Day, and the darkness He called Night. And there was evening and there was morning, a first day.

Or this passage from the Gospel of John 1:1-5 (NEB):

> When all things began, the Word already was. The Word dwelt with God, and what God was, the Word was. The Word, then, was with God at the beginning, and through him all things came to be; no

single thing was created without him. All that came to be was alive with life, and that life was the light of men. The light shines on in the dark, and the darkness has never quenched it.

In Islam, the first revelation received by the prophet Muhammad by God provides a succinct outline of the purpose of the Divine Creations (Qur'an 96:1-5):

Recite in the name of your Lord and Cherisher, Who created
Created man, out of a mere clot of congealed blood:
Recite! And your Lord is Most Bountiful
He Who taught the use of the Pen
Taught man that which he did not know.[22]

In the Hindu tradition, the Vedic hymn Rg Veda (10.90), grounds the system of social castes in the sacrificial act of a primordial being:

When they divided up the Man,
into how many parts did they divide him?
What did his mouth become: What his arms?
What are his legs called? What his feet?

His mouth became the brahmin; his arms
became the warrior-prince, his legs
the common man who plies his trade.
The lowly serf was born from his feet.[23]

These texts nowhere suggest that humans played any role in shaping the structure of reality. Human beings did not produce themselves; nor did they create light and darkness, time and space, day and night, or Brahmins and serfs. Humans did not vote these conditions into being, and they cannot vote them out of existence. Rather, the cosmos establishes the givens of existence and constitutes the prerequisites of human experience.

In religion, this cosmic structure is neither speculation nor conjecture nor provisional hypothesis. To the contrary, it is objective, factual, and true. More important, it is normative. It depicts not only how things are but also how things should be. Religion claims not only to account for this world as it is but also to perceive a structure beneath or beyond it. For instance, although the cosmos contains an array of animals and plants that humans can consume, some religions—Judaism, Hinduism, and Jainism, for example—prohibit the consumption of certain animals or plants on the grounds that eating them requires taking life or otherwise violates a deep cosmic structure. Religion's claim to know the normative structure of the cosmos shapes the character of religious behavior or at least the religious view of human behavior.

Interaction: Adhering to the Normative Cosmos

The core of religion is the human interaction with superhuman beings. These interactions are not arbitrary. Our definition stipulates that the broader culture shapes them. But another factor also applies. Religion is not merely operational. It also is purposive. Religion has goals to achieve, problems to solve, and the means to do both.

Religion operates on the assumption that humans on their own are, can be, or will be out of sync with the normative cosmic order and the superhuman beings who created, discovered, and understand it. Humans' incongruity with the cosmic order is the result either of humanity's willful intent, inherent weakness, human ignorance, or some combination of the three. Religion further claims to know how to correct and prevent this inconsonance. Religion expects human behavior—which includes attitudes as well as actions—to take the form of adherence, loyalty, fealty, devotion, or commitment to the cosmic order and conformity to its contours. It further supposes that there are serious negative consequences to humans' failure to do this and that only the religion can both explain those consequences and relieve them. Religions teach their adherents how the world should work, why it should work that way, what humans should do to live in accord with that normative structure, and what will happen to them if they do or do not do so.

A religion's knowledge of the normative nature and structure of the cosmic order is particular rather than generic. Since a religion's superhuman beings either created, discovered, or revealed that order, full and correct knowledge and understanding of it necessarily is highly specific, if not exclusive, to the religion itself. Discrete religions typically do not claim that people can randomly, accidentally, or independently acquire what the religion knows about how the universe works and how humans are to act in it. Buddhism does not teach that reading Shakespeare is the path to discovering the truth of the Buddha's teachings. Likewise, Christianity does not preach that learning computer software will demonstrate that Jesus of Nazareth is the Messiah. Each religion has its own particular sources of authority—texts, canons of scripture, revelations, sages, enlightened ones, prophets, chains of tradition, and so on—that reveal, transmit, and certify its privileged knowledge of the cosmic order. Even when religions exhibit awareness of and respect for one another—and many do—they typically do not suggest that their teachings lead to one another. Neither Judaism nor Buddhism, for instance, teaches that keeping kosher will lead one to achieve nirvana. The tendency toward exclusivity raises the stakes in religious teaching and, particularly when religion is entwined in politics, can impede interreligious communication and tolerance.

Religion assumes that only by adhering to the religion's own teachings, which entails proper interactions with its superhuman beings, can humans either repair a breach with the created order or prevent one from happening. Within religion, humans' interactions with the superhuman beings largely serve one of these two broad purposes.

The Comprehensiveness of Religion

Religion expects from its adherents—and teaches them how to achieve—cognitive recognition of, and behavioral conformity to, the cosmic order. Because of its cosmic orientation, religion is distinctively comprehensive in its scope. We can observe this trait in religion's tendency to totalize, to extend its reach. Religious teachings cover an astonishing range: cosmology (stories of the origin of the world), eschatology (stories of the end of the world), and theories of nature, birth, ethics, commerce, sexuality, suffering, and death. The most cursory perusal of the world's religions shows that there is almost no aspect of human activity—physical or mental—that religion does not touch. It emerges in the gamut of human expression: music, art, morality, intellect, ethics, sexuality, family, economics, education, politics, dress, food, and civility. Religions are full of instructions on what to wear, what to eat, whom to marry, how to do business, and so forth. Even the decision of some religions not to follow dress codes or observe food taboos is cast as made for religious reasons. For instance, the Gospel of Mark's announcement that Jesus "declared all foods clean" (7:19), makes unrestricted consumption into an act of religious principle. In a way that philosophy, politics, economics, or law does not and cannot, religion makes claims on the total human being.

Religion's comprehensiveness exceeds the worldly and the experiential. The religious cosmos includes a domain of space that humans occupy in this world and other realms of space beyond it, where superhuman beings reside. It also includes a dimension of time humans experience in this world and realms of time that both precede and follow this one.

These extraworldly realms of space and time are ordinarily invisible to humans, immune to unmediated mortal observation. Humans may see partial manifestations of these realms, but in general they are beyond routine human perception. In this respect, religious knowledge of superhuman beings differs from scientific knowledge. Scientific knowledge is based on repeatable empirical observation and is always provisional until better observations or explanations come along. By contrast, religious knowledge of superhuman beings is nonempirical, definitive, and absolute. Unlike atoms or parts of atoms, religion's superhuman beings are not material but minuscule; rather, they are immaterial and invisible. Unlike the subatomic particles or natural forces of the scientific cosmos, the superhuman beings of the religious cosmos are highly sentient. They are agents who act with purpose and respond—sometimes unpredictably—to human stimuli. The adherents of a religion know the superhuman beings are active because the privileged knowledge of their religion teaches them how to recognize a reality others cannot see. On their own, people cannot know whether a saint, a *jinn,* an angel, or a demon helped them. Only their religion can identify the superhuman agent, and that identification cannot be verified by any neutral or independent process. The proof of a religion's specialized claims about the cosmos comes from living them, not from a laboratory experiment.

Religion's comprehensiveness is temporal as well as spatial. Temporal limits define secularity. Lifetime ends with death. Extensive temporal limits—eternal or immortal—characterize religion. In some way, life continues after death. Judaism, Christianity, and Islam hold that there is resurrection of the dead. Hinduism and Buddhism, in different ways, subscribe to the doctrine of karma, or reincarnation. All these religions, with appropriate cultural variation, hold that one's life in this world is relevant to what happens after death.

To see concretely how religion's otherworldly framework shapes and motivates human behavior, consider the example of altruism, the act of serving others without benefit or at a cost to oneself. Altruism is deliberate action you perform for the sake of another person that produces either no benefit or a negative cost to you. The extreme form of altruism is self-sacrifice, giving up your life to save another, but there are countless other acts of kindness to others and care for others—the equivalent of helping older adults cross the street—that also seem to us altruistic. Perhaps because of its association with self-sacrifice, people often assume that altruism is a religious virtue. But religion's framework of eternity means that earthly experience is only a part of religion's realm. A loss in this world is not the end of the story. Compensation can come in the next world as well as, or instead of, in this one. Judaism, Christianity, Islam, Hinduism, and Buddhism all teach the value and practice of charity and beneficence. Consequently, at the very least they affirm—and must affirm—that their adherents will not suffer for following the religion's teachings, for doing what the superhuman beings commend. But religions are more ambitious than that. They typically claim that selfless action on behalf of others will be rewarded, either in this life or the next.[24] Religion's comprehensive compass means in principle and in practice that everything humans do can be religiously consequential.

Because religion covers the extended—if unobservable—realms of space and time, it can promise humans unique results. Religion not only understands the problem of human incongruity with the cosmos; it offers people an eternity—or at least extra time—in which to set things right. For example, an Islamic teaching holds that heaven and hell are permanent realms. After death, the angels Nakir and Munkar question the deceased in their graves. If one answers properly that there is only one God, and Muhammad is God's prophet, one experiences the reward of paradise in the grave. If one answers incorrectly, there is punishment in the grave. According to some reports of Muhammad's teaching (*hadith*), after the resurrection at the Final Judgment, God can still exempt people from the punishment of hell, and even an atom of faith can gain one entry into paradise.[25] This is a kind of promise no secular institution can make.

Religion as an Institution: System and Integration

Religion's power lies not only in its unusual comprehensiveness. It also has a distinctive capacity to integrate the realms of space, time, and world into a coherent structure. The discrete components of religion—myths; classifications of time, space, nature, and humanity; rituals; behavioral and food taboos; canons of scripture; nonscriptural traditions; ethics; customs; cosmologies; and eschatologies—in multiple ways reinforce one another. In Judaism, for example, the Sabbath commemorates God's creation of the world and would be meaningless otherwise. The elements of religion are not random collections. They are components of a system in which they are linked through a network of relationships that gives meaning to the system as a whole and its discrete parts as well.[26] By discerning those interrelationships, we understand how a religion works and gain insight into its rationality.[27]

An illustration of religion's integrative power is the Nicene Creed,[28] composed in the fourth century C.E. and recited in both Orthodox and Catholic liturgies:

We believe in one God, the Father, the Almighty, maker of heaven and earth, of all that is seen and unseen. We believe in one Lord, Jesus Christ, the only Son of God, eternally begotten of the Father, God from God, Light from Light, true God from true God, begotten, not made, one in being with the Father. Through Him all things were made. For us men and our salvation He came down from heaven: by the power of the Holy Spirit, He was born of the Virgin Mary, and became man. For our sake He was crucified under Pontius Pilate; He suffered, died, and was buried. On the third day He rose again in fulfillment of the scriptures: He ascended into heaven and is seated at the right hand of the Father. He will come again in glory to judge the living and the dead, and his kingdom will have no end. We believe in the Holy Spirit, the Lord, the giver of life, who proceeds from the Father and the Son. With the Father and the Son, He is worshiped and glorified. He has spoken through the Prophets. We believe in one, holy, catholic, and apostolic Church. We acknowledge one baptism for the forgiveness of sins. We look for the resurrection of the dead, and the life of the world to come. Amen.

All the elements of religion we have observed are evident in this creed. It tells us about the superhuman beings ("maker of heaven and earth," Father, Son, Holy Spirit, Virgin Mary), interactions with those beings (fulfillment of Scripture, baptism, worship, glorification), religion as an institution ("one, holy, catholic, and apostolic

Church"), realms of space ("all that is seen and unseen"), and realms of time ("resurrection of the dead" and "world to come").

In Islam, the *Arkan al-Islam,* the Five Pillars (or Foundations) of Islam, achieve the same result, though in a somewhat different way. The Five Pillars outline the basic obligations of all members of the Muslim religious community. They are present but not stated formulaically in the Qur'an, but do appear formulaically in the *hadith*—oral traditions assigned to Muhammad, his family, and companions—and in Islamic legal manuals. The Five Pillars are:

1. The *shahada* (profession of faith): "I bear witness that there is no god but God, and Muhammad is the Messenger of God." Adherents must recite this confession aloud once during their lifetime, with proper pronunciation and full cognitive awareness.
2. Prayer: the five daily prayers, recited facing the holy city of Mecca.
3. *Zakat*: the obligatory tax, used primarily to support the poor.
4. Fasting: the obligatory abstention from food, water, and sexual intercourse from dawn until dusk during the month of *Ramadan.*
5. The *hajj*: the pilgrimage to Mecca, to be made once in one's lifetime provided one is able to afford it.

The Five Pillars entail, but do not independently state, the articles of faith of the Islamic tradition. They are as follows:

- Belief in God's uniqueness (*tawhid*)
- Belief in the angels
- Belief in prophecy from Adam to Muhammad, who is the "Seal of the Prophets"
- Belief in revealed books (*Torat* of Moses, *Zabur* of David, *Injil* of Jesus, and the *Qur'an* of Muhammad)
- Belief in the Resurrection and the Day of Judgment
- *Qadr*: the measuring out of God's mercy, kindness, and testing of humanity

Together, the Five Pillars and the articles of faith integrate superhuman beings ("the uniqueness of God," Muhammad as the Seal of the Prophets, angels), interactions with those beings (profession of faith, prayer, tax, fasting, pilgrimage, God's mercy, kindness, and testing of humanity), religion as an institution (Mecca, revealed books), realms of space (the place of angels), and realms of time (resurrection). These components all reinforce one another so that the two sources combined produce a succinct and systemic account of Islam as a religion.

Diversity and Change within Religion

The recognition that religion is a system does not mean that religion is internally uniform, static, or monolithic. Not all adherents of a religion regard it with equal seriousness or necessarily take it seriously at all. Even if the superhuman beings are present at your wedding, you may not care that they are there.[29] Moreover, all religions exhibit a history of change and adaptation, and many have grown from one another. Christianity emerged from Judaism, and Islam uses elements common to both. Buddhism developed out of Hinduism. Within each of these discrete traditions, moreover, there are multiple divisions or denominations. To get a sense of the internal diversity, we merely have to list just some of the better-known divisional names in each religion: Christianity: Roman Catholic, Orthodox, Protestant, Evangelical, Pentecostal; Judaism: Reform, Orthodox, Conservative, Reconstructionist; Islam: Sunni, Shiite; Hinduism: Vaishnavah, Shaiva, Shakta; Buddhism: Nikaya, Mahayanaya, Vajrayana. To organize this diversity it might be useful to envision each of these traditions as a kind of religious family in which all members partake of a common system, structure, and heritage but understand it and adopt it in distinctive ways. Although the adherents of a religion cannot change the cosmic structure or the content of the religion's revealed truth or its privileged knowledge, they can and do interpret that legacy differently. Some of the major factors that affect these diverse interpretations are regional and tribal identities, immigration, political constraints (or the lack of them) on religion, religious pluralism, and issues of gender, social class, and ethnic heritage.

Religion as Transformative

It could reasonably be argued that religion's capacity to integrate and systematize its cosmic comprehensiveness gives it the pervasive pertinence in human life that other elements of culture do not have. Through this cosmic integration religion frees human existence from the vagaries of immediate experience. Because of its long view it anchors human experience in constancies, transcendences, and superstructures that help people know that they matter and that what they do has consequence. Religion marks off permanent structures in time and fixed orientations in space that together invest ordinary human conduct with overarching value.

The conception of religion as fealty to a transcendent cosmic order immune to human alteration is consistent with—and likely undergirds—the First Amendment's idea that religion and government are distinct realms of experience. Some of the differences between religion and secular law or politics underscore the plausibility of that judgment. Religion rewards proper attitude and action—in the routine aspects of life—as opposed to merely restraining or punishing improper behavior. Secular legal systems do not reward people for paying taxes, following the law, visiting the sick, being kind to others, and so on. Politics does not require adoption of a cosmology or an eschatology. In politics and law people simply have to give assent, or at least adapt, to the established political and legal order as the state defines it. Religion goes beyond that realm, and its rewards for and constraints on behavior are different from those of the state. The comprehensiveness of religion means that, unlike law or politics, religion is transformative, designed to create and develop a particular kind of humanity that reflects the unshakable structure of the cosmos. Religion is not simply about keeping the peace, but about creating, maintaining, and advancing a superstructure that brings distinctive meaning and purpose to human individual and collective experience. Religion's normative cosmic structure shapes and informs what humans do, and everything humans do can have cosmic implications. As Peter L. Berger says, "Religion is the audacious attempt to conceive of the entire universe as being humanly relevant."[30]

Religion Is Natural

In conceiving a "humanly relevant" cosmos, religion becomes a high-stakes enterprise. As such, it has promulgated ideas and practices of enormous insight and benefit to humanity, and it has generated extraordinary beauty in art and music. For the same reason, it also has caused misery, distrust, oppression, and death. Because of what it represents, people who accept religion are loath to give it up. Some are prepared to die, or to kill, in its name.

Behind religion's transformative impact is a critical and determinative fact. Religion is natural, an expression of our human character. Religion is a commonplace of humanity's past and a prevalent trait of humanity's global present. The First Amendment assumes the naturalness of religion and takes it as a given. Religion is historically pervasive and demographically inclusive. Throughout human history people of all types—rich, poor, educated, ignorant, smart, stupid—have made religion part of their lives. It probably does not overstate to suggest that historically religion is the norm in human experience and irreligion the exception. The more fantastic elements of religion—including but not limited to its postulated superhuman beings—certainly make it seem exotic, far-fetched, improbable, and odd, but in fact religion is a very conventional and ubiquitous piece of the mundane world it claims to transcend. As you work your way through this book, it is important to recognize that religion is as old and as consequential as any subject in the academy. Human beings have always been religious. How they have been, why they have been, and why it matters are what we study when we study religion. In the end, without the study of religion, we overlook in some very basic way an elemental part of our nature as humans and we cannot fully know either one another or ourselves.[31]

JUDAISM: BEGINNINGS

Baruch A. Levine

Religion of Ancient Israel

The Israelites of biblical times left us an exceptional narrative, the Hebrew Bible (the Old Testament), that relates how they came into being as a nation after taking possession of the promised land, governed themselves over a period of centuries, and survived empires. As part of that narrative, the Hebrew Bible projects the religion of the Israelites and describes it elaborately. The Hebrew Bible expounds on the will of the God of Israel by revealing God's plan for God's people, Israel, and for all humankind.

What is the religion's overriding concern? What makes the system self-evidently valid to the community of the faithful?

Biblical Conceptions of God

The national God of the ancient Israelites is most often designated in the Hebrew Bible by the Tetragrammaton Y-H-W-H, based on the verb *h-w-h*, "to be, exist"; in the causative stem, "to bring into existence," a meaning alluded to in the Hebrew Bible itself (Exod. 3:11-16). It is most often vocalized in the Hebrew Bible as `adonai, a form of the Hebrew `adon, "Lord." Whereas the cultural origin of the deity named Yahweh remains obscure, Hebrew inscriptions as early as the late ninth century B.C.E. and the famous Moabite-Mesha inscription from the mid-ninth century B.C.E. attest to the consonantal Y-H-W-H and its shorter forms.

1

The Israelite God-idea has evolved, expanding in response to new sociopolitical challenges. These challenges first came from the diversified population of Canaan, then from nearby nations, and finally from world empires. In this context, biblical attitudes toward Egypt are curious. Egypt was a major power in Canaan at various periods, and Egyptian expeditions traversed Canaan more than once. And yet, we find less anxiety about how Egypt might harm the Israelites and more concern over the danger of periodically relying on Egypt as an ally against Mesopotamian empires. One cannot escape the impression that the emphasis on the liberation from Egypt in biblical tradition bears a religious agenda, namely, that "the gods of Egypt" (Exod. 12:12) had been invalidated long ago, when Israel's God defeated them.

Other approaches to ancient Israelite religion tend to harmonize progressive biblical conceptions of Yahweh so as to represent universal monotheism as the original God-idea, often in cosmic terms that express age-old notions of heavenly sovereignty. So we read that Yahweh, Creator of the world and of humankind, revealed himself to the patriarchs, beginning with Abraham, later to Moses and the Israelites at Sinai and in the wilderness, and subsequently to the prophets. In contrast, critical approaches to biblical literature bring into bold relief statements about Yahweh that are better understood as henotheist, rather than as monotheist, strictly speaking. That is to say, such statements command the exclusive worship of Yahweh by all Israelites, going to great lengths to condemn paganism and idolatry, while at the same time acknowledging the existence and power of other gods worshiped by other nations. As the Israelite God-idea subsequently expanded, "oneness" came to mean that Yahweh was the only deity in all the earth (cf., Zech. 14:9).

Although the transition from henotheism to universal monotheism has been difficult to pinpoint, its clear footprints can be seen in late prophecy. Deutero-Isaiah of the Exile transmits Yahweh's declaration to Cyrus the Great: "I am Yahweh, and there is none other; except for me, there is no divine being [Hebrew `elōhîm]. I girded you with strength even though you do not acknowledge me, so that it may be known from the rising of the sun unto its setting that there is naught except for me. I am Yahweh and there is no other" (Isa. 45:5-6; this and all subsequent translations in this chapter are the author's own).

Returning to an earlier period of crisis, we perceive how First Isaiah had expounded the doctrine that Israel's God rules over all nations. This was after Jerusalem had been spared from destruction by Sennacherib, the Assyrian king who was Yahweh's "rod of rage" (Isa. 10:5-15) to punish Israel; but in time, Yahweh would bring down the arrogant conqueror. Endorsing the doctrine of submission to empires, Jeremiah, about a century later, referred to the Babylonian king Nebuchadnezzar II, who destroyed the Jerusalem Temple and exiled Judah, as Yahweh's "servant" (Jer. 25:9). In effect, First Isaiah's monotheist declaration introduced a new power concept, one that transcended military might and imperial power.

It is possible to identify three phases in the development of the Israelite God-idea: selective polytheism, Yahwist henotheism, and finally, universal monotheism.

(1) Selective polytheism. There is a fairly late tradition, preserved in Joshua 24, that the ancestors of the Israelites in Haran of Syria (Gen. 11:31) had worshiped "other gods." Of greater interest is the memory that the early Israelite settlers in Canaan proper, the patriarchs and the judges, had themselves once worshiped Yahweh, their national God, alongside familiar deities of the West Semitic pantheon, such as Baal, El, and probably a consort of Yahweh's named Asherah. We learn of this early phase primarily from biblical texts that raise objections to such practice, where both leaders and the people are admonished to worship Yahweh alone. However, there are nonjudgmental, neutral references as well. Thus, the patriarch Jacob worshiped El at Bethel (Gen. 31:13), and the Balaam orations credit El for the liberation from Egypt (Num. 23:8; 24:8). In contrast, the later poem in Deuteronomy 32 emphasizes that it was Yahweh alone who accomplished this feat: "Yahweh, alone, leads him on, and there is no other god at his side" (Deut. 32:12). Similarly, the Gideon narratives assure the hero that it is Yahweh who will bring Israel victory in battle, not Baal (Judg. 6). The confrontation between Elijah and the cult prophets of Baal epitomizes the henotheist commitment: "How long will you persist in straddling both of the hedges? If Yahweh is the [true] God, then follow him, and if it is Baal, follow him!" (1 Kings 18:21).

The prehenotheist mentality is also evident in early Hebrew epigraphy, such as in the inscriptions found at Kuntillet 'Ajrud, an ephemeral caravan site of the late ninth to early eighth centuries

B.C.E., on the southern border of Judah. These inscriptions include blessings in the name of Yahweh as well as hymns to Baal and El.

It may be that in the early stages of settlement it seemed that coexistence with the Canaanites and other elements of the population was possible, and this prospect induced a more relaxed religious policy. But many battles ensued with Egyptians and so-called Amorites, and with Canaanites and Philistines, as well as with neighboring nations in the interior such as Midianites, Ammonites, Edomites, and Aramaeans. These hostile encounters gave rise to a problematic situation: Israelites were, in fact, venerating some of the same gods that their fierce enemies were worshiping! The response of some of the religious leadership was to adopt an exclusionary policy, breaking away from the commonly shared West Semitic pantheon. One who reads Deuteronomy with this subject in mind will perceive the blatant connection between (a) enmity toward the Canaanite population and foreign nations, and (b) strict henotheism (see Deut. 7:1-11).

(2) **Yahwist henotheism.** The issue of the exclusive worship of Yahweh came to a head in the late ninth to early eighth century B.C.E., first in northern Israel, as First Hosea (Hos. 1–3) and the already cited Elijah episode in the Carmel range (1 Kings 18) both indicate. So long as the Israelites, north and south, were triumphant and reasonably secure, the promise of Yahweh, perceived as the national God, would have been fulfilled in principle, and the notion that Yahweh alone protected Israel would have retained credibility. This all changed, however, when the Neo-Assyrian Empire, under Tiglath-pileser III, followed by Sargon II and then Sennacherib, advanced on western Asia in repeated waves, beginning in the third quarter of the eighth century B.C.E. The Assyrians annexed northern Israel in 721 B.C.E., and in 701 B.C.E., after ravaging much of Judah, the Assyrian forces reached the gates of Jerusalem, as mentioned above. At this point, the henotheist God-idea would have lost its credibility because it could no longer account for Assyrian power, to which Judah had no effective military response.

(3) **Universal monotheism.** Against this historical background, the monotheist doctrine pronounced by First Isaiah is to be seen above all else as a response to empire. We note that in the history of religions there is often a lag between the promulgation of new doctrines and policies and their acceptance and implementation. There is

value, nevertheless, in tracing the origins of new ideas so as to understand the forces that produced them initially. Thus it was that for most of the following seventh century B.C.E. in Judah, the conflict between selective polytheism and Yahwist henotheism persisted under the less than devout Judean king, Manasseh. In the near-exilic period, under a more devout Judean king, Josiah, exclusive henotheism seems to have predominated in royal circles, as we may infer from the proliferation of Yahwistic names preserved on impressions of cylinder seals (objects known as "bullae"), which date from that period. And yet, Zedekiah's refusal to heed Jeremiah, and his decision to rebel against the Babylonians, suggests, among other things, that the doctrine of submission to empire had yet to override other strategic considerations. It was only during the Babylonian Exile, and afterward in the period of the return, that universal monotheism was fully endorsed by the Judean leadership whose horizons had, indeed, broadened as a consequence of dramatic historical experience. The people and their leaders were now dealing with world empires on a prolonged basis, so that when Cyrus the Great issued his edict in 538 B.C.E. allowing exiled Judeans to rebuild the Temple of Yahweh in Jerusalem, sufficient numbers of Jews ultimately maximized this opportunity.

In contradistinction to their developing God-idea, which was singular, the central concerns of the ancient Israelites were normal for a people in their circumstances. Most of all, they wanted collective security, victory over their enemies, and prosperity in the land for themselves and their "seed." We encounter in biblical literature a strong awareness on the part of the Israelites that they were immigrants in a land that had belonged to others and over which their hold was chronically threatened. The greatest blessing would be to produce generations of descendants who would inhabit the land in perpetuity. One can infer from the poignancy of this often expressed, fervent desire a deep apprehension on the part of the Israelites that they might not become "old timers" in the land (Deut. 25:1).

How do we know about this religion? What classics define the norms?

It is important to clarify that the religion of biblical Israel is nowhere practiced at the present time in all of its forms—by Jews or by others—although many of its major features survive to the present day. This situation is because the religion of biblical Israel was both nation bound and land bound. Only a people inhabiting its homeland could fulfill all of its performances and obey all of its commandments. The beginnings of what later became Rabbinic Judaism hark back to the period of the return after the Babylonian Exile (sixth to fifth centuries B.C.E.), when the national religion was being restructured to serve the needs of Diaspora Jewish communities as well as those of the restored communities in Jerusalem and Judea. Judaism taught fidelity to the revealed Torah, as it was interpreted. Jewish communities, wherever they lived, reaffirmed their identity as a people, with strict attention to their Israelite lineage. Furthermore, Judaism held to the biblical hope of national redemption through restoration to the land of Israel. For their part, Christianity, and later Islam, formed new polities and projected different eschatologies. It is most significant, nevertheless, that both Christianity and Islam continued to acknowledge the God of the biblical Israelites as the universal God. This is what makes it so important to treat the religion of biblical Israel under a separate heading, thereby directing our attention to the early emergence of universal monotheism, which constitutes its enduring, central idea. It was the capacity of the ancient Israelites to expand the God-idea in response to successive challenges that accounts for the survival of the religion of biblical Israel into late antiquity. The long-term result was that prophetic monotheism ultimately served as the common matrix of the three monotheistic world religions. Jews, Christians, and Muslims may all be identified as "the children of Abraham," after the biblical patriarch traditionally identified as the first monotheist.

Some "Need to Know" Background

Taken together, this evidence identifies the Israelites as a people composed of tribes and clans who first inhabited ancient Canaan, east of the Mediterranean, during the transitional period of Near Eastern history at the beginning of the Iron Age (ca. 1200 B.C.E.). The Israelites continued to inhabit this land throughout the Iron Age and thereafter, with some interruption and contraction. Determining the ultimate origins of the Israelites is currently an issue of scholarly debate. The approach taken here endorses the consistent biblical view that the Israelites were not native Canaanites. At the same time, it is conceded that their places of origin remain uncertain, as one may gather from differing traditions preserved in the Hebrew Bible itself. After gaining dominion over large parts of interior Canaan, the Israelites established two kingdoms—Judah and northern Israel, respectively—which, though they were separate and at times in conflict with each other, acknowledged their common Israelite lineage and identity. The Hebrew Bible records the brief existence of a united monarchy under David and Solomon, with its capital in Jerusalem. The kingdom of Judah retained its capital in Jerusalem, whereas the capital of northern Israel shifted.

The Israelites were eventually exiled from their promised land in two principal waves: first by the Assyrians in the last quarter of the eighth century B.C.E., when they annexed the northern kingdom, and then in the early sixth century B.C.E. at the hand of the Babylonians under Nebuchadnezzar II. Judeans later returned in sufficient numbers to reconstitute their life as a temple-centered community in Jerusalem and Judea under Persian imperial rule (538–332 B.C.E.), and to persevere in a similar mode under the Seleucids and early Romans. As prophecy gave way to apocalypse, there was considerable literary creativity under the Seleucids, some of it associated with the Maccabean revolt (167–164) and its long-term consequences.

The Hebrew Bible provides various self-identifications of the ancient Israelites. Two terms of reference are particularly informative in this regard: (1) Hebrew 'am, "people," is a kinship term. It configures the entire Israelite people as one large family descended from common ancestors, most notably the patriarchs Abraham, Isaac, and Jacob. In the human-divine encounter, Israel is seen as God's own family, his 'am (Exod. 3:10; 33:13). (2) Hebrew gôy, "nation," bears a territorial connotation, reflecting the reality that the Israelites possessed a land of their own (Gen. 12:1-2). Implicitly, the Israelites were an 'am from the outset, but only later became a gôy. As the Hebrew Bible tells it, monarchic government emerged as a concession to the unavoidable need for further political development (1 Sam. 8; Deut. 17:8-20). Prior to that, the 'am was governed by various types of leaders, mostly tribal or military, as for example the charismatic judges. In sociological terms, Israelite societies throughout the biblical period were predominantly patriarchal, with inheritance descending down through the male line. The status of women was generally subordinate to that of men, especially in the public domain, which is not to say that women were without considerable authority in the domestic household. In recent decades, feminist biblical scholarship has pioneered, with mixed results, a reassessment of the role of women, revealing some of the stratifying consequences of patriarchy that were either overlooked or unacknowledged in earlier scholarship.

What is the community of the faithful called? What story explains its traits?

The Will of the God of Israel for Israel, God's People

Prophets, priests, and wise teachers informed the Israelites of what it was that Yahweh demanded of them. Biblical chronicles and narratives, epic poetry, and Torah commandments often memorialize dramatic moments in Israelite history—liberation from Egyptian bondage, the formative theophany at Sinai, attainment of sovereignty in the promised land, and much more. Some of the most concise statements on the subject of God's will are associated with God's covenant, a contractual treaty enacted between Yahweh and Israel, of which there are several versions preserved in the Hebrew Bible. Fulfillment of the articles of the covenant on Israel's part will assure the realization of God's blessings and promises, whereas their violation will bring divine punishment.

Two principal objectives inform biblical declarations of God's will: the pursuit of justice and kindness, mostly emphasized by the prophets, and the pursuit of holiness, mostly emphasized by the priests. The prophets of Israel were singularly vocal in their critique of cult and ritual, and insisted on the primacy of the moral order. This does not mean that they negated the importance of holiness. What we observe in biblical statements on the subject of God's will is the attribution of the moral imperative to the God of Israel who is the supreme judge. In Israelite prophecy and law it is the God of Israel who commands the entire people directly—not only through their kings—to pursue justice and to act with kindness. The pursuit of justice is hardly unique to ancient Israel, but this objective is dramatically affirmed in biblical religion. Thus, Micah 6:6-8:

> With what shall I come before Yahweh,
>   prostrate myself before God on high?
> Shall I come before him with burnt offerings,
>   bearing yearling bull-calves?
> Would Yahweh be pleased with thousands of rams,

with myriad streams of oil?
Shall I hand over my firstborn for my offense,
   the fruit of my loins for my personal sin?
He has told you, O human, what is good,
   and what Yahweh demands from you:
It is none other than to act justly,
   and act with loving kindness,
behaving with humility in the presence of your God.

Two critical terms of extensive usage inform this prophetic oracle: *mispat*, "justice," and *hesed*, "kindness." When it came to defining the objectives of religious life within Israelite society and internationally, the prophets went beyond cultic fidelity to embrace a vision of justice and peace on an international scale. The interaction of the ethical and the ritual is most clearly evident in First Isaiah's admonition to the citizens of Jerusalem:

Cleanse yourselves; become purified!
   Remove your evil acts from before my eyes!
Cease to do evil; learn to do good!
   Demand justice; support the oppressed.
Seek justice for the orphan; take up the case of the widow.
(Isa. 1:16-17)

What is most revealing in this prophecy is the notion of moral purification. The same recasting of ritual in ethical terms informs Psalm 15, a rite of entry into the sanctified Temple:

Who may reside in your tent?
   Who may dwell on your holy mountain?
One who behaves guiltlessly and acts justly,
   and whose inward intentions are truthful. (cf. Ps. 24)

It is important to emphasize that the prophetic voice resounds in Torah law, including the priestly writings; there was no dichotomy between priest and prophet. In this connection, it would be well to examine the terms of the renewable covenant (Hebrew *berît*) between Yahweh and Israel. The formative event was the theophany at Mount Sinai in the days of Moses, following the Exodus from Egypt. Thus, Exodus 19:5-6, where Yahweh addresses the entire people assembled: "Now then, if you heed my voice and keep my

9

covenant you will be my treasured possession among all the peoples. Indeed, all the earth is mine, but you shall be my kingdom of priests and holy nation [gôy qādôs]."

The term qādôs, "holy," and related forms of the same verb were common to priests, prophets, and lawgivers, epitomized in the composite persona of Moses. He was prophet, lawgiver, and leader. In the chapters of Exodus we find codes of law and religious practice, including the Decalogue, which represent the substance of the covenant obligations. In Exodus 34:10 we read Yahweh's statement to Moses affirming Yahweh's covenant with Israel: "Then he [Yahweh] said: Behold! I am enacting a covenant in the presence of your entire people. I shall perform miracles the likes of which were never created in all the earth, nor among all the nations, so that the entire people among whom you live may behold the works of Yahweh which I am performing for you."

We find a similar sequence in Deuteronomy, where we note that in advance of a code of law there is a statement on covenantal responsibility. Thus Moses, addressing the people at Mount Horeb, another name for Mount Sinai, in Deuteronomy 5:1-3:

> Then Moses summoned all of the Israelites and said to them: Heed, O Israel, all of the statutes and judgments, which I am communicating to you this day. Study them and keep them by performing them. Yahweh our God enacted a covenant with us at Horeb. It was not with our ancestors alone that Yahweh enacted this covenant, but rather with us, we who are here today, all of us alive.

Soon after, we encounter a slightly variant edition of the Decalogue, and subsequently, the full Deuteronomic law code (Deut. 12–27). In both Exodus and Deuteronomy what we would term ethical laws mix freely with ritual duties, foremost among them the exclusive worship of Yahweh, God of Israel, and the avoidance of idolatry and paganism. A third priestly law code is preserved in Leviticus 19, which qualifies as a "mini-Torah," paraphrasing at least six of the Ten Commandments:

• "You shall be holy, for I, Yahweh, your God, am holy."
• respect for both parents; observance of the Sabbath
• prohibition of idolatry and certain forms of magic and divination
• leaving gleanings for the needy

- prohibition of fraud and dishonesty; just prosecution of the law
- prohibition of enmity; "Love your neighbor as yourself."
- offerings from the fruit of trees; prohibition against consuming blood
- respect for a woman pledged in marriage to another

What is the way of life of the community of the faithful? What are the rules of conduct? How does the way of life embody the story that this religion tells about itself?

The People of Israel and Yahweh's Design for Humankind

In the Hebrew Bible we observe a progressive tension between the expansion of sociopolitical horizons to international dimensions and a decided domestic retrenchment, as if the biblical exponents were looking inward and outward at the same time. Internally, the observance of religion, viewed as indispensable to the survival of the group, became more particularistic in the course of the biblical period, especially after the Exile, whereas social visions of the future and of Israel's place in the world order became universalistic.

The dynamic of the ongoing biblical dialogue between Israel and its God is that Israel must keep on working to establish a just and caring society, and remain true to its religious faith. The progression from henotheism to universal monotheism parallels the expansion of social horizons. Whereas henotheism aimed to consolidate the model nation, monotheism aimed to make its religious doctrine universal both in order to save that nation and to redeem the world of nations. In First Isaiah's words, the downfall of the Assyrian Empire was Yahweh's *'ēṣāh*, "plan, design," for all the earth (Isa. 14:26), and this theme was reapplied to subsequent empires that the people of Israel were to encounter. After condemning the failure of contemporary Jerusalem to fulfill its covenant with the God of Israel, as declared in chapter 1, the book of Isaiah follows up in chapter 2 with a vision of the ideal Jerusalem in global perspective:

> In the days to come, the mountain of Yahweh's Temple
> shall stand firm above the mountains,
> and tower above the hills.
> And all the nations shall gaze upon it with joy.
> And many peoples shall go and say:

11

"Come! Let us ascend to the mountain of Yahweh,
to the Temple of the God of Jacob;
   that he may instruct us in his ways,
so that we follow in his paths."
   For instruction shall come forth from Zion,
and the dictate of Yahweh from Jerusalem.
   He will judge between nations,
and reconcile conflicts for many peoples;
   they will beat their swords into ploughshares,
and their spears into pruning hooks.
   For one nation will not take up the sword against another,
nor will they even again train for war. (Isa. 2:2-4)

Experiencing Religion in Biblical Times

Most religions are best known by their practices, so that it would be well to briefly describe the experiencing and celebration of Israelite religion. In pursuit of the divine presence, temples and other smaller installations such as altars and *bamot* ("cult platforms") were erected at towns and settlements in various parts of the land where the structures, furnishings, and the space they occupied were ritually consecrated. It is this dynamic that accounts for the purification rites intended to insulate sacred space from defilement and contamination. By extension, priests and other cultic personnel were obliged to maintain a pure state of being, a norm applied as well to foodstuffs offered as sacrifices. Impurity present anywhere in the immediate community affected the cultic fitness of sanctuaries. The God of Israel demanded a sacred terrestrial environment or else he would withdraw his presence, thereby depriving the human community of ready access to his power. It is true that the God of Israel was believed to be omnipresent, as we read in Psalm 145:18: "Yahweh is near to all who call upon him; to all who call upon him truthfully." However, this assurance was apparently inadequate to alleviate human insecurity.

The sacrificial cult of Yahweh was aniconic from the outset, and pictorial representation of the deity was strongly opposed. Aniconism is not synonymous with henotheism or monotheism, but it is exceptionally compatible with these religious outlooks. An invisible deity would be less likely to be identified with—or limited to any particular power—in heaven or on earth, and this conception readily allowed for expansion of the God-idea. Though we know of other aniconic cults, the most famous being the Egyptian cult of Aten the sun god, practiced by Akhenaten, most ancient Near Eastern cults placed images and other graphic representations at cult sites, effectively making these images objects of worship. By eliminating images and other representations of the divine from their cult sites, Israelites would be more likely to avoid pagan worship altogether. Thus it is that biblical prohibitions of idolatry are invariably associated with the worship of "other gods," to employ the language of the Decalogue. The irrepressible urge to pictorialize or even symbolize the deity was driven by the primal human need for evidence of the divine presence. This mind-set is dramatized in the saga of Moses' ascent to the summit of Mount Sinai, when the people demanded to have a deity who was visible and close at hand. That episode resulted in the fashioning of the golden bull-calf, a known representation of the deity El, after whom the Israelites went astray (Exod. 32).

What we observe in biblical depictions of the God of Israel is a tendency to stop just short of pictorializing while yet avoiding it! In Isaiah's vision of the heavenly throne room (Isa. 6), there is no image, only "presence," alluded to by mention of Yahweh's robes. Cherubim proclaim Yahweh's great power as they hover over his throne on which an invisible deity is seated. Closer to an anthropomorphic conception is Ezekiel's vision of God's throne (Ezek. 1:26-28), as the prophet beheld "a likeness resembling a human form." At one point the Torah states that Moses was unique in that "he beholds the likeness of Yahweh" (Num. 12:8). It is abundantly clear, however, that the God of Israel had no desire to be represented graphically. In a sense, the human being represents the deity; the human was formed in the image of God (Gen. 1:26-27), a form conveyed by Hebrew ṣelem, "image," elsewhere a term for "idol" (Num. 38:52; 1 Sam. 6:5, 11; Amos 5:26). All who beheld the human creation would be reminded of the Creator.

What, then, if not cult images, was to be found in a proper Israelite cult site? The Hebrew Bible, in 1 Kings 6–8, describes the first Temple of Jerusalem as a roofed and walled edifice standing within a larger compound with a courtyard. The architecture and choreography of the compound reflected graduated sanctity, which was highest in the inner sanctum. We know this from restrictions of access according to which only sanctified priests were allowed entry into the Temple proper. In the tabernacle texts of the Pentateuch (Exod. 25–30; 33–40; Lev. 8–9; Num. 1–4) we also find descriptions embodying the same conception, but applied to a tentlike structure said to have been constructed in the wilderness environment during the days of Moses. According to priestly tradition the cult of Yahweh was formally initiated at that time. Information on the second Temple of Jerusalem is scattered throughout the later books of the Hebrew Bible and in apocryphal literature.

We normally have various furnishings, including the seven-branched candelabra known as the menorah, and an outdoor altar of burnt offerings. According to biblical traditions, the ark of the covenant was installed in the inner sanctum of the first Temple, but was absent from the second Temple. There was also an incense altar inside the Temple building. In earlier periods it was customary to find a cultic stele, called *maṣṣēbāh,* variously located, but in the course of time it was outlawed (Deut. 16:22). Archaeologists have unearthed a small Judean cult site at Arad in the Negeb where a *maṣṣēbāh* stood near the altar, and numerous stele have been found at other sites. There is also mention in biblical sources of the practice of positioning an Asherah, either a post or a representation of a tree, near a Yahwist altar, leading scholars to conclude that this object represented Yahweh's consort. In time, this practice was also prohibited (Deut. 16:21).

The principal act of worship in ancient Israel, as elsewhere in the ancient Near East, was sacrifice. Prayer, though an important component of Israelite worship collectively and individually, was not a sufficient mode of worship in and of itself, as it was to become in later Judaism. The primary objective of sacrificial worship was to invite or attract the deity to the human community, and once he was present, to retain his nearness. A sacrifice was essentially a gift to the deity, either voluntary or mandated, in return for which the recipient deity would hear the supplications of his people, grant them blessings, and join with them in a sacred meal known in Hebrew as *zebaḥ.* This cultic relationship is variously referred to as "communion" or "fellowship," and the relevant sacrifice was partially consumed by the altar fire and partially cooked and eaten as a meal. Sacrifice took other forms as well, most notably the *'olah,* "burnt offering," which the altar fire totally consumed and which grew in importance over the centuries. Special sacrifices were mandated in expiation of specific offenses and as such were part of the purificatory process. At both the first and second Temples of Jerusalem the public cult took place daily, with offerings in the morning and in the afternoon, with incremental features being introduced in the second Temple. Additional offerings were prescribed for the Sabbath and festivals. As for the materials utilized in sacrifice, they ranged from frankincense to pure animals from the herds and flocks, and certain fowl, to grains prepared in diverse ways and libations of wine and oil.

Through a process known as "desacralization," Israelites were expected to support the priesthood with tithes and firstfruits. This meant that in order to benefit from the produce of the land, and from the increment of herds and flocks, a portion first had to be donated "to Yahweh"—in practical terms, to the Temple and priesthood. In addition, there were prescribed ways to donate or "devote" foodstuffs and objects of value to the Temple on a voluntary basis. There is more than one biblical tradition on the history and status of the Israelite priesthood. In priestly literature, Aaron, Moses' brother, is presented as the first chief priest in the wilderness period when, according to tradition, the cult of Yahweh and its priesthood were initiated (Exod. 28–29; Lev. 8–9). From that point on, priestly status was hereditary, with priests coming from a preferred clan of the tribe of Levi. The rest of the tribe of Levi functioned as Temple servitors. Historical inquiry yields a different reality. Chief priests were appointed by the kings of Judah and northern Israel, and discharged by them when it was so desired. It is true, however, that there were priestly families wherein priestly appointments carried through generations. A well-known example was the family of Zadok (1 Kings 1). There are also indications that Levites were practitioners of priestly arts, recruited from more than one tribe.

A growing concern in henotheist circles, and later in monotheist circles, was the lure of heterodoxy at local and even national cult sites, which had the effect of polluting the exclusive worship of Yahweh by persisting in selective polytheism. Yahwist altars were even abandoned and left in ruin, as we read in the Elijah episode (1 Kings 18). Originating in northern Israel before its annexation by Assyria, and carrying over into seventh-century Judah, a religious movement arose whose objective was to close down *bāmôt* and altars, many of them long-standing, throughout the land. This movement received royal endorsement from the Judean king Josiah, who issued an edict in 622 B.C.E. restricting all sacrificial worship to the Temple of Jerusalem (2 Kings 22–23). Inevitably, Josiah's edict reflects the innovative cultic laws of Deuteronomy 12–16, where the same unification of the cult of Yahweh is mandated. There are conflicting indications as to the acceptance of this policy in the brief period between 622 B.C.E. and 586 B.C.E., when the Jerusalem Temple was destroyed. In contrast, it is clearly evident that those Judeans who returned from Babylonia endorsed it fully. They built a new temple on the same spot where the first temple had stood, and archaeologists have found little if any evidence of other temples. A rival community erected the contemporary Samaritan temple on Mount Gerizim (Shechem/Nablus).

The official decision to restrict sacrifice to a single temple in Jerusalem significantly altered the forms of Israelite, then Jewish, worship and seriously limited popular participation in the cult. At the same time, it added importance to the pilgrimage as a form of celebration and required the rescheduling of annual festival celebrations so as to alleviate the hardship of longer but inevitably less frequent pilgrimages at seasons of harvest. The Hebrew term for "festival" is *ḥag,* a cognate of Arabic *ḥaj,* which more precisely means "pilgrimage." The Torah preserves three primary cultic calendars, the oldest preserved in Exodus 23:14-19, followed by Deuteronomy 16 (cf. Exod. 34:18-26), and in turn followed by Leviticus 23, a priestly calendar. Numbers 28–30 present a late priestly calendar of the public cult. One notices scheduling changes affecting the traditional pilgrimages: the Pesah-Massot Festival in the spring, commemorating the Exodus from Egypt, and the Festival of Firstfruits, Shavuoth, seven weeks later. Even in earlier times, the third festival, that of Ingathering—Sukkoth—in the autumn of the year, was the main annual event, undoubtedly for practical reasons. We note that Solomon dedicated the Temple on that occasion so that large numbers of Israelites might be present (1 Kings 8). Long pilgrimages, whether domestic or from the Diaspora, became less and less feasible once the restriction of all sacrifice to the Jerusalem Temple became the rule.

The weekly Sabbath was a frequent yet important event. It is most probably an Israelite contribution to world civilization, referred to early on in biblical prophecy—in Hosea 2:13, quite possibly dating from the late ninth century B.C.E., and in Isaiah 1:13, dating from the end of the eighth century B.C.E. As legislated in Torah law, the

Sabbath was primarily a time when daily pursuits were to cease and desist; this is the real meaning of the Hebrew verb *sabat,* "to cease." The Sabbath also had commemorative significance, variously of the creation of the world and of the liberation from Egypt. (Compare the two versions of the Decalogue.) The Sabbath was observed in the Temple cult and also in local areas of settlement. By virtue of its behavioral restrictions, it directly affected the daily life of individual Israelites and their families.

The Sabbath and festivals were occasions for rejoicing (Deut. 12:14). In the postexilic community, the new moon of the seventh month, Tishrei (September), became the occasion of an annual convocation, and the tenth day became an annual Day of Atonement (Yom Kippurim), a day of fasting and purification. Regular celebration of every new moon, a very ancient practice, continued.

Prayer has been an important component of religious experience since earliest times, although its precise place and function in the cult is difficult to ascertain. There are numerous instances of private prayer recorded in the Hebrew Bible, as well as blessings pronounced in the name of Yahweh. Formal prayer complemented sacrifice at temples, and many of the biblical psalms were undoubtedly part of temple ritual, as their content and added captions indicate. As in most religions, prayer was of three types: petition, praise of God, and thanksgiving.

A highly visible feature of the religion of biblical Israel is its dietary code of practice, which, although it manifested itself in the cult, did not originate there. Basic to the dietary code, both cultic and domestic, was the blood taboo, which reserved blood of permitted animals for the sacrificial altar (Lev. 17:10-12, and following) and required the draining of blood from slaughtered animals consumed as food. In this context, blood was regarded as the prime symbol of life, the vitality of the soul, as stated in the postdeluvian revelation to Noah (Gen. 9:1-9). As such it was forbidden for human consumption and was demanded by the deity. The Torah (Deut. 14; Lev. 11) specifies permitted and forbidden sources of food for all Israelites. In a way, emphasis on a pure diet and the avoidance of blood helped compensate for the loss of cultic access discussed above. The family table became a substitute altar.

17

At a Glance

Classic Texts

The New Annotated Oxford Bible [Old Testament]. New Revised Standard Version. New York: Oxford University Press, 1994.

JPS Hebrew-English TANAKH, 2nd edition. Philadelphia: The Jewish Publication Society, 1999.

Important Figures

(a) Israelites

Moses: traditionally first and foremost of the prophets; the lawgiver

The patriarchs: Abraham, Isaac, and Jacob—traditionally the first monotheists

Kings of Judah: Hezekiah and Josiah—advocates of Yahwist henotheism; Manasseh—a heterodox king; Zedekiah—the last king of Judah

Israelite Prophets: Elijah, First Hosea (Hos. 1–3), First Isaiah, Second Isaiah, Jeremiah, Ezekiel

(b) Non-Israelites

Akhenaten: the Egyptian pharaoh who worshiped Aten, the sun god

Alexander the Great: conqueror of the Near East who defeated the Persians

Cyrus the Great: Persian emperor who authorized the rebuilding of the Temple

Nebuchadnezzar II: Babylonian king who destroyed Jerusalem

Sennacherib: Assyrian king, the contemporary of First Isaiah

Brief Time Line

ca. 1200 B.C.E.	Beginning of the Iron Age and the formation of new polities
eleventh through tenth centuries B.C.E.	Early formation of the Israelites, who subsequently settled Canaan
tenth through early sixth centuries B.C.E.	The overall monarchic period
721 B.C.E.	Assyrian annexation of the kingdom of northern Israel
701 B.C.E.	Sennacherib's blockade of Jerusalem
622 B.C.E.	Josiah's edict on cult centralization
586 B.C.E.	Babylonian destruction of Judah and Jerusalem; beginning of the Babylonian Exile
538 B.C.E.	The Cyrus Edict allowing Judeans to return and rebuild the Temple of Jerusalem

| 538–332 B.C.E. | The Persian period in Judea |
| 332–64 B.C.E. | Interlude, death of Alexander the Great followed by the Seleucid period, ending in 64 B.C.E. |

Important Symbols
Altars and *bāmôt,* "cult platforms"
Ark of the covenant
The Asherah—either a tree or a post representing the goddess by that name
Cherubim—in Yahweh's throne room (Isa. 6)
The *maṣṣēbāh,* "cultic stele"
Menorah—a seven-branched candelabra that stood in the Temple
The tabernacle

Glossary
'am	people
Asherah	a tree or a post, representing the goddess of that name
bāmôt	cult platforms
berît	covenant
'eḥḥād	one
'elōhim	god (generic); "divine being, divinity"
'ēsāh ('ēsâ)	design
gôy	nation
ḥag (Arabic *ḥaj)*	pilgrimage
ḥesed	kindness
maṣṣēbāh	cultic stele
menorah	a seven-branched candelabra
mišpāṭ	justice
'ōlāh	burnt offering
qādôš	holy
šāḥaṭ	to cease
Torah	the Pentateuch; Five Books of Moses
Y-H-W-H	the Tetragrammaton, pronounced "Yahweh"
Yom Kippur	the Day of Atonement

Suggestions for Further Reading
Ahituv, Shmuel. *Echoes from the Past: Hebrew and Cognate Inscriptions from the Biblical Period.* Jerusalem: Carta, 2008. (Ref.)

Albright, William F. *Archaeology and the Religion of Israel.* Baltimore: Johns Hopkins University Press, 1946.

———. *Yahweh and the Gods of Canaan.* London: Eisenbrauns, 1968.

Greenberg, Moshe. *Biblical Prose Prayer as a Window into the Popular Religion of Ancient Israel.* Berkeley: University of California Press, 1983.

Kaufmann, Yehezkel. *The Religion of Israel: From Its Beginnings to the Babylonian Exile*. Abridged and translated by Moshe Greenberg. Chicago: University of Chicago Press, 1960.

Levine, Baruch A. "Biblical Temple." In *The Encyclopedia of Religion*. Edited by Mircea Eliade. Vol. 2. New York: Macmillan, 1987. (Ref.)

Liverani, Mario. *Israel's History and the History of Israel*. Oakville, Conn.: Equinox, 2007.

Meyers, Carol. *Household and Holiness: The Religious Culture of Israelite Women*. Minneapolis: Fortress Press, 2005.

Rainey, Anson F., and R. Steven Notley. *The Sacred Bridge: Carta's Atlas of the Biblical World*. Jerusalem: Carta, 2006. (Ref.)

THE FORMATION

Jacob Neusner

What is Judaism's overriding question?

J udaism stresses the unity of God. God is one and unique, loving and just, all-powerful and omniscient. That conviction defines the dynamics of Judaism. Monotheism by nature explains many things in a single way. One God, who is benevolent, rules. Life is meant to be fair, and just rules are supposed to describe what is ordinary, all in the name of that one and only God. If one true God has done everything, then, since God is all-powerful and omniscient, all things are credited to, and blamed on, God. In that case God can be either good or bad, just or unjust—but not both. Responding to the overriding question of monotheism, Judaism systematically reveals the justice of the one and only God of all creation. God is not only God but also good. The sages of Judaism expose the justice of God. The theology of Judaism conveys the picture of world order based on God's justice and equity. The working system finds its dynamic in the struggle between God's plan for creation—to create a perfect world of justice—and human will.

Judaism makes its statement of monotheism through the narratives of Scripture. It retells the Pentateuch's story of Adam and Eve, who sinned by rebellion against God and so lost the Garden of Eden and aspire to return. It interprets the condition of Israel the holy people within the same paradigm of exile and return, beginning with the fall of Adam and the loss of Eden, with its parallel in the loss, to

a Gentile empire, of the land, Jerusalem, and the Temple in 586 B.C.E.
But, as prophecy insisted and as happened in 538 B.C.E., the sages
also underscored that through return to God Israel would recover
and keep its Eden. In the narrative of Judaism Israel has returned to
Zion and the paramount problem is how to build a community that
endures in God's sight.

How do we know about this religion? What classics define the norms?

We know about Judaism through two bodies of writings. First
come the Hebrew Scriptures of ancient Israel, which Judaism knows
as the written Torah and Christianity knows as the Old Testament.
Second are the documents of the ancient rabbis that record the originally oral tradition God revealed to Moses at Mount Sinai.

The Written Torah

The written Torah begins with the Pentateuch, the Five Books of
Moses: Genesis, Exodus, Leviticus, Numbers, and Deuteronomy. It
is written from the perspective of the loss and recovery of the land of
Israel between 586 B.C.E. (destruction of the first Temple) and 538
B.C.E., which marks the return to Jerusalem and the building of the
second Temple, and led in 450 B.C.E. to the promulgation of the
Pentateuch as divine instruction or Torah. Scripture begins with
the creation of the world; the making of man and woman; the fall of
humanity through disobedience; the flood that wiped out nearly all
humanity except for Noah, progenitor of all humanity; the decline of
humanity from Noah to Abraham; then the rise of humanity through
Abraham, Isaac, Jacob also called Israel, the twelve sons of Jacob; to
exile in Egypt and ultimately, Sinai. There, the scriptural narrative
continues; God revealed the Torah, revelation to Moses, and that
revelation contained the terms of the covenant that God then made
with Israel, the family of Abraham, Isaac, and Jacob.

The book of Genesis narrates the story of creation and then of the
beginnings of the family that Israel would always constitute, the children of Abraham, Isaac, and Jacob. The book of Exodus presents the
story of the slavery of the children of Israel in Egypt and how God
redeemed them from Egyptian bondage and brought them to Sinai,
there to make a covenant, or contract, with them by which they
would accept the Torah and carry out its rules. The book of Leviticus

portrays the founding of the priests' service of God through the sacrifice of the produce of the Holy Land to which God would bring Israel, specifying the rules and regulations to govern the kingdom of priests and the holy people. The book of Numbers provides an account of the wandering in the wilderness. The book of Deuteronomy then presents a reprise of the story, a long sermon by Moses looking back on the history of Israel from the beginnings through the point of entry into the promised land, followed by a restatement of the rules of the covenant, or contract, between Israel and God.

The Oral Torah

Rabbinic Judaism brings to the written Torah the oral tradition of Sinai. We know about Rabbinic Judaism through a law code of a philosophical character, the Mishnah (ca. 200 C.E.), and two commentaries to the code, the Talmud of the land of Israel (ca. 400 C.E.) and the Talmud of Babylonia (ca. 600 C.E.), and a score of commentaries to Scripture called Midrashim. Committed to preservation, the oral tradition, the doctrine held, was handed on from master to disciple in a chain of tradition extending down to the rabbis themselves and then also in writing in the Mishnah.

History of Rabbinic Judaism

Rabbinic Judaism took shape in two stages: first, from 70 to the fourth century C.E., represented by the Mishnah—a philosophical law code completed in ca. 200 C.E.—and earlier commentaries on the Mishnah and on Scripture; and, second, by the two Talmuds or commentaries on the Mishnah—the Talmud of the land of Israel, ca. 400 C.E.; the Talmud of Babylonia, ca. 600 C.E.; and the later Midrash compilations. The first stage set forth a Judaic religious system without reference to the challenge of Christianity; the second stage set forth a revision of the initial system, now responsive to that challenge. That fully articulated system would then form the framework for all Judaisms from the fourth to the twenty-first century. Some Judaic systems took shape in response to the rabbinic system and amplified it or added to its resources; others took shape as heresies were defined by rejection of principal parts of that same system. But so long as Christianity, and later on Islam, confronted Israel, the holy people, with critical issues, Rabbinic Judaism defined the paramount, norm-setting Judaism.

What is the community of the faithful called? What story explains its traits?

Judaism calls the community of the faithful "Israel," meaning "the people of God." The narrative of Judaism portrays Israel as the extended family of Abraham, Isaac, and Jacob, and those who have accepted a place in the covenant between the family and God. Israel also sees itself as the elected people standing in a contractual or covenantal relationship with God. The acceptance of the Torah at Sinai marks that covenant. Treating the story of exile and return as normative marked Israel as special, elect, and subject to the rules of the covenant and its stipulations.

What is the way of life of the community of the faithful? What are the rules of conduct and the rites of passage? What is the notion of sacred time and space? How does the way of life embody the story that this religion tells about itself?

The way of life of the community of the faithful emphasizes the holiness of Israel, meaning its separateness from all the other peoples of the world.

Celebrations: The Days of Awe

The first ten days of the lunar month of Tishré, in the autumn; the New Year, Rosh Hashanah; and the Day of Atonement, Yom Kippur—together called "the Days of Awe"—mark days of solemn penitence. The fifteenth day of that same month, the first full moon after the autumnal equinox of September 21, marks the advent of Tabernacles/Sukkoth. The palm branch is waved on Sukkoth in a rite praying for rain.

The story realized in the holy season of the Ten Days of Awe concerns the individual Israelite in the setting of all of humanity. It tells that the New Year commemorates the creation of the world, and on the New Year every creature comes before God to be judged in accord with deeds done in the past year. Then, ten days later, the decree is sealed. But that day is the Day of Atonement, which on its own has the power to atone for sin, so the judgment of the New Year is mitigated or even set aside by the atonement of the Day of Atonement, an occasion for forgiveness from sin. The shofar or ram's horn is sounded to call to mind Abraham's obedience to God on Mount Moriah (Gen. 22).

Restoring Eden: The Sabbath

How is Israel to regain the land, which is its Eden? Israel on the Sabbath restores the conditions that prevailed when God and Adam were last together, that perfect Sabbath when God, having perfected creation, blessed and sanctified the Sabbath day in celebration of the perfection of creation and entered upon repose. Israel's perfect sanctification of a single Sabbath day represents that repair and perfection of the world that marks the recovery of the land that is Israel's Eden. The Sabbath is a sign of the covenant. It is a gift of grace, which neither idolaters nor evil people may enjoy. It is the testimony of the chorines of Israel. And it is the most pleasant of days. Keeping the Sabbath is living in God's kingdom. Keeping the Sabbath brings the Israelite into the kingdom of God—so states a Sabbath prayer. Keeping the Sabbath now is a foretaste of the redemption: "This day is for Israel light and rejoicing." The rest of the Sabbath is, as the afternoon prayer affirms, "a rest granted in generous love, a true and faithful rest."

How does the transformation by the master narrative take place in the everyday and in the here and now? We find the answer in the actions of the pious Israelite in response to ordinary deeds routinely done.

Eating

Sustaining life, which is a gift from God, involves two matters: first, what Israelites are to eat or refrain from eating, and second, how they are to eat. Scripture, for example Leviticus 11–15, as interpreted by the rabbinic sages in the oral part of the Torah, specifies a variety of foods that may or may not be eaten. All fruits and vegetables are permitted, so too fish that have fins and scales, but not scavengers or bottom-feeders. For meat, only animals that have cloven hooves and chew the cud may be consumed by Israelites. Animals slaughtered for meat for Israelites ("kosher" or suitable meat) are killed with a perfectly sharp knife, swiftly to prevent suffering, with the recitation of a blessing; the blood is drained and the meat inspected for blemishes and indications of disease. "You shall not boil a kid in its mother's milk" (Exod. 23:19) is understood by the sages to mean not consuming dairy products for a span of time after eating meat (from two to six hours, depending on the custom); and two sets of dishes, one for meat, the other for dairy products, are required.

25

The "how" is more readily grasped. The meal presents itself as an occasion of thanksgiving, which encompasses the entirety of the story Judaism tells. To put matters simply: every time the faithful Israelite eats a meal, he or she rehearses the whole Judaic narrative—land, exile, redemption—every chapter. Blessings before eating food and an elaborate grace after meals transform the act of nourishment to a direct encounter with God, deemed to provide the food that is eaten and a reprise of Israel's condition in time and eternity. The secular facts of hunger and satisfaction now are made, in an exact sense, to *embody* exile and return, sin and remission of sin, this world and the world to come. The blessing before eating food and the grace afterward work out the meaning of a metaphor, and three meals a day transform the here and now into something other. The routine experience of hunger and satisfaction changes into a metaphor for Israel's life of anguished reality but ultimate redemption. So a meal turns into a moment of communion with the meaning of life as part of Israel, God's people.

Praying

Prayer in Judaism is obligatory three times a day and may be votive as well. The community and its members pray (1) upon rising, (2) at dusk, and (3) after dark. Public prayers encompass three important matters: to whom the prayer is addressed, the petition that is presented, and the identification of the community by whom the petition is set forth. These take shape in (1) the recitation of the creed (twice daily, morning and night) called "the Shema," meaning, "Hear...," from the first word of "Hear O Israel..."; (2) petition, at the three specified times, for the needs and welfare of the community and the individual, called "The Prayer" or "the Eighteen Benedictions" (Hebrew: *Shemoneh esré*); and (3) the situation or identification of the community in its larger setting, called "Alenu" ("It is our duty..."). These latter two prayers are said morning, dusk, and night.

The Shema

Evening and morning, Israel individually and communally proclaims the unity and uniqueness of God. The proclamation is preceded and followed by blessings. The whole constitutes the credo, "what the Jews believe." The three elements of the creed cover creation, revelation, and redemption—that is to say, God as creator of the world, God as revealer of the Torah, God as redeemer of Israel. The recital of the Shema is introduced by a celebration of God as creator of the world. In the morning, the individual, in community or not, recites these preliminary benedictions:

1. Creation of the World, attested by sunrise, sunset
   Sunrise:
       Praised are You, O Lord our God, King of the universe.
       You fix the cycles of light and darkness;
       You ordain the order of all creation;
       You cause light to shine over the earth;
       Your radiant mercy is upon its inhabitants.
       In Your goodness the work of creation
       is continually renewed day by day....
       O cause a new light to shine on Zion;
       may we all soon be worthy to behold its radiance.
       Praised are You, O Lord, Creator of the heavenly bodies.

God is made known in the Torah, the mark not merely of divine sovereignty, but of divine grace and love, source of life here and now and in eternity. So goes the second blessing:

2. Revelation of the Torah as the expression of God's love for Israel
       Deep is Your love for us, O Lord our God;
       bounteous is Your compassion and tenderness.
       You taught our fathers the laws of life,
       and they trusted in You, Father and king.
       For their sake be gracious to us, and teach us,
       that we may learn Your laws and trust in You.
       Father, merciful Father, have compassion upon us:
       Endow us with discernment and understanding.
       Grant us the will to study Your Torah,
       to heed its words and to teach its precepts....
       Enlighten our eyes in Your Torah,
       open our hearts to Your commandments....
       Unite our thoughts with singleness of purpose
       to hold You in reverence and in love....
       You have drawn us close to You;
       we praise You and thank You in truth.
       With love do we thankfully proclaim Your unity,
       and praise You who chose Your people Israel in love.

In these blessings before the declaration of the faith, then, we refer in abstract language to the concrete narratives of Creation and Sinai, and that is the main point. The narrative gives concreteness to the abstractions of theology, and the theology translates the implications of the narrative into generalizations, complete with evidence and argument. Then the liturgy turns the whole into the language of dialogue between Israel and God: "You" and "we."

In the Shema, Torah, revelation, leads Israel to enunciate the chief consequence of revelation: "Hear, O Israel, the Lord Our God, the Lord is One." This proclamation of the Shema is followed by three scriptural passages. The first is Deuteronomy 6:5-9: "You shall love the LORD your God with all your heart, and with all your soul, and with all your might." And further, one must diligently teach one's children these words and talk of these words everywhere and always, and place them on one's forehead, doorposts, and gates. The second set of verses of Scripture is Deuteronomy 11:13-21, which emphasizes that if Jews keep the commandments they will enjoy worldly blessings; but if they do not, they will be punished and disappear from the good land God gives them. The third is Numbers 15:37-41, the commandment to wear fringes on the corners of one's garments.[1]

The final component of the recitation of the Shema completes the trilogy by reciting the story of God's redemption of Israel at the sea, a model for God's redemption of Israel at the end of days.

The Prayer

The immense statement of the creed in the Shema gives way to the second of the three required components of obligatory public worship: *The* Prayer par excellence, comprised on weekdays by prayers of petition. What the community asks for, always in the plural, concerns the public welfare and covers matters we should today assign to the category of public policy as much as to personal need. In the morning, noon, and evening these weekday prayers of petition are called "the Eighteen Benedictions" (Hebrew: *Shemoneh esré*), meaning "requests concluding with a blessing." Some of these, in particular those at the beginning and the end, recur in Sabbath and festival prayers.

The introductory three paragraphs define the One to whom petition is addressed: (1) the God of the founders, who is (2) omnipotent and (3) holy.

Alenu

Every synagogue service concludes with a prayer prior to going forth, called "Alenu," from its first word in Hebrew: "It is incumbent upon us [to praise...]." The third of the three components of the communal worship, Alenu draws the community outward into the world. When Jews complete their service of worship, they mark the conclusion by making a statement concerning themselves in the world: the corporate community looking outward. Like the Exodus, the moment of the congregation's departure becomes a celebration of Israel's God, a self-conscious, articulated rehearsal of Israel's peoplehood.

Ethics

The first-century sage Hillel is cited as stating the Golden Rule in ethical terms: "What is hateful to you to your fellow don't do." That negative formulation of the Golden Rule applies to concrete relationships among ordinary people. And what is noteworthy is that classical Judaism maintains that the biblical commandment "You shall love your neighbor as yourself" (Lev. 19:18) defines the heart of the Torah, which is to say, what we should call the essence of Judaism: its ethics and its theology.

That judgment is set forth in the Talmud, the extension and amplification of the Torah, in a famous story about the sage Hillel. Hillel reformulated Leviticus 19:18, the rule of reciprocal love, in terms of action (don't do) rather than attitude (love your neighbor):

A. [In Hebrew:] There was another case of a gentile who came before Shammai. He said to him, "Convert me on the stipulation that you teach me the entire Torah while I am standing on one foot." He drove him off with the building cubit that he had in his hand.

B. He came before Hillel: "Convert me."

C. He said to him [in Aramaic]," '*What is hateful to you, to your fellow don't do.*' That's the entirety of the Torah; *everything else is elaboration. So go, study.*"
(Bavli Shabbat 31a/I.12²)

The concluding counsel, "Go, study," points to the task of elaborating the Golden Rule to cover a variety of specific ethical cases.

The Life Cycle: Birth, Puberty, Marriage, Death

Birth into the Covenant of Abraham Our Father

There are four aspects in which the medical operation of circumcision—*berit milah,* covenant effected through circumcision—is turned into an act of sanctification. When the rite begins, the assembly

29

and the *mohel* (ritual circumciser) together recite the following: "The Lord spoke to Moses saying, 'Phineas, son of Eleazar, son of Aaron, the priest, has turned my wrath from the Israelites by displaying among them his passion for me, so that I did not wipe out the Israelite people in my passion. Say therefore I grant him my covenant of peace'" (Num. 25:10-12).

Second, a chair is set called "the chair of Elijah," so that the rite takes place in the presence of a chair for Elijah the prophet. We recall that Elijah attends the Passover Seder as well, a presence when Israel assembles in the messianic hope (Mal. 4:5). The newborn son is set on that chair, and the congregation says, "This is the chair of Elijah, of blessed memory." Why Elijah here and now? The presence of Elijah attests to Israel's persistence in its unique covenant with God. For Elijah had called into doubt Israel's loyalty, explicitly complaining to God that Israel neglected the covenant (1 Kings 19:10-14). So he is required to come bear witness that Israel observes the covenant of circumcision.

We move, third, from narrative and gesture to formula, for there is the blessing said before the rite itself—that is, as the *mohel* takes the knife to cut the foreskin of the penis, these words are said to transform the act into one of sanctification: "Praised are You . . . who sanctified us with Your commandments and commanded us to bring the son into the covenant of Abraham our father."

Fourth, lest people miss the point of the stories that are called to mind, the rite makes matters explicit. This is an act of sanctification. The operation done, the wine is blessed:

> Praised are You, Lord our God, who sanctified the beloved from the womb and set a statute into his very flesh, and his parts sealed with the sign of the holy covenant. On this account, Living God, our portion and rock, save the beloved of our flesh from destruction, for the sake of his covenant placed in our flesh. Blessed are You . . . who makes the covenant.

The covenant is specific, concrete. By virtue of the rite, the child enters the covenant, meaning that he joins that unseen "Israel" that through blood enters an agreement with God. Then the blessing of the covenant is owing to the child, for covenants or contracts cut both ways.

Entering the Age of Responsibility

The advent of puberty is marked by the *bar mitzvah* rite for a young man and the *bat mitzvah* rite for a young woman, at which a young person becomes obligated to keep the commandments. *Bar* means "son" and *bat* means "daughter," with the sense that "one is subject to," and *mitzvah* means "a divine commandment." The rite is unadorned: the young person is called to pronounce the benediction over a portion of the Torah lection in the synagogue and is given the honor of reading the prophetic passage as well. In olden times it was not so important an occasion as it has become in modern America. Only when an Israelite achieves intelligence and self-consciousness, normally at puberty, is he or she expected to accept the full privilege of *mitzvah* (commandment) and to regard himself or herself as commanded by God. Judaism perceives the commandments as expressions of God's love, God's engagement with the Israelite's doings.

Marriage: Adam and Eve in Eden

The marriage rite invokes the great themes of the restoration of Israel to the land and of Adam and Eve to Eden, the matching moments that form a principal part of the master narrative of Judaism. The words and deeds of the wedding rite transform the space, time, action, and community of the "I" of the groom and the "I" of the bride into the "we" of the Israelites and of Adam and Eve. The space is contained by the *Huppah,* translated as "marriage canopy": a contained space of heaven representing heaven. Stripped down to essentials, the stories that are invoked transform the union of woman and man into the beginning of a new creation so that the woman becomes Eve and the man becomes Adam.

In this way the prophecy of the snake in Eden is realized, as the great Bible interpreter Rashi (R. Solomon Isaac, 1040–1105) explains. When the snake says, "For God knows that when you eat of it your eyes will be opened, and you will be like God" (Gen. 3:5), the meaning, Rashi maintains, is that you will become "creators of worlds." At the marriage rite a new world begins: a family in the house of Israel, the beginning of new creation of life.

Death and Resurrection

The family recites the Qaddish, a prayer of sanctification of God's name that, appropriately on the occasion of death, looks forward to the messianic age and the resurrection of the dead.

31

May the great name [of God] be magnified and sanctified in the
world which [God] created in accord with his will.

And may his kingdom come in your life and days, and in the life of
all the house of Israel, speedily, promptly.

And say, Amen.

The community says:

May the great name be blessed for ever and all eternity.

May the holy name of the blessed one be blessed, praised, adorned,
exulted, raised up, adorned, raised high, praised,

yet beyond all of those blessings, songs, praises, words of consola-
tion, which we say in this world.

And say, Amen.

May great peace [descend] from heaven, [and] life for us and for all
Israel.

And say, Amen.

He who makes peace in the heights will make peace for us and for
all Israel.

And say, Amen.

The family members of the deceased, as well as the assembled,
now shovel dirt onto the body, until the grave is filled. Then two
lines are formed leading away from the grave, and the mourners are
given the following blessing: "May the Omnipresent comfort you
among the other mourners of Zion and Jerusalem." The appeal to
Zion and Jerusalem, of course, refers to the Temple of old, which
people mourn until the coming restoration, thus a messianic and
eschatological reference—the only one. The mourners remain at
home for a mourning period of seven days and continue to recite the
memorial Qaddish for eleven months. In all we discern no appeal to
a presence other than God's, no metamorphosis of death into something more.

At a Glance

Classic Texts

The Hebrew Scriptures, also referred to as the Old Testament, the written
Torah. Concluded in ca. 450 for most of the Scriptures.

The Mishnah, comprising sixty-three tractates or topical expositions, is a
philosophical law code that reached closure in the land of Israel in ca.
200 B.C.E.

The Talmud of the land of Israel, a commentary on thirty-nine tractates—
topical expositions—of the Mishnah. Concluded in ca. 400 B.C.E.

The Talmud of Babylonia, a commentary on thirty-seven tractates of the Mishnah. Concluded in ca. 600 C.E.

Midrashim, commentaries to books of Scripture, mainly the Pentateuch and the scrolls of Ruth, Lamentations, Song of Songs, and Esther.

Important Figures

Moses: known in Judaism as "Moshe rabbenu," Moses our lord, brought the Torah down from Mount Sinai.

Characteristic Beliefs

Monotheism: belief in the oneness of God and his uniqueness

Election of Israel: belief that God chose Israel to receive the Torah and lead humanity back to Eden

Holiness of Israel: Israel is distinct from the nations of the world and is different because it serves God

Commandments: God's instructions to Israel on concrete acts of commission or of omission

Torah: instruction, revealed by God to Moses in two media, writing and memory

Essential Creeds or Codes of Conduct

Shema: the creed of Judaism, proclaiming the unity of God and his dominion over nature and history

The Mishnah with the Talmuds: the code of conduct governing the community of Judaism

Brief Time Line

586 B.C.E.	Babylonians destroyed the first Temple of Jerusalem, built by Solomon, king of Israel; Judeans exiled to Iraq.
538 B.C.E.	Persians having conquered the Babylonians permitted the Israelites to return to the land of Israel and rebuild the Temple.
450 B.C.E.	The Pentateuch was completed by Ezra the scribe and adopted as the foundation document of Judaism.
1 C.E.	Hillel stated the Golden Rule.
70 C.E.	Romans destroyed the second Temple of Jerusalem. Jewish settlement continued in the land of Israel for centuries to come.
200 C.E.	The conclusion of the Mishnah
400 C.E.	The conclusion of the Talmud of the land of Israel
600 C.E.	The conclusion of the Talmud of Babylonia

Important Symbols
The Torah—scrolls of the Pentateuch
Shofar—ram's horn sounded on the New Year
Palm branch—the *lulab* or palm branch is carried in a procession on
   Tabernacles in a rite asking for rain.
Berit milah—the covenant of circumcision

Important Rituals
Study of the Torah
Circumcision in the covenant of Abraham
Marriage rite/*Huppah*
Burial
Repose on the Sabbath
Prayer
Not eating unclean food

Glossary

Adam and Eve	the first human beings, set in paradise
Alenu	"It is our duty to praise" God for making us unique in humanity
bar mitzvah / bat mitzvah	one obligated to keep the law
berit milah	covenant effected through circumcision
Days of Awe	New Year and Day of Atonement
Eden, Garden of	paradise, created for humanity to live with God
exile and return	pattern of humanity in losing the Garden of Eden and aspiring to return to paradise
Huppah	marriage canopy
monotheism	belief in one unique God, Creator of heaven and earth
paradigm	pattern that recurs
Pentateuch	Genesis, Exodus, Leviticus, Numbers, Deuteronomy
Qaddish	prayer sanctifying God's name
Rabbinic Judaism	the Judaic religious system framed by the rabbinic sages and set forth in the documents of the written Torah as interpreted by the Oral Torah
Rosh Hashanah	the New Year, the day of judgment
Shema	the proclamation of God's unity and oneness
Sinai	the mountain in the wilderness where God revealed the Torah to Moses
Temple	the center of worship of God in Jerusalem through animal sacrifices

| Yom Kippur | the Day of Atonement, a day of forgiveness |
| Zion | mountain in Jerusalem where the Temple stood |

Sacred Spaces and Times

Spaces
The Temple of Jerusalem
The land of Israel

Times
The Sabbath
The festivals
The Days of Awe

Suggestions for Further Reading

Moore, George Foot. *Judaism in the First Centuries of the Christian Era, the Age of the Tannaim.* New York: Schocken Books, 1971.

Neusner, Jacob. *The Enchantments of Judaism: Rites of Transformation from Birth through Death.* New York: Basic Books, 1987.

Urbach, Ephraim E. *The Sages, Their Concepts and Beliefs.* Translated by Israel Abrahams. Cambridge, Mass.: Harvard University Press, 1987.

JUDAISM IN MODERN TIMES: REFORM, ORTHODOX, AND CONSERVATIVE JUDAISM; ZIONISM

Jacob Neusner

What is this religion's overriding question? What makes the system self-evidently valid to the community of the faithful?

Judaism in ancient and medieval times answered the question, How can the people of God explain its subordination to the pagan nations? It responded: Israel's condition validates its conviction about the unity and omnipotence of God, who punishes Israel's failings by placing Israel under the rule of their—and God's—enemies. This message, set forth in Scripture by Moses and the prophets, reinforced the rabbinic hegemony among the diverse systems that competed in the communities of Judaism. It set forth a powerful rationale to persuade Jews to affirm their condition as Israelites: it told them why and how they should be part of Israel the holy people and only part of Israel. But when the overriding question of how to be uniquely Israel shifted, so too the received rabbinic system met competition. Other Judaic systems in modern times emerged to ask and answer a different question. It was not, Why be Jewish and that alone? Rather, it was the question, How can one be Jewish and also something else—Jewish and a citizen of France or of Germany or of Great Britain or of the United States?

The received Judaic system built on the experience of exile and return, modified in the Oral Torah to encompass the sanctification of the life of the people as the condition of the salvation of the nation at the end of time. It competed with, and even gave way to, a number of new systems. Some of them stood in direct continuation with the received system, revering its canon and repeating its main points. Reform and Orthodoxy exemplify the Judaisms of continuation. Others of them utterly rejected the mythic structure and system of the Judaism. These are represented by Zionism—a political, not a religious, system to begin with. But Zionism above all repeated the same pattern of exile and return.

From a Nation Dwelling Alone to Individual Citizens of the Nation-state

A shift in the political circumstance of Judaism in the West, represented by the U.S. Constitution of 1787 and the French Revolution of 1789, affected Jews' thought about perennial questions. Earlier modes of organizing society recognized as political entities groups, guilds, and classes, and among them the Jews found a place. In the hierarchical scheme, with church, monarchy, and aristocracy in their proper alignment, other political entities could likewise find their location. With church disestablished, monarchy rejected, and aristocracy no longer dominant in politics, the political unit became the (theoretically) undifferentiated individual, making up the nation-state. Within that theory there was no room for a collectivity such as Israel, the Jewish people, viewed as a political unit, though (in theory at least) there might have been room for the Jewish individual, in rightful place alongside other undifferentiated individuals.

In the aftermath of the changes in Western politics in the nineteenth century, Jews indeed asked themselves whether and how they could be something in addition to Jewish. That something, to begin with, invariably found expression in the name of the locale in which they lived: whether France, Germany, Great Britain, or the United States. So, could one be both Jewish and German? Rabbinic Judaism had rested on the political premise that the Jews were governed by God's law and formed God's people. The two political premises—the nation-state and the Torah—scarcely permitted reconciliation. The consequent Judaic systems, Reform Judaism and Orthodox Judaism, each of them addressing issues regarded as acute and not merely chronic in the nineteenth century, alleged that they formed the natural next step in the unfolding of "the tradition."

Continuator Judaisms of the Nineteenth Century: Reform Judaism

From the perspective of the political changes taking place from the American and French Revolutions onward, the received system of the Rabbinic Judaism answered irrelevant questions and did not respond to acute ones. Secular nationalism conceived of society not as the expression of God's will for the social order under the rule of Christ and his church or his anointed ruler (king, emperor, czar), but of popular will for the social order under the government of the people and their elected representatives—a considerable shift. When society does not form the aggregate of distinct groups—each with its place and definition, language and religion—but rather the aggregate of undifferentiated citizens (male, white, wealthy, to be sure), then the Judaism that Jews in such a society would have to work out also would account for the difference of a different order altogether. That Judaism would have to frame a theory of who is Israel that would be consonant with the social situation of Jews who wish to be different—but not so different that they cannot also be citizens. Both Reform and Orthodoxy answered that question. Each rightly claimed to continue the received "tradition," that is, historic Judaism. Reform came first and answered forthrightly. The American Reform rabbis, meeting in Pittsburgh in 1885, issued a clear and accessible statement of their Judaism:

> We recognize in the Mosaic legislation a system of training the Jewish people for its mission during its national life in Palestine, and today we accept as binding only its moral laws and maintain only such ceremonies as elevate and sanctify our lives, but reject all such as are not adapted to the views and habits of modern civilization.... We hold that all such Mosaic and rabbinical laws as regular diet, priestly purity, and dress originated in ages and under the influence of ideas entirely foreign to our present mental and spiritual state.... Their observance in our days is apt rather to obstruct than to further modern spiritual elevation.... We recognize in the modern era of universal culture of heart and intellect the approaching of the realization of Israel's great messianic hope for the establishment of the kingdom of truth, justice, and peace among all men. We consider ourselves no longer a nation but a religious community and therefore expect neither a return to Palestine nor a sacrificial worship under the sons of

Aaron nor the restoration of any of the laws concerning the Jewish state.[1]

Here we find a Judaism answering the key questions *Who is Israel? What is its way of life? How does it account for its existence as a distinct—and distinctive—group?* Israel once was a nation ("during its national life"), but today is not a nation. It once had a set of laws that regulated diet, clothing, and the like. These no longer apply because Israel now is not what it was then. Israel forms an integral part of Western civilization. The reason to persist as a distinctive group was that the group had its work to do, namely, to realize the messianic hope for the establishment of a kingdom of truth, justice, and peace. For that purpose Israel no longer constitutes a nation. It now forms a religious community.

Continuator Judaisms of the Nineteenth Century: Orthodox Judaism

The term *Orthodoxy* in connection with Judaism first surfaced in 1795. It covers all Jews who believe that God revealed the dual Torah at Sinai. It also refers to Jews' carrying out the requirements of Jewish law contained in the Torah as interpreted by the sages through time. Obviously, so long as that position struck the generality of Jewry as self-evident, Orthodoxy as a distinct and organized Judaism did not exist. It did not have to. What is interesting is the point at which two events took place: first, the recognition of the received system, "the tradition," as Orthodoxy; second, the specification of the received system as religion. The two of course go together. So long as the Rabbinic Judaism enjoys recognition as a set of self-evident truths, those truths add up not to something so distinct and special as "religion," but to a general statement of how things are: all of life explained and harmonized in one whole account.

Affirming Torah and secular learning, Orthodox Judaism, founded in Germany in the mid-nineteenth century in response to the success of Reform, mediates between the received Rabbinic Judaism and the requirements of living a life integrated in modern circumstances. In its Western form it explained how the Jews could be both Jewish and German or French or American and so represents an integrationist Judaism. It affirmed that Jews could be both Israelites and something else. It met its fiercest competition from those who reaffirmed the received rabbinic system's conviction that Jews could be only Jewish, a self-segregationist position.

Modern or integrationist Orthodoxy maintains the worldview of the received dual Torah, constantly citing its sayings and adhering with only trivial variations to the bulk of its norms for everyday life. At the same time Orthodoxy holds that Jews adhering to the dual Torah may wear clothing that non-Jews wear and not have to wear distinctively Jewish (even Judaic) clothing, live within a common economy and not practice distinctively Jewish professions (however, in a given setting, these professions may be defined), and, in diverse ways, take up a life not readily distinguished in important characteristics from the life lived by people in general. So for Orthodoxy a portion of Israel's life may prove secular in that the Torah does not dictate and so sanctify all details under all circumstances. Since the Rabbinic Judaism presupposed not only the supernatural entity, Israel, but also a way of life that in important ways distinguished that supernatural entity from the social world at large, the power of Orthodoxy to find an accommodation for Jews who valued the received way of life and worldview, and who also planned to live their lives in an essentially integrated social world, proved formidable. The difference between Orthodoxy and the system therefore comes to expression in social policy: integration, however circumscribed, versus the total separation of the holy people from all others.

Integrationist Orthodoxy answered the same questions that Reform did but gave different answers. Reform maintained that because the Jews no longer constituted the holy people living their own distinct existence but were a religious group part of a larger nation-state, the distinctive way of life had to go. Orthodoxy held that the Torah made provision for areas of life in which a Jew could be something other than a Jew. In education, a main point, for example, the institutions of the Rabbinic Judaism commonly held that one should study Torah and that alone. Orthodoxy in the West included in its curriculum secular sciences as well. The Rabbinic Judaism ordinarily identified particular forms of dress as Judaic. Orthodoxy did not. In these and in other ways Orthodoxy formed a fresh statement of Judaism, and what made that statement distinctive is provision, for the Jew, of a life lived legitimately outside of the Judaic one—if never in violation of its norms. It follows that the point of distinction between adhering to the received system of Judaism and identifying

41

with the Orthodox Judaism that came to expression in mid-nineteenth-century Germany appeals to indicators such as clothing, language, and above all, education.

Conservative Judaism between Reform and Orthodoxy

Between Reform and Orthodoxy, the Historical School (a group of nineteenth-century German scholars of Judaism) and Conservative Judaism (a twentieth-century Judaism in America) took the middle position, each in its own context.[2] We treat them as a single Judaism because they hold in common moderation in making change, accommodation between "the tradition" and the requirements of modern life, and above all, adaptation to circumstance. Toward the end of the nineteenth century, rabbis of this same centrist persuasion organized the Jewish Theological Seminary of America in 1886–87, and from that rabbinical school the Conservative Movement developed. The order of the formation of the several Judaisms of the nineteenth century therefore is: first Reform, then Orthodoxy, and finally Conservatism—the two extremes and then the middle. The Historical School shaped the worldview, and Conservative Judaism later brought that view into full realization as a way of life characteristic of a large group of Jews. For a time nearly half, and now at least a third, of all American Jews who practice a Judaism identify themselves with Conservative Judaism.

The ambivalence of Conservative Judaism, speaking in part for intellectuals deeply loyal to the received way of life but profoundly dubious of the inherited worldview, came to full expression in the odd slogan of its intellectuals and scholars: "Eat kosher and think *traif*." "Traif" refers to meat that is not acceptable under Judaic law, and the slogan announced a religion of orthopraxy: do the right thing and it doesn't matter what you believe. That statement meant people should keep the rules of the holy way of life but ignore the convictions that made sense of them. *Orthopraxy* is the word that refers to correct action and unfettered belief, as compared to the word *Orthodoxy*, which refers to right doctrine. Some would then classify Conservative Judaism in America as an orthoprax Judaism defined through works, not doctrine. In what is called "the dogma of dogmaless Judaism," some of its leading voices even denied Judaism set forth doctrine at all.

The middle position, then, derived in equal measure from the two extremes. The way of life was congruent in most aspects with that of integrationist Orthodoxy; the worldview, with that of Reform. The two held together in the doctrine of "Israel" that covered everyone. Conservative Judaism laid enormous stress on what the people were doing—on the consensus of what one of its founders called "catholic Israel," meaning the ethnic-religious group whole. Conservative Judaism saw the Jews as a(nother) people, not merely a(nother) religious community, as Reform did, nor as a unique and holy people, as Orthodoxy did. That Judaism celebrated the ethnic as much as the more narrowly religious side to the Jews' common life. Orthodoxy took a separatist and segregationist position, leaving the organized Jewish community in Germany as that community fell into the hands of Reform Jews. Reform Judaism, for its part, rejected the position that the Jews constitute a people, not merely a religious community. Conservative Judaism emphasized the importance of the unity of the community as a whole and took a stand in favor of Zionism as soon as that movement got under way.

What separated Conservative Judaism from Reform was the matter of observance. Fundamental loyalty to the received way of life distinguished the Historical School in Germany and Conservative Judaism in America from Reform Judaism in both countries. When considering the continued validity of a traditional religious practice, the Reform asked why and the Conservatives why not. The Orthodox, of course, would ask no questions to begin with. The fundamental principle, that the worldview of the Judaism under construction would rest upon (mere) historical facts, came from Reform Judaism. Orthodoxy could never have concurred. The contrast to the powerful faith despite the world, exhibited by integrationist Orthodoxy's stress on the utter facticity of the Torah, presents in a clear light the positivism of the Conservatives, who, indeed, adopted the name "the *positive* Historical School."

The emphasis on research as the route to historical fact, and on historical fact as the foundation for both theological change and also the definition of what was truly authentic in the theological tradition, further tells us that the Historical School was made up of intellectuals. In America too a pattern developed in which essentially nonobservant congregations of Jews called upon rabbis whom they expected to be observant of the rules of the religion. As a result, many of the intellectual problems that occupied public debate concerned rabbis more than laypeople, since the rabbis bore responsibility—so the community maintained—for not only teaching the faith but, on their own, embodying it. An observer described this Judaism as "Orthodox rabbis serving Conservative synagogues made up of Reform Jews."

But in a more traditional liturgy, in an emphasis upon observance of the dietary taboos and the Sabbath and festivals—which did, and still does, characterize homes of Conservative more than of Reform Jews—Conservative Judaism in its way of life as much as in its worldview did establish an essentially mediating position between Orthodoxy and Reform Judaisms. And the conception that Conservative Judaism is a Judaism for Conservative rabbis in no way accords with the truth. That Judaism for a long time enjoyed the loyalty of fully half of the Jews in America who practiced Judaism and, while losing ground, today still retains the center and the influential position of Judaism in America. The viewpoint of the center predominates even in the more traditional circles of Reform and the more modernist sectors of Orthodoxy.

Responding to Modernity as Framed by Reform Judaism

The power of Reform Judaism to create and define the character of its own opposition—Orthodoxy in Germany, Conservative Judaism in America—tells us how accurately Reform had outlined the urgent questions of the age. Just as Reform had created Orthodoxy, it created Conservative Judaism. Reform, after all, had treated as compelling the issue of citizenship ("emancipation") and raised the heart of the matter: how could Jews aspire to return to the Holy Land and form a nation and at the same time take up citizenship in the lands of their birth and loyalty? Jews lived a way of life different from that of their neighbors, with whom they wished to associate. A Judaism had to explain that difference.

Both in Germany in the middle of the nineteenth century and in America at the end of that century the emphasis laid on "knowledge and practice of historical Judaism as ordained in the law of Moses expounded by the prophets and sages in Israel in Biblical and Talmudic writings," so the articles of Incorporation of the Jewish Theological Seminary of America Association stated in 1887. Calling themselves "traditionalists" rather than "Orthodox," the Conservative adherents accepted for most Judaic subjects the principles of modern critical scholarship. Conservative Judaism therefore exhibited traits that linked it to Reform but also to Orthodoxy, a movement very much in the middle. Precisely how the Historical School related to the other systems of its day (the mid- and late nineteenth century) merits attention because apologists insisted that this scholarship marked the Historical School off from Orthodoxy.

Zionism

Zionism, which regarded the Jews as a people lacking a state, constituted the Jews' movement of self-emancipation, responding to the failure of the nations' promises of Jewish emancipation. It framed its worldview and way of life for the Israel of its definition in response to a political crisis: the failure, by the end of the nineteenth century, of promises of political improvement in the Jews' status and condition. Zionism called the Jews to emancipate themselves by facing the fact that Gentiles in the main hated Jews. The Zionist system of Judaism declared as its worldview this simple proposition: the Jews form a people, one people, and should transform themselves into a political entity and build a Jewish state. They should found a Jewish state where Jews could free themselves of anti-Semitism and build their own destiny.

Zionism came into existence at the end of the nineteenth century, with the founding of the Zionist Organization in 1897. It reached its fulfillment, and dissolution in its original form, with the founding of the state of Israel on May 15, 1948. Zionism began with the definition of its theory of Israel: a people, one people, in a secular sense. Then came the worldview, which molded the diverse histories of Jews into a single, singular history of the Jewish people (nation), leading from the land of Israel through exile back to the land of Israel. This component of the Zionist worldview constituted an exact recapitulation of the biblical narrative, even though it derived not from a religious but from a nationalist perspective. The way of life of the elitist or activist required participation in meetings, organizing within the local community, and attendance at national and international conferences—a focus of life's energy on the movement. Later, as settlement in the land itself became possible, Zionism defined as the noblest way of living life migration to the land and, for the Socialist wing of Zionism, building a collective community (kibbutz). So Zionism presented a complete and fully articulated Judaism, and, in its day, prior to its compeller success in the creation of the state of Israel in 1948, one of the most powerful and effective Judaisms of them all.

A Judaism entirely out of phase with the received system, Zionism enunciated a powerful doctrine of Israel. The Jews form "a people, one people." Given the Jews' diversity, people could more easily concede the supernatural reading of Judaic existence than the national construction given to it. For, scattered across the European countries as well as in the Muslim world, Jews did not speak a single language, follow a single way of life, or adhere in common to a single code of belief and behavior. What made them a people, one people, and further validated their claim and right to a state, a nation, of their own, constituted the central theme of the Zionist worldview. No facts of perceived society validated that view. In no way, except for a common fate, did the Jews form a people, one people.

Zionist theory had the task of explaining how the Jews formed a people, one people. This led to the invention of "Jewish history"— that is, a past now read in a secular framework as a single and unitary story. In this way Zionist theory solved that problem by showing how the Jews all came from some one place, traveled together, and were going back to that same one place. So as a matter of secular fact, they were shown to constitute one people. Zionist theory therefore derived strength from the study of history, much as had Reform Judaism, and in time generated a great renaissance of Judaic studies as the scholarly community of the nascent Jewish state took up the task at hand. The sort of history that emerged took the form of factual and descriptive narrative. But its selection of facts, its recognition of problems requiring explanation, and its choice of what mattered and what did not—all of these definitive questions found answers in the larger program of nationalist ideology.

How do we know about this religion? What classics define the norms?

The Judaic systems of modern times produced a vast body of writing, to which reference has already been made.

What is the community of the faithful called? What story explains its traits?

Before the founding of the state of Israel in 1948, the competing Judaic systems used the word *Israel* to speak of the community of Judaism, not a geographic location. One did not *go to* Israel; one *was* Israel—an Israelite. In calling the new state "Israel," Zionism laid claim to define "Israel" as a location and a state. The received Scriptures and the liturgy of the synagogues continued to speak of "Israel" to mean the singular holy people.

What is the way of life of the community of the faithful? What are the rules of conduct and the rites of passage? What is the notion of sacred time and space? How does the way of life embody the story that this religion tells about itself?

The received way of life described in this chapter continued in integrationist Orthodoxy and in Conservative Judaism. In the Pittsburgh Platform of 1885 the Reform system introduced drastic changes in the way of life, rejecting dietary laws that separated Jews from their Gentile neighbors and rejecting customs and ceremonies that could not be harmonized with a universal system. The Columbus Platform of 1937 and subsequent statements of Reform Judaism renovated received practices.

Zionism defined its way of life in relationship to the location of its Israel, the state of Israel. A Zionist not only affirmed the peoplehood of Israel but residence in the Jewish state. A Zionist would be a Jew who lived in the state of Israel or who aspired to do so. Jews resident abroad were living in exile. That definition embodied the narrative of exile and return.

What is the worldview of the community? What is the story it tells about itself in the context of history and the Holocaust?

The worldview of the community of Judaism is shaped by the Holocaust. The Jewish experience in the nineteenth century made the question *Can the Jews be Israel and something else?* necessary. The twentieth century asked whether the Jews can *be*; what right *do* they have to live at all? And the replies, systems that took up the urgent question of the political survival of the Jewish people, came not from the master narrative of Judaism but from the ethnic consciousness of the Jews.

Two events in the middle of the twentieth century—the Holocaust, 1933–45, and the creation of the state of Israel in 1948—have added chapters to the story Judaism tells. "The Holocaust" refers to the murder, by the Germans before and during World War II, of nearly six million men, women, and children, solely because they were born into Jewish families. The state of Israel speaks of the creation of that Jewish state that Zionism aspired to bring into being. For many, the two stories form a seamless narrative. The Jews of Europe were unable to escape from the German exterminators because there was no Jewish state to afford them refuge and hope. The creation of that state in 1948 represented a solace and a guarantee that a Holocaust would never again take place.

In line with that story, Jews, both religious and secular, make pilgrimages from the United States and western Europe in two stages. First they travel to the death camp sites in Poland, such as the principal one in Auschwitz, where huge masses of Jews, as well as numbers of Poles and other conquered peoples, were murdered in gas chambers, their bodies burned in crematoria. In Auschwitz the pilgrims conduct rites of remembrance and recite the Qaddish prayer. Then they continue their journey, now to Jerusalem. They visit the Western Wall of the ancient Israelite Temple there, as well as the Holocaust memorial in Jerusalem, called Yad veShem, and other sites of renewal and rebuilding. In this way the story of holocaust and redemption plays itself out in a dramatic, personal experience.

In the state of Israel, and among overseas Jewish communities as well, a day of remembrance of the Holocaust is observed prior to the celebration of the date in the lunar calendar that marks the declaration of the state of Israel's independence. A memorial day also is observed in that same span of time for those who died in defense of the state of Israel.

How does this religion function in the world today?

Overall, about 11 percent of Jews in the United States and Canada identify with the Orthodox, 39 percent with Conservative Judaism, and 50 percent with Reform Judaism. In Great Britain, Canada, much of Latin America, Australia, South Africa, and continental Europe, most of the formal and centralized institutions are nominally Orthodox. Most of the population tends to be secular in orientation. The category "nonobservant Orthodox" covers the bulk of these Jews. As to the state of Israel, almost half are "religious" or "traditional," 36 percent define themselves as not religious, and an additional 9 percent are totally secular. About 47 percent keep separate meat and dairy dishes. Synagogue attendance in Israel is as low as in New York—about 26 percent never attend and most attend a few times a year.

At a Glance

Classic Texts

The Pittsburgh Platform of 1885 stated the theology of classical Reform Judaism.

The U.S. Constitution of 1787 forbade the establishment of a state church in the United States and afforded equal rights of religious belief to all religions.

Important Figures

Theodor Herzl (1860–1904): founded political Zionism that led to the creation of the state of Israel.

Ahad Ha'am (1856–1927): laid stress on Zion as a spiritual center.

Characteristic Beliefs

Jews may identify with Judaism and at the same time participate in modern and contemporary politics and culture.

Secular Jewishness held that Jews may reject all religious belief and remain part of the Jewish people.

The Holocaust and the creation of the state of Israel represent a continuous set of events, the latter following from the former.

Essential Creeds or Codes of Conduct

The Pittsburgh Platform

Brief Time Line

1787	U.S. Constitution and Bill of Rights
1885	The Pittsburgh Platform
1886–87	Founding of the Jewish Theological Seminary of America, center of Conservative Judaism
1897	Founding of the World Zionist Organization
1948	Founding of the state of Israel
1972	Ordination of first woman rabbi by Reform Judaism

Important Symbols

See previous chapter, "The Formation."

Important Rituals
See previous chapter, "The Formation."

Glossary

Conservative Judaism	affirms the tradition and law in practice but accepts critical historical scholarship; Judaic orthopraxy
emancipation	accords to Jews the rights of citizens to practice their religion without penalty
Holocaust	the murder of nearly six million European Jews by Germany and its allies in 1933–45
Orthodox Judaism	accepts the received tradition of Rabbinic Judaism and practices the law
the positive Historical School	see Conservative Judaism
Zionism	a political movement aiming at the creation of a Jewish state in Palestine; from 1948, a Jew who lives in the state of Israel and affirms its validity

Sacred Spaces and Times
See previous chapter, "The Formation."

Suggestions for Further Reading

Meyer, Michael A. *Response to Modernity: A History of the Reform Movement in Judaism*. Detroit: Wayne State University Press, 1995.

Neusner, Jacob. *Death and Birth of Judaism: The Impact of Christianity, Secularism, and the Holocaust on Jewish Faith*. New York: Basic Books, 1987. Second printing: Atlanta: Scholars Press for South Florida Studies in the History of Judaism, 1993.

Sachar, Howard. *A History of the Jews in the Modern World*. New York: Knopf, 2005.

CHRISTIANITY: BEGINNINGS

Bruce Chilton

The New Testament, a source of twenty-seven writings that are both provisional in the development of faith in Jesus Christ and fundamentally important, marks Christianity's beginnings. They are provisional because the New Testament does not set out any fixed creed, forms of worship, regulations for believing communities, or hierarchical structure—all characteristic features of the faith in its classic form. Yet the writings are fundamentally important because Christianity in any period can reach back to the New Testament as a dynamic and authoritative resource for determining and reforming what its true identity is.

What is this religion's overriding question? What makes the system self-evidently valid to the community of the faithful?

In a single sentence, Paul—the earliest writer in the New Testament (in this case writing around 56 C.E.), who took the message of Jesus into the Hellenistic world—summarized the message of Christianity. He said, "God was in Christ reconciling the world to himself, not reckoning their transgressions to them, and giving to us the word of reconciliation" (2 Cor. 5:19; this and all subsequent translations in this chapter are the author's own). Rather than an overriding question, the New Testament proclaims a "word," usually called a triumphant message or gospel (a *euanggelion* in Greek, or *besorta'* in Aramaic). The answer, reconciliation with God, comes with overwhelming emphasis.

51

The underlying question is implicit but powerful. Human beings commonly experience a sense of a divine power beyond themselves, transcendent of their particular circumstances. But how can their daily existence, conditioned by factors totally outside their control and often painful, be reconciled with their sense of an eternal truth to which they belong? In the passage cited, Paul called resolving this paradox "reconciliation," permitting the people who read his letters to see themselves as part of God's infinite truth. That was the profound attraction of his message.

Paul framed both his message and the question his message addressed in a vocabulary different from Jesus'. Jesus spoke less philosophically, of "the kingdom of God." This phrase was used in the Judaism of Jesus' time to speak of the promise of a time when God would overcome the injustice of this world with divine justice. To say that God would be king implied that no human being—not even the Roman caesar—would exercise a commanding role. The Kingdom was to be a time of natural righteousness and surreal peace when—in the prediction of Isaiah (Isa. 11:6)—wolf and lamb, leopard and goat, calf and lion would dwell together.

How do we know about this religion? What classics define the norms?

Whether spoken in the educated Greek of Paul or the peasant Aramaic of Jesus, the gospel was a triumphant message: the obstacles between God and humanity were being removed, the transformation of existence was under way.

For those who listened to Jesus and Paul, and responded positively to them, their message was transformative. When they joined with Jesus in Galilee to enjoy festive meals that celebrated God's kingdom as a truth that went beyond the strictures of conventional status and Roman occupation, or when they heard Paul explain to them that they belonged to God more than to any slave-owner or human master, the result was an experience of liberation.

The thrill of that experience is conveyed by the metaphors and symbols that convey it. Jesus spoke of lying back on festal couches in the manner of an ancient banquet, feasting with Abraham, Isaac, and Jacob in the kingdom of God. Paul declared that, in Christ, the old dividing lines between Jew and Greek, male and female, slave and free had been overcome.

During the period when the great majority of Jesus' followers were illiterate, teachers and new believers alike had to rely on oral tradition. Because they saw their tradition as sacred, their own acute interest—as well as their personal interpretations—shaped what they handed on to their followers. We have nothing Jesus wrote, and in all probability he was unable to write, but we have much that he said. Jesus' sayings and actions were transmitted through gospels, letters and sermons in contexts that described his life and death for contemporaries. That environment of constant interpretation surrounded the process by which the texts came to be written down.

Jesus' teachings and actions, although they were not a matter of public record at the time he lived, formed the principal model of his followers' faith and ethics. Paul's teaching was by no means wholly accepted by a majority of believers during his life, but his letters nonetheless came to provide, over time, non-Jewish Christians with a sense of how they could belong to Jesus' movement, and they served as an incentive for the transition from oral tradition to written tradition. The Gospels represent the broad commitment of Jesus' movement to educating and advancing believers in the significance of their faith, while the last writings of the New Testament raise concerns of the content of faith and its relationship to other forms of thought, such as apocalyptic speculation, philosophy, and history.

The explicit principles that determined which works would be included in the New Testament were (1) whether they derived from one of the groups of the apostles, those delegated by Jesus to deliver his message, and (2) whether they were accepted broadly by the church as a whole. The first principle meant that from the early days of Christianity believers concerned themselves with historical questions regarding how a given document emerged. The second principle committed Christians to a concern for whether, in addition to being originally connected to Jesus, a document was "catholic," that is, universally recognized (*katholikos*). These principles have been named since the second century of the Common Era, when the New Testament as we would recognize it was widely accepted. The actual listing of a table of contents that agrees with ours was all but finalized during the fourth century.

What is the community of the faithful called? What story explains its traits?

The term *church* has become dominant in order to designate the faithful, and it appears already in the New Testament. The word comes from the term *ekklesia* in Greek, where it refers to the calling out of a group for a public meeting. Ironically, in this and other cases (the original Greek for "bishop," "parish," and "priest," for example) the New Testament goes out of its way to use *secular* terms, whereas today the same words are used uniquely in an ecclesiastical context. The adjective *ecclesiastical* itself, derived from *ekklesia,* stands as the best illustration of how the language dynamics of the New Testament have sometimes been reversed. Originally, the point was to use the language of daily life to express how God was reaching in to transform human experience. Over time, the same words were used to give the impression of a special preserve, isolated from ordinary life.

Other terms in the New Testament that designate the faithful nonetheless do bear irreducibly religious senses. Paul likes to call believers "saints"—that is, "holy ones"—not because they are particularly virtuous (as Paul shows by his frequent criticism of his readers), but because they belong to God, just as Israel could be described as a royal priesthood and a holy nation. In the book of Acts, people who belong to Jesus' movement are called collectively "the Way," a term that evokes the rabbinic category of *halakhah,* or authoritative instruction.

Whatever terms appear to describe the faithful, however, the baseline of their faith is Jesus. He appears both as the subject of faith, as the person who demonstrates what it is to believe in God, and as the object of faith, as the focus of devoted commitment to God as he reshapes the world. The Gospels in the New Testament portray Jesus as both subject and object of faith, and they illustrate how the story of Christ's transforming work was adapted from community to community.

What is the way of life of the community of the faithful? What are the rules of conduct and the rites of passage? What is the notion of sacred time and space? How does the way of life embody the story that this religion tells about itself?

Within the New Testament, baptism signals the beginning of Christian life; a scene opens the book of Acts (ca. 90) that depicts the significance of baptism. At Pentecost, the Holy Spirit is portrayed as descending on the twelve apostles, including the newly chosen Mathias selected to replace Judas (Acts 1:15-26). They speak God's praises in the various languages of those assembled from the four points of the compass for the summer Feast of Harvest (called Weeks in Hebrew and Pentecost in Greek), both Jews and proselytes (Acts 2:1-12). The mention of proselytes (2:10) and the stress that those gathered came from "every nation under heaven" (2:5) clearly point ahead to the inclusion of non-Jews by means of baptism within Acts.

Peter's explanation in the narrative of the descent of the Spirit underlines this interpretation. He quotes from the prophet Joel (3:1-5 in the Septuagint): "And it will be in the last days, says God, that I will pour out from my spirit upon all flesh." "All flesh," not only historic Israel, is to receive of God's Spirit.

Pentecost is the most notable feast (in calendrical terms) of Peter and his circle. Seven weeks after the close of the entire Festival of Passover and Unleavened Bread came the feast called Weeks or Pentecost (in Greek, referring to the period of fifty days that was involved; see Lev. 23:15-22; Deut. 16:9-12). The waving of the sheaf before the Lord at the close of Passover anticipated the greater harvest (especially of wheat; see Exod. 34:22) that was to follow in the summer, and that is just what Weeks celebrates (so Lev. 23:10-15). The timing of the coming of the Holy Spirit in the recollection of Peter's circle is unequivocal (Acts 2:1-4), and the theme of Moses' dispensing of the Spirit on his elders is reflected (see Num. 11:11-29). The association of Weeks with the covenant with Noah (see *Jubilees* 6:1, 10-11, 17-19) may help explain why the coming of the Spirit then was to extend to humanity at large (see Acts 2:5-11). Firstfruits were celebrated at Weeks (see Num. 28:26), and they are taken to symbolize the gift of the Spirit and resurrection in Paul's theology (Rom. 8:23; 11:16; 1 Cor. 15:20, 23). We should expect such connections with the Pentecostal theology of Peter in one of Peter's students (see Gal. 1:18), as we should also expect Paul to be especially concerned to keep the Feast of Pentecost (see 1 Cor. 16:8; 20:16) despite what he said about calendrical observations in Galatians (see Gal. 4:9-10; cf. 2:14).

Those who entered into a fresh relationship with God by means of the Holy Spirit were themselves a kind of "firstfruits." They found their identity in relation to Christ or the Spirit as "first fruit" (so Rom. 8:23; 11:16; 16:5; 1 Cor. 15:20, 23; 16:15; James 1:18; Rev. 14:4). The wide range of that usage, which attests to the influence of the Petrine theology, reflects the deeply Pentecostal character of primitive Christianity.

Access to the covenant by means of the Spirit meant that believers entered "into the name" (*eis to onoma*) of Jesus in baptism. Also within the Petrine circle, Eucharist—the characteristic meal of Christianity—was celebrated in covenantal terms when one broke bread and shared the cup "into the remembrance of" (*eis ten anamnesin*) Jesus, a phrase associated with covenantal sacrifice. Both baptism and Eucharist are sacrificial in the Petrine understanding, involving almsgiving, and both intimately involve the spirit of God.

What is the worldview of the community, the story that it tells about itself in the context of history, the conception of divinity and the relationship of the divinity (or divinities) to the believers, and its principal ethical teachings? How do women fit into the system in its classical formulation? What are the attitude and behaviors toward persons outside the faith community?

Christianity deploys two powerful conceptions to understand itself in relation to other faiths, and that relationship is key to its address of the other questions in this subheading. The first is the metaphor of the body of Christ, embracing both the faithful and the entire cosmos. Christ, in this theology, is the animating principle of creation itself. The theme of solidarity with this body had long been a favorite of Paul's, but in Colossians (ca. 62 C.E.) Christ becomes the center of the cosmos—natural, social, and supernatural—and the very image of the God who created the world and makes the world new each day:

He is the invisible God's image, firstborn of all creation, because within him everything was created, in heaven and on earth, visible and invisible: thrones, dominions, principalities, and authorities. Everything through him and for him has been created. He is personally before all things, and all things exist in him, and he is personally the head of the body: the Church. He is the beginning, firstborn from the dead, so he becomes in all things precedent. For in him all the fullness pleased to dwell, and through him—and for him—to reconcile all things (whether on earth or in heaven), as he made peace through the blood of his cross. (Col. 1:15-20)

The range of Paul's thinking was literally cosmic, and even meta-cosmic, because the mind of Christ in his view wove all things into the primordial whole that had been their source. To Paul's mind, the fulfillment of all things had already been accomplished. Christ had mended the world, and an attuned heart and mind could join in that victory.

The second conception is the theology of the Word (the *Logos*)—the source of all human understanding, the power of creation—which Jesus personally embodied. Justin, a theologian of the second century, is the clearest theologian of the *Logos*. On the basis of New Testament sources, and writing just after the time of the New Testament, Justin crafted a distinctive view of the Divine Word (*Logos*) that conveys the truth of God to humanity. That *Logos* was Jesus Christ, understood as the human teacher who at last fully incarnated what philosophers and prophets had been searching for and had partially seen. Gnostic Christians were inclined to see that Word as a uniquely divine, ahistorical revelation of the truth, while Justin insisted with the Gospel according to John (ca. 100) that "the word became flesh and dwelt among us" (1:14). That contention only underlines by comparison how central the doctrine of the *Logos* had become to Christianity generally.

In 151 C.E. Justin addressed his *Apology* to the emperor himself, Antonius Pius. Such was his confidence that the "true philosophy" represented by Christ, attested in the Hebrew Scriptures, would triumph among the other options available at the time. Justin had been trained within some of those traditions, and by his Samaritan birth he could claim to represent something of the wisdom of the East. Somewhere between 162 and 168, however, Justin was martyred in Rome, a victim of the increasing hostility to Christianity under the reign of Marcus Aurelius.

Justin argued that the light of reason in people is put there by God and is to be equated with the Word of God incarnate in Jesus. His belief in the salvation of people as they actually are is attested by his attachment to millenarianism, the conviction that Christ would return to reign with his saints for a thousand years. That conviction, derived from Revelation 20, was fervently maintained by many Christians during the second century, in opposition to the abstract view of salvation that Gnostics preferred.

In strictly religious terms, Christianity did not compete well within the second century. Greco-Roman preferences were for ancient faiths, and the movement centered on Jesus was incontrovertibly recent. Moreover, it could and often did appear to be subversive of the authority of the emperor. After all, Christians did not accept the imperial title of *divi filius* ("Son of God"), and actually applied it to their criminal rabbi. And he was a rabbi who was not a rabbi, because the recognized authorities of Judaism did not accept Christians as among their numbers. For such reasons, the persecution of Christianity had been an established policy of state for nearly a century by the time Justin wrote.

The Christianity that Justin defended, however, was as much a philosophy as it was a religion. His claim was that the light of reason in humanity, which had already been indirectly available, actually became fully manifest in the case of Jesus Christ. Jesus, therefore, was the perfect sage, and Socrates as much as Isaiah was his prophet. In that sense, Christianity was as old as humanity; it was only its open manifestation that was recent. According to this new revelation of a primordial truth, as Paul said in his Letter to the Galatians, "There is not one Jew or Greek, not one slave or free, not one male or female; but you are all one in Jesus Christ" (3:28).

How does this religion function in the world today? What are its relationships with culture?

Jesus held that, at the end of time, God would change human life so radically that ordinary human relationships would no longer prevail. That conviction of a radical change brought with it a commitment to the language of eschatology, of the ultimate transformation God both promised and threatened. Although Jesus' eschatology was sophisticated, his commitment to that idiom of discourse is evident. Some efforts have been made recently to discount the eschatological dimension of Jesus' teaching; they have not prevailed. Periodically, theologians in the West have attempted to convert Jesus' perspective into their own sense that the world is a static and changeless entity, but that appears to have been far from his own orientation. Jesus' eschatology has proved to be a constant challenge to any notion that the status quo is a satisfactory state for human culture.

Jesus' understanding of what is to occur *to particular human beings* within God's disclosure of his kingdom typifies this challenge. Resurrection, as usually defined, promises actual life to individual persons within God's global transformation of all things. Because Jesus, on a straightforward reading of the Gospels, does not say much about resurrection as such, there has been a lively dispute over whether he had any distinctive (or even emphatic) teaching in that regard.

Still, when Jesus does address the issue, his contribution seems to be unequivocal. Sadducees, members of the priestly class in Jerusalem, are portrayed as asking a mocking question of Jesus, designed to disprove the possibility of resurrection. Moses had commanded that were a man to die childless his brother should raise up a seed for him; but suppose there were seven brothers, the first of whom was married. If they all died childless in sequence, whose wife would the woman be in the resurrection (see Matt. 22:23-28; Mark 12:18-23; Luke 20:27-33)?

Jesus' response is categorical and direct (following Mark 12:24-27; cf. Matt. 22:29-32; Luke 20:34-38):

> You completely deceive yourselves, knowing neither the Scriptures nor the power of God! Because when they arise from the dead, they neither marry nor are given in marriage, but are as angels in the heavens. But concerning the dead, that they rise, have you not read in the book of Moses about the bush, when God said to him, I am the God of Abraham and the God of Isaac and the God or Jacob? He is not God of the dead but of the living. You deceive yourselves greatly.

Of the two arguments Jesus makes, the one from Scripture is immediately fitting, an appeal both to the nature of God and to the evaluation of the patriarchs in early Judaism. If God identifies himself with Abraham, Isaac, and Jacob, it must be that in his sight they live. And those three patriarchs are indeed living principles of Judaism itself; they are Israel as chosen in the case of Abraham (see Gen. 15), as redeemed in the case of Isaac (see Gen. 22), and as struggling to identity in the case of Jacob (see Gen. 32). That evocation of patriarchal identity is implied rather than demonstrated, but the assumption is that the hearer is able to make such connections between the text of Scripture and the fulfillment of that Scripture within present experience. But that implicit logic of the argument from Scripture only makes the other argument seem all the bolder by comparison.

The direct comparison between people in the resurrection and angels is consonant with the thought that the patriarchs must live in the sight of God, since angels are normally associated with God's throne (so, for example, Dan. 7:9-14). So once the patriarchs are held to be alive before God, the comparison with angels is feasible. But Jesus' statement is not only a theoretical assertion of the majesty of God, a majesty that includes the patriarchs (and, by extension, the patriarchs' comparability to the angels); it is also an emphatic claim of what we might call divine anthropology. Jesus asserts that human relations are radically altered in the resurrection because sexual identity changes. That claim of substantial regeneration and transcendence became a major theme among the more-theological thinkers who followed Jesus, beginning with Paul. To this day, the articulation of how divine transcendence is involved with human life remains the vocation of Christianity.

At a Glance

Classic Texts

Paul's Letters to the Galatians, the Corinthians, and the Colossians are all examples of his writing to communities he helped establish in order to shape their faith. Paul's work is the earliest written contribution to the New Testament.

The Gospel According to John, called "the spiritual Gospel" as early as the second century, sets out the meaning of Christ on the basis of earlier traditions.

Justin's *Apology* marks a transition in Christianity, when the truth of Christ could be claimed as a philosophy commendable to the Roman Empire as a whole.

Important Figures

Jesus was born in Jewish Galilee and taught principally in Aramaic. His announcement of the kingdom of God brought him a wide following as a rabbi, and his prominence as a teacher who challenged the status quo brought official opposition. He confronted both priestly and Roman officials in Jerusalem in an attempt to make worship in the Temple conform to his vision. Crucifixion was the outcome, but Jesus' followers believed that he had triumphed over death.

Justin came from a Samaritan background and interested himself in the study of philosophy. Among the schools of thought available, Platonism attracted him most; but he then encountered a sage who changed his life (as he related in his *Dialogue with Trypho*, ca. 155). The sage convinced Justin that the highest good that Platonism can attain, the human soul, should not be confused with God himself, since the soul depends upon God for life. Knowledge of God depends rather upon the revelation of God's Spirit. Here is a self-conscious Christianity, which proclaims itself the true and only adequate philosophy. Justin's account of the truth of the Logos depends upon two sources of revelation resonant with each other: the Prophetic Scriptures, which attest the Spirit, and the wise reader who has been inspired by the Spirit.

Peter is the nickname that Jesus gave to one of his disciples called Simon. The word *petros* means "rock" in Greek, and corresponds to *qepha'* in Aramaic. Both terms, as well as *Simon*, are used to speak of Peter in the New Testament. Peter and his brother Andrew were fishermen from Bethsaida who settled with their wives in Capernaum. They accommodated Jesus in his early period as a rabbi. Later, Peter became one of Jesus' agents (*apostoloi* in Greek) charged with continuing Jesus' activity during a time of growing threat from Herod Antipas, the governor of Galilee. Peter headed the group of the apostles in Jerusalem immediately after the Resurrection, but then moved out from there to support the emergence of believing communities as far away as Antioch and Rome.

Paul was a Jew born in Tarsus in present-day Turkey. He went to study as a Pharisee in Jerusalem, where he acquired a reputation as a persecutor of Jesus' followers. An experience of Jesus risen from the dead converted him, and in order to fulfill the ancient prophecy of a time when Jews and non-Jews would together worship the one God, he took on Jesus' commission to reach out to non-Jews with the same forgiveness he had himself experienced. This became his guiding purpose, and Paul emerged as the single most influential thinker in the New Testament.

Characteristic Beliefs
The body of Christ
Church
Kingdom of God
Resurrection
Saints
The Way
Word of God

Essential Creeds or Codes of Conduct

The New Testament does not yet include formal creeds or ethical codes, but there are confessions of faith associated with baptism that later were formalized into doctrines and norms. Among them, one of the most striking is contained in 1 Timothy 3:16 when it speaks of Christ as "manifest in flesh, justified in Spirit, seen by angels, preached among nations, believed in the world, received up in glory." Such confessions of faith evolved into creeds that explain the relationship of Christ to God the Creator, and into ethical standards that take Christ as their touchstone.

Brief Time Line

2–16 C.E.	The birth of Jesus in Galilean Bethlehem, his childhood in Nazareth
7 C.E.	Paul is born in Tarsus in Asia Minor into a Jewish family, prospering in the profession of making tents.
16–21 C.E.	Jesus' apprenticeship with John the Baptist
21 C.E.	The death of John
24–27 C.E.	Using Capernaum as a base, Jesus' itinerancy makes him a major figure in Galilee by his twenty-fifth year.
27–31 C.E.	Herod Antipas's threat forces Jesus to skirt and crisscross Galilean territory and gather his followers in Syria.
28 C.E.	Paul departs Tarsus for Jerusalem, taking the Aramaic name of Saul, to train as a Pharisee.
31–32 C.E.	Jesus' last year in Jerusalem, age thirty
32 C.E.	Between Passover and Pentecost the Gospels attest a sequence of resurrection appearances, and the book of Acts indicates there was a series of visions during that summer. After the stoning of Stephen, Paul's vision of the risen Jesus took place (Gal. 1:15-17).
35 C.E.	The meeting of Peter and Paul in Jerusalem, and the availability of the earliest sources of the Gospels: Peter's instruction for apostles such as Paul, and the mishnah of Jesus' teaching known to modern scholarship as "Q"
37 C.E.	The removal of Pontius Pilate and Caiaphas from power
40 C.E.	The adaptation of Peter's gospel by James, the brother of Jesus, in Jerusalem
45 C.E.	In Antioch, outside of Palestine, followers of Jesus are for the first time called "Christians."
50 C.E.	Paul's First Letter to the Thessalonians
53 C.E.	Paul's Letter to the Galatians
55 C.E.	Paul's First Letter to the Corinthians
56 C.E.	Paul's Second Letter to the Corinthians
57 C.E.	Paul's Letter to the Romans

58 C.E.	Paul's Letter to Philemon
62 C.E.	Paul's Letter to the Philippians; the stoning death of James in Jerusalem, at the instigation of the high priest; Paul's Letter to the Colossians (at its earliest stage)
64 C.E.	The death of Paul and Peter in Rome during a pogrom instigated by Nero
70–73 C.E.	The burning of the Temple by the Roman troops under Titus and the end of the revolt against Rome in Palestine
73 C.E.	The Gospel according to Mark
80 C.E.	The Gospel according to Matthew
85 C.E.	The Second Letter to the Thessalonians
90 C.E.	The Gospel according to Luke; the Letter to the Ephesians; the Acts of the Apostles
92 C.E.	The Epistle of James; the First Letter of Peter
93 C.E.	The First Letter to Timothy
94 C.E.	The Letter of Jude
95 C.E.	The Epistle to the Hebrews
96 C.E.	The Second Letter to Timothy
97 C.E.	The Letter to Titus
98 C.E.	The First Epistle of John
100 C.E.	The Gospel according to John
102 C.E.	The Second Epistle of John
103 C.E.	The Third Epistle of John
105 C.E.	Revelation of John
110 C.E.	The Second Letter of Peter
151 C.E.	*Apology* of Justin

Important Symbols

During the period in question, principal symbols included the cross, the Lamb of God, and the sacrifice of Isaac.

Important Rituals

Very large numbers of Christians continued all the rituals of Judaism while non-Jewish believers were required to give up idolatry, including the eating of meat sacrificed to idols (Acts 15:20). That was so commonplace that Paul wrote that it was acceptable to eat such food (1 Cor. 8), but he was in a minority on that issue. In addition to baptism, the sacrament of being reborn in the Spirit, Christians also practiced the Eucharist. Within the New Testament, the Eucharist shows signs of developing along the lines of several types of religious meals in Judaism: (1) the meal that consecrates the beginning of a holy time, (2) festivity that takes the place of sacrifice in the Temple, (3) the blessing of a household, (4) the Passover meal, (5) the commemoration of a martyr's sacrifice, and (6) participation in the self-giving of deity.

Glossary

Aramaic	A Semitic language, ultimately the foundation of what became known as Hebrew. The inhabitants of Judea adopted the form of the language spoken during the period of the Persian Empire so that by the first century it was the principal language spoken by Jews there.
eschatology	The science (the *logos*) of last things (*eskhata*). At issue is not merely the temporal end of the world, but the purpose or end of human life.
gnostic	Derived from the word for "knowledge" (*gnosis*), refers to insight into the divine world, as compared to the purely relative awareness one might gain of this world.
gospel	The translation of *euanggelion* in Greek or *besorta'* in Aramaic and refers to the triumphant news of God's victory in this world.
Hellenistic	A term that characterizes the Greek culture throughout the Mediterranean Basin after the conquests of Alexander the Great, which gave the region a common (although far from homogeneous) linguistic and social identity.
hermeneutics	The theory of meaning, according to which authoritative texts are held to address people in their living situations.
kingdom of God	Principal subject of Jesus' preaching, concerned God's transformation of the world so that God's will would be all in all.
proselytes	People who "come in" to the community, features as the technical term for converts in Judaism.
Pentecost	One of three major feasts of Judaism, the festal sacrifice of wheat during the early summer, coming between Passover, the barley harvest in spring, and Sukkoth, the largest harvest in the autumn.
rabbinic	A term that characterizes authoritative Jewish teachers after the destruction of the Temple in 70 C.E. who developed a form of Judaism on the basis of the Torah alone, without reference to sacrifice.

| Sadducees | The priestly class in Jerusalem who claimed their inheritance from the sons of Zadok in the book of Ezekiel. |
| transcendent | What surpasses usual human experience. |

Sacred Spaces and Times

Many Christians during the period followed the calendar of Judaism (see "Pentecost" above). Whether or not they did, for the sacred calendar of Christianity the season of Passover became determinative as the season of Christ's death and resurrection.

Suggestions for Further Reading

Baumgarten, Albert I., ed. *Sacrifice in Religious Experience.* Numen Book Series XCIII. Leiden: Brill, 2002.

Brown, Raymond E. *An Introduction to the New Testament.* New York: Doubleday, 1997.

Chilton, Bruce. *Jesus' Prayer and Jesus' Eucharist: His Personal Practice of Spirituality.* Valley Forge: Trinity Press International, 1997.

———. *Rabbi Jesus: An Intimate Biography.* New York: Doubleday, 2000.

———. *Rabbi Paul: An Intellectual Biography.* New York: Doubleday, 2004.

Lang, Bernhard. *Sacred Games: A History of Christian Worship.* New Haven, Conn.: Yale University, 1997.

Nienhuis, David R. *Not by Paul Alone: The Formation of the Catholic Epistle Collection and the Christian Canon.* Waco: Baylor University Press, 2007.

Pennington, Jonathan T., and Sean M. McDonough, eds. *Cosmology and New Testament Theology.* Library of New Testament Studies 355. London: T & T Clark, 2008.

ROMAN CATHOLICISM

Lawrence S. Cunningham

The word *catholic* comes from two Greek words, *kath 'olou,* which together mean something like "universal" or "of the whole." The word does not appear in the New Testament writings but occurred first in the early second century to mean the whole church, as opposed to this or that particular Christian community. By the end of the second century, however, the word *catholic* had taken on a more precise meaning to signify what the whole (or "catholic") church, as opposed to heretical or schismatic groups, held true. In that sense, then, *catholic* becomes a synonym for *orthodox*—that is, "right believing" or "right worshiping," as opposed to the beliefs or practices of heretical communities or schismatic groups. It is in that sense that the word is used in the early creeds that profess a belief in the "one, holy, catholic, and apostolic church." At times the early Christian writers will call the Catholic Church the "Great Church," as opposed to particular dissident or schismatic communities.

What is the religion's overriding question? What makes the system self-evidently valid to the community of the faithful?

Roman Catholicism is that branch of Christianity that finds its essential unity by being in communion with the bishop of Rome, known more familiarly as the pope. Its overriding question is: what does it mean to live as a faithful follower of Jesus Christ?

This question is formalized in the authoritative Catechism of the Catholic Church. There are three essential characteristics that

67

constitute catholicity. They are: (1) the full possession of the faith handed to the apostles of Jesus Christ and their legitimate successors; (2) the full possession of the sacramental worship life intended by Jesus Christ; and (3) the union of the local bishop of the church with all other bishops including the bishop of Rome, the successor of the Apostle Peter. In a shorthand fashion we might call these three essential characteristics Catholic doctrine, worship, and church structure.

How do we know about this religion? What classics define the norms?

Roman Catholicism is shaped and known by its doctrine. The word doctrine comes from the Latin word meaning "teaching." At its most fundamental, Catholicism teaches that Jesus was the "Christ" (the word, from the Greek, means "Anointed One," from the Hebrew word *messiah*), who was the fulfillment of the promises given to the chosen people, the Jews. What the earliest followers of this Jesus believed about Jesus can be found embedded in a series of early sermons recorded in the New Testament book known as *The Acts of the Apostles*: Jesus was a mighty figure who came to earth, did marvelous deeds, was crucified, died, was buried, and rose again from the dead; and about this his followers testify. That Jesus was the resurrected Lord is economically summed up in one of the earliest professions of faith we have in the New Testament. Writing to the Christian community in Corinth about a generation after the life of Jesus, Paul wrote: "For I handed on to you as of first importance what I in turn had received: that Christ died for our sins in accordance with the scriptures, and that he was buried, and that he was raised on the third day in accordance with the scriptures, and that he appeared to Cephas, then to the twelve" (1 Cor. 15:3-5).

In order to establish a kind of baseline of what was fundamentally required to be a member of the Catholic Church, the community developed, first of all, a requirement for all those who wished to join the church to affirm their faith, and then, against the opinions of various heretics, adopted fundamental statements of faith, which we call creeds. The most famous of these is the early-fourth-century creed known as the Nicene Creed, named for the city (Nicaea) where it was adopted by the assembled bishops of the Great Church.

Fundamental Christian teaching, reflected in the creed (recited each Sunday at worship), is a brief summary of faith, but obviously the church in its preaching, in its teaching, in its efforts to convert people, and in its language of worship expands these summaries. That expansion, in all of its forms, is what is called the teaching function (known as the *magisterium*) of the Catholic Church, entrusted at the fundamental level to the bishops, whom Catholics believe to be the successors of the first apostles.

What about the Bible? Catholics believe that the twenty-seven books that make up the New Testament grew up out of the teaching of the church (i.e., there was a church before there was a New Testament), but that the New Testament (as well as the Old Testament, which together make up "The Bible") constitutes the inspired word of God and, like the Nicene Creed, is a standard against which all teaching in the church is tested. The biblical witness is preached in the church, is the resource for growth in faith, is the "check" on heresy, and with the constant preaching of the church guarantees fidelity to the gospel handed to the apostles and their successors, the bishops.

An example might illustrate how this relationship between tradition and Scripture functions. The Catholic Church holds, as a fundamental truth, that Jesus was a person who was both human and divine. What does that mean? Was he a god who assumed the guise of a human? Was he an exceptional man who seemed to have had "godlike" qualities? The Catholic Church teaches that he was truly born of Mary as a human and that in his birth he took on our humanity but preexisted as the Word of God from all eternity, as the prologue of John's Gospel clearly states. Getting that teaching "right" requires two moves: (1) to understand what the Scriptures clearly teach and (2) to articulate that belief in such a way so as to do justice to both the humanity and the divinity of Christ. When some taught that Mary was the mother of the human Jesus, only the church, in reaction, responded negatively, because such a teaching could not account for Jesus as a *person*. Hence it definitively taught at the Council of Ephesus (in the year 430) that Mary was *Theotokos*, using the Greek term that means "God Bearer"—a term still used in the Catholic (and Orthodox) Church to honor Mary in its worship. The word *Theotokos* is not found in the New Testament (neither, by the way, is the word *Trinity*) but was adopted by the church to hold the constant teaching of the church and the witness of the New Testament in correct balance.

Drawing out the witness of Scripture and the teaching of the church is called the *development of doctrine,* which means, in essence, that the truths of the gospel handed down to the apostles and their successors constantly yield new insights as well as checks against false teaching. That constant reflection is what we normally understand the task of theology to be. Theology, in the famous formulation of Saint Anselm of Canterbury, is "faith seeking understanding."

Finally, we need to make a critical distinction between tradition and traditions in Catholicism. *Tradition* means the "handing down" of the apostolic teaching whereas *traditions* mean those things that have been developed over the course of time that are not essential in the church. Tradition stands for the essential faith of the church in the trinitarian life of God, the redemptive life of Jesus, and so on, while traditions, like the use of a rosary, the celibacy of the clergy, popular devotions, going on pilgrimages, and so on are those matters that may nourish the life of the church but are not fundamental to its essential core.

What is the community of the faithful called? What story explains its traits?

The Roman Catholic Church begins its story with the life, death, and resurrection of Jesus and the community of faith who came to understand him as the Christ. To lead this community, Jesus consecrated Saint Peter as the first pope. Since that time, the leadership has been passed down through an unbroken line of succession to the present day.

In the early Middle Ages the church in the East (centered in Constantinople) broke with the church in the West (centered in Rome) and, as a consequence, the eastern church began to be called "Orthodox" and the church in the West "Catholic," even though the words are synonyms. To make matters more complicated, it became common in the modern period to speak of the "Roman Catholic Church," even though, technically speaking, the term is misleading. "Roman Catholic" means those who find their unity with the bishop of Rome (i.e., the pope), although there are Catholics who affirm that unity who are not "Roman" in the sense that they follow other rites in the church (e.g., the Byzantine).

Although it is more accurate to speak of the Catholic Church at Rome (or the Catholic Church at New York, Calcutta, Berlin, and so on), we will use the term *Catholic* to mean Roman Catholic, since that is the way in which most people understand the term. Thus, in this essay when we use the term *Catholic* we understand the word to mean that denomination, as opposed to Orthodox, Protestant, and so forth.

One final note: when someone hears the word *Catholic* it is easy to conjure up a wide diversity of images because Catholicism is a very ancient reality with an incredibly complex historical evolution. Whole books have been written on the evolution of a simple devotion like the rosary, and many histories of large topics, such as the papacy, have run into many volumes. In this brief chapter it would be impossible to give even a superficial account of Catholic history, but it is worthwhile to note how simplified (and how abstract) this exposition will be if only to warn the reader that almost everything set out in this chapter has a longer history behind it that will be assumed but not explored.

One small example might give an idea of this complexity. Everyone has seen television films set in Saint Peter's Square in the Vatican. That square, which fronts Saint Peter's Basilica, dates from the seventeenth century, as does the final work on the church. The church, however, is built over the remains of an earlier church begun in the fourth century, which, in turn, is constructed over a smaller shrine that was located in a large cemetery that dates back to pre-Christian times, in which it was believed the martyred Saint Peter was buried. Not to put too fine a point on it: present-day Saint Peter's has been a Christian worship site for nearly two millennia. The fourth-century basilica was torn down around the time that Columbus began to explore the New World.

What is the way of life of the community of the faithful? What are the rules of conduct and the rites of passage? What is the notion of sacred time and space? How does the way of life embody the story that this religion tells about itself?

Catholic Worship: Sacraments

The Catholic Church is a *sacramental* church. The word *sacrament* means a visible sign of God's grace. In that sense of the term, the created world itself is a sacrament. The early Christian writers called Jesus Christ the "Great Sacrament" because he was a visible sign of

God's gracious presence in the world. Catholics further believe that the church is a sacrament because it is a sign of Christ's continuing presence in the world. The church, in turn, mediates the redemptive race of Christ through "signs," which we call sacraments. The Catholic Church traditionally numbers seven such essential signs.

Baptism—Confirmation—Holy Eucharist

In the ancient church these three sacraments were part of a single complex in which new candidates were symbolically bathed in water, anointed with oil, and then permitted to participate in the sacred meal of bread and wine, believed by Catholics to be the true presence of Jesus Christ.

Penance (Reconciliation)

Sins committed after baptism can be forgiven through participation in the sacrament of reconciliation. This rite was first seen as a reintegration (reconciliation) into the church community after a person had committed some public sin (adultery, denial of faith in ties of persecution, and so on) that resulted in separation from the worshiping community (excommunication). Over time the practice of confession became more private and from the second millennium it was expected that each person would confess his or her sins privately to a duly authorized priest.

Anointing of the Sick

Anointing with oil those who are sick or dying is an ancient practice in the Catholic Church. Today, it is often celebrated in a communal ceremony; but for a person who is in danger of death it is done privately. The complex of prayers, giving a dangerously ill person Holy Communion after confession and the anointing with oils, is known collectively as "the Last Rites."

Matrimony

The Catholic Church considers marriage between two baptized persons before a priest and witnesses a sacrament. Such marriages are considered permanent and indissoluble. Although persons may separate and even obtain a civil divorce for grave reasons, they may not remarry in the Catholic Church. The church does recognize some reasons to annul a marriage (e.g., coercion, lack of psychological maturity, impotency, and so on). The current obligation of having a marriage celebrated before a priest is a relatively new legislation instituted because of the abuse of "private" marriages or informal forms of material consent.

Holy Orders

The sacrament by which a man is ordained a bishop, priest, or deacon is called "Holy Orders." Its essential rite is the laying on of the hands of an ordaining bishop. The bishop possesses the fullness of Orders; the priest is one who shares in those orders. Priests and bishops of the Roman Catholic Church must be celibate, a practice universal in the church for more than a millennium.

Catholic Worship: The Mass

The central worship rite of the Catholic Church uses two names to describe it: the "Holy Sacrifice of the Mass" or, more commonly today, the "Eucharistic Liturgy."

It is called a "sacrifice" because Catholics believe that it is in this rite that the once and forever sacrifice of Jesus Christ on Calvary is reenacted, remembered, and represented. The sacrificial character of the Mass explains why its clergy are called "priests": they are ordained to perform sacrifice. The two Greek words from which the phrase "Eucharistic Liturgy" derives mean the "Public Worship of Thanksgiving."

Although the ceremonies of the Mass have developed over the centuries, the fundamental structure of its worship has been attested to as early as the second century. In skeletal form the Mass is structured along two main divisions:

> The parts of the Catholic Mass, often set to music, include the following:
>
> *Kyrie Eleison* (Greek: "Lord have mercy")
>
> *Gloria in Excelsis Deo* ("Glory to God in the highest"), sung at Festal Masses
>
> *Credo* ("I believe"), sung after the reading of the Gospel and th homily
>
> *Sanctus* ("Holy, Holy, Holy"—from Isaiah 6)
>
> *Agnus Dei* ("Lamb of God..."), sung before Holy Communion
>
> At Funeral Masses it has been traditional to sing the long medieval Latin hymn that begins *Dies Irae* ("Day of Wrath").

The Liturgy of the Word

The first part of Catholic worship begins with the gathering of the people, a communal confession of unworthiness, an opening prayer, two readings from the Bible (typically a lesson from the Old Testament and one from the New Testament), and then the reading of the Gospel of the day followed by a homily from the priest and a profession of faith.

The Liturgy of the Eucharist

Offerings of bread and wine are brought to the altar and the priest recites the long eucharistic prayer, which ends with the great "Amen." The congregation recites the Lord's Prayer, exchanges the Kiss of Peace, and then Holy Communion is distributed to those in the congregation. After Communion there is another short prayer, followed by a blessing from the priest.

The Liturgy contains both parts that are used each day and those that change according to the season. The liturgical year begins with the season of Advent (four Sundays before Christmas) and then proceeds through Epiphany (January 6) to Lent, Holy Week (culminating in Easter), and fifty days later, to Pentecost. The Sundays that follow are called "ordinary Sundays," until the Advent season begins again. Woven within that calendar are feasts of the Blessed Virgin Mary and the Saints, although their feasts do not supersede the liturgical calendar described above.

Catholic Spirituality

Catholics understand the term *spirituality* to mean those who live in the spirit, as opposed to those who live in the flesh (see Rom. 8). More generically, the term means the way(s) in which Catholics grow deeper to God in the imitation of Christ empowered by the Holy Spirit. Naturally enough, the foundations of spirituality are to be found in the ordinary round of Catholic observances, such as participating in the sacramental and liturgical life of the church as well as in those ordinary exercises of daily piety like morning and evening prayer, grace before meals, and all efforts, under God's grace, to avoid sin and live a life of Christian virtue.

In the long history of the Catholic tradition, the church has recognized certain individuals and small groups who have found a particular way of living out the Christian life. The church honors those who live a life of the community of good and the life of common prayer in the monastic life. It holds up those who wish to follow the life of poverty for the love of Christ (the Franciscans) or those who wish to be formed in the *Spiritual Exercises* of Saint Ignatius of Loyola to also make an election for the greater glory of God.

These various traditions are often known as "schools of spirituality" because of their distinctive methods of prayer, their focus on particular services within the church, or the manner in which they emphasize ways to become converted more perfectly to the following of Christ. These "schools" or adaptations of them are open to men and women who are members of religious communities; they are also available as resources to nourish the life of Christian perfection. The fundamental point is, as the Second Vatican Council insisted, that all in the church are called to a life of holiness and are free to develop a life of spirituality within the unity of the church itself.

Some Characteristics of Catholicism

The Papacy

Anyone who thinks of Catholicism inevitably thinks of the pope in Rome. Catholics assert that the pope is the successor of Saint Peter, who was martyred in Rome ca. A.D. 64 in the persecution by Nero. What makes the Catholic Church "catholic" is that all bishops of this church are in union with one another and with the successor, Peter, the bishop of Rome. When we assert that the pope is infallible, we need to be very clear that the pope is not an oracle; his gift of infallibility has been exercised only twice in the past two hundred years. Infallibility does not mean that the pope gets new revelations, nor does it mean that he is always right or always moral or that he is inspired the way sacred Scriptures are inspired. It means simply that when he speaks as the authoritative head of the Catholic Church, he says in so many words, on a matter of faith or morals, that he will not lead the church astray. Infallibility, then, is a negative gift.

Catholicism and the Bible

The Catholic Church accepts both the Old Testament and the New Testament as the inspired word of God, free from all error with respect to belief and morals. Unlike many Christian denominations, it does not accept the idea that the Bible is the sole rule of faith. It believes that those who were in the church wrote the New Testament and that the church decided which books were inspired and which belonged in the canon. Nonetheless, it does maintain that the Bible is the criterion against which the church's teaching, preaching, and practice must be tested. Catholics do not typically ask, What does the Bible say? They ask, by contrast, Is what we say conformable to the witness of Scripture?

The Scriptures are the resource upon which Catholics draw for their prayer life, for the shape of their worship, for their ritual gestures (e.g., the "sign of the cross" is a gesture based on Matt. 28), for their narrative, and for their understanding of their theology. Perhaps the most used book of the Bible, apart from portions of the New Testament, is the book containing the 150 psalms of David. The Psalter, as it is known, makes up the core of the public prayer of the church.

In the United States, the standard English translation of the Bible used in all official services in the Roman Catholic Church is the *New American Version,* but for personal use, study, or the life of prayer many Catholics make use of a variety of translations such as the *Revised Standard Version,* the *New Revised Standard Version,* or the English translation of the French *Bible de Jerusalem,* known more familiarly as the *Jerusalem Bible.* Catholics are more reluctant to embrace the *New International Version* because of its evangelical tilt and its failure to contain the Deuterocanonical books of the Old Testament, which are part of the Catholic (and Orthodox) canon of the books of the Old Testament.

Mary and the Saints

Catholics believe that God alone is to be adored; Mary, the angels, apostles, martyrs, and saints are venerated because the Catholic Church believes that they are part of the church in heaven. Every Catholic Mass, at the Eucharistic Prayers, calls upon Mary and the other saints to join us as we celebrate our worship. We ask those saints, named and unnamed, to intercede for us before God in heaven. The proliferation of shrines, sanctuaries, and other locations are part of the popular devotion and piety of the Catholic faithful developed over the centuries, but the theological roots of these phenomena are deep in Catholic theology.

Multiplicity in Unity

Over the long history of Catholicism different styles of being a Catholic emerged and found a place in its tradition. There has always been space for those who wish to live a life totally focused on worship and separation from the world, as best represented in monasticism; others have sought out a life of poverty for the sake of the Kingdom in the following of Saint Francis of Assisi. These various schools of spirituality coexist within the larger church and are considered ways of following Christ. It is also important to remember that under the large umbrella of Catholicism there are different "styles" of being Catholic. Irish Catholics are not quite the same as Mexican Catholics, just as exuberant charismatic Catholic worship is in a style quite different from the manner of the old Latin Mass offered before the reforms of the Second Vatican Council. These diverse styles and these quite different schools are still part of the unity of the church. There are also other rites of the Catholic Church that are in union with the bishop of Rome. Byzantine, Ruthenian, Melkite, and other such Catholics have their own canon law, their own customs, and their own liturgical rites.

The diversity of styles, schools, and devotional practices underlines the Catholic notion of tradition with a small "t." Within the unity of sacramental and devotional life there is a vast multiplicity. One may be a good Catholic and never go to a shrine to Mary or say the rosary or become a monk, but one cannot be a good Catholic and deny the trinitarian nature of God or refuse to go to Mass or to receive the sacraments.

Catholic Morality

Every religious tradition demands that its adherents practice a way of life conformable to its teaching. Catholicism preaches a morality that is a synthesis of the ethics it receives from the Jewish tradition. It honors the Ten Commandments given by God to Moses on Sinai; it honors the prophetic connection between belief and the demands for social justice. Much of what Jesus preached must be seen against the tradition in which he was formed. Beyond that basic context, Catholics believe that Jesus himself is a model for behavior. In other words, Catholics ought to be first followers of Jesus and then followers of his teachings. Finally, within the Catholic moral teaching is a robust theory of natural law—that is, within the human psyche, however attenuated by sin, is an impulse to do good and to avoid evil. It sees that natural impulse as one implanted in the very structure of human beings who are, in the words of Genesis, created in the image and likeness of God. Natural law, in the final instance, is clarified and made concrete in the light of the biblical tradition and, more particularly, in the example of Jesus.

Finally, Catholicism also stipulates laws for the right order of the church. Those church laws legislate matters such as proper times of fasting, the discipline of having celibate clergy for priests, regulations concerning when attendance at Mass is obligatory, the prerequisites for those who wish to marry in the church, and so on. Catholic morality has always insisted that morality is both individual (each person must answer before God for his or her actions) and social, in that each person lives in community and has a responsibility not only to a particular community like the Catholic community but also to the larger human community. As a consequence, the Catholic moral tradition is, by its very character and of necessity, both ecumenical and interreligious.

Again: Sacramentality

As we insisted earlier in this chapter, the Catholic Church puts a strong emphasis on the sacramental—the view that all visible signs somehow reflect the presence of God mediated to us by that which is visible. It is for that reason that Catholicism has always had a strong orientation toward the visual. Catholic churches use the visual arts extensively: there are crucifixes (i.e., crosses with a body attached), statues or icons of Mary and other saints, visual narratives in stained glass windows, and so on. It is that kind of atmosphere in which the Liturgy—celebrated with vestments, candles burning, and incense wafting smoke toward heaven—is celebrated.

Individuals and families also honor the sacramental way. It is common for Catholics to wear religious medallions, just as it is usual for a Catholic family to have crucifixes over beds and sacred art on their walls. Most practicing Catholics identify themselves as Catholics living within a parish. Traditional parishes include not only a church building for worship but frequently a school, a social center, a home for the local priest, and so on. The church is located within the parish, and in that local church there are always prayers for the local bishop and the bishop of Rome (the pope). It is also from the local parish that much of the moral, spiritual, and material support of the worldwide needs of the church comes. In that way the local church is simultaneously local and universal, which is to say, catholic.

What is the worldview of the community?

Let us think of an "ideal" American Catholic. What does his or her life look like? Most likely these persons were baptized shortly after birth and if their parents were practicing Catholics they soon began to accompany their parents to church (Catholic churches are typically filled with squirming or crying young children). Perhaps they were enrolled in a Catholic grammar school. Around the age of six they were prepared to make their first Holy Communion, and when entering their teen years the local bishop confirmed them on his visit to the parish. A small percentage might go on to a Catholic college, but their next big rite of passage would be marriage and the beginnings of their own families. Toward the end of their days they would be prepared for death by the church's sacraments and buried after services in their parish.

Along the way most Catholics would absorb some Catholic ways of doing things. They would pray morning, evening, and before meals. They would pick up rudiments of doctrine in catechism classes. In the United States they would have to learn that not everyone believes the way they do. It is not uncommon for many to become inactive either through simply drifting away from their early upbringing, or from disagreements with some aspect of Catholic teaching, or by marrying someone of another faith when that other person had stronger beliefs than they themselves possessed.

Many Catholics would engage in various charitable works offered by the church; others might visit monasteries for spiritual retreats; still others might find companionship in activities sponsored by Catholic organizations. In previous generations they may well have been born, raised, and died in what some have called the "Catholic ghetto," but that is less likely the case today. They will notice today that many of their fellow Catholics speak Spanish as a first language, or that their parish priest is a refugee from Vietnam. Separation from their Protestant neighbors would be less strained than was the case a couple of generations ago, and most would be startled if they ran across anti-Catholic prejudice, which was more common then than it is today.

Observers of the Catholic scene today would soon see that among this idealized picture of who Catholics are there is, despite their fundamental unity, a bewildering variety: Catholics are no longer reducible to the fabled blue-collar working class (one quarter of the House of Representatives and a majority of the Supreme Court are Catholic). There are liberals, conservatives, and the politically indifferent; there are poor and rich Hispanics; there are ethnic enclaves;

there are suburbanites. What holds them together is that when they go to Mass on Sunday they all stand and affirm in the words of the Nicene Creed: "I believe in the one, holy, catholic, and apostolic faith."

At a Glance

Classic Texts
Catechism of the Catholic Church
Saint Augustine of Hippo, *On the Trinity*
Saint Anselm of Canterbury, *Why God Became Man (Cur Deus Homo)*
Saint Bonaventure, *The Mind's Journey to God (Itinerarium Mentis in Deum)*
Saint Thomas Aquinas, *The Summa Theologiae*
John Henry Newman, *An Essay on the Development of Christian Doctrine*

Important Figures
Jesus Christ
Saint Peter (Cephas)
Mary, mother of Jesus
The pope (Bishop of Rome)
Saint Francis of Assisi
Saint Ignatius of Loyola

Characteristic Beliefs
Jesus was a person who was both human and divine.
All bishops are in union with one another and with the successor Peter, the bishop of Rome.
The pope is infallible.
The Bible is the inspired word of God, free from all error with respect to belief and morals.
Mary (the mother of Jesus), the angels, apostles, martyrs, and saints are venerated.

Essential Creeds or Codes of Conduct
Nicene Creed

Brief Time Line
ca. 2 C.E.	Birth of Jesus
31–32 C.E.	Jesus' last year in Jerusalem
ca. 35 C.E.	Meeting of Peter, James, and Paul in Jerusalem

ca. 45 C.E.	In Antioch, outside of Palestine, followers of Jesus are called "Christians" for the first time.
ca. 50 C.E.	Council of Jerusalem
64 C.E.	Death of Peter in Rome
325 C.E.	First Council of Nicaea
381 C.E.	Nicene Creed
476	Fall of the western Roman Empire
1054	Split between eastern Orthodox Christianity and western Roman Catholicism
1205	Saint Francis of Assisi becomes a hermit, founding the Fransiscan order of friars.
1473–81	Sistine Chapel built
1517	The 95 Theses of Martin Luther begins German Protestant Reformation.
1531	Our Lady of Guadalupe in Mexico. According to tradition, when roses fell from a cactus cloth, the icon of the Virgin of Guadalupe appeared imprinted on the cloth, which resulted in the sudden, extraordinary success of the evangelizing of ten million Indians in the decade of 1531–41. This constitutes the most successful evangelization ever.
1534	Ignatius of Loyola founds the Jesuit order.
1545–63	Catholic Council of Trent, counterreformation against Protestantism, clearly defines an official theology and biblical canon.
1566	Roman Catechism
1582	Saint Terese of Avila
1592	Clementine Vulgate of Pope Clement VIII replaces Sistine Vulgate of 1590, standard Latin Catholic Bible until reforms of the Second Vatican Council.
1854	Immaculate Conception is defined as Catholic dogma.
1869–70	Catholic First Vatican Council asserts doctrine of Papal Infallibility.
1933	Catholic Worker Movement founded
1950	Assumption of Mary decreed by Pope Pius XII
1950	Missionaries of Charity founded by Mother Teresa
1962–65	Catholic Second Vatican Council, announced by Pope John XXIII in 1959, produces sixteen documents that become official Roman Catholic teaching after approval by the pope. Their purpose is to renew "ourselves and the flocks committed to us."

| 1992 | Catechism of the Catholic Church |
| 2005 | Death of Pope John Paul II, election of Pope Benedict XVI |

Important Symbols
Bread and Wine
Crucifix

Important Rituals
First Holy Communion
Sign of the Cross
Rosary

Glossary

apostolic teaching	The core teaching of Jesus Christ as taught by the first followers of Jesus and preserved in the Christian tradition.
charity	From the Latin *caritas,* it means self-giving love that is directed first to God and then to others.
doctrine	A formula expressing a core teaching as, for example, the doctrine of the Holy Trinity.
gospel	Literally meaning "good news," the word first expresses the apostolic teaching and later refers to four books that are included in the New Testament.
heresy	Literally the word means "to split" but is used for any teaching that contradicts the doctrine held by the church.
magisterium	A Latin term meaning "teaching authority," used to describe the traditional teaching of the college of bishops in the Catholic Church.
Mass	Common term for the central act of Catholic worship; also called the "Eucharistic Liturgy."
Orthodox	The literal meaning is "right doctrine and right worship," as contrasted with heretical.
pope/papacy	refers to the bishop of Rome who is the central figure in the college of Catholic bishops.
rosary	A beaded cord used as a devotional device to honor the Blessed Virgin Mary.
sacrament	a visible sign instituted by Jesus Christ to bestow grace.
saint	Anyone who lives in the state of God's grace and, more restrictively, any person who is ven-

	erated publicly in the public worship of the church.
Second Vatican Council	The last general council of all the Catholic bishops who met to legislate church matters for the whole church; it ended its sessions in 1965.
Theotokos	The Greek term, adopted at the Council of Ephesus, to describe the Virgin Mary as the "God bearer."
Trinity	The term describes the unity of God in three persons: Father, Son, and Holy Spirit.

Sacred Spaces and Times

Basilica of Saint Peter in Rome
Mass
Sacraments
Baptism
Confirmation
Holy Eucharist
Penance
Anointing of the Sick
Matrimony
Holy Orders
Vatican

Suggestions for Further Reading

Catechism of the Catholic Church. New York: Paulist, 1994 (an authoritative account of Catholic belief).

Cunningham, Lawrence. *Introduction to Catholicism.* New York: Cambridge University Press, 2009.

McBrien, Richard, ed. *The HarperCollins Encyclopedia of Catholicism.* New York: HarperCollins, 1995 (a comprehensive resource).

O'Collins, Gerald, and Mario Ferrugia. *Catholicism: The Story of Catholic Christianity.* New York: Oxford University Press, 2003.

Ratzinger, Joseph. *Introduction to Christianity.* San Francisco: Ignatius, 1990 (a survey of the Catholic faith by the current pope, Benedict XVI).

Von Balthasar, Hans Urs. *Credo.* New York: Crossroad, 1990 (a meditative study of the creed by an eminent theologian).

ORTHODOX CHRISTIANITY

J. A. McGuckin

What is Orthodoxy's overriding question?

Orthodox Christianity is an ancient expression of the Christian tradition. It reflects the main features of the religion as it was established over the first few centuries following the New Testament era, predominantly in the Greek-speaking half of the Roman Empire. It is, for this reason, also called Eastern Orthodox Christianity, though it shares many fundamental features with Western Catholicism. Before the late nineteenth century, Orthodoxy used to be predominantly based in Greece, the Balkans, and the Slavic lands (although it was once the main form of Christianity in the Middle East, in Africa along the length of the Nile, and by the seventh century had penetrated down the Silk Road even into China). But in the twentieth century, Orthodoxy became a global phenomenon, with more Greek Orthodox living in America, western Europe, and Australia, for example, than in mainland Greece.

Orthodox Christianity lays great stress on the central concept of the eternal Divine Word of God (or *Logos*), the second person of the Trinity, personally entering into human life as Jesus of Nazareth for the rescue of an ailing world. This coming in the flesh of the Divine Word is called "the Incarnation" (enfleshment) and is seen in Orthodoxy as God's primary work of rescue for the creation. Orthodox teachers saw the Word bringing the powers of the divine condition into his own human life as Jesus Christ, which did not just energize Jesus alone, but also served as a "test case" for the

85

remodeling of all humanity, in and through Jesus as God-Man. By coming personally into the flesh, the Divine Word was understood to have refashioned a defective humanity (fallen from grace) into redeemed humanity (graced anew with divine favor). Orthodoxy calls this process of cosmic redemption by the strong term of "deification by grace." As one of the leading fourth-century Orthodox fathers, or sages, once said: "He [the Divine Word] became a human, that we humans might become gods" (Saint Athanasius, *On the Incarnation*). This key term does not signify the pagan notion of abolishing the distinction between God and the creature, but instead poetically tries to describe the work of grace in which God reenergizes humankind and gives it back the power of communion with God that it lost through long ages of forgetfulness and error. Orthodoxy believes that by losing the mindfulness of God, death entered into the world and humanity lost its original gift of immortality. Consequently, with the coming of God the Word into the flesh, humanity was remade on the lines of the Word's own humanity, a human life perfectly united with the divinity, which was unable to be overpowered by death (as shown in the Resurrection). The Word's coming to the world meant that the human race was gifted once again with the potential for a divine communion and the promise of immortality. This master idea of saving deification (God's merciful coming down to earth and humankind's reorientation to God because of it) is the heart and core of Orthodox Christianity. Most other things are commentary upon it.

In telling this story Orthodoxy assumed the ancient Scriptures of Israel to itself, though now it retold them in a way that focused all attention on the centrality of the story of Christ's incarnate ministry (it read them christocentrically). After the fourth century C.E. Orthodoxy also composed a series of creeds and major statements from international councils of bishops that were held between the fourth and eighth centuries. These texts, which are almost all in Greek, would eventually become part of the foundational mind-set of nearly all later forms of Christian religion.

How do we know about this religion? What classics define the norms?

We know about Orthodox Christianity through an extensive set of literatures deriving from the church's origins in the Near East, especially in the time of the late Roman Empire. The Gospels themselves were first issued in Greek, and from the end of the first century early Christian writers began to assemble in Greek, Latin, Coptic, Syriac, and Armenian a massive body of Christian theological, historical, and poetic literature that remains the core of the Orthodox Church's "library." Some of it was circulated as instructional literature meant to provide authoritative frameworks for the international church— especially the creeds and conciliar decrees (the Creed of Nicaea dating to the fourth century is still recited at many Christian Eucharists all over the world each Sunday)—though much of it circulated chiefly among the Christian intellectuals, especially the early patristic theologians (called the "fathers") who were usually bishops of the church, and it is rarely read outside the monasteries today. The literature can be broadly classified into scriptural commentary, doctrinal writings of the fathers, creeds and conciliar statements, liturgical texts, and ascetical literature (or the spiritual writings of the monks about the inner life). Among the latter category are many little-known gems.

Scriptural Commentary

Orthodoxy produced a very large collection of patristic commentaries on the Bible. They tend to interpret the large vistas of biblical stories in a way that consistently focuses on the story of Jesus as promised Messiah. The Law and the Prophets are read as looking forward to Jesus; the Gospels, Acts, and Letters are read as leading out from Jesus into the formation of his new community, the church, presenting his Spirit to the world. It prefers these writings, generally speaking, to the many forms of biblical criticism that have grown up in the Protestant world in the modern era.

Writings of the Fathers

Important Orthodox bishops of the Golden Age (fourth to ninth centuries) left a set of theological treatises outlining classical forms of Orthodox teaching. These have normative status in the Orthodox Church. Chief examples are the writings of the Egyptian fathers, saints Athanasius and Cyril of Alexandria; the Cappadocian fathers, saints Basil of Caesarea, Gregory of Nyssa, and Gregory of Nazianzus; and the Syrian fathers, such as Saint John Chrysostom. Composed in Greek and Syriac mainly, the works are available in many languages today. Orthodoxy also gives the same "patristic" status to the writings of the Latin Church's fathers, such as the saints

Pope Leo the Great and Saint Gregory the Great. It acknowledges the Christian richness of Saint Augustine but does not regard his theological work as having been without its flaws and does not give him a high ranking in importance.

Creeds and Councils

In the time of the Byzantine Empire, any international level disputes over church life were settled at major gatherings of bishops known as ecumenical councils. Orthodoxy regards the first seven of these (held, respectively, at Nicaea in 325 C.E., Constantinople in 381 C.E., Ephesus in 431 C.E., Chalcedon in 451 C.E., Constantinople in 553 C.E., Constantinople in 681 C.E., and Nicaea in 787 C.E.) as having the highest doctrinal authority in the church after the Scriptures. Their decisions and teachings are held up to be the central definitions of Orthodox thought and life.

Liturgical Texts

The chief collections of the formal prayers of the Orthodox Church are its Eucharistic Liturgy (Communion service). This exists in several different forms used on different occasions. The Liturgy of Saint Chrysostom is the normal Sunday rite, and the longer more solemn Liturgy of Saint Basil is used in the Lenten time of preparation for Pascha (Easter). There are also liturgies attributed to Pope Gregory the Great and Saint James of Jerusalem that are used less frequently. Formal prayer services also grew up from the fourth century onward and are used daily in monasteries and weekly in most parishes. Vespers (*Hesperinos*) is the evening prayer of the church, and day or dawn service (*Orthros*) is the equivalent of Matins. There are extensive books of liturgical prayers for almost every occasion in the collection of prayer books known as the Horologion, the Triodion, the Pentecostarion, the Octoechos, and the Menaion. The smallest of these is many hundred pages long; the largest runs to several volumes.

Ascetical Writings

Over the course of many centuries Orthodox monks and clergy produced a very large body of writings about the life of the Spirit, meditation, and prayer. These collections are known as the *Niptic* writings, from a word meaning "mindfulness," or the *Paterika*, a word that means "writings of the fathers." One of the most well known of these collections is the five-volume set of texts on prayer known as the *Philokalia*, which is one of the few yet available in

English. In this genre of literature are many hymns and poems, several of which have been abstracted for use in the public Liturgy. Some of them are set to beautiful and ancient music. One example is the third-century hymn called "Gladsome Light," sung when the sun's light started to fade at dusk signaling (in ancient times) the vesperal beginning of the new day:

> O Jesus Christ, the Gladsome Light of the Immortal Father's holy
>   Glory;
> the Heavenly, Holy, Blessed One;
> As the Sun declines, we see the light of evening,
> and sing our hymn to God, the Blessed One.
> Worthy are you, Our glorious Lord, through each and every moment,
> that joyful songs should hymn you.
> You are the Giver of our Life, and so the world gives glory.

Orthodoxy, after the first millennium, tended to look back more and more to this ancient body of foundational literature, not so much developing it to the future by constant addition but rather holding on to it in a conservative and protective way. This is why Orthodoxy often appears very concerned with tradition and precedent, not innovation. It is, nevertheless, a living and energetic body of the faithful with subtle and differentiated traditions within it (such as the Russian, Greek, Romanian, or Serbian forms of Orthodox church life), each with its own emphases but all bonded together in a family of churches called the wider Orthodox communion, sometimes known as the "sister churches" of the Orthodox world. Nevertheless, several centuries of past domination, first by the fifteenth-century Ottoman Islamic power and then in modern times under harsh Communist rule, tended to wreck the continuity and freedom of the Orthodox Church's universities and schools, and contributed to the traditionalist mentality. Throughout many hard times it was the Liturgy, or set public prayers of the Orthodox (they do not vary and have rarely been changed over many centuries), that provided its body of believers with the fundamental tenets of their faith and a continuing sense of identity. Many Orthodox commentators say that a close study of the Orthodox Liturgy reveals all the constitutive elements of its foundational literature in miniature.

What is the community of faithful called? What story explains its traits?

Orthodoxy calls the body of faithful believers "the church" (*ekklesia*), a word from the old Greek version of the Bible meaning "called out by God." Orthodoxy sees this calling out as an election story following on in a universal way from the particular election story that characterized Israel's covenantal choice by God. Orthodoxy sometimes calls the church the "new Israel" to evoke this, seeing the scriptural stories as an organic outgrowth of God's gifting of salvation to the world through the Law and the Prophets, and in Jesus as a new covenant (literally a "new testament") given universally to the Gentiles who put their faith in him as risen Lord and Savior.

What is the way of life of the community of faithful? What are the rules of conduct and the rites of passage? What is the notion of sacred time and space? How does the way of life embody the story that this religion tells about itself?

The Orthodox community's way of life stresses the need for repentance and purification from the ever-present tendencies to conform to the "ways of the world" (meaning the negative aspects of human attitudes such as vainglory, self-importance, violence, and so on). Instead, Orthodoxy attempts to help the believer "conform to the mind to Christ" (Rom. 8:29; 12:2) by the practice of mercy, repentance, and constant focus on the glories of the coming kingdom of God, the eschatological "eighth day" when it is believed that the Lord's Prayer (the "Our Father") will be fulfilled and God's will "shall be done on earth as it is in heaven." Orthodoxy's major celebrations turn around Pascha (Easter), a feast that celebrates the passion and resurrection of Jesus as the making of the covenant that established the church and as the definitive sign of God's mercy over the world. Pentecost, fifty days after Pascha, is another major celebration noting the gift of the Holy Spirit to the body of believers. The year is broken up with many other great feasts commemorating Jesus' work—such as Christmas (December 25), the baptism of Jesus (January 6), and the Transfiguration (August 6; see Mark 9:1)—or the memory of the saints (the dormition or "falling asleep" of the Virgin Mary, August 15), or the Feast of the Apostles (June 29). Now there is not a day in the whole year that in the church's calendar does not mark a lesser feast of a saint. But the spirit of celebration is also muted by several seasons of repentance and fasting, notably the forty days leading up to Pascha (Great Lent). Wednesdays and Fridays are also observed as days of fasting to recall the passion of Christ and the need for individual repentance. Consumption of meat, dairy foods, and luxuries, such as wine, is not allowed on these days.

What is the community's worldview? What is its conception of divinity and of the relationship of the divinity to the believers? What are its principal ethical teachings? What are the attitudes and behaviors toward persons outside the faith community?

The Orthodox see themselves as an eschatological community of witness. Eschatology is a worldview that is very strong in the New Testament literature and that focuses on the decisive act of God that brings an end to one age (the disobedience of the world) and ushers in another age (the kingdom of God in which evil shall be ended and the will of God shall be perfectly fulfilled). The church sees itself as the sign of the eschaton (literally "the latter days" or the "consummation of the ages"; see Matt. 24:14; 28:20) in the present world order where obedience to God is not yet fully established. It sees itself, therefore, as the companion to the angels of God, as the earthly counterpart that must seek to fulfil the will of God "as it is done in heaven" (the Lord's Prayer)—that is, perfectly by the angels. It fulfills this task partly through the offering of worship and prayer unfailingly to God, and especially through the attempt to live out an ethical life marked by Christ's own witness of mercy, love, and peace. Christ's life sets to the Orthodox the pattern of the life of holiness. The ethical literature of the church has been extensive, mainly propagated before the twentieth century in the form of sermons in church services, from the clergy to the people. The church advocates a common standard of mercy and humility to all, and, through the practice of the virtue of hopeful repentance (*Metanoia*), calls on all its believers to constantly repair the tendency to human fallibility and selfishness. Orthodoxy expects the faithful to attend Divine Liturgy at least once a week and to observe the church's rules for moral living and for domestic fasting and prayer.

Prayer Rituals

Monastic communities pray seven times a day in organized services called "the Hours," of which Vespers and Matins are the chief services. Devout Orthodox laypeople set up in the easternmost corner of their houses and private rooms (the corner facing Jerusalem where Jesus rose from the dead) a small shelf that contains their icons (religious images) of Christ and the saints. Oriented this way, they will say morning, evening, and night prayers, often offering incense before the icons as symbols of veneration to the Divine Trinity: God the Father, Son, and Holy Spirit. Orthodox Christians do not worship images; they believe that offering "veneration" to the icon is a form of worship that can be given to the One God alone (in Trinity). Orthodox also venerate the icons of Mary and the saints by bowing before and kissing the icons. This again is an Eastern custom of veneration, not worship. It is practiced by Orthodox Christians to show signs of respect and love for Christ's saints as those who model the righteous life to believers and those who, living in the next age of God's glory already, are believed to be able and willing to assist the believer in all things that contribute to the life of grace. All prayer services begin with the Trisagion Prayers (so called from the three-fold repetition of the acclamation "Holy"; see. Isa. 6:3), which culminate in the Lord's Prayer, and of which these are the chief other elements:

> O Heavenly King, the Paraclete, the Spirit of Truth who is present everywhere,
> filling all things, Treasurer of Good and Giver of Life, come and dwell in us,
> cleanse us of every stain, and save our souls, O Good One.

> Holy God, Holy Mighty, Holy Immortal, have mercy on us. (Said three times.)

> All-Holy Trinity, have mercy on us. Lord, forgive us our sins. Master, pardon our transgressions. Holy One visit and heal our infirmities for your Name's sake.

Rituals of the Life Cycle

Orthodoxy celebrates the death of the believer as a time of sadness but one that is also a time of hope that the individual church member might be led through the mystery of the death of Christ himself to the experience of new life and resurrection. One of the chief funeral hymns puts the paradox in this way: "We make our sad pilgrimage to the grave, but even so we sing the song Alleluia, Alleluia,

Alleluia, believing that You, O Lord, who put the divine image in humanity, will not allow that image to be lost." Marriages are celebrated with great ceremony involving a common cup of wine, a sharing of honey to symbolize the sweetness of love, and the crowning of the bride and groom with garlands. The priest leads the couple in procession three times around the cross and the book of Gospels to signify the couple's oath of loyalty and love to each other. Baptism celebrates the believer's entrance into the community of faith. It is performed with the full immersion of the believer, underwater three times, in the name of the trinitarian God. After emergence from the water (spiritually signifying death and rebirth), the newly baptized person is anointed with sacred oils (*Chrism*) signifying his or her priestly and regal status as a recipient of the gift of the living spirit of God. By the laying on of a bishop's hands, in solemn ceremonies of prayer and consecration, the spiritual leaders of the community are ordained as deacons, priests, or bishops. Those seriously ill are anointed with blessed oil seven times by the assembled priests of the area. At the celebration of the Divine Liturgy the faithful (who fast and pray beforehand to prepare for this as a solemn moment) receive the eucharistic bread and wine (Communion), which is regarded as the real presence of the Lord. These chief rituals of prayer and celebration are called "the sacraments" of the church (called by the Orthodox "the holy mysteries").

How does this religion function in the world today? What are its relationships with culture?

In ancient times, from the extensive turning of the Roman Empire to Christianity in the fourth century and on into the high medieval period, Orthodox Christianity was a globally present form of Christian religion that made immense contributions to world culture in art, music, literature, philosophy, and social philanthropy. In the Christian imperial capital at Constantinople the first formally arranged hospitals, orphanages, and homes for older adults were built and state funded. After the progressive weakening of the Greek Roman Empire, the political fortunes of Orthodox Christianity began to wane. In 1453 Constantinople (Istanbul), the center of operations for the Eastern Orthodox world up to that time (just as Rome was the center for Western Catholicism), fell to the ascendant Islamic powers of the Ottoman Turks, and from then on until the late nineteenth century, with the notable exception of czarist Russia, Orthodox Christianity had to exist as a tolerated but heavily taxed religious system whose missionary efforts were legally forbidden and whose institutions were often suppressed. In the last five hundred years or so Orthodoxy has developed less of a culture-making spirit and fostered more of a culture-protecting mentality, conservative in character, and turned more to mystical inwardness than zealous social operations. Russian Orthodoxy, which served as an international protector and developer of the Orthodox world after the fall of Byzantium, itself fell before totalitarian Communism and suffered a deep eclipse for most of the twentieth century. In present times, since the last decade of the twentieth century, the eastern European world has opened up once more and world Orthodoxy has emerged as a surviving and still-living force. In recent plebiscites 90 percent of Romanian people declared themselves to be Orthodox Christians after the fall of the Communists, who had once declared Orthodoxy to be observed only by a minority of uneducated peasants. Of a (roughly) estimated two billion Christians in the world at present, Orthodox Christians number about three hundred million, making them the second-largest distinct Christian group after Roman Catholics (with whose culture and teachings they share a considerable amount). Orthodoxy's cultural and wider societal influence is in the course of being reconstituted in many lands now emerging from the shadows of totalitarianism.

At a Glance

Classic Texts

The Orthodox Church takes the Scriptures as its fundamental charter, giving precedence of place over all to the Gospels and generally interpreting all Scripture Christocentrically—that is, looking to and from the redemptive story of Jesus as the interpretative key of all. Other foundational texts are the writings of the fathers, the early bishops and saints of the church, who composed biblical commentaries and doctrinal treatises. Central to all Orthodox teaching are the decisions, creeds, and rules (canons) of the seven ecumenical councils, which are regarded as the highest textual authority in the church after the Scriptures. Most of these texts relate to the details of the doctrinal, or theological, message of the church. Other writings make up the very large library of Orthodox texts such as liturgical prayer books in many volumes or the spiritual writings of the monastics (called ascetical literature). Liturgical texts shape and specify the formal church services, which are never varied by individual clerics but followed carefully in terms of ancient ritual forms. The spiritual writings stress the need for regular repentance among Christians because of human fallibility but also speak much about practices of prayer and mysticism and the potential for the individual believer to reach life-giving communion with God (the state of salvation called "deification by grace").

Important Figures
Between the fourth and tenth centuries several great saints of the Eastern Church, and also several from the Latin Church (which was then regarded as part of the inner family of the Orthodox churches), came to enjoy an especially authoritative status. They were known as the fathers or the patristic theologians. Leading figures among them are: Saint Athanasius and Saint Cyril of Alexandria, Saint Basil of Caesarea, Saint Gregory of Nazianzus, Saint Cyril of Jerusalem, Saint John Chrysostom, Saint Ambrose of Milan, Saint Cyprian of Carthage, and many others whose writings define central doctrines concerning the Divine Trinity, the person and work of Jesus, or the nature and mission of the church.

Characteristic Beliefs
The Orthodox Church celebrates the chief event of salvation as the coming into a personal human life, within history, of the second person of the Trinity, the Divine Word of God. This doctrine is known as the Incarnation. All things in Christian religion seen individually or partially, such as the cross, the Resurrection, the teachings of Jesus, or the sacraments and rituals of the church, are understood as commentary upon this central mystery of God's outreach to the world in and through the person of Jesus, the divine presence that was "reconciling the world to himself" (2 Cor. 5:19).

Essential Creeds or Codes of Conduct
The chief creed of the church after the Scriptures is the Creed of the Council of Nicaea. It was published in 325 C.E., in what is now Iznik in Turkey, under the direction of the first Christian Roman emperor, Constantine the Great. The Nicene Creed was meant to put an end to considerable wrangling over the status of the person of Jesus (was he a divinely honored being within the Godhead or a created being, albeit a high angel of God?). The creed established classical Orthodox teaching that Jesus was, "God from God, light from light, true God from true God." The Orthodox insistence that God was one, and could be none other than one, led to further elaborated creedal statements and theological clarifications in ancient times (the formularies, or *Ektheses,* of the ecumenical councils) elaborating the doctrine of the Divine Trinity: God has only one being or essential nature, specified in three divine persons (the hypostases of Father, Son, and Holy Sprit),

who are each divine in the unity of the single divine being of God the Father and not each constituting three different parts of a single Godhead or each setting up three distinct gods. The doctrine of God in Orthodoxy, therefore, is one of complex unity.

Brief Time Line

ca. 6 B.C.E.	Birth of Jesus of Nazareth.
ca. 29 C.E.	Death of Jesus; foundation of the church in Jerusalem.
150 C.E.	Establishment of basic rules for Christian communities in the key imperial cities of Rome, Alexandria, and Antioch, which lay down important patterns for the subsequent development of Eastern Orthodox Christianity.
300	Emergence of a clear pattern of dioceses, large areas of territory, led by a single ruling bishop with the assistance of clergy called priests and deacons.
400–900	The Golden Age of Orthodox Christian writing and practice under the protection and encouragement of Christian emperors. Ascetics establish a great communal movement called monasticism; theologians produce a large body of patristic writings that gain high authority in the Orthodox Church.
1000–1200	Eastern Orthodoxy has growing conflict with Western Catholicism, centered largely on the issue of how much authority, worldwide, can be commanded by the Roman popes. Orthodoxy acknowledges the pope as the symbolic leader of the Christian world but with a status as "first among equals" among the great bishops of the Orthodox world. The claims of the papacy for a higher juridical authority lead to rupture with the western Catholic Church. The Orthodox and the Catholics blame the rupture on each other.
1300–1800	Orthodox independence in the old territories of the eastern Roman Empire is progressively lost to the expanding forces of Islam. Orthodox churches lose territory, schools, and status. After the sixteenth century only Russia is left as a free Orthodox country and it assumes the leadership of the Orthodox world.

1800–1900	Greece begins the fight for independence from its Ottoman Islamic masters, and parts of the Orthodox world assert their independence by rebuilding their own free Christian cultures, a process that has notable signs of success in the Greek Diaspora, such as in the United States.
1917	The great and expansive Russian Orthodox Church, as led by the czars who see themselves as the successors of the Christian Roman emperors, falls captive to the Bolshevik Revolution that overthrows the feudal social organization of the czars and savagely suppresses Christian Orthodoxy with numerous martyrdoms.
1989–	The progressive democratization of the old Communist empire and the slow revival of the political and intellectual fortunes of Orthodox churches in eastern Europe.

Important Symbols

Important symbols include the cross, on which Jesus is depicted in serene majesty (not in the torture often seen in Latin crucifixion art), and the icon, of Christ or the saints, which is a religious art panel painted in accordance with ancient and strict rules of procedure, that is often used in church ritual.

Important Rituals

Important rituals include: the Sunday Eucharist; the chief sacraments ("mysteries") of baptism, confession, anointing, marriage, and ordination; and many forms of blessings of objects (homes, vehicles, water, natural places, and so on) using holy water and incense as symbols of the process of God's progressive deification by grace of a deeply blessed created order.

Glossary

ascetical	To do with a penitential seeking after a spirit of humility; a main theme of the monastic movement and a literature dedicated to mysticism and prayer.
conciliar	From the general assemblies (international councils) of the ancient Orthodox Church; the first seven of these, all held in the East, were given an immensely high legislative status for later Orthodoxy.
divinization	The concept that by the incarnation of the Word of God into human flesh, that which was mortal and creaturely in the human race was raised to a new ontological level of the potentiality of divine communion—a sharing in

the life of God, by grace; the God-Man of Jesus, incarnate *Logos*, became a paradigm of how the human race was brought into life-giving communion with God as the source of its being.

fathers
Chief theologian bishops of the early centuries who wrote important theological and liturgical works that have become authoritative for Orthodoxy.

hypostasis
A word that in conciliar and patristic thought signified "truly real," not merely symbolical; it is used to connote the "real presence" of Christ in the sacraments and also to describe how the three divine persons (hypostases) were but One God in the Christian Trinity, a central doctrine in Orthodoxy.

icon
A religious panel painting of Christ or one of the saints, often used in Orthodox ritual; the reverence shown to the image is theologically understood as passing directly to the one depicted, meaning that the image is not worshiped but that the figure it depicts is venerated through the medium of the icon.

incarnation
Literally means "coming into the flesh"; the doctrine that the earthly Jesus was the physical embodiment of no less than the Divine *Logos* of the Father; in a wider sense, the doctrine that teaches the atonement of the whole human race by the incarnation of one of the Trinity among it.

liturgical
Liturgy was the Greek word for public ceremony. It comes to be the chief designation of the Orthodox eucharistic ritual and sacraments (known as "the mysteries"). Liturgical literature is said to be especially demonstrative of the spiritual character of Orthodoxy.

Logos
The Greek term for "Divine Word," or the eternal Divine Wisdom: the second person of the Trinity.

saint
The word literally means "holy person." Orthodoxy regards the saints as the supreme teachers among Orthodoxy, those who embody the truths of religion by showing the transformative character of the gift of the spirit of God in the re-shaping of their own lives after the model of Jesus.

Silk Road
An ancient caravan road from the Roman Empire through Baghdad eastward to China; a major route of commerce in antiquity and thus a major highway for missionary endeavors.

Trinity The word means "three-in-oneness." It connotes the central Orthodox Christian doctrine that God is one being in three hypostases (subsistences), each of whom is divine but not parts of the Godhead or independent gods. God is one in a complex unity of communion. God is Father, Son, and Holy Spirit: all three are one. The mystery resists logic and mathematics and is a way of expressing the New Testament doctrine of the three-fold energies of God as recounted in the story of Jesus and the charismatic effect of his passion and resurrection in the service of witnessing the unique fatherhood of God in and through his Spirit-filled sonship.

Word of God Synonym for *Logos* (see above) and also a Christian Orthodox synonym for Divine Wisdom, understood as the preincarnate person of the Savior.

Sacred Spaces and Times

Orthodox Christians have always regarded the Holy Land as the primary place of pilgrimage, especially Jerusalem, which was the site of the mystical events relating to Jesus' passion and resurrection. Many ancient Orthodox pilgrim sites still exist in the Holy Land. Other than this, Constantinople (now Istanbul) was regarded as a holy place because of the numerous sacred shrines and relics it once contained. Rome is also regarded as a major Christian holy place because of the shrines of the martyrs it still contains. Today the Orthodox regard Moscow as an important place that contains numerous relics and shrines, and also Mount Athos, a venerable monastic colony in Greece.

Suggestions for Further Reading

Bettenson, Henry S. *The Early Christian Fathers.* London: Oxford University Press, 1963.

———. *The Later Christian Fathers.* London: Oxford University Press, 1970.

Evdokimov, Paul. *The Art of the Icon: A Theology of Beauty.* Torrance, Calif.: Oakwood, 1990.

Hapgood, Isabel Florence. *Service Book of the Holy Orthodox-Catholic Apostolic Church.* New York: Association Press, 1922.

McGuckin, John A. *Standing in God's Holy Fire: The Byzantine Tradition.* Maryknoll, N.Y.: Orbis, 2001.

———. *The Orthodox Church: An Introduction to Its History, Doctrine, and Spiritual Culture.* Oxford: Blackwell-Wiley, 2008.

Meyendorff, John. *Byzantine Theology.* New York: Fordham University Press, 1974.

Ware, Timothy. *The Orthodox Church.* London: Penguin Books, 1987.

Wybrew, Hugh. *Orthodox Liturgy: The Development of the Eucharistic Liturgy in the Byzantine Rite.* London: SPCK, 1989.

PROTESTANTISM

Martin E. Marty

Protestants, in their many varieties, together made up the majority religious complex in the United States through the colonial period down to the early twenty-first century, when it began to lose that place. Protestantism, that complex itself, is made up worldwide of more than thirty thousand varieties, usually called denominations or church bodies. Strictly speaking, Protestantism is not one of the world religions, but is part of the larger whole called Christianity. However, as organized and experienced, it is sufficiently different from the other two largest faith communities—Orthodoxy, often called Eastern Orthodoxy, and Catholicism, sometimes referred to as Roman Catholicism to warrant separate treatment.

Curiously, whoever consults directories such as the historic version called "the yellow pages" of the phone book or listings on the Internet will hardly find the designation "Protestant." More than two hundred church bodies, most of them Protestant, are listed in the annual *Yearbook of American and Canadian Churches,* but only one—the seven-thousand-member group called Protestant Reformed Churches in America—includes the word in its name. Religious statistics are always hard to register, and Protestantism is an especially difficult case because it has no single center, no authority to which all Protestant groups feel responsibility, and not even a precise definition of what it is to be Protestant.

Protestants in their Anglican (in the United States usually called Episcopal) form arrived with English colonists to Virginia in 1607 and were followed by the familiar New England Puritans and a constant flow of immigrants who brought their versions of Protestantism from Europe, Asia, Africa, and Latin America. They have this in common as one of the three main Christian branches: they are all Western Christians, as opposed to the Eastern Orthodox. They do not accept the authority of the pope, to whom more than one billion people worldwide and one fourth of the American population give allegiance. Most of them share a cluster of beliefs but display a wide variety of forms by which they are governed and in which they are organized.

Many Protestants do not like the name that they have inherited since it sounds negative and became their designation almost accidentally. Some German princes "protestated" against a policy of the Holy Roman Empire in 1529, over issues long forgotten and quite irrelevant to church life around the world. Yet the name stuck, and demographers, statisticians, strategists, opinion makers, and the public at large still use it. Protestants like to think that part of their message calls them to "protest" against injustice and the expression of untruth, but more often their signal teaches and ways of life are affirmed.

To those who view Protestantism as a whole, it comes in several families of churches. Thus, alongside the inherited "mainstream Protestant," as these "standard-brand" types have come to be called in recent decades, there is a large and burgeoning network called "Evangelical." In turn, it includes a form called Pentecostalism, which is the fastest-growing version of Protestantism around the world today. Add to these the heirs of what is often called the Radical Reformation of the sixteenth century, out of which the modern Baptist churches sprang. The independent streak that has been characteristic of Protestantism from its beginnings in Europe in the sixteenth century leads many to resist being characterized by any name or description by their own. A Pentecostal group in Guatemala would have difficulty seeing itself in any company called "Protestant" alongside Anglicans who use formal patterns of worship and church organization.

Finally, in a preliminary statement of Protestant core beliefs, we discern this: its members, however concerned with laws and morals they may be, believe the most important experience of God that gives meaning to life is divine *grace*. They believe it is a gift that they do not earn by doing "good works" that impress God; but they also believe that "faith is active in love," which is a way of saying that "good works" follow faith. Their faith and God's grace result from the birth, death, and resurrection of Jesus Christ, whom they see as the only one who mediates or connects between God and humans. Those who experience grace through faith gather in communities called "churches," which, taken together, make up the "one, holy, catholic, and apostolic" church.

Beyond that, it is hard to generalize. List most Orthodox and Catholic teachings and you will find that almost all of them find some match in some Protestant communion somewhere in the world. Protestants stress their belief in and cherishing of the Bible, but find that contemporary Catholicism also regards it as central—though when Protestantism was born, Catholicism appeared to be less devoted to the Bible. Most Protestants are less devoted to the saints than are Orthodox and Catholics, though they may honor many of them. Finally, the only thing that all Catholics adhere to that Protestants do not is papal authority. Protestants like to summarize their way of belief and life as being characterized by Christian freedom, variously expressed.

American Religion and Protestantism

Awareness of what we know as the Western Hemisphere, once called "the discovery of America," occurred almost precisely when Protestantism was being born. This birth occurred among English Bible translators who created controversy by making the sacred Scriptures available to ordinary people, thus undercutting many forms of church authority. Many date the birth of Protestantism to what one scholar called "the revolt of the junior faculty at Wittenberg University in Germany." The leader among numerous colleagues there was Martin Luther, who also stressed devotion to the Bible and the focus on grace and faith. This occurred three decades after the discovery of America, though Luther and his counterparts in Switzerland, and in other places where "Reformed" Protestantism was born, showed little awareness of the Americas, which were being explored, claimed, exploited, and "churched" by Spanish and Portuguese Catholics.

The split of the English church from Rome under King Henry VIII and the rise of England as a colonial power occurred in the decades before the planting of the Church of England (the Anglican or Episcopal Church) in Virginia and other southern colonies in 1607 and the Pilgrim and Puritan arrivals in 1620 and 1630. Meanwhile, the Dutch Republic was becoming a colonial power and also estab-lished itself, especially in what became New York, soon after. From then and through the colonial era most colonists and immigrants were from Protestantized nations of northern Europe and the British Isles, and they opposed Catholic colonization. It is estimated that when the nation was born, between 1776 and 1787, there were only about thirty thousand Catholics and three thousand Jews in all thir-teen colonies.

Some of these Protestants were "established," which meant that the public paid taxes to support them and that they had influence and privilege in lawmaking, moral judgments, and practices. However, although the northern Puritan or Congregational Protestants in the North and the Anglican or Episcopal Protestants in the South were legally established, many who came to the middle colonies—among them Quakers in Pennsylvania or opponents of establishment—separated church and state and minimized or cut state support. What came to be called "the voluntary church" was invented and, after long constitutional struggles in the colonies and later the states, prevailed everywhere. Still, non-Protestant faiths suf-fered, by rule of law or not, as Protestants were privileged and pros-pered. They put their stamp on many American institutions with themes and practices that have endured even among Americans who are not Protestant. In company with the national founders who were often called "Enlightenment" figures, they helped produce what kept being called the "separation of church and state" and an ever-increasing religious liberty.

In one sense, the new American nation helped advance or com-plete the Reformation begun in Europe, from which came a constant flow of immigrants who quickly learned that if their faith and churches were to survive, it was up to them to spread their faith and build institutions. As the frontier moved progressively west, so did they. Through setting up schools and colleges, planting churches, forming voluntary agencies of mercy, and for morality as they saw it, they shaped much of American culture. It often seemed—not least of all to Protestants—hard to know where "Protestant" ended and "American" began. Although many Protestants showed prejudice to others—or to one another—and participated in what today they would call "the great sins of the nation," especially against Native Americans and Africans whom they enslaved, they also produced much that is good in the United States. Understanding Protestantism became ever more important to the non-Protestant half of the nation.

Protestants in their "voluntary churches" sent missionaries and evangelizers with every group of migrants on the frontier to the West and to many immigrants. They left their mark with the hundreds of thousands of steeples, towers, and high-roof lines that signaled their sanctuaries were almost everywhere. They took part in spreading the teachings of the Bible and inventing ways to articulate and enforce their understandings of its ethical calls. They established hospitals, orphanages, charitable organizations, and provided themes for stories and poems by literary figures.

Their patterns of organization were varied. The two most efficient spreaders of the word, the Baptists and the Methodists, used very different means and invented very different forms of government. Neither had been strong in colonial America, and Methodism itself was just being born. Then came the opening of the gaps through mountains toward the west and the spread of villages and cities. Baptists were fiercely independent: the local churches were just about the highest authority they would recognize. They often encouraged and licensed unlettered "Spirit-filled" adventurers to go out on their own to set up churchly shop in the new communities. The Methodists, however, were highly organized and efficiently governed. They formed collectives that sent their pastors and evangelists out as itinerants, subject to control. They were joined by Episcopalians, who were governed by bishops, and others who did church business, planning, and moral teaching through a variety of organizations, some of them so light that they were almost anarchic.

Characteristically, in all of these cases, the central act was the worship of God; but these churches also chartered and equipped members to share social life and engage the surrounding world, often with acts of mercy but sometimes with oppressive judgmentalism expressed through local as well as larger anti-Catholic moves and movements. Most of them—some Baptists temporarily excluded—built seminaries to train ministers and evangelists. Ministers were to take care of the many needs of members and local communities. Evangelists, often in large outdoor gatherings, would hope to fire up individuals to make a commitment to Jesus Christ and form communities.

In the twentieth century many American Protestants cooperated with one another through various councils, federations, and associations. Some of them merged with one another. In the middle of the century, leaders of interfaith movements found Protestants speaking and working with Jews and Catholics. After the Second Vatican Council (1962–65), they were permitted to engage in formal theological talk with Catholics. Some of their own internal divisions resulted from nothing more than the fact that their members arrived in different boats at different times from different shores where there had been different national expressions of church life. Early in the twentieth century, Lutherans worshiped using almost twenty different languages. They found that cultures, practices, and even doctrines differed among them, and many of the differences persist.

Some Protestant groups were "native born," which means they grew up on American soil and made few references to their European ancestry. The Christian Church (Disciples of Christ), born on the frontier, is one of these. Such groups stress the belief that "where the Bible speaks, we speak; where the Bible is silent, we are silent." Still, most accents of their faith line up congruently with many forms of English and Scottish Protestantism. At the opposite end of the spectrum are groups like Presbyterians, Lutherans, and the Reformed, who try to shape their contemporary witness in the light of and with devotion to sixteenth-century documents such as the Westminster Confession or the Augsburg Confession. Here again, for all the seriousness of their intent, they make some adaptations to the American culture, its possibilities and prohibitions, as they formulate beliefs and practices through their centuries in America.

What is this religion's overriding question? What makes this system self-evidently valid to the community of the faithful?

The overriding question for Protestants can be put in terms posed by Martin Luther, John Calvin, and others: how can I find or be found by a gracious God? Protestantism was not born to deal with the question of the existence of God, and most Protestants do not make that their central question today. The existence of God was and is somehow part of their "given" world—though they may be free to doubt it and to raise questions. The Protestant issue is: how does this existent God, who is invisible and in most ways inscrutable, accessible to my community and me? How does a God who often seems distant, remote, eclipsed, and somehow judgmental display a friendlier bearing to me and mine—and maybe to people even beyond our community of faith?

Protestants believe that there is divine law, through which the will of God is asserted for human good: "Thou shalt not steal. Thou shalt not kill." These "thou shalt nots" can apply to the most intimate and small details of life—in marriage and the family, in business and learning. Protestants believe that they will all fail to meet the mark of the divine standards. They have a Bible that tells them that God can punish the faithless and the ones who harm others or neglect to do God's will. Their overriding questions are: How can the merciful face of God show itself to me? How can I experience the love of God in a faith that says, "God is love"? When I have gone wrong, how do I find forgiveness?

Since Protestants of all kinds of personality—some "sin sick" and some more naturally open to grace—believe that they all need God's rescue, by devotion to God's Son, Jesus Christ, they believe that they will discern this benign face and action of God and, through for-giveness, be empowered to serve the neighbor, "the other"—something they are all called to do. They find all these accents self-evident because of the central place the Bible (the Hebrew Scriptures and the New Testament) has played and plays in the teachings of the church that have shaped them, at least partially, and which they have made their own, even if imperfectly. In sum: somehow the Bible is *huge* in making these transactions self-evident.

How do we know about this religion?

We know about this religion in several ways. First, by using their eyes and ears, modern people, two thousand and more years since these ancient Scriptures were written, will find contact with it almost inevitable. The Bible remains the best-selling book, year in and year out, and millions do read it. The churches of this religion dot the landscape and cityscape with steeples and doors of buildings stately and small. Through modern media of communication, many Protestants advertise their presence and what they have to offer. Their agencies of justice and mercy do what they can to be recognized and to have their stories get out.

The second way to answer this question is to say, "Consult the Bible," as Protestants have said since the sixteenth century when *sola scriptura*, "Scripture alone," became their battle cry against church tradition and Catholic authority. Admittedly, expecting a modern community of faith to literally replicate the world of the Bible would be absurd, even if some Protestants try to give the impression that they are doing so. The presence of so many hundreds—indeed thousands—of kinds of Protestants, all of whom appeal to the Bible yet differing enough in their interpretations to stay apart, makes it hard to suggest that one finds all about this faith by referring to their central authority. Still, almost all of them, from ecstatic Pentecostals who "feel" the Holy Spirit to rather liberal church bodies, find that they have no choice but to address their world through what the prophets and poets, the evangelists and letter writers in the Bible set forth. Some church bodies say that the Bible is the only source and norm for their teaching.

What is the community of the faithful called? What story explains its traits?

The Protestant Reformers of the sixteenth century all devoted themselves to "the whole Bible." By this they meant the sixty-six books that believers considered to belong to the "canon" of authoritative writings in the early Christian centuries. Since the canon was decided upon through two centuries of study and debate, this meant that, more than many of them wanted to admit, some form of church tradition entered in. Tradition comes from the Latin words for something being "handed down," and the sixty-six books did not hand themselves down. Some Protestants are uncertain about whether some of these books should belong to the canon. Most of them formally reject "apocryphal writings," which did not make it into the canon but which Catholicism especially honors and from which Protestant scholars also learn more about how the Bible, including the New Testament, was formed. Still, one addresses or "settles" arguments among Protestants more on the basis of their reading the Gospels of Matthew, Mark, Luke, and John or the Letters of Paul than they do on their citing of the gospels of Thomas and other long-known and sometimes recently discovered texts that some cherish.

For all intents and purposes, then, the canonical Bible is the definer of what this community is called. The Scriptures for them includes books of the Hebrew Scriptures, which they call the Old Testament. In the early church some dissenters, called "heretics," such as Marcion, rejected the Old Testament as being a legalistic, primitive document. Sad to say—tragically to say—many Protestants (they are called "Evangelicals" in Germany) repudiated those Scriptures in their effort to purge the memories of Israel of old (or new) and distance themselves from Jews. Those terrible exceptions aside, it is fair and honest to say that most Protestants, through five centuries and everywhere, regard the Old Testament as having full authority.

However, on the basis of their belief in it and identification with its themes, some Protestants have thought of themselves or called themselves "the new Israel." Although there is some New Testament warrant for calling themselves that, most Protestants avoid the term because of their growing sensitivity to Jews and Judaism, and because some anti-Semitic groups preempt those words and use the phrase in their propaganda. So Protestants accept the gift of Israel and, thanks to joint Bible study and interfaith activity, both Christians and Jews want to affirm their heritage. A twentieth-century pope said, "Spiritually we are all Semites, and Catholic and Protestant official and informal teaching pays ever more attention to the prophets and other legacies to them of Israel."

At the same time, something "new" went on, which Protestants seized and from which they got the name for their community: "the church." In the New Testament it was sometimes called the *ecclesia,* which derives from the Greek for the people "called out"; or *koinonia,* the fellowship; or even "the way" of life and teaching. However much these inform the community, though, none of them stand a chance against the winning term *church,* which Protestants share with the Orthodox and the Catholics. Protestants use the word *church* for the building in which they worship and for the act of worship (as in "we are going to church"). They ordinarily use the name for a congregation, and speak of the denomination of which they are a part as "their church."

Theologically, although they may not always cite the term, Protestants believe they are part of the "one, holy, catholic, and apostolic church." Often they will refer to the teachings of Paul the apostle, in the New Testament, and speak of the church as being "the body of Christ." These are ways of saying that they believe their being right with God is a social or communal activity. Just as God dealt with Israel as a community—one cannot picture an individual member of Israel saying, "I found God as my personal Savior," as some Protestants who stress their individualism do—most believe that their life with God finds them part of a community. Strict sectarian Protestants think that God deals fully only with them, but most Protestants see the community of faith far beyond their congregational or denominational boundaries.

What story explains the traits of this community? First of all, the biblical story beginning with Genesis and Exodus does. Whereas literalists use the first chapters of Genesis as a scientific text and get into arguments with evolutionists over it, most Protestants read the opening books as answers to the question, How did God's people come to be God's people? With Jews, Muslims, and—one hopes and expects—all other Christians, Protestants see themselves as "children of Abraham" and use the story of Abraham as the father of faith in the One God, and thus their father. They find significance in the stories of the Passover and the wilderness experience. They make much of certain biblical figures such as David, historically perceiving him as the author of many of the poetic psalms, which they regularly use in worship. They revere and hear messages from the eighth-century prophets, and listen to figures like Isaiah, Jeremiah, and Amos as shapers of their ethics and announcers of the call of God.

That is chapter 1 of their story. Chapter 2 they get from the New Testament, which they share with all Christians. Characteristically they explain themselves with variations on the first verse of a New Testament book by an unknown author, the book of Hebrews: "Long ago God spoke to our ancestors in many and various ways by the prophets, but in these last days he has spoken to us by a Son" (1:1-2a). God has spoken to us through Jesus, the son of Mary, the central figure of the Gospels, and through the faith, the creed, and Protestant witness. In this story Jesus is called "Christ," meaning "anointed." The Hebrews verse goes on "...whom [God] appointed heir of all things, through whom he also created the worlds. He is the reflection of God's glory and the exact imprint of God's very being, and he sustains all things by his powerful word" (1:2b-3).

That might be called a story that explains the faith—the Christian faith, not a Protestant exclusive—though, as broad and reaching as it is, it does not contain all the main explanatory features. Still, some markers are there. Jesus is God's Son. That is the point at which these "children of Abraham" in one story have a story that separates them from Jews and Muslims. Many of them could share lessons from the teachings of Jesus in the Gospels, but none of them could believe the divine claims that undercut monotheism, the belief of one God, in their view. One could find fifty parallel texts to the one cited here, but what they add up to in Protestant faith can be condensed in a sentence something like, "The human Jesus is the exalted Lord."

How that came to be explanatory in the story would be chapter 3, the worlds of believers, disciples, followers of the way, witnesses, and, for most Protestants, people who gather as members of the church. Believers from the first had to ponder and debate how the human Jesus, who was really human and did not merely seem to be so, was also the exalted Lord. Beginning with the letters of Paul, a rabbinically trained figure who recognized a call to be a disciple, they learned to focus on the event of Jesus' self-giving in the Crucifixion— Rome's most cruel punishment—and the Resurrection, the rising from the dead, an event that, however interpreted, meant the living presence of Jesus among them. Also as part of chapter 3 they experienced this presence through the Holy Spirit, who came to them on Pentecost, the birthday of the church.

Chapter 3, part 2, extremely meaningful to most Protestants, less so to a minority, was what we might call a creed-making period, when at councils the scholars and bishop worked to relate Father, Son, and Holy Spirit in the divine Holy Trinity. But the accent in the life of the church that triggered Protestants came through the story of reformers. They argued that God's free gift of grace had been captured, packaged, and bartered by a corrupt church, and Protestantism was born when the Scriptures, now available to all, were "opened" to reveal that grace was not something to be bartered but was free.

With that, on another Protestant note, while almost all of them kept professional, trained, ordained, and church-regulated ministries, they also proclaimed what was called "the priesthood of all believers." This meant a dispersal of the powers the church claimed and experienced. Every believer was now a "priest," though they were not all called to the office of ministry. Protestants have very different ways of preparing, credentialing, monitoring, and relating to ministers—the clergy—but they do believe that priestly power and acts are widely shared among the baptized. So Protestants in general have seen too much power-sharing with those they call "the laity."

The traits that derive from, or are supposed to derive from, these stories include: (a) the evidence of the experience of the love of God;

(b) the desire to extend that love to the neighbor; (c) a freedom in establishing church structures; (d) a freedom from most church law and regulation of private life; (e) a sense of having voluntarily chosen to participate in the life of God, in ways not regulated by law and church authority; (f) a desire to have the Bible more than councils of the church decide what matters in life. Obviously, because there are thousands of Protestant denominations, there are thousands of ways of realizing or revising these, but they are broadly characteristic.

What is the way of life of the community of the faithful?

Much of the answer to this is implied in the stories just told, but some features should stand out:

First, central to the Protestant way of life is the act of worship, pursued in a great variety of ways. Most gather every Sunday, "the Lord's day," and worship in private prayer and Scripture reading as well. Protestantism is devoted to "the word," as preached, spoken, taught, and conversed about.

Although the word is central, most Protestants observe sacraments in their way of life. Whereas Orthodoxy and Catholicism have more, Protestants celebrate only two. For them sacraments demand visible means—water for baptism and bread and wine for the Lord's Supper or Holy Communion. They stress that faith in the word of God is what makes a sacrament effective, especially as a "means of grace."

Not a means of grace but characteristic of Protestantism through the centuries is that it has been a singing movement. Virtually all branches of the Reformation were born with and gave birth to distinctive forms of music: hymns, carols, chorales, anthems, and more.

Most Protestants believe that they are supposed to be personal witnesses to what happens in community, in transactions with God. Those called "evangelical" or "evangelistic," no doubt the most prominent and news-making form of Protestantism in the twenty-first century, make a big and bold point of telling others what God has done for them in Jesus Christ and trying to convince them to respond to God's call. The church is not considered a closed society or a finished product.

Beyond this, Protestants have always been perceived as activists. They may not make the religious world's best meditators or contemplatives; they are supposed to be restless when they see evils and ills and they are expected to be alert in faith to help bring about healing and justice.

The language of being "stewards" is common to Protestantism, especially in the United States where the disestablishment of religion, the separation of church and state, and the voluntary church model dominate. In Europe, the tax-supported churches stress the giving of alms, but in the United States virtually everything churches do they must do on their own. This means providing places of worship and keeping them up, paying the salaries of clergy and other staff, and supporting charities and works of justice. So most Protestants put energies into having the way of life issue in regular, preferably weekly donations—"offerings"—for local and global needs.

Protestants are expected to carry their witness and way of life over into the structures of society. Historically they have been very family centered, expecting that the teachings and behaviors of the senior generation be imparted to the children. Much of the Protestant ethic has drawn on family models. At the same time, some versions have produced "social gospels" for society at large, in which both on a voluntary charitable basis and in cooperation with governments and secular agencies they are to give time, money, and certain kinds of allegiance with nonchurch organizations and endeavors.

What is the worldview of the community?

Protestants believe that God's good creation has been blighted by human wrongdoing, a belief that should lead to pessimism but does not. Instead they believe that thanks to God's gracious activity in Jesus Christ, fully a human among us, the human race is honored and chartered to serve the purposes of God in the world.

Protestants therefore tell the story of God meeting humans not by overpowering them but by meeting them in weakness, as in the infant Jesus of the Christmas story, the hospitable Jesus who dealt with outcasts, the dying and abandoned Jesus who calls out in agony yet is seen as triumphing. They tell the story of heroines and saints, heroes and adventurers, artists and laborers who are empowered to follow this Jesus into all walks of life.

This worldview relies upon a specific vision of divinity: although a few Protestants are uneasy with the rather abstract language of the Trinity, most confess faith in a creator (Father), a redeemer (Son), and an advocate (the Holy Spirit). They do not have the ability to know the mind of God, which is shrouded in mystery, so they have no explanation of the origin of evil. Their story is more about how to live in the face of it.

The principal ethical teachings are set forth in the Ten Commandments, but Protestants also believe that people who do not know the Ten Commandments can serve God. "Loving one's neighbor as one's self" guides them. They are to be "a Christ to the neighbor in all their dealings." This does not mean that they have unchanging applications to meet all the demands that come to them through history, but they do say, with biblical writers, that in their ethic "the love of Christ controls them."

In classic formulation, one cannot disguise the fact that the voice of Protestantism has not by any means always advanced the cause of women, and male clerics and scholars throughout the centuries made the most of biblical texts that limited the roles of women. Yet, barely hidden in the Bible, roles of women are huge and potentially liberating. In the Gospel accounts they were the first witnesses to the resurrection of Christ. In modern times their role has been reinterpreted and the Scriptures are being reread.

Some Protestants are exclusivist sectarians—that is, anyone outside their part of Protestantism is to be kept at a distance and disdained. Most Protestants do not believe that all faiths are teaching the same thing, that "we are all in different boats heading for the same shore." They have to leave the shore to God's care. But they have long known that God works among those who do not know God, for the sake of civic and humanitarian life. And more and more of them are in hospitable relations of give-and-take with members of other religions.

At a Glance

Classic Texts
The Hebrew Scriptures (The Old Testament)
The New Testament
Ancient creeds about the nature of Jesus Christ
The Westminster Confession
The Augsburg Confession

Important Figures
Abraham
Jesus Christ

Marcion
Martin Luther
John Calvin
Henry VIII

Characteristic Beliefs
The Bible as the word of God
Faith in Jesus Christ as the Son of God
Grace given through the work of Christ
Belief in the power of the Holy Spirit
Gathering the individual believers into community
Expressing religious freedom

Essential Creeds or Codes of Conduct
The Apostles' Creed
The Nicene Creed
Protestant creedal confessions, Westminster and Augsburg

Brief Time Line
eighth century B.C.E.	Time of the prophets
first century	Life of Jesus; writing of the New Testament
third century	Development of the biblical canon and early creeds
1517	Beginning of the Lutheran Reformation
1607 and 1620–30	Arrival of Protestants in colonial America

Important Symbols
Whereas individual churches have symbols, Protestantism as a whole does not. It shares with other Christians the cross of Jesus Christ. See also an open Bible and the cup and plate or loaf for the sacraments.

Glossary
anointed	dedicated by God for a special purpose; in Greek, *Christos,* as in "Christ"
apocryphal writings	ancient scriptural texts not regarded by all Christians or many Protestants as being on the same level as the approved "official" Scriptures
apostolic	intending to be faithful to the teaching of the apostles of Jesus
Catholic	in Protestant life does not mean Roman Catholic but means the universal church

crucifixion	Roman punishment executed by exposing a person nailed or tied to a cross
Ecclesia	the Greek word ("called out") for the church
Enlightenment	an eighteenth-century movement of thought devoted to reason and science, influential among America's founders
establishment	churches as expressions of government, supported by law, taxes, and privilege
Evangelical	of the Christian gospel (*evangel*); now seen as a conservative Protestant party
itinerants	Methodist and other missionaries and pastors given assignments and frequently moved by church officials
monotheism	the belief that there is only one God
ordained	set aside with church sanctions for special ministry to the believing community
Pentecostalism	another Protestant party; celebrates the Holy Spirit
Sacraments	sacred acts ordained by God, which use visible means like water and bread and wine to impart grace or give expression to faith
Sola scriptura	the belief that the Bible alone is the authority for faith

Sacred Spaces and Times
Spaces
Protestants respect historic sites associated with moments in their history, but most do not consider spaces sacred. They would rather say that all God's creation is sacred, although many would give special notice to Holy Land sites connected with Jesus Christ's activities.

Times
Most Protestants celebrate the church year, especially the half of the calendar year that includes Christmas, Easter, and Pentecost. Many also mark "saints' days" and other times in which the faithful are recognized.

Suggestions for Further Reading
Anderson, Robert Mapes. *Vision of the Disinherited: The Making of American Pentecostalism*. New York: Oxford University Press, 1979.
Balmer, Randall. *Mine Eyes Have Seen the Glory: A Journey into the Evangelical Subculture in America*. New York: Oxford University Press, 1993.
Dillenberger, John, and Claude Welch. *Protestant Christianity*. 2nd ed. New York: Macmillan, 1988.

Handy, Robert T. *A Christian America: Protestant Hopes and Historical Realities.* New York: Oxford University Press, 1984.

Hunter, James Davison. *Evangelicalism: The Coming Generation.* Chicago: University of Chicago Press, 1987.

Hutchison, William R., ed. *Between the Times: The Travail of the Protestant Establishment in America, 1900–1960.* Cambridge: Cambridge University Press, 1989.

Marty, Martin E. *Protestantism.* New York: Holt, Rinehart, and Winston, 1972.

———. *Protestantism in the United States: Righteous Empire.* 2nd ed. New York: Scribner's, 1986.

Mead, Sidney E. *The Lively Experiment: The Shaping of Christianity in America.* New York: Harper & Row, 1963.

Morgan, David. *Protestants and Pictures: Religion, Visual Culture, and the Age of American Mass Production.* New York: Oxford University Press, 1999.

Roof, Wade Clark, and William McKinney. *American Mainline Religion: Its Changing Shape and Future.* New Brunswick, N.J.: Rutgers University Press, 1987.

ISLAM: BEGINNINGS

Th. Emil Homerin

Islam is the second-largest religion in the world today, with more than a billion adherents. Though most often associated with Arabs and people living in the countries of the Middle East, Islam is also the faith of significant populations in Africa, Europe, China, and the United States. The largest contemporary Muslim population in the world is in Indonesia, with about 235 million Muslims, followed by India's Muslim minority of 175 million, and then Pakistan's Muslim population of 150 million. Though the vast majority of Muslims today are not Arabs or even speakers of Arabic, the origins of Islam are firmly rooted in Arabia of the seventh century C.E.

What is this religion's overriding question? What makes the system self-evidently valid to the community of the faithful?

For Muslims, the overriding question is how to create a just society based on belief in God (*Allah*) and the undertaking of good deeds. For the earliest Muslim community, this required the elimination of polytheism and idol worship, and the restructuring of society based on Qur'anic principles and the traditions of the prophet Muhammad. This would be a daunting endeavor since Arabian religion and society had been founded centuries earlier on the blood of one's ancestors and the custom of the tribe.

According to Muslim tradition, the Arabs are descendants of Abraham through his firstborn son, Isma'il (Ishmael). Over time, the Arabs adulterated Abraham's monotheistic faith with idolatry, such that by the sixth century C.E. Arabian religions were generally poly-theistic, often involving the veneration of an idol. A common ritual was a tribal pilgrimage to circumambulate a sacred stone called a *baetyl,* from *bet 'el,* "house of the god." Among the most famous stones was the Black Stone in the Ka'bah at Mecca, which would become the sacred site for Muslim pilgrims. Sacred stones were usu-ally found in a rectangular sanctuary (*haram*). These sanctuaries were to be inviolate, and so the towns and cities containing them often became safe staging posts for caravans and trade. Pilgrimage to these sanctuaries usually required a prohibition on violence and might include fasting, sexual abstinence, and sacrifices to the gods. The senior men of the tribe usually led the religious rites for other tribe members; these religions were not universal faiths, but particu-lar to a specific kin group. Surviving Arabic inscriptions contain prayers for health, prosperity, and victory in battle, offer thanks to a deity, or request forgiveness for transgressions. Such acts aimed pri-marily to assist the present life of the tribe, not the individual, by securing the blessings of the deity.

The ancient Arabs also believed in jinnis, ghouls, and other super-natural beings thought to inhabit desolate waste places. Jinnis, in par-ticular, interacted with humans by inspiring poets as well as diviners (*kahin*), who sometimes fell into trances and gave oracles or carefully observed the flight and cries of birds for omens. For most pre-Islamic Arabs life was governed by a capricious fate, which determined every person's death. Moreover, most Arabs probably did not believe in a resurrection; the afterlife was a gloomy, reduced existence. Faced with life's uncertainties, the Arabs maintained a code known as *muru'ah* ("manliness"), which embodied social standards as to what was hon-orable, including hospitality, generosity, bravery, and courage. Protecting the tribe's women and children was of paramount impor-tance to the existence and prosperity of the tribe, which was to be ensured by the practice of blood vengeance. Ironically, securing revenge often led to further bloodshed and sometimes to a prolonged vendetta. As a result, Muslims have often called the pre-Islamic period the *al-Jahiliyah,* the "Age of Impetuosity," during which quick tempers and grudges prevailed over forbearance and prudence.

However, by the sixth century C.E. other notions of life, death, and the afterlife made their way to the Arabian Peninsula, often carried by merchants, monks, and missionaries from Syria, Mesopotamia, and Ethiopia. Several northern Arab tribes converted to Christianity, and there was a Christian community in Najran near the Yemen. Jews had also migrated into Arabia, perhaps fleeing Roman rule, and Jewish settlements arose in the towns of Khaybar, Yathrib (Medina), and Tayma' in the Hijaz region of western Arabia, and farther south at San'a. Significantly, a few Arabs at this time appear to have renounced polytheism to embrace monotheism but without conversion to Christianity or Judaism. Nevertheless, by the sixth century C.E., most Arabs continued to worship their gods and goddesses and held fast to their tribal traditions.

How do we know about this religion? What classics define the norms?

Essential to Islam are the Qur'an and the prophet Muhammad, who was born in Mecca around 570 C.E. He was a member of the Quraysh tribe, which was in charge of the pilgrimage to the sanctuary containing the Ka'bah. Muhammad was orphaned young and raised by Abu Talib, his paternal uncle. Together, they worked as merchants on caravans of western Arabia. During this time, Muhammad married a prosperous widow named Khadijah, with whom he had four daughters. According to tradition, Muhammad was a well-respected member of the Quraysh, but he was troubled by the injustice he saw involving orphans and the poor in his society, while harboring doubts about tribal religion. Sometimes Muhammad would go alone to a cave outside of Mecca to reflect on these matters, and there, perhaps in the year 610 C.E., he received a revelation from God, which began: "Recite in the name of your Lord who created, created the human from a clot of blood. Recite, for your Lord is the most generous, who taught by the pen, taught humanity what it did not know!" (96:1-5).

Muhammad returned to Mecca where he soon began to call people to worship the one true God and to reform themselves and society. Muhammad rejected idolatry and called for economic and social justice for all, and warned of an awesome judgment day. Muhammad continued to receive revelations from God through Gabriel, the spirit of revelation, helping establish and regulate the young Muslim community for twenty-two years until the prophet died in 632. Collected together after the Muhammad's death, the Qur'an ("the recitation") contains 114 *surahs* ("chapters") ranging from 3 to 286 verses. The Qur'an tells a number of stories similar to some found in the Bible, but the Qur'an is not a sustained narrative recounting the sacred history of a people, as in Genesis and Exodus, nor does it narrate the life of its prophet as do the Gospels. Rather, the Qur'an declares itself to be God's revelation sent down as "guidance for humanity." Thus, the Qur'an is the fundamental guide for Muslims who strive to live in accordance with God's revelation.

Yet many aspects of the faith, including important details regarding prayer, pilgrimage, and alms, are not explicitly described in the Qur'an, and so Muslims have turned to their second essential source for additional religious knowledge, the accounts of Muhammad's life known as the prophetic *hadith* (*al-hadith al-nabawi*). Each hadith is usually prefaced by a chain of known authorities (*isnad*) who attest to the validity of its content (*matn*):

> Abu al-Walid related that Shu'bah related from al-Ash'ath, who said he heard it from Mu'awiyah ibn Suwayd ibn Muqarrin, who heard it from al-Bara' ibn 'Azib, may God be satisfied with him, who said: "The Messenger of God, may God bless him and give him peace, ordered seven things for us and forbade us from seven things. He ordered us to follow the funeral procession, to visit the sick, to accept invitations, to fight for the oppressed, to fulfill vows, to return greetings, and to bless one who sneezes. He forbade us silver utensils, silver dishes, gold rings, silk, silk brocade, brocade, and cloth combining flax with silk."[1]

When compiled in a narrative form, hadith traditions on Muhammad's life resemble a Christian Gospel. But in addition to this important function, hadith, such as the one above, may instruct on matters of right and wrong as well as give advice for following the straight path to God. In addition to the prophetic hadith is a smaller body of hadith traditions known as "Divine Sayings" (*al-hadith al-qudsi*), which many Muslims believe are the words of God revealed to Muhammad but not found in the Qur'an for various reasons. Many of these sayings relate to matters of the Day of Judgment, mysticism, and sanctity.

What is the community of the faithful called? What story explains its traits?

During the early years of Muhammad's prophetic career in Mecca some Arabs embraced his message, but powerful members of

Muhammad's Quraysh tribe opposed him, saying he was possessed. Muhammad hoped to convert his entire tribe to Islam, but their persecution of him and his followers forced Muhammad to leave Mecca in 622 and immigrate with his small community to the city of Yathrib, about 250 miles to the north. This immigration, the *hijrah,* marks year 1 on the Muslim calendar, thus designating a crucial stage in the development of the young religion. Muhammad had been invited to live in Yathrib by a number of wrangling tribes of Arab polytheists and Jews. Hoping to settle their disputes peaceably, some of them asked Muhammad to serve as a mediator, and they gave Muhammad and the Muslims their own status as an independent tribe. But in contrast to traditional Arab tribes, Muhammad formed his *ummah,* or community, largely on religious affiliation, not blood. Furthermore, many of the revelations that he received in Medina speak to important issues of identity, including diet, marriage, inheritance, and other matters essential for establishing and organizing a community of believers. Muhammad was a prophet to his people and their political and military leader as well, and after several years of warfare with the Quraysh and other tribes in the region, Muhammad and the Muslims were victorious over Mecca, whose inhabitants converted to Islam. Muhammad continued to receive revelations and expand the Muslim state until his death two years later in 632.

What is the way of life of the community of the faithful? What are the rules of conduct and the rites of passage? What is the notion of sacred time and space? How does the way of life embody the story that this religion tells about itself?

According to Islamic tradition, God sent Muhammad as his final prophet to reaffirm the message of all earlier prophets—from Adam to Abraham, Moses to Jesus—to believe in the one God, his angels, the prophets and their revelations, and the Judgment Day. Believers are to submit to God's will, hence, the name of the religion, *Islam,* "to submit," while a Muslim is "one who submits." God also charges persons to do good deeds and establish a moral order for which the Qur'an gives general principles for guidance as well as important rituals and rules for regulating personal and public life. The consumption of pork and alcohol is forbidden, as is gambling, prostitution, adultery, murder, and other criminal offenses. Muslim men and women should dress and act modestly, and they are encouraged to marry and procreate. Polygamy is permitted, and a Muslim man may marry up to four women at a time provided he can treat his wives equally; he is also allowed concubines. Wives and concubines may be drawn from the Muslim, Jewish, Christian, or other monotheistic communities, but a Muslim woman is permitted to marry only one Muslim man at a time, probably to ensure the male bloodline and the Muslim religion of any offspring. Muhammad was monogamous during Khadijah's lifetime, but following her death in 619 C.E. the prophet contracted a number of marriages, some of which formed important alliances between the prophet and members of the Arab community. Though discouraged by the Qur'an, Muslims are allowed to divorce their spouse, and both parties are permitted to marry others, as are widows and widowers.

As for religious rituals, the five daily canonical prayers (*salah*) reaffirm a believer's personal relationship with God. Following Muhammad's practice, prayers are to be said in the early morning, noon, midafternoon, sunset, and evening. These prayers are preceded by ablutions and the creation of a ritual space, if only a prayer rug facing Mecca. Thus, sacred time and space are established for the required recitation of particular religious statements and a series of bodily positions and prostrations. Prayers may be performed in private or in public, and the Qur'an underscores the importance of Friday noon congregational prayer by suspending all commercial activities prior to the prayer.

The Qur'an often pairs prayer with almsgiving, linking prayer's vertical dimension to God with a Muslim's horizontal relationship to fellow believers. The Qur'an calls for an annual tithe on one's possessions (*zakah*) to be used for the good of the Muslim community and for the poor, in particular. Muslims also undertake a fast (*saum*) during the month of Ramadan, when they are to refrain from eating, drinking, and sexual relations during daylight hours. This helps to recall humanity's dependence on God as well as the plight of the less fortunate. At the end of Ramadan is the "Feast to Break the Fast" ('Id al-Fitr), which includes a congregational prayer and donations to the poor.

Another sacred time occurs during the *Hajj*, or the pilgrimage to Mecca, which is to be undertaken once during a lifetime if a Muslim is financially and physically able to do so. The Hajj takes place annually during the first two weeks of Islam's twelfth lunar month. Again following Muhammad's practice, pilgrims perform required rituals that underscore the unity of the Muslim community as pilgrims worship together as one. Significantly, the Hajj serves as a preview of the Day of Judgment when all of humanity will be gathered together before God. Like Ramadan, the Hajj ends with a holiday, the "Feast of Sacrifice" ('Id al-Adha), which is joyously celebrated for three days and, if possible, with the sacrifice of an animal to be shared with others.

Whereas these rites and rituals join Muslims together, often in peace and harmony, the Qur'an also warns that Muslims may be required to join in a *jihad,* or "struggle," in order to defend Muslims from attack or oppression by non-Muslims. Jihad originally developed as a response to Quraysh polytheists as they sought to destroy the early Muslim community by exiling them from Mecca:

> Permission to fight is granted to those who have been oppressed. God has power to give them victory. They were driven out of their homes for no other reason other than they declared, "God is our Lord." If God did not defend some people by means of others then surely monasteries, churches, synagogues, and mosques, where God's name is mentioned often, would be destroyed. God will surely help those who help Him, for He is powerful, mighty! (22:39-40)

The Qur'an exhorts Muslims to defend themselves and their faith, and for those who sacrifice their property or lives for this cause, God will give them a more precious heavenly reward.

What is the worldview of the community, the story that it tells about itself in the context of history, the conception of divinity and the relationship of the divinity (or divinities) to the believers, and its principal ethical teachings? How do women fit into the system in its classical formulation? What are the attitude and behaviors toward persons outside the faith community?

The Qur'an does not have a clear narrative structure or a sure chronology for individual revelations, but its major themes are clear. First is monotheism, that there is one god, *Allah,* a word best translated into English as "God" with a capital "G."

Qur'an 1: *The Opening*
In the name of God the compassionate, the merciful,
praise be to God, lord of the worlds,
the compassionate, the merciful,
master of the day of reckoning,
You we worship, and to You we turn for aid.
Guide us along the straight path,
the road of those whom You have blessed,
not those with anger against them,
nor those who are astray!

The Qur'an declares many times that God is one, not one among many—as was the case with the pagan Arabs—but the one and only: "Your lord is God who created the heavens and the earth in six days. Then, He sat upon the throne dispensing all affairs. Who can intercede with Him save by His permission? He is God, your Lord, so worship Him. Will you not take heed?" (10:3).

God is all-knowing, all-powerful, the lord and master ruling over his creation, and this fact is reflected in the Qur'an's frequent use of the royal "we" when God speaks: "We have not created the heavens and all that is between them save in truth and for an appointed time. But the ungrateful who were warned, turn away!" (46:3). Images of God as king resonate with the Bible, which may reflect the shared Semitic traditions among Jews, Christians, and pagan Arabs in Arabia at this time. Judaism, Christianity, and Islam share in a common religious heritage, as they believe in one God who has made a covenant with his people and to whom he gives laws for leading a righteous life.

Yet, there are substantive differences in their interpretations of key themes, including the covenant and monotheism. The Qur'an clearly states that God's covenant is not with a chosen people, such as the Jews, but with every human being. As to different conceptions of monotheism, the Qur'an declares: "God: there is no deity but Him, the living, the eternal. Drowsiness does not touch Him, nor sleep" (2:255). In contrast to the book of Genesis, where God rested on the seventh day of creation (Gen. 2:3), in the Qur'an God is unique and not in any way human. The Qur'an is again in stark contrast to Genesis regarding the creation of Adam. The Qur'an states: "[God] created him from earth and then said to him 'Be!' and he was" (3:59); and again in 40:64: "God created the earth as a dwelling for you and the sky as your roof, and He shaped you in the best of forms." However, the Qur'an never says that God created man in God's own image (Gen. 1:27). Such a notion could undermine God's uniqueness and justify the very polytheistic practices that Muhammad opposed. The Qur'an instructs Muhammad to declare: "This is God, my Lord, to whom I turn and place my trust, originator of the heavens and the earth.... There is nothing like Him, the all-seeing, all-knowing!" (42:10-11).

In support of God's uniqueness, the Qur'an denies Christian doctrines of Jesus as the Son of God, something the Qur'an takes quite literally. The Trinity is also an unacceptable compromise with monotheism. According to the Qur'an, some people believed that there was a trinity consisting of God, Jesus, and his mother, Mary. Even though Jesus was a great prophet and his mother an honored virgin, the Qur'an rejects the Trinity as akin to polytheism, where others share a divine status with God. The Qur'an unequivocally declares God's oneness, though there are other supernatural beings. God created angels who serve him as messengers and guardians and who surround his throne. God also created from fire jinnis, who fly through the heavens and interact with humans. Some jinnis believe in God and obey him, though others do not and so will suffer in hell. Perhaps, the latter are the satans mentioned in the Qur'an who are led by Iblis, also known as Satan, humanity's primordial enemy:

> Whoever does a good deed, whether they are male or female, and who believes, We will resurrect them in a sweet life, and reward them with something equal to the best that they did. So when you recite the Qur'an, seek refuge in God from Satan, the accursed. But he has no power over those who believe and trust in their Lord. His power is only over those who take him as their patron and over those who make him an equal [with God]. (16:97-100)

This passage addresses two important corollaries of monotheism—individual moral responsibility and personal immortality—which were in clear contrast to the polytheistic religion of Arabia that primarily served the present life of the tribe, not the individual worshiper. As part of his prophetic mission, Muhammad brought Qur'anic revelations that forbade vendetta and regulated blood-vengeance, and he replaced the primacy of tribal affiliation with membership in the larger community of believers. Now, individual men and women who believe in the one God and perform good deeds will enter the gardens of paradise and be reunited with their believing loved ones.

But to attain this immortality, individuals must submit to God and his will. However, humanity often forgets this charge because of basic human weaknesses, including pride, greed, narrow-mindedness, and despair. At the root of them all is selfishness, which may result in acts of injustice that strain and may even sever the covenant with God and fellow human beings. Satan exploits these weaknesses in order to lead humans astray. But in his mercy God sends messengers to humanity to remind them that God cares for his creation, to reaffirm God's will, and to warn of an awesome Judgment Day. The prophets try to rouse in humanity a mindfulness of God (*taqwa*), for although people are free to act, judgment upon that action, and the standard by which it will be judged, belongs to God: "Oh, you who believe, be mindful of God. Let each person consider what they have set aside for tomorrow. Be mindful of God, for He knows what you do. The residents of hell and those of heaven are not equal, for the residents of paradise will be the winners!" (59:18-19).

This final judgment, however, should not be regarded as a promise of gleeful vengeance so much as a present warning for people to mend their ways, to try to right the wrongs that they have committed, and to seek justice in the world while there is still time. Further, many passages reveal a God of mercy and compassion: "Say (to them Muhammad): 'If you love God, then follow me, that He may love you and forgive your sins, for God is forgiving and merciful'" (3:31). The Qur'an also states that creation is a blessing from God, and that humanity should dwell peacefully in the world and enjoy life. This applies to both believing men and believing women who are spiritually equal in the eyes of God:

> Indeed, men and women who submit, believing men and believing women, devout men and devout women, truthful men and truthful women, patient men and patient women, humble men and humble women, men who give alms and women who give alms, men who fast and women who fast, men and women who are chaste and remember God often, God has forgiveness for them and a great reward! (33:35)

In social terms, however, the Qur'an appears to envision a world in which men and women have rights, though men "are a degree above" women (2:228); thus men are required to support women and children. For this reason, a son will receive twice the amount of inheritance as a daughter. Moreover, as noted above, while a Muslim woman is allowed to marry only one Muslim man at a time, a Muslim man may have up to four wives, in addition to concubines, and they may be Muslim, Jewish, Christian, or a member of another monotheistic faith.

Such a close relationship as marriage between faiths draws attention to the ambiguous position of Jews, Christians, Zoroastrians, and other non-Muslim monotheists in the Qur'an. The Qur'an collectively refers to them as the "People of the Book" (*Ahl al-Kitab*), since they have previously received a revelation from one of God's many prophets. In the Qur'an, God commands Muhammad to say, "I believe in whatever book God has sent down!" (42:15), and the Qur'an names the Psalms of David, the Torah brought by Moses, the Gospel of Jesus, and the Qur'an. Yet, in spite of this underlying unity, the original revelations may be altered over time as humans ignore God's commands and tend toward their own desires, thus corrupting God's original revelation to a community, as was the case when the followers of Jesus began to believe in the Trinity. In addition, sectarianism arises, obscuring the truth that God's covenant is with all of humanity and not just with a single faith community.

Yet, despite such disagreements, the Qur'an explicitly recognizes the existence and rights of Jews, Christians, and other non-Muslim monotheists who strive to lead a pious life: "Those who believe [i.e., Muslims], and those who are Jews, Christians, and Sabians, whoever believes in God, the Last Day, and does good deeds, they will have their reward from their Lord. They have nothing to fear nor will they grieve" (2:62).

This recognition of religious diversity, however, should not be construed as religious equality, and the Qur'an warns Muslims against aligning too closely with those of other faiths lest Islam be compromised (2:120; 5:51; 5:82).

> Fight those who do not believe in God, the last day, and who do not forbid what God and His messenger have forbidden, and who do not practice the religion of truth among the people given the Book, until they pay tribute out of hand and are humbled. (9:29)

Oh, you who believe, do not take Jews or Christians as allies for some of them are allies of one another. For one who makes alliances with them, is one of them, and God does not guide an oppressive people. (5:51)

Muslim tradition claims that these two passages were revealed late in the prophet's life after several Jewish tribes joined with the pagan Quraysh to oppose Muhammad. Therefore, while the Qur'an acknowledges and respects the rights of other monotheistic religions based on past revelations, it asserts the superiority of the Muslim faith proclaimed by Muhammad.

How does this religion function in the world today? What are its relationships with culture?

From Islam's beginnings in the Qur'an and the life of the prophet Muhammad, the faith would quickly develop and spread throughout the world to become the second-largest religion today. This development and Islam's relationships to culture will be addressed in subsequent chapters on the Sunni and Shi'i traditions of Islam.

At a Glance

Classic Texts
The Qur'an
Prophetic Hadith
Divine Sayings

Important Figures
The prophet Muhammad (570–632)
Abu Talib, uncle who raised Muhammad
Khadijah, first wife of the prophet
Iblis / Satan

Characteristic Beliefs
Belief in one God
Doing good deeds
Establishing a just society
Overcoming selfishness
Satan as the enemy of humanity
God's forgiveness
Obeying God's commandments leads to eternal life.

Essential Creeds or Codes of Conduct
The commandments and revelations of God contained in the Qur'an
Qur'anic creeds: 2:177; 2:285; 4:136

Brief Time Line
ca. 570	Muhammad is born
ca. 610	The revelation of the Qur'an begins
622	The *hijrah* or emigration of Muslims from Mecca to Medina
630	Mecca falls to Muhammad; Meccans convert to Islam
632	Muhammad dies; prophecy ends

Important Symbols
The Ka'bah
Black Stone of Mecca

Important Rituals
Canonical Prayer (*salah*)
Pilgrimage to Mecca (*Hajj*)

Glossary
Ahl al-Kitab	monotheists who are not Muslims
Allah	God
baetyl	a sacred stone
al-hadith al-nabawi	traditions of the prophet Muhammad
al-hadith al-qudsi	sayings of God not found in the Qur'an
Hajj	the canonical pilgrimage to Mecca
haram	a sanctuary
hijrah	emigration of Muslims from Mecca to Medina in 622
Jahiliyah	Age of Impetuosity
jihad	"struggle" in defense of Islam and the Muslim community
kahin	diviner; soothsayer
muruᶜah	code of honor
Qur'an	"recitation"; the Muslim book of God's revelations to Muhammad
salah	canonical prayer
saum	fasting
surah	a chapter of revelation
ummah	the community of Muslim believers
zakah	the annual tithe

Sacred Spaces and Times
Ka'bah of Mecca
The five daily canonical prayers
The Feast to Break the Fast (*'Id al-Fitr*)
The Feast of Sacrifice (*'Id al-Adha*)

Suggestions for Further Reading
(a) The Qur'an

Ali, Ahmed. *Al-Qur'an: A Contemporary Translation.* Princeton, N.J.: Princeton University Press, 2001.

Cook, Michael. *The Koran: A Very Short Introduction.* New York: Oxford University Press, 2000.

Rahman, Fazlur. *Major Themes of the Qur'an.* 2nd ed. Chicago: University of Chicago Press, 2009.

(b) The Life of Muhammad

Cook, Michael. *Muhammad.* New York: Oxford University Press, 1983.

Guillaume, Alfred. *The Life of Muhammad.* New York: Oxford University Press, 1955.

Peters, F. E. *Muhammad and the Origins of Islam.* Albany: State University of New York Press, 1994.

(c) Hadith

Graham, William A. *Divine Word and Prophetic Word in Early Islam.* The Hague: Mouton, 1977.

THE SHI'I TRADITION

Liyakat Takim

What is Shi'i Islam's overriding question?

L
ike Sunni Islam, the stress in Shi'ism is the belief in the unity
of God. God is One, unique, all-powerful, omniscient, and,
above all, incomparable to any created being or thing. God not
only creates every living thing but also communicates to human
beings by sending prophets or messengers. Thus, Shi'ism shares with
Sunnism the essential beliefs of Islam: one God, the prophets (from
Adam to Muhammad), and the Day of Judgment. Contrary to Sunni
Islam, Shi'i theology further insists that good and evil are categories
that can be known directly through reason, independently of revelation. Reason tells us that since God is the Creator, he is not only
good (evil cannot be imputed to God) but also just, a view that is
anchored on many verses in the Qur'an. Shi'ism also emphasizes the
doctrine of free will over predestination. Indeed, the justice of God
is an essential article of faith in Shi'i theology.

Shi'i beliefs in monotheism, God's justice, and free will are based
primarily on Qur'anic verses like the chapter of unity (chapter 112)
and other verses that insist God is One and incomparable. Shi'i
beliefs are also premised on numerous *ahadith* (traditions) reported
from the prophet Muhammad and Imams.

How do we know about this religion? What classics define the norms?

Since they emerged only after Muhammad died in 632 C.E., information on the early Shi'is and their beliefs are to be found in a wide range of Sunni and Shi'i sources. The presence of the early Shi'i community and its beliefs are documented in juridical, biographical, heresiographical, hagiographical, exegetical, and polemical texts. Many Shi'i beliefs are based on verses of the Qur'an. Historical works like those of Tabari, Masu'di, Baladhuri, and others mention the rise of the supporters of 'Ali b. Abi Talib (d. 661). The presence and political stance of the early Shi'is are also found in various biographical works like those of Ibn Sa'd's *Tabaqat*, al-Dhahabi's *al-Mizan al-I'tidal,* and other works. Shi'i beliefs are also stated and refuted in Sunni polemical and heresiographical works. They are of course stated in detail in Shi'i works too. There are a number of Shi'i *hadith* texts, starting with the time of Kulayni's (d. 939) *Usul al-Kafi,* that elaborate on Shi'i beliefs and practices.

What is the community of the faithful called? What story explains its traits?

The term *Shi'i* refers to the partisans of 'Ali, the cousin and son-in-law of Muhammad. After the prophet died, the early Shi'is claimed that 'Ali was the only legitimate successor to Muhammad, having been designated by him at Ghadir Khum and on other occasions. They further restricted leadership of the community to the family of the prophet, the *ahl al-bayt*. Such leadership was designated by the term *Imam* and is believed to pass on from father to blood successor. The basis of the Shi'i belief in the principle of succession through the family of the prophet can be traced to numerous utterances that Muhammad is reported to have made in favor of 'Ali.

Shi'is also believed that the rights of 'Ali and the family of the prophet were usurped by the companions of Muhammad. This meant that, from the very beginning, Shi'ism rose as a dissenting group in opposition to the Muslim majority. This dissent manifested itself in different forms during the course of Shi'i history. Initially, Shi'i protest expressed itself by contesting Abu Bakr's succession to the prophet, advocating instead the succession of 'Ali. Later conflicts between 'Ali and Mu'awiya (d. 679), Husayn (d. 680), and Yazid

(d. 684), and the various Shi'i revolts against both the Umayyad and 'Abbasid caliphs, were further manifestations of these differences. Political opposition and rebellion against a central government formed the basis of the development of a distinct sectarian movement that postulated its own concept of religious authority and leadership.

Shi'is believe that God sent twelve Imams to guide humankind after the prophet. The first Imam is 'Ali and the last one is the messiah, also called Muhammad al-Mahdi, who will reappear at the end of time to establish peace and justice on earth. In Shi'ism, religious identity is conceived in terms of devotion to the Imams. Various traditions cited in Shi'i sources accord complete authority to the Imams. They are referred to as "the Imams of guidance and justice." God guides people through them; they are the pillars of religion and life for humankind. Soteriology, as envisaged in Shi'ism, is contingent on the recognition of and loyalty to the Imams in general and to the Imam of the time in particular.

Three principles encapsulate the charismatic authority of the Imams: *nass, 'ilm,* and *'isma.* The doctrine of divine designation (*nass*) stipulates that 'Ali had been designated by the prophet to succeed him, inheriting, in the process, his many traits. Thus, 'Ali's authority, and that of the subsequent Imams, is legitimized through the act of designation (*nass*). The question of *nass* is important because it links the Imams in a concatenated chain culminating in the ultimate source of authority, the prophet.

The authority of the Imam is also measured by the *'ilm* (divinely bestowed knowledge) that he had reportedly inherited from the prophet. The possession of divinely bestowed knowledge is important in the study of the Shi'i concept of religious authority because, in the absence of any political investiture, this was the only factor that could prove the claim to imamate when disputes arose regarding the identity of a true successor of an Imam.

The Shi'is maintain that the *'ilm* of an Imam is transmitted in a concatenated chain to all subsequent Imams. Thus, although the authority of an Imam can, theoretically, be inherited by any one of a number of his sons, it is the belief in the divinely inspired knowledge that restricts the authority to a particular individual. *'Ilm* acts as a mitigating factor, ensuring that only one candidate among several contenders for the imamate can inherit the Imam's authority. The twin principles of *nass* and *'ilm* thus become a focal point in the Shi'i theory of leadership because they guarantee and protect the divine message from adulteration by transmitting it through a divinely protected chain of authority. Acknowledging the correct Imam becomes equivalent to accepting the original source of authoritative guidance, the prophet.

To serve as exemplary models, the Imams, like the prophet, are believed to possess the trait of immunity from sins (*'isma*). *'Isma* is important in the Shi'i concept of authority and essential to the Imams' mission to set paradigmatic precedents, because the community cannot follow one whose actions are immoral or sinful. The principle of *'isma* also means that, as exemplary models, the pronouncements of the Imams acquire normative force and, together with the actions and sayings of the prophet, are regarded as the primary source of law after the Qur'an.

What is the way of life of the community of the faithful? What are the rules of conduct and the rites of passage? What is the notion of sacred time and space? How does the way of life embody the story that this religion tells about itself?

Shi'i Muslims share with Sunnis the major Islamic festivals (*eid al-fitr* and *eid al-adha*) and seasons such as Ramadan and the pilgrimage to Mecca. However, the Shi'i calendar is punctuated by other religious holidays that Sunni Muslims do not commemorate. This is because the Shi'i notion of sanctity and holiness is markedly differently from that of other Muslims. Sunni religious events are confined to daily or weekly prayers and annual events in which Muslims from different ethnic backgrounds congregate. Shi'is, however, have their own calendar of days wherein venerated Imams and holidays are clearly marked as distinct from profane time. Besides holding daily, Friday, and *eid* prayers, Shi'i communities hold numerous functions to commemorate the martyrdom of Husayn, the third Shi'i Imam. Together with members of his family and friends, on the day of *'Ashura,* Husayn was brutally killed by the orders of a tyrannical ruler called Yazid (d. 684) at Kerbala, Iraq, in 680 C.E. For Husayn, Yazid had established an unjust and corrupt society and had violated all moral and religious norms. When asked to accept Yazid as his ruler, Husayn responded that he would never submit to oppression and tyranny.

The massacre of Husayn was an important milestone in Shi'i history because it affirmed notions of injustices endured by the family of the prophet and exacerbated a passion for martyrdom. It also inspired the Shi'is to defy oppressive rulers. Every year, during the first ten days of the first month of the Islamic calendar (called *Muharram*), Shi'is will mark Husayn's martyrdom with a series of lectures and the performance of various acts of devotion that are premised on culturally generated symbols and rituals.

An important ritual in the month of Muharram is that of flagellation. In Shi'ism, *flagellation* is a composite term that includes the use of swords and knives to cut the head (*tatbir*), the use of chains (*zanjir*), and the striking of the chest (*ma'tam*). *Tatbir* is the most violent of these acts and is practiced by only a small portion of the Shi'i community. *Ma'tam* or *latmiyya* designates the formal ritual acts of breast-beating and self-flagellation that are generally undertaken by all Shi'i groups.

A key element in the commemorative gatherings is a lecture and recollection of the martyrdom of Husayn in Kerbala, called *majlis*. The *majalis* (plural of *majlis*) are lamentation assemblies where the stories of the martyrs of Kerbala are recited for the evocation of grief. Narratives associated with the Imams are often heard in the *majlis*. These gatherings have also been used to recount the persecution endured by the Shi'i Imams, evoking, thereby, the emotions of the audience. In addition, their virtues, miracles, and valor are recounted.

Other holidays include the day of *Arba'in* (the fortieth day after the death of Husayn). Devout Shi'is will also mark the birth and death anniversaries of the prophet Muhammad and of every Imam. Often, a death anniversary will be marked by a lecture mourning for and remembering the dead Imam. The birth anniversary of an Imam will also be marked by remembering the virtues and character of the Imam.

Shi'is are also encouraged to visit the tombs and shrines where the Imams are buried. The presence of the Imam in the grave provides the Shi'is the opportunity to experience the *baraka* (blessings) that pervades the Imam because it is believed that his shrine is an important channel for the transmission of divine blessings. Touching the shrine of the Imam or any object associated with it is seen as an effective medium to experience this *baraka*. Pilgrimage to the shrine of an

Imam is an integration of a series of rituals that begin with pre-entrance etiquette (*adab*) and other acts of devotion that attest to and cement the deep emotional attachment that the Shi'i has with the Imam.

Shi'is will also mark the day of Ghadir. It is believed that when he was returning from his last pilgrimage, the prophet Muhammad stopped in the middle of the desert at a place called Ghadir and designated 'Ali b. Abi Talib as his successor. This event is important for Shi'is because it refutes the Sunni contention that the prophet did not appoint a successor and that Abu Bakr was legitimately chosen by the community to succeed the prophet. Shi'is also mark the event of *Mubahila*. It is reported that, on this day, the prophet brought his family to Najaran when that Christian community challenged him to an imprecation. The Christians reportedly preferred to sign a peace agreement rather than imprecate against the *ahl al-bayt*. Shi'is will also mark the important event of *layl al-Qadr* in the month of Ramadan. It is believed that the Qur'an was revealed on this night.

Shi'is share with Sunnis the major rituals that Muslims are required to perform. These include the daily and Friday prayers, fasting during the month of Ramadan, paying the poor tax, and the performance of the annual pilgrimage to Mecca.

Like many other religions, Shi'ism has taken on distinctly indigenous forms in the different lands where it has spread. The practices of "popular Shi'ism" are where the differences within the Shi'i community are most pronounced. Popular practices are often the most important agents in spreading a religion in lands where it is foreign. After the establishment of the Safavid Empire in Iran in 1501, Iranians created a popular-based ritual called the *taziyeh,* a dramatic reenactment of the events at Kerbala. Subsequently, the *taziyeh* has assumed different forms as various Shi'i groups have expressed their devotion to Husayn in a myriad of culturally conditioned forms. In the Indo-Pakistani subcontinent, for example, *taziyeh* refers to a replica of the tomb of Husayn that is constructed, paraded in processions, and then kept in special sanctuaries within the precincts of the mosque. In Iran, the same term signifies passion plays that depict the events in Kerbala. In Lebanon, *taziyeh* refers to a gathering or procession to mark Husayn's martyrdom.

It is these genres of distinctive Shi'i symbols and icons that create Shi'i space and identity. These visual words and symbols convey the message that distinguishes Shi'i from Sunni Islam; they also affirm the authority of 'Ali and his descendants, the Imams, and that salvation is attained through the recognition of the *wilaya* (authority) of the Imams.

Eating

The origins of Shi'i law are attributed to the sixth Imam, Ja'far al-Sadiq (d. 765). Highly respected in the Sunni sources, al-Sadiq was reportedly the author of thousands of legal and theological traditions that were recorded by his disciples and documented in later Shi'i literature like those of al-Kulayni, Ibn Babuya, and Tusi. These sources also indicate that Ja'far al-Sadiq was responsible for the formulation and crystallization of the Shi'i doctrine of the imamate. The Shi'i school of law (called *Ja'fari*) is named after him. Shi'is observe the same dietary restrictions as Sunnis do. Pork is forbidden, as is carrion. Only meat that has been slaughtered in a prescribed manner may be consumed. Animals are slaughtered with a sharp knife, swiftly, to reduce suffering. Certain veins are cut and the blood is drained. The name of God is invoked before the slaughter, and the slaughterer must face Mecca. All fruits and vegetables are permitted; so too are fish that have fins and scales, but not scavengers.

Praying

Prayers are to be offered five times every day. However, Shi'is are allowed to combine the noon and afternoon prayers as well as the evening and night prayers. Thus, the five prayers are offered three times a day. The community and its members pray (1) before the sun rises, (2) in the afternoon, and (3) after night has fallen. Prayers are offered by facing Mecca and are composed of three positions: standing up erect, bowing, and prostrating. The opening chapter of the Qur'an (called the *fatiha*) is recited in every prayer. There are other mandatory prayers that must also be offered. These include Friday prayers, prayers over the dead, and prayers when there is an eclipse or a natural catastrophe like an earthquake, hurricane, or tornado. In addition, there are several voluntary prayers that the faithful are recommended to offer.

Birth

The birth of a child, male or female, is a special and joyous occasion. The child's head is shaved on the seventh day after birth. At this point, it is recommended to give some money to charity. Boys are circumcised preferably within a week of birth. There is no legislation for female circumcision.

Entering the Age of Responsibility

There is no specific rite to mark the advent of puberty. Girls attain puberty when they begin to menstruate, whereas boys attain puberty when they ejaculate or turn fifteen. At this point, the young person becomes obligated to observe religious commandments such as prayers, fasting, and so on.

Marriage

As in Sunni Islam, marriage is highly recommended in Shi'ism. A famous tradition from 'Ali, the first Shi'i Imam, states, "Whoever gets married has performed half of his or her religious obligation. The other half lies in being morally upright." Marriage is seen as a contract between two consenting adults. Thus, both parties are entitled to stipulate conditions to the contract. Both parties are to strive to their utmost to create a harmonious familial environment; if there is a conflict, both parties should appoint arbiters to resolve their differences.

For all Muslims marriage is intrinsically interwoven into family life. God instituted marriage to create a prosperous family unit and, ultimately, a morally upright human society. Families that are ingrained with virtue are to share their spiritual riches with other families.

Divorce in Shi'ism

Although not prohibited, divorce is highly discouraged, especially as it causes great difficulties for children. Shi'i laws on divorce treat women more favorably than their Sunni counterpart. This is because Shi'is do not accept the triple divorce (*talaq*), which Sunnis adopted, as a valid form of divorce. Shi'i rejection of this form of divorce is favorable to women since the triple divorce allows the husband the right to unilaterally pronounce the divorce in one setting.

Shi'i law considers invalid any repudiation during a menstrual period or when the woman is pure but cohabitation has taken place since her last period. In addition, Shi'i law also requires the presence of two male Muslim witnesses during the divorce and allows the man to take back his wife during the waiting period (*'idda*). Even after the waiting period ends, the couple can get back together by solemnizing a second marriage.

Since the husband normally initiates the divorce proceedings, women's rights to seek divorce are more circumscribed. Shi'i law allows a woman to seek divorce under the *khul'* (at the instigation of the wife) form of divorce. *Khul'* can be finalized with the husband's consent. For it to be valid, the wife has to petition for divorce and is also required to offer some form of compensation to the husband (such as the return of the dowry). The wife can also nullify the marriage under certain circumstances without obtaining a formal divorce. Nullification is possible if the husband has no sexual organ, is impotent or insane, or if he has leprosy or leucoderma.

Overall, it is correct to state that Shi'ism encourages young adults to marry when they are able to and to create a harmonious familial environment. Verses in the Qur'an are invoked at the time of performing the marriage. Since there is no priesthood in Islam, in some countries in the West women sometimes conduct their own marriages (*'aqd*).

Death

The Islamic view of death is overall positive. Death is seen as a return to the Lord. Hence, when someone dies, Muslims recite a verse from the Qur'an stating, "From God we come and to Him we shall return." Death is seen not as the end of life but as only the end of the appointed period during which human beings are tested. It is a transitional phase in which the *ruh* (spirit) is separated from the body. Thus, death is an essential part of Allah's creation and signifies the continuation of a different form of life. To signify this transition from a physical to a spiritual form of life the Qur'an talks of angels receiving and interrogating the dead (4:97). The term *barzakh* (barrier) is used to refer to purgatory (the period between death and the Day of Judgment), although the term is used in a different context in the Qur'an.

Death is also part of the broader Qur'anic vision of the purpose of God's creation of human beings. They are tested in this world; death signifies the end of the testing period. Death is also a manifestation of God's power, for he decides the appointed time (*ajal*) for every person. He also decides when the Day of Judgment (*qiyama*) will take place.

When a person is about to die, she or he is made to recite the *shahada*, if possible. This is the testimony that there is only one God and that Muhammad is his prophet. The person is made to sleep so that her or his feet face Mecca. After death, the body is washed three times and shrouded in white clothing. Prayers are offered for the dead and then the body is buried facing Mecca. The family of the deceased, as well as the assembled, shovel dirt onto the body until the grave is filled. In most cases, a mourning period of forty days is observed and the death anniversary is marked.

What is the worldview of the community?

Shi'ism is built around the concept of *wilaya* (authority). Ultimately, all *wilaya* emerges from God, who designates special individuals to proclaim (the prophets) and protect the message (Imams). As he inherits the comprehensive authority from the prophet, the Imam is also believed to exercise both juristic and spiritual authorities over the lives of his followers. It is believed that the prophet transmitted the *wilaya* to 'Ali and subsequently to the rest of the Imams. The *wilaya* enables the Imam to provide salvation to his followers and to guide them in both the exoteric and the esoteric sense.

The pervasive and comprehensive *wilaya* of the Imam led Shi'ism into becoming a distinctive movement based on loyalties to and identification with spiritually authoritative human beings. At the nexus between the divine and the human, the Imam is considered to be the exclusive and legitimate, religious and spiritual heir of the prophet who endeavored to re-create his ideal community and to have acted as intermediary with God. In addition, the Imam is believed to have replicated the prophetic paradigm, which was centered on an heir of the prophet living within the Muslim community. As his authority resonates strongly with that of the prophet, the Imam becomes an extension of the personality of the prophet.

How does this religion function in the world today? What are its relationships with culture?

Shi'ism has become a major political force in the Middle East since the Iranian Revolution in 1979. Ayatollah Khamenie promulgated the idea of *wilaya al-faqih*, the rulership of the jurist. The establishment of an Islamic government in Iran and the enhanced power of the Shi'is in Iraq and Lebanon (because of the rise of Hizbollah) have made Shi'ism a major political force today. Shi'is in other parts of the

Muslim world, such as Saudi Arabia and Bahrain, have also sought to reclaim their rights. However, other Shi'i scholars like Ayatollah Seestani have rejected the concept of a theocratic state ruled by religious scholars.

Since the 1960s, Shi'is from all over the world have migrated to the West looking for greater economic and educational opportunities. Immigration to the West means that, like other Muslim immigrants, many recent Shi'i arrivals see Islam through a cultural prism, a lens that they have been accustomed to. Immigrants tend to impose the homeland culture in the West by determining how the mosques are run or what is an acceptable dress code, language, or behavior.

The Shi'i community in the West is constituted in a different environment in which Shi'is form a conglomerate of disparate ethnic groups. This confluence of Shi'is sharing common space has proved to be problematic. Increased emigration from various parts of the world has resulted in the Shi'i community in the West becoming more fragmented as ties to common origins, ethnicity, and culture have replaced bonds of common faith.

Despite the common beliefs and practices that characterize the global Shi'i community, the unity of the community evaporates in the face of ethnic, linguistic, and national differences. Nowhere in the world is the ethnic diversity in the Shi'i community as evident as it is in America. Major cities like New York, Los Angeles, Houston, Detroit, Washington, and Chicago are characterized by disparate Shi'i centers established along ethnic lines. In addition, Shi'i communities mark events like the martyrdom of Husayn and enact Muharram rituals based on their own culturally generated symbols and modes of expressions. Thus, Muharram rituals construct additional boundaries that further segment the Shi'i community.

At a Glance

Classic Texts

The Qur'an is believed by Muslims to be the word of God. Shi'i beliefs are often derived from Qur'anic verses.

al-Kafi fi 'ilm al-Din is one of the earliest Shi'i collections of traditions reported from the prophet and Imams. Muhammad b. Ja'far Kulayni (d. 939) compiled this work. Shi'i beliefs regarding the imamate are explicitly stated in this work.

Risala al-I'tiqad is a brief theological work written by Ibn Babuya stating basic Shi'i beliefs regarding God, the prophets, and the Imams.

'Awa'il al-Maqalat, written by Muhammad b. Muhammad al-Mufid, is an eleventh-century theological tract that outlines some of the essential beliefs of Shi'ism.

Historical texts of figures like Ibn Sa'd (*Tabaqat*), Tabari (*Ta'rikh al-Muluk*), and al-Dhahabi (*Mizan al-I'tidal*) all indicate the presence and activities of the supporters of 'Ali and other Imams.

Important Figures

Muhammad b. 'Abdullah	Considered by all Muslims as the founding and final prophet of Islam.
'Ali b. Abi Talib	The first Shi'i Imam who, the Shi'is believe, was appointed by Muhammad to succeed him.
Husayn b. 'Ali	The third Shi'i Imam; martyred in the plains of Kerbala in 680 C.E. by a tyrannical ruler, Yazid b. Mu'awiya.
Ja'far al-Sadiq	The sixth Shi'i Imam and founder of the Shi'i school of law, called Ja'fari.
Muhammad al-Mahdi	The twelfth Shi'i Imam is believed to be in occultation since 940 C.E. He is the messiah who will reappear at the end of time to establish the kingdom of justice and equality.
Abu Bakr	The first caliph and successor to Muhammad; Shi'is believe he usurped the position that was supposed to have been occupied by 'Ali.
Yazid b. Mu'awiya	The Umayyad caliph responsible for the killing of Husayn.

Characteristic Beliefs

Belief in one God and the prophethood of prophets, starting with Adam and ending with Muhammad.

Belief in God's justice, free will, and questioning on the Day of Judgment. After judgment, the faithful and those who have performed good deeds will be rewarded with heaven, whereas others will be punished in hell.

Belief in twelve Imams beginning with 'Ali and ending with the twelfth Imam, al-Mahdi. Shi'is believe that the messiah will return at the end of time. They also accept that the Imams are appointed by God, free from sin, and have been bestowed with divinely inspired knowledge.

Obedience to and observance of God's commandments (revealed in the form of the law—*shari'a*) will result in salvation.

Essential Creeds or Codes of Conduct
The commandments and revelations of God contained in scripture and hadith literature
Articles of Faith as outlined above

Brief Time Line
570	Birth of Muhammad, the prophet of Islam
632	Death of Muhammad
661	'Ali b. Abi Talib is murdered while praying in a mosque in Kufa.
681	Husayn, the third Shi'i Imam, is martyred in Kerbala.
765	Death of Ja'far al-Sadiq, the sixth Imam, who founded the Ja'fari school of law
870	Birth of the twelfth Imam in Samarra, Iraq
874	Death of Hasan al-Askari, the eleventh Imam. Al-Mahdi enters a minor occultation. During this period, he communicates with specially appointed agents.
940	The twelfth Imam enters a prolonged occultation. He is expected to return at the end of time.
1501	The Safavid Empire is established in Iran. Shah Isma'il, the first Safavid king, establishes Shi'ism as the state religion.

Important Symbols
The *Ka'ba*: all Muslims pray toward this cubical structure in Mecca.

Dharih refers to the shrines where the Imams are buried. Shi'is visit the shrines of the Imams to pay homage. They also consider it meritorious to be buried in Najaf where 'Ali is buried.

Dhu'l-Jinah was the horse of Husayn in Kerbala. A picture of the horse is often displayed in some lamentation assemblies.

Dhu'l Fiqar is the sword of 'Ali and Husayn. It is also displayed in some assemblies.

'Alam (lit. a flag) is displayed in the form of a palm. The *'alam* symbolizes the bravery and courage of 'Abbas, the half brother of Husayn, who was also killed in Kerbala.

Important Rituals
Five daily prayers, Friday prayers, prayers over the dead, and prayers during natural catastrophes
Fasting during the month of Ramadan
Performance of Hajj, the pilgrimage to Mecca at least once in one's lifetime

Muharram rituals: these may include various forms of self-flagellation, processions, and lectures

Glossary

ahl al-bayt	the family of the prophet Muhammad
'Ashura	signifies the day when Husayn was killed in Kerbala
baraka	blessings derived in numerous ways, including at the shrines of the Imams
'ilm	divinely-inspired knowledge of the Imam
'isma	belief in the infallibility of the Imam
majlis	assemblies where the faithful gather to mourn for Husayn
ma'tam	flagellation by hitting the chest
Muharram	the first month of the Islamic calendar, when Husayn was killed
nass	principle of designation of the Imam
qiyama	the Day of Judgment
tatbir	striking of the head during the mourning ceremony
taziyeh	a reenactment of the events in Kerbala
wilaya	belief in the spiritual and temporal authority of the Imams
zanjir	refers to the chains used to strike the body

Sacred Spaces and Times

Spaces

Jerusalem: The first direction of prayer. Muhammad is said to have ascended to the heavens for the night journey from Jerusalem.

Kerbala, Iraq: This is where a famous battle took place in 680. The caliph Yazid's forces killed Husayn, the grandson of the prophet, because he refused to pay allegiance to Yazid. Husayn and his family members and companions are buried here. Kerbala has become a focal point for Shi'i visitation.

Mashhad, Iran: The site where the eighth Imam, 'Ali al-Rida, is buried. Millions of Shi'is visit this site every year.

Mecca: The location of the Ka'ba and the place where Muhammad was born. This is the holiest place for all Muslims.

Medina: Muhammad migrated to Medina in 622 and died there in 632 C.E. Four other Shi'i Imams are buried in a cemetery in Medina.

Najaf, Iraq: Site where 'Ali b. Abi Talib was buried after he was killed in nearby Kufa.

Samarra, Iraq: The tenth and eleventh Imams are buried here. It is also believed that the twelfth Imam entered into a state of occultation in Samarra.

Times

Arba'in: the fortieth day after Husayn's death

'Ashura: the day when Husayn was killed in Kerbala

Eid al-Adha: the twelfth Islamic month, marks Abraham's intended sacrifice of Ishmael

Eid al-Fitr: marks the end of Ramadan

Eid al-Ghadir: when Muhammad appointed 'Ali to succeed him

Layl al-Qadr: the night of power in Ramadan; it is believed that the Qur'an was revealed on this night

Muharram: the month when Husayn was killed in Kerbala

Shi'is also mark the birth and death anniversaries of the prophet, the twelve Imams, and of Fatima, the daughter of Muhammad.

Suggestions for Further Reading

(a) Kerbala and Muharram Rituals

Ayoub, Mahmoud. *Redemptive Suffering in Islam*. New York: Mouton, 1979.

Pinault, David. *The Shiites: Ritual and Popular Piety in a Muslim Community*. New York: St. Martin's Press, 1992.

———. *Horse of Kerbala: Muslim Devotional Life in India*. New York: Palgrave, 2001.

Schubel, Vernon. *Religious Performance in Contemporary Islam: Shi'i Devotional Rituals in South Asia*. Columbia: University of South Carolina Press, 1993.

(b) Hadith

Newman, Andrew J. *The Formative Period of Twelver Shi'ism: Hadith as Discourse between Qum and Baghdad*. Richmond: Routledge, 2000.

(c) History

Donaldson, Dwight. *The Shi'ite Religion*. London: Luzac & Company, 1933.

Jafri, Syed. *The Origins and Early Development of Shi'ite Islam*. London: Longman, 1976.

Madelung, Wilferd. *The Succession to Muhammad: A Study of the Early Caliphate*. Cambridge: Cambridge University Press, 1997.

Modarressi, Hossein. *Crisis and Consolidation in the Formative Period of Shiite Islam: Abu Jafar ibn Qiba al-Razi and His Contribution to Imamite Shiite Thought*. Princeton, N.J.: Darwin Press, 1993.

Momen, Mojan. *An Introduction to Shi'i Islam: The History and Doctrines of Twelver Shi'ism*. New Haven, Conn.: Yale University Press, 1985.

al-Mufid, Muhammad b. Muhammad. *Kitab al-Irshad*. Translated by I. Howard. London: Balagha and Muhammadi Trust, 1981.

al-Tabari Muhammad b. Jarir. *Ta'rikh al-Umam Wa'l-Muluk*. 8 vols. Beirut: N.p., 1983.

(d) Shi'i Beliefs and Practices

Dakake, Maria Massi. *The Charismatic Community: Shiite Identity in Early Islam*. Albany: State University of New York Press, 2007.

Kohlberg Etan, ed. *The Formation of the Classical Islamic World: Shi'ism*. Burlington, Vt.: Ashgate, 2003.

McDermott, Martin. *The Theology of Shaykh al-Mufid*. Beirut: Dar al-Mashreq, 1978.

Tabatabai, Sayyid Mohammed Husayn. *Shi'ite Islam*. Albany: State University of New York Press, 1975.

Takim, Liyakat. *The Heirs of the Prophet: Charisma and Religious Authority in Shi'ite Islam*. Albany: State University of New York Press, 2006.

(e) Shi'ism in America

Takim, Liyakat. "Multiple Identities in a Pluralistic World: Shi'ism in America." In *Muslims in the West: From Sojourners to Citizens*. Edited by Yvonne Yazbeck Haddad. New York: Oxford University Press, 2002.

———. *Shi'ism in America*. New York: New York Press, 2009.

Walbridge, Linda. *Without Forgetting the Imam: Lebanese Shi'ism in an American Community*. Detroit: Wayne State University Press, 1997.

(f) Theology

Amir-Moezzi, Mohammad Ali. *The Divine Guide in Early Shi'ism: The Sources of Esotericism in Islam*. Edited by David Streight. Albany: State University of New York Press, 1994.

Kulayni, Muhammad b. Ya'qub. *Al-Kafi fi 'Ilm al-Din*. Tehran: Daftar Farhang Ahl al-Bayt, n.d.

Moussavi, Ahmad Kazemi. *Religious Authority in Shi'ite Islam: From the Office of the Mufti to the Institution of Marja'*. Kuala Lumpur: Institute of Islamic Thought and Civilization, 1996.

al-Mufid, Muhammad b. Muhammad. *Awa'il al-Maqalat fi al-Madhahib wa'l-Mukhtarat*. Tabriz: N.p., 1950.

Sachedina, Abdulaziz. *The Just Ruler in Shi'ite Islam: The Comprehensive Authority of the Jurist in Imamite Jurisprudence*. New York: Oxford, 1988.

(g) Visitation (Ziyara) to the Shrines of the Imams

Abu Zahra, Nadia. *The Pure and Powerful*. Reading, Berkshire, U.K.: Ithaca Press, 1997.

Takim, Liyakatali. "Charismatic Appeal or Communitas? Visitation to the Shrines of the Imams." *Journal of Ritual Studies* 18, no. 2 (2004): 106–20.

Talib, al-Sayyid Husayn. *Guide to Ziyarat: Selected Supplications*. Translated by Liyakatali Takim. Toronto: Mebs Printing Plus, 2000.

THE SUNNI TRADITION

Th. Emil Homerin

Islam arose in the Arabian Peninsula in the seventh century C.E. and quickly spread from Arabia throughout the Middle East, then into Africa, Europe, and eventually to the Americas. Islam also moved east to the Indian subcontinent and then on to Indonesia, Malaysia, and China. Today, the majority of Islam's more than one billion adherents live in Asia and Africa, though sizable Muslim communities are found in nearly every country in the world. Significantly, approximately 85 percent of all Muslims belong to the Sunni tradition.

What is this religion's overriding question? What makes the system self-evidently valid to the community of the faithful?

Like all Muslims, Sunnis seek to live in accord with God's revelation and guidance for humanity contained in the Qur'an. In addition, Sunnis strive to follow the tradition (*sunnah*) of the prophet Muhammad and his pious companions (*salaf*).

In 630 C.E., Muhammad and the Muslims conquered Mecca, which would serve as the spiritual center of Islam because of the Ka'bah in the holy sanctuary there. Muslims pray toward Mecca, where they also perform the *Hajj* pilgrimage. According to Muslim tradition, Muhammad returned to Mecca in 632 for his "farewell pilgrimage," which established many of the Hajj rites and rituals still observed today. Further, some Muslims believe that during the farewell pilgrimage the prophet named his successor at a place known as Ghadir of Khumm, where he received this revelation:

149

"O messenger, make known what has been delivered to you from your Lord, for if you do not, you will not have delivered His message. God will preserve you from the people; God does not guide a faithless people" (5:74).

Muhammad then stated that after he died 'Ali ibn Abi Talib (d. 661), his cousin and son-in-law, should lead the Muslims. However, the authenticity of this tradition is disputed, and most Muslims do not accept it. Instead, following Muhammad's death, his companions elected a new leader who then became the caliph, or vice-regent. The Muslim majority has claimed that this election was in accord with the *sunnah,* or "custom," of Muhammad and his close companions, and so they are known as *Sunni* Muslims. However, a significant minority has held that Muhammad designated 'Ali and 'Ali's male descendants as his rightful heirs, and this "party of supporters" (*shi'ah*) came to be called the Shi'i or Shiite Muslims. Though the initial difference between Sunni and Shi'i was over issues of succession, in time many Shi'i came to venerate these special descendants of 'Ali as sinless spiritual authorities who were to govern the community and regulate religious life as the chosen *Imam* ("leader").

How do we know about this religion? What classics define the norms?

Whatever the authenticity of the tradition of Ghadir of Khumm, 'Ali was not elected Muhammad's immediate successor, though Sunnis number him among the four "rightly guided caliphs." First was Abu Bakr (d. 634), Muhammad's father-in-law, who solidified Muslim rule in the Arabian Peninsula. 'Umar ibn al-Khattab (d. 644) succeeded Abu Bakr, and he extended Muslim rule to Egypt, Palestine, Syria, Iraq, and Iran. A slave assassinated 'Umar, after which 'Uthman ibn 'Affan (d. 654) was elected caliph. Under his rule the Muslim empire expanded into North Africa and Afghanistan. More significantly, according to tradition, 'Uthman formed a committee of experts to collect and codify Muhammad's revelations, which they arranged into the standard text of the Qur'an still used today. Though many Muslims regarded 'Uthman as a pious man, other Muslims, incensed by 'Uthman's alleged favoritism toward his own Umayyad clan of the Quraysh, assassinated him.

'Ali then succeeded 'Uthman. Perhaps wishing to avoid further bloodshed, 'Ali refused to punish the Muslims who had plotted against 'Uthman. He was opposed by the Umayyad clan and others who wanted revenge for 'Uthman's murder. 'A'ishah, one of the prophet's widows, and other prominent Muslims attacked 'Ali, but 'Ali defeated them and their army at the Battle of the Camel in Iraq in 656. Still, 'Uthman's nephew Mu'awiyah (d. 680), the governor of Syria, would not recognize 'Ali's authority. Their forces clashed on several occasions, including at the Battle of Siffin in 657, but these confrontations and attempts to negotiate a settlement resolved little. Then 'Ali was assassinated by one of his former supporters who held that compromise with the godless Mu'awiyah was totally unacceptable. 'Ali's oldest son, al-Hasan (d. 670), was then named caliph, but he abdicated to Mu'awiyah.

Having secured the caliphate, Mu'awiyah moved the capital of the empire north to Damascus and founded the Umayyad dynasty. Often regarded as a line of tyrannical Arab kings, the worst of the Umayyads was probably Mu'awiyah's son Yazid (d. 683), who laid siege to Mecca, burned down the Ka'bah, and had 'Ali's second son, al-Husayn (d. 680), killed. Despite their faults, the Umayyads spread and stabilized Muslim political authority by creating a more professional army and centralizing political authority, with Arabic as the official language of state.

The Umayyads' despotic rule discriminated against non-Arab Muslims, and this fomented a revolt in 750 when the Umayyads were overthrown by a coalition of Muslims—Arabs and non-Arabs but especially Persians. The new rulers were descendants of Muhammad's uncle, 'Abbas, hence the name of the dynasty, the 'Abbasids. The 'Abbasid caliphs built a new capital, Baghdad, which was more centrally located within the vast and increasingly diverse Muslim empire. Muslim culture grew more cosmopolitan and confident under the early 'Abbasids as the scholarly community became more specialized, and by the ninth century distinct religious disciplines formed around aspects of Islamic belief and practice, including Qur'anic commentary, theology, philosophy, and mysticism. The 'Abbasid period also witnessed the emergence of the Sunni tradition.

What is the community of the faithful called? What story explains its traits?

Sunni and related terms appeared in the eighth century C.E. to designate those scholars who sought guidance from Muhammad and the pious ancestors regarding legal and ritual matters not clearly detailed in the Qur'an. Often the Sunni tradition has been called *Ahl al-Sunnah wa-l-Jama'ah*, "the people of tradition and community." Essential to the Sunni tradition is the *sunnah* as related in hadith, originally oral accounts of the earliest Muslims but which came to be increasingly focused on Muhammad's custom alone. Scholars collected the traditions, evaluated their reliability, and collected and arranged the sound traditions according to either their chains of authority (*isnad*) or their subject matter (*matn*), as was the case with two of the most important collections, one by al-Bukhari (d. 870) and the other by Muslim ibn al-Hajjaj (d. 875). Whereas early Sunnis were united in their reliance on hadith, Sunnis have never been a monolithic group and there have been significant differences among them, especially regarding law.

In the seventh through ninth centuries Muslims experienced rapid change, which generated questions regarding many aspects of life and society. Religious thinkers aimed to establish the obligations of the faith, ritual, and law, the latter often an ad hoc affair to help administer a growing empire. Of particular importance was the development of jurisprudence (*fiqh*), undertaken by religious scholars collectively called the *'ulama'*, "those who know (the law)." The Qur'an provided some legislation on important matters, including marriage, divorce, and inheritance, which Muslim scholars addressed along with other subjects in their attempts to establish laws for the community that were based on the Qur'an, the custom of Muhammad, and the early Muslim community. The use of analogical reasoning (*qiyas*) and the consensus of the scholarly community on legal issues (*ijma'*) augmented the Qur'an and the *sunnah*. Legal scholars known as *muftis* consulted these sources to formulate informed opinions (*fatwa*) on new questions of law. Though not legally binding, these opinions could be useful to the judge (*qadi*) who ruled on legal matters. There were a number of Sunni legal traditions, but over time they were condensed into four prominent schools—the Maliki, Hanafi, Shafi'i, and Hanbali—named after important scholars. Two of these scholars, al-Shafi'i (d. 820) and Ahmad ibn Hanbal (d. 855), stressed the prophetic hadith as second only to the Qur'an as a source of law, and this became a fundamental principle of the classical Sunni tradition.

What is the way of life of the community of the faithful? What are the rules of conduct and the rites of passage? What is the notion of sacred time and space? How does the way of life embody the story that this religion tells about itself?

Sunni scholars sought to implement the Qur'an's moral and legal imperatives within the Muslim community through the *shari'ah,* or "divine law," which encompasses personal, communal, and ritual life. Accordingly, within the *shari'ah* all acts may be classified into one of five categories: obligatory (e.g., five daily prayers), recommended (feeding the poor), neutral (what shirt to wear today), reprehensible but permitted (divorce), or forbidden (murder). However, this system should not be construed as arid legalism. Rather, for many Sunni Muslims, the *shari'ah* enumerates the moral and ethical norms that are to shape society and guide believers to know right from wrong so believers may succeed in this life and the next.

Sunni scholars also codified important religious rituals into the "Five Pillars of Islam." They began with the Muslim profession of faith (*shahadah*): "I bear witness that there is no deity but God, and I bear witness that Muhammad is the apostle of God." The first part of this statement declares one to be a monotheist, while the second distinguishes one as a Muslim. The second pillar is the five daily canonical prayers (*salah*) proceeded by the call to prayer and ablutions.

The Call to Prayer

God is most great! God is most great!
God is most great! God is most great!
I bear witness that there is no deity but God!
I bear witness that Muhammad is the messenger of God!
Come to prayer. Come to prayer.
Come to success. Come to success.
God is most great! God is most great!
There is no deity but God!

The Friday noon prayer is of special importance, for the Qur'an commanded that all commerce be suspended until the prayer is concluded. Within the Sunni tradition, Muslims are urged to say this prayer in a public congregational mosque and to listen to a sermon exhorting them to piety. The third pillar is the annual tithe on a person's possessions (*zakah*), which is to be spent for the good of the Muslim community, especially the less fortunate. The fourth pillar is the fast (*saum*) during the month of Ramadan, ending with the "Feast to Break the Fast" (*'Id al-Fitr*). The fifth and final pillar is the Hajj, or canonical pilgrimage to Mecca, which concludes with the "Feast of Sacrifice" (*'Id al-Adha*).

In addition, drawing from the Qur'an and the prophetic *sunnah*, scholars classified foods as either forbidden (*haram*) or permitted (*halal*) and set the proper procedures for slaughtering livestock, which include reciting the name of God over the animal as it is killed. The Qur'an forbids consumption of alcohol, pork, blood, carrion, and food sacrificed to another deity. All seafood is permissible, though some Sunnis have avoided shellfish. Although not mentioned in the Qur'an, Sunni jurists have also forbidden the consumption of predatory birds and beasts, dogs, donkeys, and insects.

Sunni scholars also developed rites and ceremonies regarding the life cycle, which were often influenced by local as well as prophetic custom. When a child is born, a Muslim man recites the call to prayer in the baby's right ear. When a child learns to talk, he or she is taught basic religious phrases in Arabic, and ideally the child will begin to read the Qur'an at around age seven. When a Muslim boy reaches puberty, he will be circumcised, though the age and accompanying rituals vary from one Muslim culture to another. In some Muslim countries, particularly Egypt and the Sudan, girls are also circumcised based on a prophetic tradition that some Sunni scholars have recently called into question.

The Qur'an exhorts Muslim men and women to be modest in dress and conduct, and to marry and procreate. Polygyny is permitted, and a Muslim man may marry up to four women at a time provided he can treat each wife equally; he is also permitted concubines. Wives and concubines may be from other monotheistic communities, though within the Sunni tradition Muslim men are encouraged to marry Muslim women. A Muslim woman may be married to only one Muslim man at a time to ensure the paternity and Muslim faith of any offspring.

The Qur'an permits divorce, and the classical Sunni tradition allows a man to repudiate his wife by saying three times, "I divorce you!" A woman has no such rights, and classical Sunni law makes it difficult for a woman to obtain a divorce except in cases where a husband is impotent or if he abandons her for more than a year. However, beginning in the twentieth century, governments of many Sunni-majority nations passed legislation making the divorce process more equitable and less cumbersome for women. Divorced men and women may remarry, as may widows and widowers.

Death rituals vary among Sunni communities, reflecting local as well as prophetic traditions. Ideally, a dying Muslim will face toward Mecca and recite the profession of faith. Often the thirty-sixth chapter of the Qur'an, *Ya Sin*, is recited, telling of the Day of Resurrection and the promise of paradise. The corpse is washed and wrapped in a shroud, which may be the Hajj garments if the person had completed the pilgrimage, and burial usually occurs within twenty-four hours, with the body interred facing Mecca. Sometimes burial is preceded by a prayer service in the home or mosque, or at the gravesite.

According to the Qur'an, God creates all humans, assigns their life spans, causes them to die, and then re-creates them on the Day of Resurrection to be judged according to their beliefs and actions, and rewarded or punished for eternity.

However, there are several ambiguous verses of the Qur'an, including 14:27: "God confirms those who believe in the firm word in this life and the next." Whereas the "next life" in the last verse would appear to mean paradise, some Sunni scholars have read it as referring to "states in the grave" based on hadiths in which the prophet relates accounts of the recently deceased who are visited in the grave by two angels. They test the dead person's faith, and if the deceased testifies to the oneness of God and the prophethood of Muhammad, she or he will pass a comfortable period in the grave and, after judgment, ultimately enter paradise.

If the deceased cannot do this, the angels will torture her or him in the grave until Judgment Day when the condemned will be dragged into hell. Further, some Sunni scholars have stated that most believing Muslims too will be punished either in the grave or later in hell in order to work off their past sins. Still, a number of hadith relate that God has given the prophet Muhammad the power of intercession and that he will eventually intercede to save all Muslims, even the vilest sinners who, nevertheless, will first burn in hell for a time before entering paradise.

What is the worldview of the community, the story that it tells about itself in the context of history, the conception of divinity and the relationship of the divinity (or divinities) to the believers, and its principal ethical teachings? What are the attitude and behaviors toward persons outside the faith community?

Since 630 and the Muslim conquest of Mecca, a defining feature of the Muslim community has been its success. Though Muhammad and Muslims have experienced discrimination at times, for centuries Muslims dominated their neighbors politically, culturally, and religiously. As a result, many Sunni Muslims have regarded their way of life as the straight path blessed by God, to which others are invited to follow. In stark contrast to Western stereotypes, Islam did not spread by the sword, and Muslim rulers did not require conquered people to convert if they could be considered monotheists. Further, during the seventh through tenth centuries C.E., Christians, Jews, and Zoroastrians comprised the majority of the population in Muslim domains. These subject peoples were classified as *Ahl al-Dhimmah*, "protected people." In exchange for paying taxes on their land and a special tax that exempted them from military service, the protected people were permitted significant latitude regarding their religious beliefs and practices. However, they were not to seek converts to their faiths and they were to recognize the authority of the Muslim state and abide by its civil laws.

At its apex in the ninth century, 'Abbasid rule stretched from Spain in the East to India in the West, but control over such a far-flung empire gradually eroded. In the tenth century, other Muslim empires arose to challenge 'Abbasid rule, including a new Umayyad caliphate in Spain and the Fatimid Shi'i caliphate in Egypt and Syria. Sunni regional governors in Iran, Afghanistan, and India also challenged 'Abbasid central authority and founded their own dynasties. Soon, the 'Abbasid caliphs had little real power and for more than a century a Shi'i military dynasty known as the Buyids controlled the Sunni caliph. Then, in the eleventh century, a Turkish people, the Seljuqs, migrated from the Asian steppes, and in 1055 a Seljuq leader entered Baghdad and declared himself *sultan* ("sovereign"). The Seljuqs recognized the caliph's significance to the Sunni Muslim community, but the Seljuq sultans managed political and military affairs in their efforts to reunify and expand the Muslim empire. The Seljuq sultanate vigorously promoted Sunni Islam by patronizing Sunni scholars and mystics, and by funding *madrasahs,* schools for religious higher education. Since Sunni Islam lacks a central religious authority and a formal ordination, the *madrasahs* help to maintain the scholarly lineage and to train Sunni religious professionals. The Seljuqs period is also important because as Turkish peoples joined the Muslim population Turkic became a major language, along with Arabic and Persian, for the expression of Islam and its cultures.

Finally, the Seljuq expansion alarmed Christians throughout Europe, leading to the Crusades, though Muslim armies generally fended off their Christian foes. However, beginning around 1220, Mongol armies began to conquer the northeastern provinces in present-day Pakistan, Afghanistan, and Iran. The Mongol hordes razed the land until they reached Baghdad, where, in 1258, they sacked and burned the Muslim capital, killing thousands, including the 'Abbasid caliph. Muslims were stunned, for pagans now ruled them. Overwhelmed by despair, many Muslims felt that the end of time was near. However, the Mongols were eventually stopped, and some converted to Islam, but their invasion had resulted in massive destruction among Muslims, who, like the Europeans, were also ravaged by plague in 1348. Less confident than in the past, the Sunni community felt threatened by these trials that God had sent.

Still, all was not lost as merchants and missionaries continued to spread Sunni Islam into Africa, India, Indonesia, and China, and many populations gradually became Sunni Muslim. A major feature of this Sunni Islam was a devotional spirit as Muslim mystics developed spiritual practices of meditation and prayer to draw closer to God. Particularly important as a guide was the life of the prophet Muhammad, the beloved of God. On his birthday (*Mawlid al-Nabi*), Sunni Muslims have traditionally recited poems praising him and seeking his intercession in worldly and heavenly affairs. Muslims have also sought the intercession of Muhammad's spiritual heirs, the Muslim saints. Although the Qur'an does not articulate a doctrine of sainthood, several verses contain the word *wali* (plural *awliya'*), as the Qur'an declares that all pious Muslims are God's *walis,* or "protected friends" (7:34). But by the ninth century, many Sunnis believed *wali* referred specifically to pious persons with God-given spiritual power (*barakah*) to perform miracles (*karamat*). God could also inspire these saints with new insights into the meaning of the Qur'an and divine law, and so they posed a persistent problem for conservative Muslims who wished to establish God's unchanging laws for society. One conservative Sunni theologian, Ibn Taymiyah (d. 1328), stridently opposed any belief that weakened the fundamental distinction between God and his creation, upon which monotheism was based. Thus he vociferously condemned Shi'ism and the cult of the saints as idolatry and deviations from God's truth, which could be found only in the Qur'an, the traditions of Muhammad, and codified in Sunni law. Other Muslims countered that saints are not worshiped; rather, the saints are venerated in order to receive God's grace and forgiveness. Like a king surrounded by his courtiers, God is close to his favorite companions, the prophets and the saints, whom he allows to intercede with him on behalf of others.

How does this religion function in the world today? What are its relationships with culture?

Sunni Islam experienced a resurgence beginning in the sixteenth century with the rise of the Ottoman and Mughal Empires. The Mughals spread Islam and Muslim culture throughout India, while the Ottomans expanded their empire to include parts of eastern Europe as well as present-day Turkey, Syria, Palestine, Egypt, and Arabia. Both dynasties patronized Sunni learning, poetry, arts, and architecture, and they applied Islamic principles and law to administer Muslim society. However, by the eighteenth century the expansionist economies of both empires had reached their limits and decline set in, hastened by the rising European colonial powers, especially Russia, France, and England. Ottoman and Mughal administrators introduced military and governmental reforms to shore up their states, while some Sunni religious leaders sought moral reforms to realign their communities with God.

One of the more influential reformers was Muhammad ibn 'Abd al-Wahhab (1703–91) in central Arabia. A conservative of the Hanbali law school, Ibn 'Abd al-Wahhab believed that Muslims had corrupted their faith. Inspired by the works of Ibn Taymiyah, he condemned Sufism, Shi'ism, and any belief or practice that he viewed as compromising God's oneness (*tawhid*). Ibn 'Abd al-Wahhab denounced saint veneration as idol worship and he rejected religious innovation, including the celebration of the prophet's birthday. Ibn 'Abd al-Wahhab held a largely literal interpretation of the Qur'an accompanied by independent legal reasoning (*ijtihad*)—though restricted by hadith—and Hanbali law in what came to be known as the Wahhabi movement. A defining feature of this and similar movements is an overtly political agenda, often accompanied by militancy. Ibn 'Abd al-Wahhab recruited a tribal chief, Muhammad ibn Sa'ud (d. 1765), and together they created a state based on this "purified" form of Islam. Their mission was carried on by their successors who sometimes massacred other Muslims whom they regarded as infidel pagans. Many Muslims condemned such extremism, yet the Saudi state brought security to the Holy Land of Mecca and Medina while calls for jihad appealed to some reform-minded Sunnis.

Other Sunni reformers in the nineteenth and twentieth centuries also endeavored to free Islam from local non-Muslim religious practices and to establish through education—not through violence—a Muslim community based on Islamic law. These Sunni "modernists" attempted to forge new interpretations of Islam, claiming that the Qur'an, the *sunnah,* and the Islam of the prophet were fully compatible with reason and modern society. These reformers actively promoted Western-style education, which they believed could free Muslims from blindly following normative tradition. Many of these reformers also fought to free Muslims from foreign influence and rule. Since the nineteenth century, various European powers and the United States have occupied or controlled Muslim lands, and in response many Sunni Muslims, including some religious leaders, have supported independence and nationalist movements.

This resistance has continued. During the Iranian Revolution in the 1980s, the Shi'i leader Ayatollah Khomeini (d. 1989) denounced the United States as the great Satan, while Sunni militants, including the Egyptian Sayyid Qutb (d. 1966), Osama bin Laden, and the Taliban rallied against what they see as the corrupt, imperialist, and Zionist West, calling for jihad as the mandatory sixth pillar of Islam. Much of their anger undoubtedly arises from colonial experiences. Yet over the centuries many Muslims have viewed non-Muslims as spiritual inferiors. Although the Qur'an praises numerous biblical figures, including Moses and Jesus, it sometimes denounces Jews and Christians as being obstinate and deceitful. Further, Sunni Islam's political and material success over the centuries gave Sunnis confidence in the truth and supremacy of their faith. However, over the last century Western hegemony and globalism have left many Muslims on the defensive, feeling helpless and humiliated.

Today, most Muslim-majority nations are politically independent, but many bear colonial legacies, including economic dependence on the West and Western prejudice against them based on color, ethnicity, and religion. This is also the case for the millions of Muslims living in western Europe, many who came as guest workers beginning in the 1960s. Moreover, Muslims who have lived in eastern Europe since the Ottoman period have been persecuted by ultranationalist states such as Serbia and Bulgaria. Muslim populations of Canada and the United States have faired better. Since the 1800s, Muslims have lived in North America, though most Muslims came to America as immigrants in the 1960s in search of jobs and higher education. Further, many African Americans converted to Islam after World War II, asserting that they were returning to their ancestral faith. Although Muslims have been a visible part of American society for decades, they continue to be the targets of suspicion and racism, especially since the destruction of the World Trade Center towers on September 11, 2001.

For many Sunni Muslims today, religious life continues to be based on the Qur'an, the *sunnah* of the prophet, and the ways of their ancestors. They pray daily, assist the poor, fast during Ramadan, and hope to go on Hajj. Millions of Sunni Muslims worldwide still venerate Muhammad and the saints and seek their intercession. Yet elsewhere, as in Saudi Arabia, religious tolerance and many traditional religious practices are scorned as more literal-minded clerics set the tone for religious practice. Unfortunately, this exclusivism overshadows Sunni Islam's message of justice and compassion that is still to be found throughout the contemporary Muslim world as Muslims have joined their voices to those calling for peace and cooperation. For them, jihad is not a holy war against non-Muslims and Shi'is but a struggle to free oneself from selfishness, to aid the oppressed, and to establish the social justice called for by the Qur'an.

At a Glance

Classic Texts
The Qur'an
Collections of the prophetic hadith by al-Bukhari and Muslim ibn al-Hajjaj

Important Figures
The prophet Muhammad
'Ali
Mu'awiyah
al-Bukhari
Muslim ibn al-Hajjaj
Ibn Taymiyah
Ibn 'Abd al-Wahhab
Sayyid Qutb

Characteristic Beliefs
Belief in one God
Following God's commandments and the way of Muhammad leads to eternal life.
Muhammad's intercession and that of the saints

Essential Creeds or Codes of Conduct
Qur'anic commandments
Fiqh Akbar I (in Williams below)

Brief Time Line

632	Muhammad dies; prophecy ends
661	'Ali assassinated; beginning of the Umayyad Empire
680	al-Husayn ibn 'Ali is killed
750	'Abbasid Revolution
1055	Seljuqs take Baghdad
1096	First Crusade
1258	Mongols sack Baghdad and kill the 'Abbasid caliph
1348	Black Death
1350	Rise of the Ottomans (until 1920)
1525	Rise of the Mughals of India (until 1857)
1920–48	Muslim independence and nationalist movements
1967	Six-Day War
1973	Arab-Israeli War
2001	Destruction of the World Trade Center towers; start of the Second Gulf War

Important Symbols
The Ka'bah and the Black Stone of Mecca

Important Rituals
Canonical prayer (*salah*)
Pilgrimage to Mecca (*hajj*)
Visiting saints' shrines

Glossary

Ahl al-Dhimmah	"protected people"; non-Muslims living under Muslim rule
hadith	a tradition usually of the prophet Muhammad
Hajj	the canonical pilgrimage to Mecca
Imam	Sunni: a prayer leader; Shi'i: the divinely chosen leader of the Muslim community
jihad	"struggle" in defense of Islam and the Muslim community
madrasah	a school for religious education
Qur'an	"recitation"; the Muslim book of God's revelations to Muhammad
salaf	pious ancestor, especially among Muhammad's companions
salah	canonical prayer
saum	fasting
shahadah	the profession of faith
shari'ah	divine law
tawhid	God's oneness; monotheism
'ulama'	Muslim scholars, especially of law
wali	a Muslim saint
zakah	the annual tithe

Sacred Spaces and Times

Ka'bah of Mecca
Mawlid al-Nabi (the prophet's birthday)
Mosques and shrines
The five daily canonical prayers
Ramadan

Suggestions for Further Reading

Coulsen, Noel. *A History of Islamic Law*. Edinburgh: University Press, 1964.

Denny, Frederick. *An Introduction to Islam*. 3rd ed. Upper Saddle River, N.J.: Pearson Prentice Hall, 2006.

Esposito, John L., ed. *The Oxford History of Islam*. New York: Oxford University Press, 1999.

Rahman, Fazlur. *Islamic Methodology in History*. Karachi: Central Institute of Islamic Research, 1965.

Watt, W. Montgomery. *The Formative Period of Islamic Thought*. Edinburgh: University Press, 1976.

Williams, John Alden. *The Word of Islam*. Austin: University of Texas Press, 1994.

HINDUISM

Douglas Brooks

What is this religion's overriding question? What makes this system self-evidently valid to the community of the faithful?

Hinduism, the predominant indigenous religion of the Indian subcontinent, stresses a hierarchy of relationships focused on divine and human interaction elaborated in formally constructed and implicit social institutions, texts, popular beliefs, and practices. Diverse and complex literatures evolving over the past four thousand years portray a highly developed organization of the cosmos that manifests in social structures, particularly the caste system, and sanctions inequitable power relationships with special emphasis on the diversity and plurality of forces that create, sustain, and transform relationships.

There is no singular dogmatic claim defining Hindu relationships to this cosmos of power and the divine. Hindus may believe in one god, many, or none. The essence of cosmos may be with or without qualities, attributes, or purpose. Hindus may be monists (belief there is only one reality despite appearances), pantheists (God is reality), or panentheists (God pervades all things and also extends beyond), and just as likely monotheists or polytheists: what is important are the processes of an ordered, hierarchical universe, the principles that govern the nature of relationships, and human possibilities involving bondage, empowerment, and ultimate liberation. The overriding question of Hinduism is, How will human beings live and act in a

163

cosmos that binds them to a hierarchy of relationships and, ultimately, experience liberation from the processes of bondage?

The overriding question of Hinduism raises two issues. First, how
do human beings create the relationships that secure an advanta-
geous place within the universe that has created them from within its
hierarchies and by its own principles? This question is answered by
engaging the notion of Dharma. Dharma, which derives from the
root *dhr*—meaning "to maintain, secure, make firm"—governs the
natural and social order. Dharma refers to the deepest principles of
existence and moral order prescribed in the sacred texts, enacted in
convention and custom, and as the relationship between normative
(ought) and normal (what is common). Dharma is natural and moral
law ordained by the cosmos itself and self-evidently revealed through
nature and by the sages who ascertain its meaning for human beings.
There is no escaping the Dharma that governs the universe any more
than a Hindu can be born without caste, gender, or other features
that circumscribe the processes of a life's journey through the cycles
of time.

The cycles of time, called *samsara,* fetter and control one's choices
and destiny according to the processes of causality in action called
karma. Karma is *action* and provides explanation for the processes
of time and identity. Everything exists in bondage to karma until one
is freed from its determinations. Hinduism's second great issue
derives from the first: how does a human being master the process of
karma and achieve liberation or *moksa?* The nearly infinite variety
of interpretations of Dharma, which operates according to the laws
of karma, stand in juxtaposition to the attainment of ultimate liberation. A Hindu life enjoins both the fulfillment of one's Dharma in
the world and the pursuit of liberation from *all* terms that define the
cycles and processes of existence. Are Dharma and *moksa* comple-
mentary or contradictory? Hindus puzzle over this with almost every
imaginable consideration from solution of the problem to embrace
of the paradox itself.

The Meaning of the Word Hindu

The word *Hindu* is Persian in origin, deriving from *Sindhu,* the
Sanskrit word for the river Indus, and referred to peoples living
beyond the river in lands that are today both Pakistan and India.
Hinduism came about as a descriptive category invented by Western
colonialists of the seventeenth century to distinguish those who

maintained the indigenous subcontinental religion in contrast to Muslims, Christians, Sikhs, and other minorities. A modern reformist, the first president of India, Sarvepalli Radhakrishnan, interpreting for an English-speaking audience, entitled his book *The Hindu Way of Life* to emphasize the comprehensive sociocultural breadth of traditions and practices that extend into every facet of a Hindu's life. Like others, Radhakrishnan used the term *Dharma* or the compound *sanatana dharma*, "eternal religion," to bring Hindus within the linguistic parameters of those who similarly express a desire to distinguish beliefs and practices as religious, not merely social, cultural, or political.

Whether one is a Hindu reformist, a textual historian, or an anthropologist, the issue of creating a relatively coherent identity for all that expresses Hinduism remains a daunting and even controversial task. Nonetheless, there is a history of sources, principles, institutions, and social structures that provides all who seek to encompass the breadth of Hinduism with a common project, one that places the vast diversity of orthodoxies (correct views) in relationship to evolving orthopraxes (correct practices), which establish individual, cultic, communal, regional, and even universal Hindu identity. Scholars, like Hindus themselves, can map clearly traceable developments in history, thought, social organization, cultic affiliation, and practical behaviors to create a distinctive, continuous Hindu identity over the past four thousand years. Being Hindu has never been confused with what any particular individuals or groups might believe, profess, or practice. This almost limitless diversity of forms and expressions has often been touted as a feature of Hindu tolerance, though it might just as well be seen as another feature of living in a cosmos that is itself filled with nearly infinite possibilities and the presence of dynamic powers that each express their own interests and create their sense of place in larger structures and identity through relationships.

There is at least one predominantly Hindu culture outside of the Indian subcontinent, on the island of Bali, Indonesia, and modernity has brought elements of Hindu culture, theology, and practice into new forms of religion practiced globally. Nepal is also predominantly Hindu. *Hinduism,* however, as a term does not provide meaningful self-identification for many—perhaps still even the majority of Hindus. Clearly, Hindus know they are Hindus. They unambiguously distinguish themselves from other religious affiliations—whether they use the term *Hinduism* or do not—and, according to recent studies by Pew, are among the least likely of those with religious affiliations in North America to pursue conversion or to reject their traditional identity. Hindus comprise as much as 70 percent of the population of contemporary India, though such a geographical boundary does not address the extent of Hindu presence over the past four or even five millennia in what is today Afghanistan, Pakistan, Nepal, and over a considerable range of south and southeast Asia. Hindus globally comprise significant minorities in many countries, especially in Malaysia, Singapore, and North America.

How do we know about this religion?

The story of Hinduism begins in three distinctive pre-Hindu movements that provide sources, causes, and traceable origins leading to familiar expressions of Hinduism for at least the past thousand years. These three movements are known as (1) the Indus Valley civilization, (2) Vedism, and (3) Brahmanism. From these movements we enter into Hinduism properly speaking beginning about 400 B.C.E. with the period of the epics (*itihasa*) and ancient mythologies (*Purana*) and, ultimately, move through the development of innumerable theologies (*siddhanta*), god and goddess cults, and the complex relationship between exoteric devotionalism (*bhakti*) and more esoteric matters involving yoga, alchemy, Tantra, and other eclectic traditions. We derive our understanding of popular and practical beliefs from texts, archaeological studies, anthropology, and the process of legacy whereby much that is archaic and, in substance, pre-Hindu persists as part of the larger scope of Hinduism.

The Indus Valley

In the middle of the third millennium B.C.E., the Indus Valley civilization developed a complex social, civic, and political life, reaching its fulmination around 2000 B.C.E. A late contemporary of Egypt and Mesopotamian civilizations, its primary locus was the swath of the Indus River and its estuaries, though it certainly extended over much of today's Pakistan, likely as far east as contemporary Delhi in India, and south toward the Narmada River. There is no evidence of any singular cause for its decline and eventual eclipse, but this seems to have occurred by 1600 B.C.E., that is, *before* the introduction of the

Veda with the migration of the Aryan peoples. The two major archaeological city sites are Mohenjo-Daro, in modern Sind, and Harappa, more than three hundred miles to the north, following a path once made by the Ravi River (known as Parushani or Iravati in Vedic times). These sites demonstrate social and political coherence with evidence of common religious values and practices.

Perhaps the most important evidence of religious life in the Indus Valley civilization is the presence of public great baths along with arrangements for other bathing, drainage, and sewage systems. The dimensions, construction, and design of these venues suggest sophisticated civic organization and important roles for ritual in cultic life. Although we can surmise no more than widespread concern for ritual purity, there is a remarkable similarity in design with later Hindu temple tanks used for purification, further suggesting the approaches familiar to pilgrimage fords (*tirtha*).

Common in nearby villages are terra-cotta female figurines suggesting strong cultic interest in fertility and goddesses both benign and terrifying. This connection with the feminine divine is critically connected to the importance of goddesses in Hinduism since goddesses play only minor roles in Vedic. In the Indus Valley civilization we find strong indications of an autochthonous origin for goddess traditions.

More controversial are the steatite seals that bear both images and some form of inscription. Recent scholarship has argued that this imagery is not, in fact, a script encoding language but rather an example of a nonlinguistic symbol system serving a multilingual culture. No effort to decipher this symbolic system or script has been yet able to prove the Indus Valley culture to be literate or to establish relationship to indigenous Dravidian languages. Other imagery on the seals has provided more viable links to later Hindu concerns: powerful male animals—especially bulls, composite human-animal figures, female figures apparently linked to goddesses, and a controversial figure in apparently a yogic posture are all indications of relationship to divine power and human interaction. In the most important example, a seated figure appears on a raised platform with an erect phallus or pillar of fire before him (or that is part of him). He wears a buffalo's horns and ornaments suggesting association with yoga, the ithyphallic figure Siva, and other associations with sacrifice, ritual protagonists, victims, and demonic antagonism. Such "substratum" theories of association between these and other Indus Valley elements are sometimes considered derived solely from later Hindu sources. What remains beyond any doubt is that these archaic autochthonous religious values are deeply significant in later Hinduism.

Vedism

Despite recent efforts to explain the early sacred literature of Hinduism called the *Veda* (literally, "knowing"), which is the essential revelation or *sruti* ("that which is heard"), as subcontinental in origin along with the Vedic language (and therefore its legacy in the Sanskrit language), most scholars agree that this formidable body of oral and written material, which reached its present form between 1400 and 400 B.C.E, originated with so-called Aryan peoples, migrants with Indo-European origins who arrived about 1500 B.C.E. Unlike the remnants of the Indus Valley whom they met, the Aryans were a mobile, conquering, and assimilating culture without specific locale or settled agriculture. Their gods, like their society, were organized into hierarchies and relationships of role-distributed power serving cosmic and social purposes. The organizing principle, shared with other Indo-European societies, in which three social functions—priests (*brahmana*), warriors (*ksatriya*), and agriculturalists and merchants (*vaisya*)—provided the structure for human and divine interactions, was instantiated mythically in the concept of the cosmic "person" (*Purusa*) whose ritual dismemberment created the world, its natural order, and society's basic organizational principle. To these three social interactive groups was added a fourth, the *sudra*, or servile (*dasa, dasyu*, "slaves"), who were at first demonized as the Aryan's foes and then incorporated into the greater structure of society. This program of hierarchical social inequity is the origin of the later caste system that elaborates on these four social estates (*varna*). The cosmos provides the macrocosmic model for the organization of the social world while the sacrificial process describes the hierarchies and the necessity of sustaining order in an entropic universe.

The essence of the Veda, in which the chant describing the cosmology of the person appears, is the *Rgveda Samhita,* a collection of 1,028 such hymns extolling the powers and roles of the gods and the cosmic order (*rta*), which they protect. From the *Rgveda* is then derived *Yajurveda* (sacrifice formulas) and *Samaveda* (melodies) *Samhitas* to which is added a fourth Veda, the *Atharvan* (named after the sage providing its content). By 1000 B.C.E. these poetic sacrificial formulas were organized by the priests into specific branches (*sakha*), memorized verbatim, and then elaborated into three further Veda categories: *Brahmana* (rituals), *Aranyaka* ("forest texts," largely ritual speculation), and *Upanisad* (contemplative insight). Vedic religion was reconstructed from the *Rgveda* chants.

Although much of Brahmanism's ritual is suggested in the *Rgveda*, the focus of the hymns is the pantheon of deities, including Indra (the general of the gods and upholder of the cosmic order) and various others such as Mitra, the twin Asvins, Surya the sun, and Vayu the wind, all of whom have relationships to gods appearing across the expanse of Indo-European and Indo-Iranian cultures. But most important to human beings are Agni, the god of fire who receives and conveys sacrificial offerings to the other gods, and Soma, who provides the deathless (*amrta*) elixir from a plant said to inspire the visionary insight (*dhi*) that brought the Vedic poets (*kavi, rsi*) into contact with the cosmos's innate resonance in the form of the utterances or *mantras* that make up the chants themselves. These sacred formulas and utterances are regarded to be manifestations of the goddess of speech, Vac, who ensures human prosperity and the final prospect of heaven (*svarga*) through maintenance of the luminous cosmic order (*rta*).

Though the gods are said to be thirty-three in number, the Veda proposes a vast polytheistic, polyvalent universe of divine hierarchies in which there is a basic opposition between forces of light, the gods (*deva*), and antagonistic powers, the *asura*, likely ranked first gods in the Veda but brought into demonic roles in later Hinduism. All of the gods are praised similarly for their brilliance, power, and beneficence, and often serve multiple roles in the perennial contest of interests that shape order and stave off the always-advancing prospect of chaos. The significance of other gods important to later Hinduism, particularly Visnu; Siva, usually called Rudra in the Veda; and the goddess(es) is less in their frequency of appearance than in their emergent roles: Visnu for his part in the perseverance of order, Siva for his powers of dissolution, and the goddesses for their material presence as nature.

Brahmanism

The priests' role in systematizing the Veda for the sake of acquiring more direct access to the power (*brahman*) that determines the fate of celestials and mortals, the living and the dead, leads to the *Brahmana* texts, which provide the liturgy and exposition of the ritual by which the sacred power of the *mantras* can be put to use. The division of rites into domestic (*grhyasutra*) and solemn (*srauta*) establishes the ritual as the means of controlling the energies of the cosmos. It is said that the priests by their ritual knowledge are more powerful than the gods who, like the demons, are reduced to being part of the process by which *all* forces are placed in subordination to the ritual. In domestic rites the priests use a single fire sacrifice to establish relationships with ancestors, gods, and what are termed "others," including living humans, which empower the processes of life from conception to birth, coming of age, marriage, and death. There are sixteen principal rites of passage, including the well-known *upanayana* investiture in which boys of the three upper estates (*varna*) become "twice-born" (*dvija*) and therefore full participants in the Vedic-based rites. It is in the solemn rites, however, that the cosmic implications and complexities of the ritual are realized. Some rituals may take up to two years to fulfill, with the promise of tasting immortality (*amrta*) and heaven (*svarga*). At the heart of the solemn rites is the consolidation of the immortal as one's self (*atman*) through ritual action (*karma*) that identifies with the god Prajapati (Lord of Creatures). Perfect ritual prevents participation in Prajapati's own transient nature and therefore in one's own redeath. Some portion of this thinking is invariably connected to later Hindu ideas concerning the processes of redeath and rebirth—that is, the larger issue of reincarnation (*punarjanman*), which is addressed not only through ritual but also through behaviors of asceticism (*tapas*), meditation (*dhyana*), and appeal to other forces, including the grace of god(s). It is in some measure the failure of Brahamanic ritual to provide consistent and demonstrable results, instead claiming efficacy is unseen (*apurva*), that instigates further reflection upon how to address the cycles of *samsara* and the problems associated with *karma*.

Emergent Classical Hinduism

Later Hindu traditions called *Vedanta* treat the last portion of the Veda, the *Upanisads,* as its true end (-*anta*), providing ultimate insight regarding the source and origin of the power in which the gods, the ritual sacrifice, and indeed the whole cosmos resides. Whereas the *Upanisads* cover a vast array of hierarchies and homologies used to weave together a universe warp and weft, it is the relationship between the macrocosmic *brahman,* the eternal (*nitya*) that is the All (*sarva*), and the microcosm of self (*atman*) as the human essence, the soul inhabiting a mortal body, that provides the link to eternity. The gods are thus reduced to essence, no longer players in the negotiations with karma but, rather, irrelevant to the highest task of liberation through the discovery of essence. In later Hinduism the equation that *brahman* is *atman* creates a speculative foundation for the relationship between divine and human.

The *Upanisads* also introduce an innovation in achieving the *brahman* is *atman* equation, namely, asceticism as the key to making the secret, deeper connection (the literal meaning of *Upanisad* is "to sit nearby") by dissociation with transience and transcendence of karma. Motivated by desire (*kama*), karma must be controlled and conquered not merely by correct karma but also by knowledge (*jnana*). Knowledge is more than the *Brahmana's* ritual perfection, though the *Upanisads* continue to support proper ritual; knowledge is more specifically the unity experience of *brahman atman,* by which one is extricated from the cycles of death and rebirth (*samsara*). Such insight and personal experience must begin with instruction from a qualified teacher, a guru in possession of both understanding and the experience itself. No longer does the ritual itself create the power of karma and coerce the gods' cooperation to affect the desired results, the *Upanisad's* ascetic (*muni*) has made the vow (*vratya*) to disavow the transience of the material world (*prakrti*) (encoded in the saying *neti, neti,* "not this, not that," in *Brhadaranyaka Upanisad,* 2.3.6) and identify the self with the eternal essence, the person or soul (*purusa*) that abides in all things as their substance and nature (encoded in the saying *ahambrahmasmi,* "I am Brahman," in *Brhadaranyaka Upanisad* 1.4.10). The ascetic's authority is established by his own relationship to desire (*kama*). The seer becomes *yoked* in such knowledge and experience, thus using the process of yoga—engagement, joining, union—as the primary means of transforming relationship to the world and achieving final liberation. There is in later *Upanisads,* particularly *Svtasvaratara* and *Isa Upanisad,* the suggestion that loving commitment (*bhakti*) and the grace (*krpa, anugraha*) of the divine play a crucial role in liberation. Thus by 400 B.C.E. the *Upanisads* set the stage for the elaboration of yoga and devotion as twin pillars of classical Hinduism in later literature and in popular practice.

Classical Hinduism: Texts and Popular Devotionalism

With the rise of ascetical practices new religions begin to take shape during the period of the *Upanisads* (ca. 800–400 B.C.E.), particularly Buddhism and Jainism, which strategize the problems of *samsara,* desire, and karma using their own metaphysical and experiential models. About 400 B.C.E. we begin to see the emergence of the Hindu epics, *Ramayana* and *Mahabharata,* as well as the Ancient Lore (*Purana*), which will provide much of the mythic content then further developed in the pantheon of gods expressed in art, architecture, and new forms of ritual and devotion.

A key to classic Hinduism is the canonical distinction between the immaculate Veda as *sruti* or "what is heard," because it is without authorship (*apaurusheya*), and *smrti,* "what is remembered" through powers of reflection by individual authors, some of whom are celestial, others human. Virtually any topic from law to mythology can be given significant amplification as *smrti* so long as it does not contravene or reject *sruti* explicitly. With this distinction comes amplification in vernacular literatures and regional interests that expand the pantheon to include gods, seers, saints, philosophers, and charismatics, bringing them into greater local focus and relationship with community lives, calendars, and other features of regional history, language, and culture. Oral traditions of storytelling and commentary, legend and custom merge in complex social relations and create a merging, assimilation, and cross-fertilization between local or "folk" elements appearing in vernacular languages and the pan-Indian use of the Sanskrit language.

What is the community of the faithful called? What story explains its traits?

The community of the faithful, called *varnasramadharma,* or "caste and life-stage law," serves as the basic structure for Hindu society. Certainly the rise of alternative non-Hindu ascetic traditions and encounters with outsiders (the Sanskrit word for "barbarian," *mleccha,* carries the same connotation as the Greek—that is, people who can't speak properly) are central to this modeling. To the four basic social estates of priests (*brahmana*), warriors (*ksatriya*), merchants (*vaisya*), and servants (*sudra*) are added four corresponding life stages (*asrama*): studentship (*brahmacarin*), "householderhood" (*grhasthin*), forest dwelling (*vanaprasthin*, a kind of intermediary state), and renunciation (*sannyasin*). The proliferation of castes (*jati*) is first explained as mingling between *varnas* but more likely evolves through notions of ritual purity and endogamy as a basis for hierarchy. Every Hindu belongs to the hierarchies that are locally defined by caste (*jati*, "social birth group"), but such distinctions are not necessarily universally recognized and gain significance primarily in terms of proximate relations.

There is some original correlation between caste and life stage— that is, ideally speaking, students would study Veda and related materials, householders would perform the requisite domestic and solemn rites, the forest dwellers would be vested in the *Aranyaka* portions of Veda, and the *sannyasin* would follow the renunciate's path to liberation taught in the *Upanisads*. But this paradigm gives way to Hindu society's more basic tension between Dharma and *moksa,* which poses a dual norm of worldly householder and otherworldly renouncer-ascetic. What appears, then, is a Dharma world of rigorous hierarchies, in which caste is rooted in the distinguishing principles of purity, auspiciousness, and social interaction, and a putative otherworldliness for renunciates who no longer abide by or are subject to the terms of Dharma because of their dedicated pursuit of liberation (*moksa*) and their efforts to remove themselves from karma's imposed terms.

In modern India we see the social organization of caste providing fundamental localized identity and the continued presence of the *sannyasin* as a social institution and spiritual ideal. Hindus practically assign meaning to caste structurally even as the claim for its intrinsic reality is made by appeal to the cycles of karma and destiny (*daivya*).

Although much has been made of modern efforts to diminish the influence of caste, it is no more possible to ignore as a feature of Hindu society than is the greater relationship to the order of a powerful universe presenting itself through hierarchies. What we do find are some Hindus claiming that within the hierarchical universe one can gain power over it and transcend its delimiting terms from any station in society and even at any stage of life (*asrama*).

What is the way of life of the community of the faithful?

The Hindu's way of life is encapsulated in the *purusarthas*, or four human aims. First presented in the law manuals known as *Dharmasastras*, discussed at length in the epics, and implied across the breadth of Hindu literature, these four goals mean to be wholly integrated into the caste and life-stage model (*varnasramadharma*). There is also a specialized literature for each aim, beginning with the *Dharmasutras* and *Dharmasastras*, which form the foundation for understanding law and customary behavior—that is, Dharma. Issues of statecraft and material pursuits regarding wealth, possessions, and acquisition provide the second aim, called *artha,* with an important subject manual attributed to Kautilya, also known as Chanakya (ca. 350 B.C.E.). Regarding sensual pursuits, Hindus cite the *Kamasutra,* which is attributed to Vatsyayana (ca. 400 C.E.). This is ironic because of his association as a commentator on the Verses on Logic, that is, Gautama's *Nyayasutra.* These three aims, law (*dharma*), wealth (*artha*), and love (*kama*), form the triadic group, or *trivarga,* and set in some opposition to the fourth aim, *moksa,* or "liberation." Whereas such organization suggests the appositional tension between householder and renunciate, the treatises regarding *moksa* do not exclusively belong to or espouse renunciation as a requisite. Such treatises or *sastras* take up a wide variety of philosophical views (*darsana*) and theological standpoints (*siddhanta*) in order to direct the process by which householder or renunciate can follow a path toward liberation. Although Dharma is often cited as the aim that best captures the sense of every Hindu's role in the world, it is one's relationship to *kama*—to desire—that can be considered just as pivotal.

What is the worldview of the community, the story it tells about itself in the context of history?

The Hindu worldview is expressed primarily through devotion (*bhakti*). A Hindu seeks to have *darsana*, or visionary experience of the divine, through actions (*karma*), knowledge (*jnana*), and love (*bhakti*), and seeks a relationship of grace (*anugraha, krpa*) in which there is an exchange, reciprocity, and direct experience of the divine. Acts of worship (*puja*) and other forms of offering, such as asceti-

174

cism, alchemy, sacrifice, and mystical exertions, are largely encompassed by devotion.

Devotionalism and Esotericism: The Maturation of the Hindu Worldview

The dominant and ubiquitous practice of loving devotion known as *bhakti* defines the majority of popular religious expressions as well as the *smrti*-based or *smarta* religion that appears in the epics *Mahabharata* and *Ramayana*, the mythologies of the *Purana*, and the oral lore that encompasses the supposed 330 million gods. Hinduism's focal point worldview centers on *bhakti* as relationship: in love, participation, and connection with the divine through worship (*puja*), exchange of gifts as manifestations of grace (*prasada*), and recognition that the gods can, by their powers, provide what humans need and truly want. Whether this is the descent of Visnu through the ten *avataras* (and especially as Rama and Krsna), Siva as the yogi transcending and commanding the entirety of forces that define existence, or the goddess in her beneficent (*saumya*) or horrific (*aghora*) forms, devotion to these divine sources of grace is the principal expression of the Hindu worldview. Virtually any approach toward the divine can express *bhakti*; the key is commitment, offering, and appeal to the power that can transform one's relationship with embodied life and fulfill the promise of liberation or paradise as reward. It is important to note that devotional practice may involve offerings to one or many gods or goddesses, celestials, saints, or other demigods. Whatever other practices might be undertaken (learning, asceticism, and so on), the *bhakti* tradition asserts that devotion is the *sine qua non* of all practices, paths (*marga*), and views (*darsana*).

Tantra: Esoteric Worldviews

Tantra means "loom" and "extension," and these meanings taken together form a picture of mystical worldviews and esoteric practices that loom Vedic, Brahmanical, and other views and also create canons and concepts well beyond the boundaries of devotionalism. The Tantra instigates its own canon of scriptures called *Tantra*, *Agama*, *Samhita*, and *Yamala*, and involves closely held secrets of initiation and cultic participation. Beginning with familiar cosmologies—the essential paradigm of the gods, goddesses, celestials, and saints—the Tantric worldview asserts a visionary experience that often challenges social norms, that is, orthodox and orthoprax values. Tantric practice (*sadhana*) is rooted in transmissions from teachers (*guru*) in lineages that claim a more direct, expeditious, and complete experience of the divine, promising both sovereignty over the material world through the acquisition of powers (*siddhi*) and final liberation (*moksa*). Whereas all elements of the divine pantheon may be appropriated in Tantric theologies, a special role is assigned to the goddess and goddess-centered (*sakta*) practices. Tantra's reputation for black magic and social transgression has not diminished the extent of its influence.

How does this religion function in the world today?

Although Hinduism's origins are subcontinental, it is today a world religion. There are elements of Hinduism that include evangelistic expressions of devotion. Postcolonial reformist traditions known as Neo-Hinduism have made efforts to assign values and concepts that bring Hinduism into structures familiar to Western monotheisms. But Hinduism rarely seeks to spread doctrine or to advance ideas in ways comparable to other religions that share themselves with the world community. Since there are long-standing communities of Hindus outside India, it would be an error to identify the religion as ethnically "Indian," though there remains controversy within Hinduism regarding adoption or conversion of persons or cultures that are traditionally non-Hindu. Within India and beyond, Hinduism flourishes in temple attendance, pilgrimages that draw tens of millions, and other expressions of a Hindu's everyday experience.

Conclusion

Hinduism encompasses such an enormously diverse and historically rich body of teachings, practices, and communities that it may be beyond any singular definition. For every expression of Hindu life there is likely a counterexample in worldview or a contradiction in ideology or practice.

Two focal points emerge for understanding Hinduism. First is the canon—written, oral, and visual—of the gods, goddesses, demigods, and saints. However these expressions take shape and wherever they are appropriated, we can identify their origins and forms from within Hindu traditions. Second, the social system of caste that informs custom, belief, and practice maintains a critical role in identity, even when the issue is rejection, transcendence, or irrelevancy. Hindu matters cannot be framed without considering the relationship of caste to social and divine power and authority; encompassing caste are also matters of gender, age, ethnicity, and virtually all forms of social identity.

At a Glance

Classic Texts

Veda, including the *Rg, Yajur, Sama,* and *Arthava* Vedas and related corpus of *Brahmana, Aranyaka,* and *Upanisad*

Dharma or legal texts, ritual or Kalpasutras, including *Grhya-* and *Srautasutras*

Epics *Ramayana* and *Mahabharata,* including the *Bhagavadgita,* which is included in the *Mahabharata*

Nyayasutra, Vaisesikasutra, Mimamsasutra, Vedanta (Brahma-) sutra, Yogasutra

Purana (Ancient Lore), *Tantra, Agama, Samhita,* and *Yamala*

Characteristic Beliefs

A hierarchy and plurality of existence orienting nature and society

A principle of order and law inherent to existence

The concept of karma or causality that governs the process of recurrent existence and reincarnation

The concepts of action, knowledge, and devotion that empower human beings to follow the law and achieve liberation from the bondage of perpetual death and rebirth

Essential Creeds or Codes of Conduct

Laws contained in *Dharmasutras* and *Dharmasastras*

Teachings contained in epics and *Bhagavadgita*

Brief Time Line

2000 B.C.E.–1600 B.C.E.	Indus Valley civilization
1500 B.C.E.	Vedism
1000 B.C.E.	Brahmanism
800 B.C.E.	*Upanisads*
400 B.C.E.	Epics *Ramayana* and *Mahabharata*
400 B.C.E.	Classical Hinduism
200 B.C.E.	Rise of Devotionalism
400 C.E.	Rise of Tantra

Important Symbols
OM, the symbol of eternity
Svastika, the symbol of wellness and auspiciousness

Important Rituals
Agnistoma, Agnicayana: portions of the larger Vedic sacrifice described in general by the *yajna*

Upanayana: one of the so-called sixteen *samskaras* or rites of passage, this being the rite of initiation that permits listening and learning Veda to males

Diksa: the general term for initiation that may include any formal instruction from a guru

Glossary

bhakti	devotion, love, commitment
Brahmanism	ritualism based on scriptures claiming the absolute authority of perfect actions
guru	teacher
karma	action, particularly ritual action, and the laws of causality
mantra	sacred utterances endowed with power
moksa	liberation from bondage
samsara	the process of recurrent death and rebirth into the bondage of transient reality
smrti	all scriptural sources not *sruti* that provide remembrance and further reflection
sruti	revelation and the canon of the Veda, understood as resonantly inherent in the universe
varna	literally, "color"; the term for the four social estates that give rise to caste (*jati*)
Veda	corpus of authoritative scripture and concept of a knowing universe
yoga	engagement, union, connection, the process of discipline in action, knowledge, and devotion

Sacred Spaces and Times
Ganges River, northern India
Benares, also known as Kasi and Varanasi, holiest city of the Hindus, on the Ganges River

178

Suggestions for Further Reading
(a) **Vedism**
Gonda, Jan. *The Ritual Sūtras*. Wiesbaden: Harrassowitz, 1977.
————. *Vedic Literature (Samhitas and Brahmanas)*. Wiesbaden: Harrassowitz, 1975.
Jamison, Stephanie W., and Michael Witzel. "Vedic Hinduism." In *Electronic Journal of Vedic Studies*, 1992.
Witzel, Michael. "The Development of the Vedic Canon and Its Schools: The Social and Political Milieu." In *Electronic Journal of Vedic Studies*.
————. "Rgvedic History: Poets, Chieftains and Polities." In *The Indo-Aryans of Ancient South Asia*. Edited by George Erdosy, 307–54. New York: Walter de Gruyter, 1995.

(b) **Brahmanism**
Heesterman, J. C. *The Ancient Indian Royal Consecration: The Rājasūya Described According to the Yajus Texts and Annotated*. 's-Gravenhage: Mouton, 1957.
Jamison, Stephanie W. *The Ravenous Hyenas and the Wounded Sun: Myth and Ritual in Ancient India*. Ithaca, N.Y.: Cornell University Press, 1991.
Staal, Frits, et.al. *Agni: The Vedic Ritual of the Fire Altar*. 2 Vols. Delhi: Motilal Banarisidass, 1983, 1984.

(c) **Classical Hinduism**
Biardeau, Madeleine, et al. *The Hinduism Omnibus*. New York: Oxford University Press, 1993.
Biardeau, Madeleine. *Hinduism: The Anthropology of a Civilization*. New York: Oxford University Press, 1990.
Doniger, Wendy. *The Hindus: An Alternative History*. New York: Penguin Press, 2009.
The Thirteen Principal Upanisads. Translated by Robert E. Hume. Oxford: Oxford University Press, 1931, 1984.

BUDDHISM: BEGINNINGS

Mario Poceski

In the course of its long history, which began in northern India some twenty-five centuries ago, Buddhism spread to a great variety of cultural and geographical regions, gradually becoming one of the world's great religions. Over the centuries rich arrays of doctrines, practices, texts, and traditions developed and spread across much of the Asian continent, all of them ostensibly inspired by the life and teachings of the historical Buddha. Consequently, it might be appropriate to think and write about the religion in plural terms, keeping in mind that we are dealing with a multiplicity of Buddhisms. In this chapter, the first of three chapters on Buddhism, we will focus on the early Buddhist traditions as they grew during the lifetime of the Buddha and the subsequent few centuries.

The opening sections of the chapter are loosely organized in terms of the traditional Buddhist scheme of three refuges (or jewels): the Buddha and his quest for transcendence of the imperfections that characterize humanity's everyday predicament, the teachings (Dharma) that explain the nature of reality and delineate the path to spiritual liberation, and the community of disciples (Sangha) who aspire to follow the Buddha's example and put his teachings into practice. That is followed by a brief historical survey of the early growth of the religion and the emergence of a number of distinct schools of Buddhism that produced the earliest versions of the Buddhist canon.

What makes the system self-evidently valid to the community of the faithful?

The Buddha's Quest and His Mission

The Buddha was born as Siddhārtha Gautama. Traditional sources depict him as a prince, son of the ruler of the Śākya people, although modern historians have suggested that the Śākyas might have had a republican form of government. There is no scholarly consensus on the exact dates of the Buddha's life, although often they are given as ca. 480–400 B.C.E. The various traditional narratives about the life of the Buddha seamlessly weave together elements that today we may perhaps place into the categories of myth, legend, and history, but his historicity and the main story line of his life are fairly well established. Although traditional sources depict the Buddha's awakening and ensuing ministry as unique events in human history and imbue them with supreme cosmic significance, much of the religious outlook and vocabulary of the Buddha and his disciples reflected the intellectual horizons and socioreligious milieu of ancient India.

The Buddha lived during a transitional period in Indian history that was marked by momentous and far-reaching changes, which in the religious arena were reflected in the emergence of new movements that rejected the Vedic tradition and the authority of Brahmanic orthodoxy. That included refutation of the normative system of social stratification that existed at the time, in which the priestly class (Brahmins) enjoyed highest social status, as well as denial of the efficacy of Vedic rituals. The early Buddhists and other similar groups formed communities of religious seekers that abandoned society and lived peripatetic lives dedicated to the pursuit of higher spiritual knowledge. Known as *śramanas* (seekers), the members of these groups often supported themselves by means of mendicancy.

During his early years the future Buddha led a life of wealth and privilege. He married at a young age and after a short time his wife gave birth to a son. Disenchanted with the limitations and purposelessness of everyday existence, Siddhārtha decided to give up everything and assume the austere life of a religious ascetic. According to Buddhist lore, his decision to leave the comforts of the palace and embark on an arduous spiritual journey was made after a series of excursions among the local populace, during which he saw "four signs": a corpse, a sick person, an old man, and a meditating monk.

Traditional accounts describe how the young Siddhārtha embarked upon a bold spiritual quest aimed at realizing the true nature of reality and solving the essential problem of human suffering. The early years of assiduous practice included study with famous religious teachers and performance of various forms of austerities. Ultimately Siddhārtha gave that up and sat under the *bodhi* (enlightenment) tree, determined not to get up until he had reached a definitive realization of the ultimate truth of existence and had found a solution for the fundamental spiritual ills that befell humanity. Finally, as the full moon was gracing the sky in the month of May, the story goes, he awakened to the true nature of reality, thereby becoming the Buddha (literally "awakened one") of this age.

Subsequently the Buddha's disciples came to construe the attainment of Buddhahood as the highest perfection and most complete realization of ultimate reality. A Buddha was deemed to be free from all obscurations and impurities, yet imbued with an overabundance of positive qualities, including wisdom and compassion. Traditional Buddhist cosmologies see the historical Buddha as one in a long lineage of awakened beings whose main function is to bestow upon humanity ultimate knowledge and supreme guidance about a path of practice that leads to transcendence of ordinary attachments and imperfections and culminates in the realization of the final goal of nirvana. Thus while the Buddha's appearance in this world is understood to be of enormous significance, an epochal event that changed the course of human history, he is not unique in terms of the nature of his insight and knowledge or in regard to the spiritual qualities he embodies. The Dharma realized and taught by him is deemed to be eternal, being grounded in the true nature of reality. There is only one universal reality—the Buddhas simply awaken to it and then teach others about it.

Soon after his awakening the Buddha initiated his public ministry, which lasted until his passing away some forty-five years later at the age of eighty. During this period the Buddha traveled widely across an area that corresponds to the northeastern part of modern India, preaching to a multitude of individuals with diverse backgrounds, from kings to commoners. His teachings touched on a wide range of topics but primarily revolved around his exposition of a path of spiritual practice, which led to self-transcendence and liberation from imperfect mundane or *samsaric* existence. After contracting a stomach illness, the Buddha passed away peacefully, surrounded by his disciples. According to established belief, that marked his entry into final nirvana, the deathless realm of the unconditioned, which is the ultimate goal of the Buddhist path. The Buddha's passing away became a frequent motif in Buddhist art, often represented by statues or paintings of a reclining Buddha. The Buddha did not appoint a successor, which meant that the monastic order and the lay community were left without a central source of ecclesiastical authority, which as we will see had lasting ramifications for the subsequent development of Buddhism. Instead, he is said to have advised his disciples to follow the Dharma (meaning both the teachings and the essential truth that the teachings point to) and the Vinaya (monastic code of discipline), as well as to rely on their own experience.

After the cremation of the Buddha's body, his relics were purportedly divided among various groups of followers; subsequently relic worship became an important feature of Buddhist devotional practice. Early Buddhists did not produce anthropomorphic representations of the Buddha. For a few centuries after his passing away, the Buddha's religious persona and his awakening were primarily represented in somewhat abstract terms: by the *bodhi* tree, the Dharma wheel, and the *stūpa,* which became major objects of worship. Later, perhaps starting around the first century B.C.E., statues and paintings of the Buddha emerged, and over the centuries they remained key forms of artistic representation and central objects of cultic adulation. During this period there was also an emergence of popular accounts about the Buddha's previous lives, when he was a *bodhisattva* engaged in single-minded practice that included the performance of many virtuous acts motivated by supreme compassion. These stories became a distinct literary genre known as the *Jātakas.*

While within the Buddhist community the Buddha's unique presence in the world was primarily understood in human terms, inevitably there was also a parallel process of deification. From early on, reflections on the nature and significance of Buddhahood became fertile subjects of philosophical debate and contemplative practice; later traditions, especially Mahāyāna, introduced novel ideas on these topics and made them important parts of their doctrinal systems. The Buddha's life story remained an important point of reference for subsequent generations of Buddhists throughout history. As later generations of pious followers evoked and venerated the great sage, many of them also felt compelled to follow in his footsteps by embarking on the transformative path of spiritual practice that he initially taught.

How do we know about this religion? What classics define the norms?

Doctrinal Perspectives

The Buddha did not leave any written records. The earliest information about his teachings comes from texts that were first put into writing long after his passing away. The early Buddhists redefined and adopted into their system a number of key elements from normative values and worldviews that were prevalent in ancient India. That included the notions of karma (literally "action") and rebirth. Humans and other beings, including those who dwelt in the various hells and heavens, were believed to continuously transmigrate in the cycle of birth and death (*samsara*). Transmigration was perceived as a natural process of ongoing change that was primarily regulated by the law of karma, according to which wholesome deeds—which can be verbal, physical, or mental—lead to good results, including favorable rebirth. The same principle applies to unwholesome deeds, which inevitably lead to bad results either in this life or in future lives. The process of reincarnation does not have a beginning, but it can come to an end. That is accomplished by the realization of intuitive knowledge into reality and the attainment of the unconditioned realm of nirvana, which cannot be described by way of words or concepts.

The basic doctrinal perspective of Buddhism is often defined in terms of the "middle way" and the "four noble truths," which are said to have been the contents of the Buddha's first sermon. In its basic formulation, the notion of middle way implies avoidance of extremes, especially those of ascetic mortification and sensual indulgence. The four noble truths are: suffering or imperfection (the original Sanskrit term, *duhkha,* encompasses both meanings), the origin of suffering, the cessation of suffering, and the path that leads to the cessation of suffering. The first truth depicts suffering or imperfection as an essential part of life that defines the human predicament.

The second truth explores the causes behind it, which can be traced back to insatiable desires and attachments, which themselves are caused by fundamental ignorance of reality. The third truth points to the ultimate solution of the basic problem, namely the end of suffering and imperfection, which is equated with the realization of nirvana. The final truth delineates the path of spiritual practice that leads to the final goal of nirvana. The path of practice is often described in terms of eight elements, the "noble eightfold path" (see sidebar), but there are also other taxonomies, such as the three trainings: morality, meditation, and wisdom.

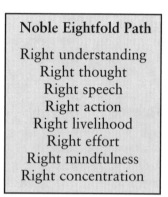

Noble Eightfold Path

Right understanding
Right thought
Right speech
Right action
Right livelihood
Right effort
Right mindfulness
Right concentration

Another feature of the early Buddhist worldview—which can be described as being unequivocally nontheistic—was avoidance of metaphysical speculations or dogmatic assertions regarding such topics as the origin of the world and the existence of a creator deity. Instead, there is a marked focus on dealing with the immediacy of human life and articulating a compelling course of spiritual practice that involves far-reaching personal transformation. There is also a marked preference for talking about reality in terms of abstract principles or psychological categories, such as impermanence and the lack of reified self (in persons and things). The primary center of attention revolves around practical soteriology rather than speculative abstractions or sanctimonious articles of belief. That is accompanied with an emphasis on self-reliance and personal experience, at the expense of belief in the spiritual potency of an external salvific agency.

From what we can tell, another trend in early Buddhism was a latent aversion to all sorts of dogmatic thinking, including unreflective attachment to religious beliefs, rituals, and doctrines. That is symbolized by the popular simile of the raft, which is to be abandoned after it has served the purpose of facilitating the crossing of a turbulent river. In the same vein, all religious teachings—including those enunciated by the Buddha—are provisional and are not to be grasped as constituting the ultimate truth, which by definition is ineffable. They are to be abandoned once they have served their purpose, namely after they have guided the disciple through the turbulent waters of *samsaric* existence and have made it possible to reach the other shore of nirvana. The value of religious teachings is thereby primarily defined in functional or practical terms: they are true if they bring about genuine personal transformation, which involves the elimination of mental impurities and the actual achievement of spiritual liberation. Conversely, even the most profound teachings can become obstacles to realization if they are made into fetishes and become objects of emotional or intellectual attachment. These kinds of ideas often fostered a sense of ecumenicalism and respect for other religious traditions. That helped instill a general attitude of tolerance toward alternative paths, although it goes without saying that throughout history many Buddhists fell short of abiding by such lofty ideals.

What is the worldview of the community, the story that it tells about itself in the context of history, the conception of divinity and the relationship of the divinity (or divinities) to the believers, and its principal ethical teachings? How do women fit into the system in its classical formulation? What are the attitude and behaviors toward persons outside the faith community?

Establishment of Religious Community

One of the defining features of Buddhism is the preponderance of monasticism. Buddhism has a somewhat unique status among the major world religions in terms of the central roles monks and monasteries play in it. From its inception, Buddhism was a tradition founded by a monk, and his monastic disciples primarily transmitted its teachings and practices, especially in the course of its early history. The Buddha's initial disciples formed the nucleus of a new monastic order (Sangha), which played crucial roles in the subsequent growth of Buddhism. According to traditional Buddhist lore, some members of the Buddha's own family, including his aunt, wife, and son, also entered the monastic order. Buddhist monks were known as *bhiksus* (mendicants). Although entry into the monastic order implied abandonment of social ties and worldly attachments—which among other things involved the observance of celibacy—the order did not set itself in opposition to the prevalent political and socio-economic systems because its institutional survival was dependent on the patronage it received from the social elites and the general populace.

The Vinaya, a collection of teachings and precepts meant to regulate the everyday life and behavior of monks and nuns, organized monastic life and practice. Buddhists in ancient India created a number of different versions of the Vinaya, some of which are still normative for present-day monastics such as those in the Theravādin, Chinese, and Tibetan traditions. The creation of distinct versions of the Vinaya was related to the formation of separate schools of Buddhism. The number of monks' rules differed somewhat among the various schools. For instance, the Theravāda Vinaya lists 227 rules, while the Dharmaguptaka Vinaya, which became prevalent in China and the rest of East Asia, has 250 rules.)Nuns (*bhikṣunī*) have additional rules, a total of 311 in the case of the Theravāda tradition. Notwithstanding the differences in the number and the interpretation of specific regulations, on the whole the core monastic precepts are fairly similar across the various Indian Buddhist traditions; the same can be said of the overall structure of their Vinayas. That seems to point to the early origins of core parts of the Vinaya, even though the extant texts we have today were compiled a number of centuries after the Buddha's lifetime and reflect the historical circumstances and intuitional needs of the monastic groups that created them.

In general, the Vinaya extols and codifies a disciplined way of life dedicated to the pursuit of moral excellence and higher knowledge, making allowances for both eremitic and coenobitic (communal) variations of the monastic vocation. At the same time, throughout Vinaya literature there is an overriding sense of concern about securing the laity's support. Many rules are aimed at making sure that members of the order do not alienate or upset their lay patrons, whose support of the monastic community was perceived to be an important source of religious merit. Whereas the Vinaya rules and other canonical sources were meant to serve as blueprints for monastic life, throughout Buddhist history there were often notable discrepancies between idealized archetypes and actual monastic practice, with many monks failing to adhere to canonically sanctioned mores and ideals. Recent research has also indicated that monastic and lay attitudes and practices often were not as sharply distinct as it was once taught. Furthermore, monks were supposed to support themselves by mendicancy, which brought them in close contact with the laity. Even when that was not the case, as in actual practice monasteries often had other sources of income and support, the economic viability and institutional survival of the monastic order was predicated on lay support. In return, monks were expected to minister to the religious needs of the laity. That included the performance of rituals and the preaching of the Dharma.

One of the important decisions made by the Buddha was to allow women to enter the monastic order. The fist nun was the Buddha's own aunt and foster mother, Mahāprajāpatī Gautamī, who according to traditional accounts made the initial request to the Buddha to allow women to enter monastic life. That was a major step in the direction of gender equity, a decisive event that can be construed as a significant paradigm shift within the context of ancient Indian society. At the same time, the nuns' order was set up in a manner that made it junior and subordinate to the monks' order. A number of the Buddha's female disciples were warmly remembered by the Buddhist community, and over the centuries both monastic and lay women made important contributions to the growth of Buddhism.

Besides his monastic disciples, the Buddha also attracted numerous lay followers who came from all walks of life, from poor people to royalty. Throughout history the majority of Buddhists belonged to the laity, and the story of Buddhism must take into account their religious needs, practices, and aspirations.

In theory, there was no essential distinction between the clergy and the laity in terms of their ability to realize the highest truths of Buddhism and enter nirvana, although monastic life was commonly perceived as being spiritually superior and more conducive to serious study and practice. The monks' renunciation of worldly pleasures and their virtuous way of life allegedly made them deserving of lay patronage, while the laity also benefited from the symbiotic relationship by being able to accrue merit by their making of offerings to the monastic Sangha. Consequently, lay patronage was essential for the growth and flourishing of Buddhism, in India and elsewhere, including China and Southeast Asia.

> **Five Precepts for the Buddhist Laity**
>
> Abstention from killing
> Abstention from stealing
> Abstention from sexual misconduct
> Abstention from lying
> Abstention from consumption of alcohol

Early Buddhist literature and epigraphic sources provide a wealth of materials that address the everyday concerns of the laity and shed light on their religious observances and aspirations. Some of the popular expressions of Buddhist piety included the worship of *stūpas* and relics, although these were not necessarily restricted to the laity. Another area of major concern was the practice of morality, which was codified by way of the five precepts (see sidebar on page 189). Together with the formal taking of the three refuges—in the Buddha, the Dharma, and the Sangha—the ritualized taking of the five precepts was a key expression of religious faith and commitment. Another popular practice was going on pilgrimages to various holy places, including those associated with key events in the Buddha's life, such as Bodhgayā, the site of the Buddha's awakening. Also important was the performance of good deeds such as charitable giving and compassionate concern for others. Throughout history, the laity's basic attitudes and practices have to a large degree been influenced by concerns about the accumulation of merit, which purportedly helps secure happiness in this life and favorable rebirth in the next one.

Growth of Buddhism as Pan-Asian Religion

During the Buddha's lifetime Buddhism was a regional tradition, as his followers formed only one among the many religious groups that flourished on the Gangetic plain of northern India. Its spread across the Indian subcontinent and beyond was a gradual and protracted process. The earliest archaeological and epigraphic evidence about the emergence of Buddhism as a major religious tradition comes from the reign of King Aśoka (r. 268–232 B.C.E.), the famous ruler of the Mauryan dynasty who united much of India under his imperial rule. Later Buddhist traditions celebrated Aśoka as a paradigmatic Buddhist monarch. He became a prominent model of a pious and compassionate king whose acts were worthy of emulation, while his contributions to the growth of Buddhism became the stuff of legend. Among his many celebrated accomplishments was the sending of missionaries to other lands, including the island of Sri Lanka to the south. Aśoka's son Mahinda, who had previously joined the monastic order, led the Sri Lankan mission, and ever since the island nation has been a Buddhist stronghold. Traditional accounts also make mention of missionaries who departed toward the Middle East, some of them supposedly going as far west as the eastern shores of the Mediterranean, although there are no independent sources to confirm that they actually got there.

Within a few centuries of the Buddha's passing away, the growth of Buddhism as a major religious tradition and its integration into the multifaceted socioreligious milieu of ancient India were accompanied by its spread to other lands. With its universalist ethos and its compelling message about spiritual transformation and human perfectibility, Buddhism was eminently suited to become India's major export religion. An important factor in its spread to a variety of geographical and cultural areas was the ability of Buddhist teachings, practices, and institutions to adapt to diverse local conditions. Buddhist missionaries proved adept at tailoring their message and making allowances for indigenous religious sentiments and cultural predilections.

There is evidence that Buddhism already had established its presence in the western reaches of Central Asia, which roughly corresponds to the area of present-day Afghanistan, as early as the time of Aśoka. Over the next couple of centuries Buddhist monks and monasteries became prominent fixtures throughout much of Central Asia. Buddhism flourished in the area for many centuries, as can be seen from the numerous monuments that grace the local landscape, only to disappear with the Islamization of Central Asia, which started during the seventh century. Farther east, Buddhism first entered China during the first century C.E., and from there it was exported to Korea (fourth century) and Japan (sixth century).

Other parts of Asia where Buddhism was successfully transmitted include Southeast Asia, Tibet, and Mongolia. In all these lands Buddhist institutions and practices became major elements of local social and cultural life. Other major developments in the cultural sphere were the flourishing of diverse forms of Buddhist art across much of Asia. The astounding variety, timeless beauty, and striking creativity of Buddhist artistic expressions is readily evident in innumerable statues, paintings, *stūpas,* cave sanctuaries, and monastic complexes. All these remain enduring testaments to the vitality and lasting relevance of Buddhist teachings and ideals, as well as to the richness of the cultures that produced them.

Diversity of Perspectives and Traditions within Early Buddhism

The Buddha did not leave a successor, and the monastic order was set up in a decentralized manner without one source of instituitional authority or centralized ecclesiastic structures. He also did not place emphasis on rigid adherence to a creed or dogma, nor were there any principal texts sanctioned to serve as sacred repositories of divine revelation or absolute truth. This set of circumstances fostered a spirit of relative intellectual openness within the early Buddhist community and created opportunities for the emergence of divergent approaches and perspectives. While the unity of the Sangha was regarded as an admirable ideal, in actual practice from early on there were prominent centrifugal forces that led toward the fragmentation of Buddhism. The same can be said of the later history of Buddhism, which was typically marked by remarkable diversity. After a while a number of autonomous schools or traditions (*nikāya*) developed, all of them with their own interpretations of the Buddha's essential message. The various schools diverged in terms of their doctrinal perspectives, religious practices, monastic conducts, and institutional arrangements.

Buddhist historical records depict the gradual demise of unity within the early Buddhist community, and the emergence of distinct schools, in terms of a series of schisms. Initially, the Sangha's unity was allegedly affirmed during a Buddhist council that took place soon after the Buddha's passing away, where his teachings were initially codified, although modern scholarship questions the reliability of such traditional accounts. With time the latent fissures within the monastic order only gradually grew wider and more pronounced. That became clearly evident during the second council, said to have been held about a century after the first one, when two major groups emerged, each with its competing claims to authority and legitimacy. That was followed by subsequent splits and divisions, which were primarily occasioned by the emergence of divergent views about particular points of doctrine or monastic discipline. We can surmise that other centrifugal forces were also at work, including the impact of local customs, the use of different languages, and the development of discrete forms of ritual practice. Notwithstanding their competing claims to orthodoxy, the various schools of early Buddhism also had much in common.

Buddhist texts make mention of eighteen early schools that emerged within the first few centuries of Buddhist history, although the exact number is not known and probably there were more than that. Some of the better-known schools are the Mahāsāmgika, the Sarvāstivāda, the Sautrāntika, and the Theravāda. The early schools developed their own canons and codes of monastic discipline. By and large they coexisted peacefully, although often they had their main strongholds in different geographical areas. Yet another important division within Indian Buddhism occurred with the emergence of the Mahāyāna tradition, which developed its own distinctive ideals, doctrines, texts, and practices. During the early centuries of the Common Era some of the early schools continued to flourish alongside the nascent Mahāyāna movement, with monks belonging to different schools sometimes living in the same monastery. Collectively the various schools comprised a diverse and multifaceted Buddhist milieu, which over the centuries experienced numerous changes and adaptations.

Canon Formation

As stated above, the Buddha did not leave any written records and there was never a unified collection of sacred writings that was accepted as authoritative by all Buddhists. The initial process of canon formation was linked with the aforementioned emergence of various Buddhist schools, which created their own bodies of scripture. These texts were initially transmitted orally; subsequently they were committed to writing in a variety of canonical languages, such as Pāli and Sanskrit. The linguistic diversity became even more pronounced when Buddhism was transmitted to other parts of Asia where the canon was translated into a number of local languages. Among these, especially noteworthy are the Chinese and Tibetan versions of the canon, which are immense in scope and contain a remarkable variety of texts. Although some Buddhist schools, such as the Theravāda, did close their canon at some point—albeit after complex processes of canonization that stretched over a number of centuries—one of the hallmarks of Buddhist scriptural collections is that they are open canons. That was especially true of the canons of Mahāyāna and Tantra, whose followers were arguably the most prodigious and prolific producers of sacred texts the world has ever known.

Normative Buddhist accounts trace the initial codification of the canon back to the first Buddhist council, which is said to have been attended by five hundred senior monks and presided over by Mahākāśypa, one of the Buddha's senior disciples. At that time, the Buddha's close disciples supposedly recited his teachings from memory. The collection of scriptures, or *Sūtra Piṭaka,* was recited by Ānanda, the Buddha's close relative and personal attendant. These were primarily discourses attributed to the Buddha, although some were also credited to his eminent disciples. The second part of the canon, which consists of texts about monastic discipline, or *Vinaya Piṭaka,* is said to have been recited by Upāli, another senior disciple. To these, at a later date, a third section consisting of scholastic treatises, or *Abhidharma Piṭaka,* was added by the members of certain schools of early Buddhism, thus arriving at the classical tripartite division of the canon known as "three baskets," or *Tripiṭaka.* The differences among the Abhidharma collections produced by various Buddhist schools—collections that were products of monastic scholasticism aimed at systematizing and interpreting the teachings contained in the scriptures in terms of carefully crafted categories— is especially noticeable.

In contrast to the traditional narrative about the canon's early origin, modern scholarship interprets the formation of the Buddhist canon(s) as a gradual process that unfolded over a very long period. The basic tripartite structure of the canon was later expanded, for instance in the case of the Chinese canon, which came to include numerous texts composed in a number of other genres, many of them written by prominent Chinese monks. To sum up, the Buddhist canons are large and diverse collections of texts. They contain an immense variety of materials composed at different times and places, and often differ in terms of their content, form, and language. However, throughout these vast bodies of religious literature there are some common themes, including an overriding concern with explicating a path of practice and realization that leads to transcendence of the mundane realm and attainment of spiritual liberation. The same can perhaps be said of Buddhism as a whole, which can be approached and discussed in terms of both its intrinsic unity as well as its essential and far-reaching diversity.

At a Glance

Important Figures

Ānanda: the Buddha's close relative and key monastic disciple who for many years served as his personal attendant

Aśoka (r. 268–232 B.C.E.): the famous ruler of the Mauryan Empire in ancient India, celebrated as a great supporter of Buddhism

Siddhārtha Gautama (c. 480–400 B.C.E.?): the historical Buddha, also referred to as Śākyamuni (sage of the Śākyas)

Mahāprajāpatī Gautamī: the Buddha's aunt and the first Buddhist nun

Essential Creeds or Codes of Conduct

Prātimokṣa: the core list of monastic precepts, which are elaborated in great detail in canonical Vinaya literature

Five precepts (*pañca-śīla*): the basic ethical rules for laypeople

Important Symbols

Bodhi tree (*Ficus religiosa*): the tree of awakening under which Siddhārtha Gautama attained Buddhahood

Dharma wheel (*dharma-cakra*): symbolizes the teachings of the Buddha; the wheel's eight spokes represent the eightfold path

Lotus flower: symbol of purity

Stūpa: monumental structure with spherical shape that commemorates the Buddha and his awakening; *stūpas* often contain relics or other sacred objects such as scriptures

Important Rituals

Bowing and making of offering to the Buddha

Taking the three refuges in the Buddha, the Dharma, and the Sangha

Receiving the five precepts

Monastic ordinations (*upasampadā*)

Sacred Spaces and Times

Bodhgayā, the site of the Buddha's awakening

Lumbinī, the place where the Buddha was born

Various monastic sites and cave complexes, such as Ellora in India and Longmen in China

Buddha's birthday: In Theravāda countries it is celebrated as Vesak, which falls on a full-moon day in April or May and also marks the Buddha's awakening, renunciation, and passing away.

Observance days (*poṣadha* in Sanskrit and *uposatha* in Pāli): the full moon, the new moon, and the two nights in between those two, when Buddhist followers commit themselves to ethical observances and spiritual practices

Suggestions for Further Reading

Buswell, Robert E., ed. *Encyclopedia of Buddhism*. New York: Macmillan Reference, 2004.

Gethin, Rupert. *The Foundations of Buddhism*. Oxford: Oxford University Press, 1998.

Harvey, Peter. *An Introduction to Buddhism: Teachings, History, and Practices*. Cambridge: Cambridge University Press, 1990.

Hirakawa, Akira. *A History of Indian Buddhism: From Śākyamuni to Early Mahāyāna*. Translated by Paul Groner. Honolulu: University of Hawaii Press, 1990.

Lamotte, Etienne. *History of Indian Buddhism: From the Origins to the Saka Era.* Louvain-la-Neuve: Université catholique de Louvain, Institut orientaliste, 1988.

Lopez, Donald S., ed. *Buddhist Scriptures.* London: Penguin, 2004.

Strong, John. *The Buddha: A Short Biography.* Oxford: Oneworld, 2001.

THE THERAVADA TRADITION

Kristin Scheible

Buddhism began in India, when Siddhattha Gotama,[1] after years of ascetic meditative practice, became awakened and initiated his teaching of the *dhamma,* or doctrine, actively changing the religious landscape of fifth-century B.C.E. India. Theravada Buddhism considers itself in a direct line of transmission from this model teacher and moral exemplar. The majority of secondary sources on Theravada Buddhism, in fact, begin with a detailed description of the Buddha's biography, indicating the centrality of this model, exemplar Buddha to the faith. Buddhism may have begun as a local meditative tradition surrounding the charismatic didactic presence of a central figure, the living and teaching Buddha ("Awakened One"), but it rapidly evolved into a translocal institution with mutually supportive lay and monastic branches and various culturally and philosophically diverse sects. Whereas Mahayana Buddhism has flourished in East Asia and Vajrayana dominates much of the Himalayan cultural area, Theravada is the predominant religious form in Sri Lanka and the continental Southeast Asian countries of Thailand, Burma (Myanmar), Cambodia, and Laos. There are also Theravada groups in Nepal, Indonesia, India, and throughout the West, totaling well over one hundred million adherents.

What is this religion's overriding question? What makes the system self-evidently valid to the community of the faithful?

Theravada Buddhism inherits its general understanding of the way of the universe from India. With other Indic religious traditions, such as Hinduism, Jainism, and Sikhism, it shares terms and concepts such as *samsara* (the endless round of birth and rebirth, the "wandering on" of lifetimes that include birth stations as humans, divinities, hell beings, animals, and others), *kamma* (literally "action," the system or even law that governs samsara and dictates moral value to intentions and actions of the individual), and even *dhamma* (in the Theravada context this applies especially to the Buddha's teachings and religion; in pan-Indic usage Dharma has a more abstract meaning encompassing notions of law, duty, order, truth, morality, religion, and so on). Given the structure of the knowable world, samsara, and the unavoidable suffering or "dis-ease" that is both symptomatic and constitutive of the round of birth, life, aging, illness, death, rebirth governed by the laws of kamma, the central overriding question that drives the faith is, What is to be done by me to eradicate dis-ease?

Theravada Buddhism considers each individual empowered and responsible for immediate and ultimate ethical transformation. Each person controls through her intentions and actions her own proximate ethical development as well as ultimate self-awakening (*bodhi*) and liberation from the binds of samsara, which is nibbana. Every individual is a being in the throes of moral development based on intention, action, and consequences (*kamma*). Kamma is often understood to be a law, in impact and truth similar to the law of gravity, that dictates the moral dimension to any action (*kamma* literally means "action"), whether bodily, articulated, or intended. Each action, big or small, is determined to be skillful (*kusula*), unskillful (*akusula*), or neutral, and to produce "fruit" or consequences. Skillful actions result in earned merit (*punna*) for the practitioner, while negative actions accrue demerit (*papa*). The measure of one's skillfulness, therefore, has an impact on the type of birth one is able to achieve and how far one may progress on the path to liberation from samsara. Through one's moral development, one may hope to achieve the most conducive birth station from which to achieve awakening (*bodhi*), which is a deep and directly experiential understanding of the true nature of reality, seeing things as they truly are.

One's ignorance of this governing system propels one to repeat offenses and thus perpetuate the round of rebirth, the continuation of samsara. The only means of release from the binds of samsara call for a path of action to cultivate the right mind-set and behaviors to ultimately, through many lifetimes of perfecting the ten *parami* (perfections; virtues such as generosity), lead to *nibbana* (translated variously as "extinction" and "unbinding").

In short, Theravada Buddhism is predominantly an ethical system that asks what is to be done by each individual in this life. The question at stake is, How do I eradicate the fundamental, experiential disease (*dukkha*, frequently translated as "suffering") in this world and in myself?

Whereas the ultimate goal of self-cultivation, nibbana, takes numerous life cycles to realize, one must first begin by conscientiously choosing to begin the path of action, the thing that is to be done. There is a path that is clearly articulated throughout the *suttas* (core Buddhist texts, sermons in the canon), beginning with the Buddha's very first sermon, the Dhammacakkappavattana Sutta ("Turning the Wheel of the Dhamma Sutta"). This path is called the "noble eightfold path" and comprises the fourth noble truth. The Buddha's articulation of the four noble truths explicitly outlines the diagnosis and prognosis for human moral development, and they make the goal and the path self-evident for the community.

Most interpretations of Theravadin doctrine begin with the Dhammacakkappavattana Sutta, delivered soon after the Buddha's own awakening. Whereas it is true that this short sermon contains the fundamental rubric for all future teachings, and that it therefore represents the most central teaching of the tradition, it bears observation that this was a sermon delivered to a special audience—the group of five ascetics with whom the Buddha had been pursuing awakening through severe meditative and ascetic practices—and not an ordinary, unprimed audience. In spite of its primacy, the Four Noble Truths are not creedal formulations or compulsory articles of faith, but rather a road map or guide for the internal, experiential, and direct discovery of each practitioner. The framework moves, as many have pointed out, much in the way an observant doctor moves through the process of observation, determination of origin or cause, diagnosis, and then prescription. The Four Noble Truths are:

1. All life entails dukkha, or "dis-ease." (This can be physical or mental suffering, distress, discontentment, anxiety, stress, or pain.)

2. There is a cause for the dukkha, which is thirsting or craving (*tanha*). (This is craving for concrete sensual things as well as for states of becoming and nonbecoming—anything that might induce attachment or desire.)
3. There is an end to dukkha (which is renouncing the craving).
4. The Noble Eightfold Path is a practical path for the elimination of the craving and the eradication of dukkha. The path entails right view, right resolve, right speech, right action, right livelihood, right effort, right mindfulness, and right concentration.

Several texts elucidate the path and clarify actual, practical methods to attain the eight right attitudes and behaviors expressed above. This pathway is further understood to represent categories of moral discipline (*sila*): right speech, right action, and right livelihood; meditative concentration (*samadhi*): right effort, right mindfulness, and right concentration; and wisdom (*panna*): right view and right resolve. Through successful implementation of the Noble Eightfold Path, the individual, through lifetimes, benefits from the cumulative ethical transformation, experiences *bodhi* (awakening), and becomes an *arahant* (a person who has destroyed the roots of dukkha—namely greed, hatred, and ignorance; an awakened being). The Buddha is not considered to be a salvific figure able to rescue others from the binds of samsara. Rather, he is seen to have been an arahant who then used his profound, experiential understanding of "the way" to describe and teach a practical path for others to follow in order to discern what to do in life.

How do we know about this religion? What classics define the norms?

What we know of the Theravada as a distinctive Buddhist tradition is colored by scholarship from the nineteenth and twentieth centuries. There has been much discussion in academic circles lately as to when and who first used the actual designation "Theravada" as a name to denote a circumscribed school of Buddhist thought. Debates aside, we do see Buddhism that evolved with particular regional and doctrinal characteristics in other locations. We know about this form of the religion because it is a vibrant living tradition with established, even thriving monastic and lay institutions and practices.

Most important, the recognition of the particular classics that define the norms varies little: the Tipitaka, the canon preserved in Pali, is central in the construction of the tradition. This collection, the "three baskets," comprises the Vinaya Pitaka, or "basket of monastic discipline"; the Sutta Pitaka, or "basket of discourses"; and the Abhidhamma Pitaka, "the basket of higher teachings." The written Tipitaka is a more recent phenomenon, having been first inscribed on palm leaves in Sri Lanka during the first century B.C.E. According to the tradition, its oral precedent was initially articulated at the First Council held by the Buddhist *Sangha* (community) shortly after the Buddha's death and was preserved through memorization and oral recitation within the Sangha. Tradition holds that the Buddha's disciple Ananda reported to that body of gathered monks the entirety of the sermons (*suttas*) while the disciple Upali recounted the entirety of the monastic code (*vinaya*). The Tipitaka is not revered as gospel, revelation, or even scripture; it is rather a repository of guidelines for proper behavior and understanding.

The Sutta Pitaka alone is a vast collection of texts, grouped in five major sections or *nikayas*: Dighanikaya ("Long Discourses"), Majjhimanikaya ("Middle-length Discourses"), Samyuttanikaya (2,889 "Grouped Discourses"), Anguttaranikaya (a section ordered in sets of numbers), and Khuddakanikaya ("Group of Small Texts," a collection that holds some of the most well-known Buddhist texts such as the Dhammapada and Jataka tales). The Vinaya Pitaka not only lists the 227 monastic rules, but also conveys colorful contextual stories to explain them.

Much as in other religious traditions that have core scriptures, commentaries began to augment the canon. At the time of the fifth-century commentator and translator extraordinaire Buddhaghosa, local versions maintained in Sri Lanka were translated into the translocal language of Pali, signaling the authoritative preeminence of Sri Lanka as the center of the Theravadin world. Buddhaghosa is also responsible for the Visuddhimagga ("Path to Purity"), perhaps the most significant Theravada text beyond the Tipitaka. Visuddhimagga leads the practitioner through seven steps of purification (in terms of virtues, the mind, knowledge, and views), and like other Buddhist texts is organized around the categories of moral discipline (*sila*), meditative concentration (*samadhi*), and wisdom (*panna*).

A genre of historical texts, the *vamsas* ("chronicles"), further complements the canonical and other extracanonical texts. An example is the fifth-century Mahavamsa, a rerendering of elements from the earlier Dipavamsa, which details the coming of the *sasana* (the entire tradition of the Buddha, the dhamma, and the Sangha) to the island of Sri Lanka and the relationship through time between Buddhism and the secular rule of the island. The vamsas also amplify through narrative examples and give historical context to the practices and norms that distinguish Theravada. Beyond the commentaries and chronicles, there are numbers of handbooks, subcommentaries, anthologies, cosmological texts, law texts, and collections of stories and poetry.

What is the community of the faithful called? What story explains its traits?

Technically, *Sangha* refers to the monastic community of the faithful, the *bhikkhus* (monks) and *bhikkhunis* (nuns). Although in the West it is common to hear the term *Sangha* used to denote any group of Buddhist practitioners or congregation of meditators, this is a recent, even spurious development. It is also important to note that the bhikkhuni Sangha has died out in Theravada countries, although there are movements to reinstate the ordination lineage as well as bolster alternative renunciant paths available to women, such as the *dasa sil mata* ("Ten Precept Mothers") in Sri Lanka, *thila shin* in Burma, and *mae ji* in Thailand. Traditionally, the fourfold Sangha includes not only the bhikkhu and bhikkhuni, but also the especially devout laymen (*upasaka*) and laywomen (*upasika*). The Buddha himself proclaimed that his dhamma, or teaching, was impermanent (*anicca*) and like every other conditioned thing prone to eventual decay. The Buddha's own biography can be understood as a structural blueprint for his followers, and the story of the creation and evolution of the Sangha itself illustrates one core understanding held by Theravada Buddhists to be a mark of all existence, that of *anicca* (impermanence).

Around the fifth century B.C.E., the Bodhisatta (pre-Buddha) was born as Siddhattha Gotama, a prince of the Sakya clan in a region of northeast India. He lived a life of luxury that he later rejected and renounced in order to explore asceticism as a possible venue to awakening. Neither the extreme luxury and comfort of his former life nor the extreme denial and restriction of the latter asceticism proved to be conducive to awakening. Despite these obstacles, he found value in his practice of the *majjhima patipada* ("middle path"). As he preached, he began to attract and ordain followers, his *savakas* (or disciples, literally "listeners"). The story of the lineage and continued importance of the technology of proximity to the Buddha is encased in the very rendering of the suttas. Each canonical sermon begins, "evam me sutam," "Thus was heard by me." This phrase, as it came to be used, refers to the Buddha's right-hand disciple Ananda, who was also his cousin and attendant, and his recollection of the Buddha's sermons.

Buddhism spread rapidly as the Buddha recommended that his disciples move away, "no two in the same direction," to preach on their own. By the time of the Mauryan king Asoka (third century B.C.E.), Buddhist communities were prevalent and received royal patronage. During Asoka's reign, a Buddhist mission was led by the monk Mahinda (who may have been Asoka's son) to bring the dhamma to Sri Lanka.

The story of the Sangha's practices mirrors the life story of the Buddha: just as the Bodhisatta made a pronounced break from his family life, so must every aspiring monk break family ties; just as the Bodhisatta cut his hair as he began his spiritual path, so must each novice and monk shave his head; just as the Buddha begged for sustenance, so must the members of the Sangha, and so on. Just as the Bodhisatta himself took vows to focus his agency on the act of perfecting himself, so do Buddhists first take vows (similar to the vows the Buddha had articulated on his own initial path). *Upasaka* and *upasika* (virtuous laypeople) vow to observe the five precepts (*pancasila*): not to take the life of sentient beings, not to take what is not given (not to steal), to refrain from sexual misconduct, to refrain from false speech, and to refrain from using intoxicants. To enter the Sangha, and thus increase one's ability to follow the path, one can then become a *samanera,* or novice, by undertaking the *pabbajja* ("going forth," or lower ordination) and vowing to follow the full ten precepts. As long as one is over the age of twenty, one can be eligible for the higher ordination, *upasampada,* at which point one becomes a bhikkhu. The levels of the Sangha to some degree reflect the increased levels of dedication and intention the Buddha applied in his own search for and development of awakening.

The Sangha's purity is paramount, reflected in the periodic gatherings to reaffirm its shape and constitution. Practically speaking, the Sangha gathers twice a month for Uposatha as a sort of check-in, but throughout history there have been a series of councils for periodic assessment of the purity of the dhamma and Sangha. Nonetheless, there are several quite distinctive sects of the Theravada.

What is the way of life of the community of the faithful? What are the rules of conduct and the rites of passage? What is the notion of sacred time and space? How does the way of life embody the story that this religion tells about itself?

The most basic mark of the faithful, the element that identifies one as being Buddhist, is the sincere act of taking refuge in the Buddha, dhamma, and Sangha called the "Triple Refuge" or "Three Jewels": "Buddham saranam gacchami; Dhammam saranam gacchami; sangham saranam gacchami" ("I take refuge in the Buddha; I take refuge in the dhamma; I take refuge in the Sangha"; spoken aloud three times). To take refuge means to cultivate the right mind-set, which initiates the path. This path is one of action, which embodies both the central question of the tradition, What is to be done? as well as the story the religion tells about itself (the Buddha was a teacher and exemplar who actively sought the truth and encouraged others to actively seek and follow the path to it). The Theravada Buddhist path is one distinguished by a variety of degrees: laypeople follow the precepts, which changes the laypeople's behaviors, which may lead to ordination (temporary or occupational). For those who do ordain, *patimokkha* (the 227 further rules) and three additional precepts are observed.

The ideal way of life set forth in the Noble Eightfold Path is as much an ethical call to action as a practical plan for it. The three middle elements of the Noble Eightfold Path—namely, right speech, right action, and right livelihood—represent the basis for virtuous moral conduct (*sila*). These right behaviors correlate with the occupational path one has chosen to follow: observant laywomen and laymen articulate and adhere to the Five Precepts (*pancasila*): to refrain from taking the life of living creatures, taking what is not given, sexual misconduct, inappropriate or incorrect speech, and using intoxicants. On full- and new-moon Uposatha days, monks gather to confess any transgressions and collectively recite the *patimokkha*, the code of discipline comprising 227 rules of conduct. It is a time where there is an increased intensity to lay practice as well. The laity undertake the more rigorous eight precepts (*atthasila*) where the third precept is expanded to include all sexual activity rather than only sexual misconduct, as in the five precepts, and three more: abstaining from eating after noon; abstaining from entertainment such as dancing, music, and singing, and from beautifying the body with cosmetics, perfumes, or garlands; and abstaining from lying on high or comfortable beds. In Sri Lanka, the full moon Poya (Uposatha) holiday is a public holiday where businesses remain closed in observance.

Theravada rituals are distinguished by monastic teaching and chanting as well as the giving of offerings by laypeople. Beyond the rituals enacted during the Uposatha gatherings, annual holidays and occasional rituals, such as those in remembrance of the dead, bring the broader fourfold community together (bhikkhus and laypeople). In the Theravada notion of sacred time, time (conventionally measured by the lunar calendar) and ethics are intertwined. The dhamma is in decline, and it becomes harder for people to do the right thing as time progresses. The calendar varies within different Theravada cultures, though several of the holidays take similar shape. Visakha Puja (April/May) is a spring holiday to celebrate the occasion of the Buddha's birth. His awakening and his *parinibbana* (final passing) are said to have occurred on the same day. Asalha Puja (mid-summer, July) recalls the Buddha's first sermon and marks the beginning of the Rains Retreat (*vassa*) for the monks. Pavarana and the Kathina ceremony (the eleventh lunar month, October) ends the *vassa* (Rains Retreat) and is the time when laity provide cloth for robes, and other gifts, to the Sangha.

The Theravada notion of sacred space marks the landscape with *stupas*, sites where the Buddha, his life story, and his dhamma can be recalled and venerated. The places in India closely connected to the events of the Buddha's life, such as his birthplace and the sites of his *bodhi* (awakening) and final passing (*parinibbana*), are popular pilgrimage sites. Many countries also preserve a sense of their own preordination as sacred space. In Sri Lanka, the Mahavamsa, the chronicle that preserves the history (or mytho-history) of the island, opens with an account of the Buddha's own visitations to the island: this chronicle declares that shortly after his awakening the Buddha scanned the universe for a fitting place for his dhamma, setting his sights on the island of Lanka. The Buddha then made a visit to prepare it as a future place to shine by clearing it of its *yakkha* (demonic) inhabitants through fear and then peace. He returned to stop an impending war between *nagas* (semidivine serpent beings) and convert hoards of them to the dhamma. He returned a third time at the request of a particularly devout naga. With each visit, the story maintains that the Buddha left behind something to mark his presence: a tree, footprints, and relics. The fifteenth-century northern Thai chronicle Camadevivamsa follows similar structural and rhetorical patterns, tells the story of buried Buddha relics in Thailand, and claims a preordained status for the nascent kingdom of the seventh-century queen Cāma.

Theravada practice thrives where there are signs of the Buddha; there is an express need to see bhikkhus, *viharas* (monasteries, or wats), and *stupas* (relics or monuments, cetiya, dagoba, pagodas) to help focus the mind on the path. The daily religious life of lay Theravada Buddhists varies greatly, but there are common general practices that can be followed even in the absence of a community. This includes daily veneration in one's home at a shrine consisting of a Buddha image, a vase for flowers (their beauty honors the Buddha but also helps turn one's mind to *anicca*, impermanence, as they inevitably die), and incense (perfume also helps focus the mind and is said to be like the virtues one cultivates through the path, pervasive and sweet). Homage to the Buddha is paid through bodily posture and *anjali* (hands pressed together as in prayer), and articulated through chants, such as "namo tassa bhagavato arahato samma-sambuddhassa," "Homage to the Blessed One, Arahant, Perfectly Awakened One."

What is the worldview of the community, the story that it tells about itself in the context of history, the conception of divinity and the relationship of the divinity (or divinities) to the believers, and its principal ethical teachings? How do women fit into the system in its classical formulation? What are the attitude and behaviors toward persons outside the faith community?

At the base of the Theravadin worldview is the understanding that ignorance (*avijja*) binds us to repeat lifetime after lifetime in the rounds of samsara and the laws of kamma govern the process of rebirth. Each individual is therefore responsible for his or her own moral, intellectual, and spiritual development. This worldview is expandable from the individual to the broader community so that the story it tells about itself in the context of history is one of a community that responsibly and faithfully follows the leader or teacher who discerned the path that leads to awakening and nibbana. Legacy and legitimacy matter, and have historically influenced the connection between the Sangha and various rulers in Theravadin countries. The function of mutual legitimation has origins in the primary sources and the Buddha's biography itself.

Theravada Buddhists understand the world to include many levels of deities, but all deities (*devas*) are subject to the same binding qualities of samsara as every human. In other words, there is no singular, transcendental, creator, adjudicating God, but there are many opportunities for one to be born a god for a time before taking another birth. The enduring object of faith, the Buddha, is not a god, but a teacher and exemplar.

The principal ethical teachings (especially the Noble Eightfold Path: right view, right resolve, right speech, right action, right livelihood, right effort, right mindfulness, right concentration), explained in the first section of this chapter as the entirety of the Theravada tradition, can be thought of as primarily ethical teachings, the central question being, What needs to be done? In practical teachings an emphasis is also placed on the generation of *metta* (loving-kindness), which one must learn to be able to extend to all sentient beings— from one's own mother, to one whom one feels neutral about, to one's enemy.

As traced in the third section of this chapter, women have played an important and yet diminished role in the tradition. Although Buddhists and scholars alike are still debating the ability of women to fully ordain in the Theravadin countries where the bhikkhuni Sangha has disappeared, there are established, traditional roles for very dedicated women. Laywomen also play an important role in the tradition as the monks rely on alms, traditionally doled out by the women in the home. Throughout the early texts, images of women as meditative devices abound, especially the rotting corpses of once beautiful courtesans. Seeing a beautiful woman subject to decay illustrates the lesson of *anicca,* impermanence. Soteriologically speaking, a woman cannot become a Buddha directly from her female birth, however, and must instead hope to be reborn in a male form.

There is no singular, pervasive attitude or behavior toward persons outside the faith community. Generally speaking, *avijja* (ignorance) leads individuals through various rebirths; to be born human is a rare opportunity to take advantage of the special circumstances for self-cultivation. It is only in a human birth that one can be confronted with so many choices in one's actions and then take responsibility for one's choices and actions; a lion, for example, kills because it is in her nature, but a human can avoid negative actions with agency, effort, and vigilance. A Theravada Buddhist, then, may regard people of other faiths or those outside the faith community with a degree of ambivalence. On the one hand, there may be regret, remorse, or even pity felt toward a being who is seemingly incapable of following the dhamma, one who because of ignorance continues to behave in counterindicated ways and who further harms his potential to cultivate himself by wrong or unskillful actions. One might think this would provoke a sense of proselytizing or missionary behavior, but Theravada resists active proselytizing—each individual must begin the process of self-cultivation on his own terms, engaging with his own self to determine what is right and good. On the other hand, in many Theravadin cultures there is a practical distrust of the other, many times amplified and buttressed by certain readings of Buddhist materials. For example, the more than a quarter of a century long, ethnically rooted civil war in Sri Lanka, pitting the majority Sinhalese Buddhists against the Tamil minority, was directly fueled by rhetoric and perceptions drawn from the historical chronicle of the island, the fifth-century Mahavamsa.

How does this religion function in the world today? What are its relationships with culture?

In Sri Lanka, the Theravada has endured centuries of colonial influence, even miraculously recovering a vital tooth relic that was destroyed centuries ago by intolerant Portuguese. During their colonial rule, the British imposed a school system and governmental structures that could have threatened the legitimacy of the Sangha, but ultimately did not. The Thai constitutional monarchy has always maintained a very close relationship with the Sangha; the king is identified as a defender of the faith (*dhammaraja*), an idea that began with the founder of the kingdom of Sukhothai in 1238. Since 2007 (though some would say longer), after public and peaceful demonstrations, bhikkhus have faced repression from Burma's military government. In all three countries, Theravada culture is dominant. As Theravada moves into the West, there is not as much historical or cultural support for its institutions, such as almsgiving and support of the Sangha, or often for the Sangha itself. In the West, one sees *vipassana* meditation groups and centers for Insight Meditation that offer retreats and workshops to a primarily Western audience.

At a Glance

Classic Texts
Tipitaka (Vinaya Pitaka, Sutta Pitaka, Abhidhamma Pitaka)
Dhammapada
Jataka
Visuddhimagga
Dipavamsa and Mahavamsa

Important Figures
The Buddha, Siddhattha Gotama (fifth century B.C.E.)
Ananda
Asoka
Buddhaghosa
Mahinda

Characteristic Beliefs
anatta
anicca
Buddha, dhamma (teaching), and Sangha (monastic community): "the three jewels"
dukkha
Four Noble Truths
kamma
metta
Noble Eightfold Path
samsara
sila, samadhi, and panna (moral cultivation, mental discipline, and wisdom)

Essential Creeds or Codes of Conduct
The precepts
For monks, the *patimokkha,* 227 rules of monastic conduct
The Triratna (triple refuge, "three jewels")

Brief Time Line

fifth century B.C.E.	Buddha lived and taught in India.
ca. 480 B.C.E.	The First Council, held during the Rains Retreat after the *parinibbana* of the Buddha, where the entire body of the Buddha's dhamma was recited.
ca. 380 B.C.E.	The Second Council, held in Vesali, to address controversial points of *vinaya*; the first schism between the Mahasanghika and traditionalist Sthaviravada (precursor to modern Theravada) occurs.
ca. 250 B.C.E.	The Third Council, convened by Asoka in Pataliputta, leading to further schism between the Sarvastivadin and Vibhajjavadin (even more directly connected to the modern Theravada) sects.
247 B.C.E.	Asoka sends forth Buddhist missions; Mahinda brings the dhamma and *sasana* to Sri Lanka, and the king is converted. Mahinda then establishes the Mahavihara (Great Monastery) in 240 B.C.E. where the Vibhajjavadin community becomes known as the Theravada.
100 B.C.E.	A Fourth Council is held in Sri Lanka where Mahavihara monks write the Tipitaka for the first time. Theravada first appears in Thailand and Burma about this time.
fifth century C.E.	Buddhaghosa collects and translates into Pali various Sinhala commentaries on the Tipitaka and composes his meditation manual. Buddhadatta and Dhammapala also compose commentaries and sub-commentaries.
1050 C.E.	The Bhikkhu and Bhikkhuni Sangha in Anuradhapura (Sri Lanka) die out; in 1070 a contingent from Burma come to reinstate the lineage.
thirteenth century	Theravada spreads to Cambodia and Laos.
1753	Bhikkhus from the Thai court reinstate the lineage that had once again waned in Sri Lanka (this begins the Siam Nikaya).
1803	Sri Lankan monks are ordained in Burma and begin the Amarapura Nikaya.

1828	Thailand's Prince Mongkut founds the Dhammayut Sect.
1868	A Fifth Council is held in Mandalay, Burma.
1881	The Pali Text Society (PTS) is founded and begins transliterating and translating the canon and other Theravada texts into Roman script and Western languages.
1956	Buddha Jayanti Year, celebrating twenty-five hundred years of the dhamma.
1958	Dr. Ariyaratne founds Sarvodaya Shramadana, a grass-roots social justice movement in Sri Lanka.
1970s	Ajahn Chah establishes a forest monastery in Thailand for training Western monks and the Insight Meditation Society is founded in Cambridge, Massachusetts. Theravada becomes a presence in the West as Westerners ordain.
1996	The contested ordination of eleven women in Sarnath (the location in India of the Buddha's first sermon) revives the Theravada bhikkhuni sangha.

Important Symbols
Chedi/dagoba/thupa
Bodhi tree
Buddhapada (footprint relics)
The Buddha
Relics

Important Rituals
Taking Triple Refuge in the Three Jewels
Pabbajja and *upasampada* ordination levels for monastics
Daily remembrance of the Buddha (by veneration of Buddha's image, lighting candles and incense, and presenting offerings of flowers, and so on) in a shrine room or dedicated space
For laity, performing *dana* (acts of generosity) toward the Sangha

Glossary

anatta	"no-self," sometimes rendered "no soul," characteristic of all existence
anicca	"impermanence," sometimes called "flux," characteristic of all existence
arahant	a person who has destroyed the roots of *dukkha*—namely greed, hatred, and ignorance; an awakened being, the goal of one's practice

bhikkhu or *bhikkhuni*	monk or nun; member of the Sangha
bodhi	"awakening," commonly translated as "enlightenment"
Bodhisatta	"Being of Awakening," a pre-Buddha, one on the way to Buddhahood
Buddha	"Awakened One" or "Enlightened One," a descriptive epithet rather than a name
dhamma	the teaching or doctrine
dukkha	"dis-ease," commonly translated as "suffering," characteristic of all existence
Four Noble Truths	core of philosophy: all is "dis-ease," there is a cause (craving) and an end, which is a path one follows to cultivate the self
kamma	"action," the law of cause and effect
Noble Eightfold Path	the path one follows to cultivate the self, the fourth noble truth
Paticcasamuppada	"Dependant Coarising" or "Codependent Origination"
patimokkha	the 227 monastic rules
parami	Perfections, ten virtues to cultivate through practice, such as Generosity
samsara	"the wandering on," the realm of birth, life, death, and rebirth
Sangha	the Buddhist monastic community
sasana	the Buddha, dhamma, Sangha, and everything that supports the tradition itself
sutta	"sermon," didactic texts in the Buddha's words
vinaya	monastic text, comprising both the monastic code of conduct and context for it

Sacred Spaces and Times

Spaces

All sites in India that are associated with the Buddha's life story, especially his awakening

All monasteries (*vihara, wat*) where the Sangha resides

All *stupas,* dagobas, pagodas, and *chedis* where there is direct access to the Buddha's relics for veneration

Times

Visakha Puja (April/May)

Asalha Puja (mid-summer, July)

Pavarana and the Kathina ceremony (the eleventh lunar month, October)

Uposatha (observed at the full and new moons; for some the quarter moons as well)

Suggestions for Further Reading

Carrithers, Michael. *The Forest Monks of Sri Lanka: An Anthropological and Historical Study.* New York: Oxford University Press, 1983.

Gombrich, Richard F. *Theravada Buddhism: A Social History from Ancient Benares to Modern Colombo.* London and New York: Routledge & Kegan Paul, 1988.

Payutto, Phra Prayudh. *Buddhadhamma.* Translated by Grant A. Olson. Albany: State University of New York Press, 2007.

Spiro, Melford E. *Buddhism and Society: A Great Tradition and Its Burmese Vicissitudes.* 2nd exp. ed. New York: Random House, 2007.

Swearer, Donald K. *The Buddhist World of Southeast Asia.* Albany: State University of New York Press, 1995.

Tambiah, Stanley J. *The Buddhist Saints of the Forest and the Cult of Amulets.* New York: Cambridge University Press, 1984.

Wijayaratna, Mohan. *Buddhist Monastic Life: According to the Texts of the Theravada Tradition* New York: Cambridge University Press, 1990.

Translations of selected primary sources, especially those of Thanissaro Bhikkhu, available at www.accesstoinsight.org.

THE MAHAYANA TRADITION

Mark L. Blum

Upon the death of Shakyamuni, the founder of Buddhism, his disciples were so numerous and spread out over such a large area of India that the leaders of the community scheduled a large convocation (usually translated as "council") to plan their future. Despite coming from a royal family himself, Shakyamuni repudiated the notion that family lineage had any religious significance and thus, despite his son being a member of the clergy, there was no attempt to assert the authority of the son or any family member to lead community after his death. To this day this doctrine has held firm after his disappearance in all Mahayana societies, with the exception of Japan.

Buddhism as a whole continued to expand throughout South Asia, and some believe that by the dawn of the Common Era it had become the largest religious movement in India, if not in south Asia as a whole. By the third through second centuries B.C.E., it was divided into at least twenty schools of interpretation, some large enough to have their own orders with their own canons. What became known as Mahayana Buddhism began as a movement at that time that evolved eclectically, absorbing a variety of hermeneutic traditions and cults, and that was openly more inclusive of lay believers and their religious needs and practices. It needs to be stated, however, that many Mahayana Buddhist believers today reject this scenario entirely, instead insisting that the Mahayana *sutras,* or scriptures, were simply another set of sermons by Shakyamuni that were played down in the first centuries of religion after the founder's death. However, the so-called School of the Elders, or Theravada, whose great antiquity is universally recognized, does not recognize any Mahayana sutra as canonical.

A small note about language is in order here, because the *lingua franca* of Mahayana texts is Sanskrit, even if most of the extent texts are written in a variety of Prakrit or Middle Indic forms. The Mahayana movement arose as urban India was transitioning from an oral to a written culture; this resulted in much longer texts than had been seen previously and also in a Sanskritization of those texts to make them more accessible to educated populations throughout south Asia. Consequently, the Sanskrit forms of Buddhist jargon will be used here, often resulting in differences with the same words found in the Theravada chapter, such as *karma* instead of *kamma, Dharma* instead of *dhamma,* and so on.

What is this religion's overriding question? What makes the system self-evidently valid to the community of the faithful?

There are two core religious issues in Mahayana Buddhism that are not fundamentally different from those found in Theravada Buddhism, as discussed in the preceding section. They are: how to escape from samsara, the endless cycle of birth and death (*samsara*), and how to eliminate "dis-ease" or suffering (*duhkha*).

However, while the basic Indian presumption of actions (*karma*) having moral consequences remains basically intact, Mahayana Buddhism shows far less concern with ethics and morality than its Theravada counterpart. This can be attributed to two categories or dimensions of cultural expression. The first we might call devotional: the belief that an individual's karma can be changed by the production of merit through praxis and the intervention of divine others. The second is philosophical: a fierce attack on the presumptions of causality stemming from a more transcendent perspective on the Buddhist truth of nonself. It is argued that the presumed cause-and-effect relationship that lies at the heart of karmic theory in fact represents only the mundane understanding of truth and that the "higher" understanding of the nature of reality is based on such a thoroughgoing rejection of individuality in any sense that the idea of discreet events of determined moral value has become untenable.

As a result, the overriding religious concern for many Mahayana Buddhists has been access to the sacred and its salvific power, often pushing concerns for maintaining proper morality to the periphery. Morality is never explicitly rejected, but there is such a strong tendency in Mahayana intellectual thought to focus on the liberated, awakened, or "nirvanic" perspective that it limits the relevance of morality to the realm of a mundane truth "merely instrumental" for its expediency in enabling the individual to attain liberation by accessing sacred power. Nevertheless, the ultimate goal is the attainment of buddhahood, which transforms the individual into a buddha utterly devoted to helping others with an infinite capacity for compassion and wisdom.

In Mahayana Buddhism, there is a significantly different notion of "buddha" itself. We may infer that over two or three centuries following the death of the founder, the instantiation of his dispensation in the *Sangha*, or religious community, gradually lost its ability to convince the population as a whole that its presence alone made the religion self-evidently true. In the Mahayana movement we see new forms of praxis emerging, many among the lay followers themselves, that reestablish links to "buddha" as a tangible, historical presence. One of these is devotional *puja* offerings at *stupas* that contained the relics of Shakyamuni; another is the arising of a new understanding of "buddha" such that there are many buddhas in many places existing all at the same time, ultimately leading to the conclusion that at its core "buddha" is an ahistorical principle. This difference is clearly illustrated in the two versions of a scripture called the *Mahaparinirvana Sutra*, which describes the circumstances of Shakyamuni Buddha's death. In the early, original text, he gets food poisoning, suffers from diarrhea, and his eighty-year-old body finally succumbs to illness and he dies. The sutra communicates the religious message that all things are impermanent, but the Buddha's legacy lives on through his teachings, he tells those gathered at his last sermon, "Cling to my teachings, not to me." But in the Mahayana version, Shakyamuni affirms that yes, he is disappearing from view by passing into nirvana, but no, this is not because he is old and his body has physical limitations. The message of this sutra is to ridicule the very idea that he even needs nourishment from food to maintain his body; here the Buddha is revealed as a human manifestation of nirvana itself. In the Mahayana paradigm, therefore, there are many such manifestations—many buddhas. Whereas in the original cosmology of Buddhism there was only one buddha per age, in the Mahayana there are essentially an infinite number of buddhas functioning at any place and time.

In this sense, what makes the religion self-evidently valid is that it is able to show how nirvana is not a distant ideal, but a sacred presence manifest in this world, on other planets, in other dimensions, and so forth. This is accomplished in a number of ways. Doctrinally this is expressed in the teaching that the world of transmigration characterized by "dis-ease," or samsara, *is* in fact nirvana, and nirvana *is* samsara. Attaining liberation is therefore no longer a matter of escaping from this reality characterized by limitation and unpleasantness into another reality characterized by freedom and bliss, but awakening to the reality of the sacred dimension of nirvana within oneself. The difficulty in attaining this nirvanic awareness is addressed with myths of "pure lands" where particular buddhas or divine bodhisattvas live in paradisic settings, extending invitations to individuals to seek immediate rebirth there in their postmortem state, for these pure lands have conditions ideal for religious awakening and for becoming a buddha oneself. These narratives of salvation are common in Mahayana literature and always include ritual or meditative means to access those realms.

Materially, it is sacred scriptures and sacred art, and at times sacred invididuals, that embody this truth. The scriptures are revered as objects of devotion no less than the art, but because Mahayana scriptures are often abstract and symbolic, and visual culture is a more plastic medium, the sacred is often more accessible to the community of believers in its visual forms. Pilgrimages are common, for example, to stupas or pagodas where either relics of buddhas or saints are buried, enshrined on altars, or placed within the images; but certain images are also considered so powerful merely to gaze at that even without relics they are perceived to endow the pilgrim with faith and enough merit to ensure them a favorable rebirth.

Art plays a central role in another way by stroking the believer's imagination of what that sacred dimension of reality looks like in the form of scenes depicting a buddha preaching in his pure land or the layouts of a hot or a cold hell or the realm of hungry ghosts.

Historical depictions of individuals who indeed achieved salvation by personal integration into the sacred are another means by which the truth of the religion is made evident. Portraits or statues of patriarchs that remind the pilgrim that the truth has been passed down over generations to his or her own time express this iconographically. It is also expressed through literature in sacred biographies of eminent clerics or in collections of stories either by or about pious individuals who also attained liberation, the latter usually after death by achieving rebirth in the pure land of a buddha or bodhisattva.

How do we know about this religion? What classics define the norms?

Mahayana Buddhism defines itself by the same concept of the "three jewels" that was developed in earlier iterations of Buddhism and that we also see in Theravada Buddhism: the founder (the Buddha), his teachings (Dharma), and the community that live by those teachings (Sangha). All three are taught as equally valuable in the transmission of the authority of religion for the world. We know of the heritage of Mahayana Buddhism through the continuation of all three lines of approach over time, in some cases down to the present day and in others through literary evidence of broken lines of transmission. The role of the Sangha in preserving the tradition is crucial to the entire enterprise, as active participation in the Sangha always presumes a commitment to transmit all three jewels to the next generation.

Religious scripture abounds in Mahayana Buddhism for many reasons. First is the "cult of the book" that is apparent in many Mahayana sutras, where the transition to a written culture in India is seen in the sutra's exhorting its reader or believer to "copy this sutra" and give it to others. Second is the fact that paper was invented in China soon after the introduction of the religion there. Third is the fact that printing was apparently invented in China in order to duplicate Buddhist scriptures, as the world's oldest extant book is the *Diamond Sutra* produced in China in the ninth century. Translation also played a large role in the cultural history of the religion. Enormous time and resources were put into first translating the Buddhist sutras into Chinese and then Tibetan and then arranging to have wooden blocks carved so each text could be printed and collected in a canon called *Tripitaka,* as it is also called in Theravada Buddhism. Although we have only sparse examples of Indic language texts, near complete canons in Chinese and Tibetan were printed and copied repeatedly—the whole canon at the expense of the state for each dynasty as a way of preserving the Dharma and thus earning merit for king and nation.

These Mahayana canons in translation contain texts that cannot be found elsewhere, so the origins of many works are unknown. The canons are extremely large, the standard core of the Chinese canon used today by scholars being 55 volumes, with each volume ranging more than 1,000 pages, and totaling more than 2,100 texts. The expanded version that includes Japanese texts reaches 85 volumes and 2,900 texts. In addition, individual schools of Buddhism in some nations have also created their own interpretive canons, a process that began in Japan in the seventeenth century and is still in print today, ranging from 35 to 100 volumes. In Tibet, the core Indian canon, known as the Kanjur, is 85 volumes, and the supplemental interpretive canon, called the Tanjur, reaches 224 volumes and more than 3,600 texts. Although there has been some control over this material within individual schools in each Mahayana country, in general the Mahayana Buddhist canon is considered "open," which is why it is so voluminous.

From the standpoint of all but the most serious scholar, the idea of reading through the entirety of the canon of one's affiliated tradition or lineage is clearly impossible. As a result, each "school" or lineage of the tradition defines itself by which texts it holds most sacred. In China, the number of sutras and the difference in their content led to an intellectual debate that continued for centuries in the medieval period over the order that the Buddha must have given these sermons and why, and which one represents his final word.

Moreover, because of terseness and the mythical dimension to a great many Mahayana sutras, they require an unpacking of their symbolism and jargon. Therefore the Sangha has the responsibility of not only preserving the books themselves but also studying and understanding them, and passing that knowledge on generation after generation.

What is the community of the faithful called? What story explains its traits?

The community of faithful is called the *Sangha*. But unlike the Theravada Buddhist tradition, in Mahayana Buddhism the lay-monastic distinction is deconstructed at times. Based on what we read in the Pali canon, in early Buddhism anyone who felt a serious commitment to the religion was expected to ordain as a religious, and there were even traditions of interpretation that claimed it was impossible for a lay believer to attain the goal of becoming an *arhat* (*arahant*) and remain outside the monastic community. One of the most famous Mahayana sutras, the Vimalakirta, however, is about a lay believer who upbraids all the senior disciples of Shakyamuni, all of them monastics, for their narrow-minded interpretations of his teachings. A lay believer in the Mahayana therefore regards the Sangha to be of critical importance in maintaining the Dharma, but need not feel he or she cannot achieve salvation without taking the tonsure, which in most cases requires one to live outside of one's family. Thus when we speak of the "Sangha" in Mahayana Buddhism, it often includes both clerics and lay.

Despite this, the monastic rigor required of ordained clerics in all Mahayana Buddhist countries outside Japan continues to this day. In fact, the Vinaya precepts for the Sangha are typically pre-Mahayana in origin, but this has not caused any serious problems. In this sense, the basic rules of monasticism such as celibacy and when food can be taken are consistent between Theravada and Mahayana Buddhism, at least as ideals. A lay believer is much more willing to make donations to the Sangha when he or she feels the monks or nuns in a community are keeping the precepts and engaging in diligent practice.

The basic narrative around which the Mahayana Sangha operates is not appreciably different from that of Theravada Buddhism. That is, the precepts and practices that make up Sangha life stem from the time when it was formed under Shakyamuni's direct leadership. The part of the canon that pertains to monastic life is called the Vinaya and is centered on specific rulings made by Shakyamuni and how these rulings were interpreted. As Buddhism moved east, however, the Indian model underwent a number of changes, most noticeably in a reduction in the number of precepts in certain traditions, from around 250 to 80 in China, and a tradition in Tibet of many individuals' undergoing only the first stage of ordination, thereby technically remaining novices wherein fewer restrictions apply.

Japan, however, is a notable exception. From its arrival on Japanese soil, the institutional concept of the Sangha, reflective of Indian cultural values, clashed with Japanese assumptions about spirituality. Unlike the Indians or the Chinese, the Japanese had no tradition of regarding their bodily functions as inherently disruptive or in need of control, so complete removal from society and renunciation of physical pleasures such as sex, alcohol, music, or art was expected only during "retreats," though these could go on for years in some cases. Throughout the medieval period, Japanese Buddhist clergy were frequently involved in artistic activities, including poetry, music, calligraphy, and theater, and there is scant evidence that this weakened them in the eyes of the public. In the thirteenth century, the monk Shinran was released from his vow of celibacy by his teacher, initiating a sectarian line since that time that limits celibacy and other restrictive precepts to a period of training before final ordination. With its married clergy, this sect, called Shin Buddhism, slowly grew to become the largest Buddhist denomination in Japan, and today remains arguably the most devout. The vast majority Buddhist clergy in Japan today are not celibate

What is the way of life of the community of the faithful? What are the rules of conduct and the rites of passage? What is the notion of sacred time and space? How does the way of life embody the story that this religion tells about itself?

Practice must be viewed differently depending upon whether the individual is a professional religious or a lay believer. For ordained members of the clergy living in settled communities, there are many precepts that need to be observed, as well as daily sutra recitations, rituals, and, for some, daily meditation. Ordination also follows more or less the traditional two-stage origination. But whereas most Mahayana monastic communities also depend upon donations for their financial well-being, in East Asia the traditional Indian practice of daily begging has long been defunct. Where it does survive, it does so as a form of ritual discipline rather than as a means to secure food. Instead monastic communities have developed their own means of support, usually in the form of either direct support from the state or from a group of donors, or in tilling the land, either by the monastics themselves or by farmers who rent temple lands. Rites of passage for monastics consist primarily in the two stages of ordination: first to novice and next to full cleric.

For the lay community, aside from living by a set of five principles of the religion (no lying, stealing, harming life, improper sexual activity, or anything injurious to the Sangha) and supporting the clergy, religious activities are usually focused on a vegetarian life-style—traditional in China, Korea, and Japan—and on rituals that mark the calendar when the lay community journeys to particular temples. Examples of these days are the spring and fall equinox; the birthday of Shakyamuni; and in East Asia, memorials held on the death anniversaries of saints and ancestors, or recent family members. Vegetarianism was strongly extolled in certain Mahayana scriptures such as the *Mahaparinirvana Sutra* and strictly observed by the devout in premodern times, but was interpreted differently in each country, a common view being that the rule applied only to four-footed animals, freeing people to eat fish and fowl. Chinese Buddhist lay believers continue to hold this precept highly, and outside Tibet food served within monasteries is still largely expected to be vegetarian, though in Japan this too seems to be fading.

In all Mahayana countries the principles of the noble eightfold path were largely ignored in favor of various other principled systems of practice, most commonly the six "perfections" (*paramita*): charity, morality, patience, effort, meditation, and wisdom. There is no custom of regular attendance to temples for prayer or worship on a weekly basis by the lay community, as there is no notion of a Sabbath. But lay believers frequently make formal offerings to the Buddha and the Sangha to support the monastics and generate merit (*punya*), and at festival time temples can get very busy.

What is the worldview of the community, the story that it tells about itself in the context of history, the conception of divinity and the relationship of the divinity (or divinities) to the believers, and its principal ethical teachings? How do women fit into the system in its classical formulation? What are the attitude and behaviors toward persons outside the faith community?

Historical consciousness in Mahayana Buddhism is not particularly strong. In fact, it is usually evident only in discussions of decline, for one recurring theme in many Mahayana scriptures is the implication of the gradual weakening and eventual disappearance of the religion in the centuries following the time a buddha was active or when a sermon was given. Indeed, this theme was particularly resonant in East Asia where it was picked up and included in a great many of the indigenous scriptures written in China that profess to be translations from Sanskrit. There is strong concern for "the Buddhist world" in both Indian and Chinese sutras that speak of this "decline of the Dharma," because recognizing the decline of the Dharma should inspire greater commitment to the teaching and even greater acts of piety, and also because it allowed for new interpretations, for in the final period of decline (*mofa/mappo*) the Dharma is virtually impossible to understand in the traditional way. The opposite notion that affirms the Mahayana Dharma as a religious truth transcending history also exists, but despite sectarian divisions on this point in either case lineage played an important role in demonstrating to the world that understanding of the Dharma had not been entirely lost.

Divinity is expressed in two distinct forms: gods, or those beings who reside in one of many heavens that Buddhism assumed from pre-Buddhist Indian religion; and the Buddhist pantheon of buddhas, bodhisattvas, "protectors," and so forth. The former have supernatural power as deities, but they are consistently depicted as in need of spiritual guidance from buddhas. This is because Buddhist heavens are still part of samsara and one's time there is limited. At the end of one's lifetime in heaven, one dies and undergoes rebirth and redeath again in any one of six realms. So the gods in the heavens are also seeking nirvana, which as a goal lies outside samsara. There are demons and hostile deities in Buddhist myths, but ultimately all are converted to Buddhism and function to defend and promote the religion in their own realms, which include the realms of ghosts and hell beings, and of course in the human realm as well, where the religion is always in some danger from its enemies, both seen and unseen.

There is no creator god who stands outside creation, for creation itself is just another manifestation of samsara. In this sense, Mahayana continues a pre-Mahayana distinction between phenomena that have been created and those that have not. To be "created" (*samskrta*) means to have been brought into existence by karmic means (and in the case of humans and animals, also through sexual intercourse) and therefore to have a limited life span. The few "uncreated" (*asamskrta*) phenomena include buddhas, space, and nirvana. These are permanent and unchanging; it is explained that because they have no beginning they also have no end. Indeed one of the core paradoxes is how a person, who is created, can "enter" or "achieve" nirvana, which is uncreated. One very popular Mahayana "solution" to this is to posit a "buddha-nature" in all living beings that is itself uncreated. That is to say, all created life-forms also embody the uncreated: as stated above, nirvana is not separate from samsara; they are but two dimensions of the same reality.

The status of women in the Mahayana is generally favorable because of its strong emphasis on universal spiritual potential regardless of family, religious ties, or gender. Unlike the Theravada tradition, for example, the monastic lineage for women is alive and well in all Mahayana countries except Tibet, where it has also died out. Mahayana sutras contain a number of passages meant to deconstruct traditional norms of class and gender in India, such as the serpent princess (an animal!) in the *Lotus Sutra* who attains buddhahood despite another Buddhist monk's saying this is impossible for women. But resistance toward the idea of women leaving their traditional family-nurturing roles has tenaciously remained in the Buddhist culture in all Mahayana countries from India to Japan, particularly in East Asia where Confucian ethical norms held sway. The demands of celibacy also led to misogynistic writing in which women are blamed for the sexual impulses that arise in the hearts of monks, and nunneries never achieved the status of the most eminent monasteries. But although we do not have very much in the way of exegetical treatises or essays written by women prior to the modern period, and women were forbidden from living in male-only monasteries, women have long enjoyed their own lineages of teachers and students that continues to the present day.

Regarding the question of how Mahayana Buddhist belief and culture has responded toward persons of other faiths, like all forms of Buddhism, Mahayana is known for absorbing local religious traditions and allowing its believers to engage in rituals at non-Buddhist shrines and temples. Unlike most other major religions, despite a very clear intellectual tradition that rationalized the fusion of religion and politics in a positive way, there have been few instances of reactionary responses when this fusion did not take place. Although in some scriptures there is mention of taking up arms in defense of the religion, in fact this rarely occurred. The exception is Tibet and Japan, but this is sectarian violence between Buddhist groups, not between Buddhists and non-Buddhists. Nonbelievers are at times called "heretics," but rather than being seen as a threat to Buddhism, they are typically dismissed as wrongheaded and pitied for the many future rebirths they will have to endure before attaining liberation.

225

There are no examples of crusades to capture land deemed to belong exclusively to the sacred tradition of Mahayana, probably because the notion of fixed sanctity lying in a particular geographical location (such as a mountain) is usually shared in Mahayana countries with followers of other religions. Even the five pilgrimage sites in India have not been under the exclusive control of Buddhists for more than a millennium.

Rather than being located in one or more divinities, the Mahayana sutras preach a salvific truth called *Dharma* that explains the nature of the sacred reality as independent of time, space, or history. There is no sacred Buddhist nation, therefore, but Buddhism can sanctify a nation. This sacred reality is contrasted with how reality is seen by "ordinary persons" (*prthagjana*), a pejorative term for dull-witted individuals who believe in their "common sense," meaning they do not question the validity of their own emotions or opinions, or the descriptions of the world that hold sway in society. The truth of this Dharma-nirvana-buddha way of seeing the world is referred to by a number of phrases that seem unique to Mahayana Buddhism and that have proved difficult to put into English: emptiness, suchness, thusness, naturalness, things-as-they-are-ness, and so on. To explain:

(a) Emptiness (*shunyata*): all identifiable phenomena—for example, a molecule identified as "water"; a mobile vehicle identified as "automobile"; an individual living being identified as "dog" or "George Washington"; a collective of individuals identified as "Californians" or the "New York Giants"—are real only on a contingent basis. They could break apart at any moment and regroup with other like elements to form new phenomena with new identities and names. Therefore they are "empty" of any permanent, true self-nature. To see the truth of emptiness to see the reality of this as a whole, to see how this principle lies embedded in all existence, both physical and mental.

(b) Nothingness: a parallel concept to emptiness, this term stems from Chinese language expressions of emptiness that use the Chinese word *wu* as a negative. This principle of the radical deconstruction of identity operates more or less as emptiness, but Chinese Buddhist writings often prefer this term because of its Daoist roots.

(c) Suchness or thusness (*tathata, dharmata*): these refer to the sacred dimension or aspect of "things" as they truly are, not as we think or hope they are—that is, the "nature" of reality independent of human understanding. These terms may be used in a general sense, for example, "this is the nature of all buddhas," or they may occur in reference to a particular, concrete phenomenon. While also built on the doctrine of emptiness, these terms have the advantage of affirming empirically perceived existents *as they are* as sacred.

How does this religion function in the world today? What are its relationships with culture?

Until recently the dominant narrative concerning Mahayana Buddhism in the modern world was how it was damaged during recent centuries of political and cultural imperialism first from the West, then from Japan, and subsequently from China after the revolution in 1949. The hundred years prior to the end of World War II also saw serious political suppression of Buddhist institutions and beliefs internally in all Mahayana nations except Tibet. Since the war, there has been a slow but steady recovery in Korea, Japan, and Taiwan; but in China, Tibet, Mongolia, and Vietnam there has been serious destruction of all aspects of the religion.

In Japan and Taiwan the postwar period has produced a number of new Buddhist movements, some of which have grown into sizable institutions creating traditions of social engagement and even colleges. In keeping with their traditional view of monasticism in each society, in Taiwan this "new Buddhism" is dominated by monastics (especially women), while the Japanese form is almost entirely lay.

Political suppression of Buddhists in China in the first forty years after the 1949 revolution came from an ideologically driven materialist agenda based initially on Soviet principles. Senior monks were jailed with only show trials for many years, monasteries and nunneries were turned into factories or torn down, and a great many valuable art pieces were destroyed or damaged. Under Soviet influence, Mongolia and Vietnam carried out similar policies that, if anything, were even more oppressive, with thousands of monks executed in Mongolia for treason.

But with the fall of the Soviet Union, and the Communist parties in China and Vietnam sacrificing ideology for pragmatism, under government supervision Mahayana Buddhism is currently making a strong comeback in China, Mongolia, and Vietnam. There remains a serious problem within these religious communities, however, in that essentially two generations passed without proper study and training of the clergy in meditation, ritual, and the complexities of Buddhist doctrine. In Tibet, however, the Chinese government's suppression of the Buddhist clergy continues unabated today, as the clergy there is far more hostile to government supervision and most Tibetans regard Buddhism as a symbol of their national identity. Despite Chinese propaganda to the contrary, there are no credible signs that Chinese suppression has weakened the devotion of the Tibetan people to their religion. One interesting, if politically tragic change has been the emergence of the Dalai Lama, the traditional religious and political leader of the greater Lhasa region, as the first worldwide spokesman for Buddhism as a whole, the very idea of which was inconceivable in the past. Interestingly, his form of Buddhism, called the Gelug school of Vajrayana, is no impediment to his acceptance by distinctly different sectarian traditions in other Buddhist countries. It is also worth noting that the political suppression of Mahayana Buddhism in the modern period may be seen as part of a long historical struggle over the legal independence of monastic communities under Confucian legal norms. It also reflects the fear in government that Buddhism provides an alternative ideology to state control because temples and monasteries have served as staging grounds for revolutions in the past, especially in China.

At a Glance

Classic Texts
Amitabha Sutra
Garland (Flower Ornament) Sutra
Mahaparinirvana Sutra
Mahavairocanasutra
Sutra on Perfect Wisdom
Lotus Sutra
Diamond Sutra

Vimalakirti Sutra
Yogacarabhumi

Important Figures

Asanga (fourth century C.E.): brother of Vasubandhu, author of Yogacara treatises
Bodhidharma (early sixth century): founder of Chan/Zen tradition in China
Chinul: influential Korean master of the Son/Zen school
Dignaga (480–540 C.E.): founder of Buddhist logic
Dogen (1200–1253): founder of Soto school of Zen in Japan
Kumarajiva: central Asian scholar famous as elegant translator of Mahayana sutras into Chinese
Milarepa: beloved Tibetan Buddhist poet
Nagarjuna (250–350 C.E.): founder of Madhyamaka school
Shinran (1173–1262): founder of Shin school of Pure Land in Japan
Tsong kha pa (1357–1419): systematized Tantric Buddhist thought in Tibet
Vasubandhu (fourth century C.E.): author of treatises of Yogacara school
Xuanzang: Chinese pilgrim who walked to India and then brought back scriptures
Zhiyi (538–597): founder of Tiantai school of Buddhism in China

Characteristic Beliefs

bodhisattva
buddha
buddha-nature
emptiness
decline of the Dharma
dharmadhatu
esoteric
exoteric
merit
rebirth or transmigration
rebirth in the Pure Land
suchness
tathagatagarbha

Essential Creeds or Codes of Conduct

Six perfections: goals of praxis for lay and monastics
Samadhi: trance meditation that produces religious attainment
Merit-making: sacred acts encouraged by the religion
Skillful means: the expediencies that are used to instruct and lead others to understanding

Monastic precepts: rules and restrictions governing behavior of monks and
　　nuns
Lay precepts: rules and restrictions governing behavior of lay believers

Brief Time Line

460–380 B.C.E.	Shakyamuni Buddha lived in India.
first century B.C.E.	Mahayana movement arises; first Mahayana sutras are composed.
first century C.E.	Mahayana Buddhism arrives in China; first Chinese sutra translations are made. Sutras on the Buddha Amitabha/Amitayus begin to appear in India.
second century C.E.	Buddhism is established in Vietnam.
50–250 C.E.	Kushana Kingdom (central and north India, Pakistan, Afghanistan, south Persia, central Asia, and Tarim Basin in northwestern China) uses Mahayana Buddhism as a symbol of translocal unity.
250–450	Middle period of Mahayana sutra composition in India.
364	First catalog of sutras in China, evidence of indigenous sutras already being written in China that claim to have come from India, labeled "forgeries" or "doubtful."
401	Kumarajiva arrives in China from Kuche.
third century	Madhyamaka school of Mahayana Buddhism is established in India.
fourth century	Yogacara school of Mahayana Buddhism is established in India.
fifth century	Mahayana Buddhism is established in Korea.
sixth century	Mahayana Buddhism is established in Japan.
seventh century	Mahayana Buddhism is established in Tibet.

Important Symbols
buddha
Bodhisattva
wheel of transmigration
vajra

Important Rituals
Taking triple refuge in the three jewels
Two stages of ordination
Goma fire ritual

Monastery or temple visits as pilgrimage
Donations by laity to monasteries or temples; donations by monasteries or
    temples to administrative headquarter temples

Glossary

anatman	nonself
bodhi	awakening, enlightenment
Bodhisattva	a seeker of bodhi
buddha	a fully realized or awakened one
cakravartin	religious king/king of religion; one who rules a kingdom or religious community by the authority of his religious virtue
karuna	compassion
nirvana	goal of all Buddhists
original enlightenment	doctrine that religious truth is inherent in all living beings
paramita	perfection, the perfected form of praxis
prajna	spiritual wisdom
puja	offerings or other ritual acts of charity that create punya
punya	virtuous merit
refuge	ritual act of commitment to the Buddhist path
samsara	nonnirvanic realm of transmigration
sattva	all living or sentient beings in all six realms of samsaric existence (hells, hungry ghost, animal, human, asura, heavens)
three jewels	the Buddha (founder and other buddhas as well), Dharma (teachings), Sangha (community)

Sacred Spaces and Times

All monasteries and temples
Sacred mountains in each country
Stupas
Buddha's birthday
Spring and fall equinox
Death anniversaries of founders of lineages and monasteries or temples
Ullambana festival / Obon

Suggestions for Further Reading

Dayal, Har. *The Bodhisattva Doctrine in Buddhist Sanskrit Literature*. Delhi: Motilal Barnarsidass, 1932, numerous reprints.

DeBary, William, ed. *The Buddhist Tradition: India, China, Japan*. New York: Columbia University Press.

Dutt, Nalinaksha. *Mahayana Buddhism.* Delhi: Motilal Barnarsidass, 1978.

Robinson, Richard. *Early Madhyamika in India and China.* New York: Samuel Weiser, 1978.

Williams, Paul. *Mahayana Buddhism: The Doctrinal Foundations.* 2nd ed. London: Routledge, 2008.

DAOISM

Mark Meulenbeld

What is this religion's overriding question?

Daoism revolves around the notion of Dao, literally a "Way,"
or a "Course." It refers to the abstract and impersonal force
that engenders the cosmos and every being in it. The Dao
constitutes a natural order that eternally structures the dynamics of
birth, life, and death. As the universal "Way" of growth, early Daoist
writings emphasize that this natural order is always already present
in every being: our heart "knows" how to beat, and no tree needs to
be told how or when to grow leaves. As one thus need not search for
the Dao outside oneself, one similarly does not require instruction in
religious dogmas or orthodox teachings in order to attain it. Indeed,
Daoist texts are fond of presenting Daoism with the paradox of a
"teaching without words." Some of the most famous stories in
Daoism tell of humble people, such as a kitchen aide or a physically
disabled person, who have found the Dao without the help of teachers, simply by diligent practice.

Language is largely presented as a second order phenomenon: it is
not natural, but imposed externally via social interaction, and it
always carries other people's views of the world. Language, furthermore, has a differential function: it distinguishes, it names, and it
"captures" things in a web of words. In short, a surplus of language
obscures the one source of which we all partake, and which connects
all beings equally: the Dao. Among the great minds of early Daoist

literature, it was the fourth-century B.C.E. author known by the name of Zhuang Zi who attempted to express the vexing burden of language in contrast to the freedom of natural being:

> Once I, Zhuang Zi, dreamt that I was a butterfly, a butterfly fluttering about happily, utterly content, and innocent of knowledge about Zhuang Zi. Yet, suddenly I awoke and started to realize that I still was Zhuang Zi. Now I don't know whether it has been me dreaming that I was a butterfly, or a butterfly dreaming that it was me. Yet there must be a difference—we will call this the "Transformation of Things." (*Zhuang Zi*, 2.8)

As language is thus thought to have its limits for the human being, Daoists have put great emphasis on unlearning: as a product of language, all conventional knowledge is thought to be relative and subjective. Indeed, by forgetting about conventional truths just like Zhuang Zi's butterfly above, Daoists hope to transcend the fissures and entanglements of worldly knowledge and return to the undifferentiated purity of the universal Dao.

This religious ideal of reunion with the Dao could be achieved by what Zhuang Zi calls "transformation" (*hua*). It is impossible to fully understand this concept without taking the notion of cosmogony into account. Daoists imagine all worldly beings—the "Myriad Things"—as the tangible outcome of the cosmogonic process that originally is initiated by the Dao. The *Daode Jing*, the ancient Daoist "Classic of the Way and Its Virtue," offers the following glimpse into cosmogony: "The Dao begets the One; the One begets the Two; the Two beget the Three, and the Three beget the Myriad Things" (*Daode Jing*, 42). While on a most basic level the "Myriad Things" is simply meant as a catchall phrase to include every imaginable being that exists in the world, the term also connotes the more complex concept of differentiation: the distinctions that are made between individual existences, in name as well as in actual matter ("man," "tree," "butterfly," and so on). From the perspective of cosmogony, differentiation is the turning point in the transformative process started by the Dao. In other words, before humans grew into individual existence in this dimension they share with all the other "Myriad Things," they were all connected to a unified dimension *before* differentiation ("the One").

If one were to represent the process of cosmogony with a line that has two poles, then worldly existence would be situated at one end—the pole of being; the other pole would be nonbeing. Somewhere in between being and nonbeing the moment of differentiation would take place. We can mark this line with several crucial stages that together form the transformative process of cosmogony: from (A) the Void of nonbeing, emerges (B) the Dao, which produces (C.1) the singularity of being that is differentiated by (C.2) *yin* and *yang* into (C.3) the tripartite cosmos of heaven, earth, and man.

Stage A, the Void, is permeated with the quiet emptiness of non-being and nonaction. It is from here that (B) the Dao emerges and initiates the process of becoming. The Dao thus causes the fundamental transition from nonbeing to being: it gestates (C.1) the great singularity of Hundun, a primordial soup of creative energies that hustle and bustle within one totality ("the One"). This is a stage of full potential for becoming, because the process of differentiation has not yet drawn the limits of individual existence. But the Dao consists of (C.2) the two cosmic aspects of *yin* and *yang* ("the Two"), and before long, this hodgepodge of swirling energies settles down in a process of (C.3) cosmic differentiation: the bright energies rise up to form heaven (*yang*: male), the turbid energies sink down to form earth (*yin*: female), and in between them the human being is born, thus constituting "the Three." The individual human being has emerged, but the perfect oneness has thereby disappeared. It is a common theme in Daoist poetry to lament the loss of this pure and unified oneness of being.

As the religious ideal of "transformation" entails a reunion with the Dao, and thus a return to the cosmic origin of the Great Void, "transformation" thus looks suspiciously like the final absolution of death. However, the goal to attain reunion with the Dao is not necessarily understood as an ultimate objective that decisively liberates an individual from mortal existence. Although death is indeed also understood as a renewed entrance into the regenerative process that allowed the Dao to produce life, Daoists would rather strive to attain the Dao by repeated practice of self-cultivation: the differentiation caused by cosmogony can be undone within one's own body. Certain of the earliest known Daoist meditative excursions aim at a temporary "re-creative" presence in proximity of the Dao, sharing the Void in which the Dao would grow, so that the practitioner might renew himself or herself. Instead of a final liberation, however, when the meditative journey is completed the Daoist practitioner returns to conventional earthly existence. The concept of "transformation," then, can be applied to the cosmogonic progression from nonbeing to being, but also the other way around, to the regression of an individual being toward the cosmic origin, from which he or she could then re-create himself or herself again.

Moreover, although the earliest Daoist classics are silent on this topic, ritual manuals from later periods show that union with the Dao is also attained during all major Daoist rituals, including those performed on behalf of a community of devotees. Nowadays, the empty Void in which the Dao is thought to emerge, devoid of language and characteristics, is taken literally and transferred onto the Daoist altar: a wooden structure or a scroll painting representing the celestial "Golden Gate" (*Jin Que*) is positioned centrally on the altar. The Golden Gate (embodying a great void) allows access to the cosmic origin, and thus to proximity of the Dao. The union of the Daoist priest with this primal cosmic force lies at the core of Daoist ritual. In order to get there, the Daoist must literally "transform" his or her body (by temporarily abandoning his or her social persona), and meditatively enter the Void. By means of this recreation near the original cosmic center, the Daoist is aligned with the Dao and becomes the central node in the cycle of energies that flows through the "Myriad Things." Subsequently, the community is liberated from stale or stagnant energies, the kind of cosmic hindrances that might otherwise cause drought and disease.

How do we know about this religion? What classics define the norms?

The history of Daoism is complex because it did not originate from a single founder but emerged from a variety of ancient religious practices that each reflected the customs and beliefs of particular local traditions. As such, there has never been any centralized orthodoxy or any dogma that defined the norm or divided hairsplitting fundamentalists. During the classical period of China, a body of writings has come to represent much of what Daoists claim as their own. It cannot be stressed enough that there is no Daoist equivalent of a single authoritative text, such as the Bible. Instead, there are many different texts that all provide different visions on the ineffable reality of the Dao. These texts, although often referred to as the "philosophical" texts of Daoism, were relevant within an intellectual environment that qualifies as "religion" no less than "philosophy" and whose practitioners would moreover engage in physiological practices that aimed at prolonging life.

First and foremost, the text now known predominantly as the *Daode Jing,* the "Classic of the Way and Its Virtue," was originally named after its alleged author, Lao Zi, the "Old Master." Most sources portray Lao Zi as a senior contemporary of the other great sage of ancient China, Kong Zi, better known in the West as "Confucius," and date his life to the sixth century B.C.E. The *Daode Jing* contains attempts to hint at the ineffable reality of the Dao. In terse stanzas it stipulates an awareness of the limits of language, especially for expressing the ultimate truth of the Dao (ch. 1); it argues for the relativity of conventional values (ch. 2) and the natural order that requires no such conventional knowledge (ch. 3); it presents emptiness as an ideal (chs. 4, 5, 11); it directs the gaze of practitioners away from worldly matters (ch. 20); and it attempts to describe the condition that has brought forth all being (ch. 25).

The other classic of Daoism is the collection of myths, short stories, parables, metaphors, and jokes that is named after its main author, Zhuang Zi, "Master Zhuang." Zhuang Zi lived during the fourth century B.C.E. In what is considered by many to be among the greatest works of world literature, the author portrays a variety of characters as spokespersons to elaborate many of the ideas already contained in the Lao Zi's *Daode Jing.* The tone of Zhuang Zi's work is often lighthearted, and he seems to self-consciously present a thoughtful alternative to the formal ritualism of Kong Zi, often putting Daoist words into Kong Zi's mouth. The most accomplished seekers of the Dao in *Zhuang Zi* are persons with deformed physiques, such as cripples, hunchbacks, and those with potbellies. The suggestion made over and over again is that the Dao must not be sought outside one's own body—every body can discover the Dao within oneself.

Indeed, the self was thought to constitute an inner world, a complete universe unto itself. Both Lao Zi and Zhuang Zi place a premium on the practice of "ordering the inner cosmos" with the much broader aim of "ordering the empire." The idea is that only sage persons who know how to make their own bodies cohere with the natural order of the Dao will be able to accomplish order in their empire. In other words, much of the political metaphors in *Daode Jing* or *Zhuang Zi* make sense only if applied to the parallel effect that physical ordering of the self (inner cosmos) has on the greater order in the empire (outer cosmos).

Other Daoist books rely heavily on the above authors. The "Prince of Huainan," *Huainan Zi* (second century B.C.E.), for example, is a testimony of the early spread and popularity of Daoist lore, showing the deep intertwinement of the world of philosophical ideas and the world of religious practice. Later Daoist traditions have produced a tremendous variety of scriptures, ranging from the intricate meditative visualizations of the "Inner Classic of the Yellow Court," *Huangting neijing* (second century C.E.), to the ritual almanacs of the Celestial Master tradition that was founded by Zhang Daoling at the end of the Han dynasty, around the second century C.E. However, the Daoist Canon (*Daozang*, "Repository of the Dao"), compiled around the year 1445 of the Ming dynasty, constitutes the greatest monument of Daoist scriptures. It is in this collection that we find almost fifteen hundred texts on all kinds of topics, from philosophical treatises and exalted hymns to ritual compendia, manuals for curing diseases, biographies, hagiographies, and almanacs for divination.

What is the community of the faithful called? What story explains its traits?

Chinese religions have not shown the same kind of exclusive "faith" in religious denominations that readers with a Western background may be used to. Although many Daoists have at least since the early imperial times publicly defined themselves in distinction from other traditions, at the same time they have almost always been open to interaction with other religions. Early Daoist movements, such as the Celestial Masters, would have rather rejected the popular religious practice of sacrificing offerings of meat to the gods of local village temples than wage wars against the followers of Kong Zi. Later, they would also not be opposed to appropriating certain ideas from Buddhism.

Paradoxically, although much of the rhetoric of post-Han dynasty Daoist movements was directed against the bloody sacrifices of local religious cults, it seems that the Daoist *ecclesia* had taken on the function of the religious specialists of local communities, providing ritual services such as rain prayers, ritual therapies, exorcisms, or local temple ceremonies. Notwithstanding the abstract nature of the Dao, and the proverbial quest to transcend language, the ritual procedures of Daoism were highly lettered and thoroughly bureaucratic. The meditative journeys that brought Daoists in proximity to the Dao were often conceptualized as official visits to the highest celestial authorities. On behalf of their patrons, Daoists would present written requests before the celestial throne. Some have therefore characterized Daoists as "supernatural administrators" of the Chinese people.

In sum, while these ritual professionals clearly considered themselves to be Daoist, the lay members of the communities to which they belonged may have had many religious identities or none at all (while devoutly participating in services to local divinities). It was, and still is, common practice for laypersons to participate in a Daoist ritual one day while visiting a Buddhist temple the next day. It was the ritual attachment of Daoists to nondenominational local communities—negotiating the local cult in the face of the larger celestial empire—that made them into the "custodians" of local religion. Daoists thus had strong ties with their local community, and although they defined themselves as Daoist, they did not intend to convert the members of the village in which they lived. Indeed, during most of its history Daoism had been an esoteric religion, meaning that one had to pass through several stages of initiation that each required strict training and profound familiarity with ritualized procedures. Some episodes of proselytism notwithstanding, the appellation of "Daoist" was reserved only for initiates; only the performance of Daoist services in communal services would ultimately define one as being a Daoist. Such a definition would include reclusive hermits as well as immortal mountain-dwellers, because their hagiographies tell us that they, too, radiated the virtue of the Dao into the communities that surrounded them.

The foremost tradition of Daoism is called *Zheng Yi*, often translated as "Orthodox Unity," or "Authentic Unity." This epithet has become the general appellation for Daoist traditions nowadays. The movement to which it was first applied, the Celestial Masters, is traditionally thought to have been founded by Zhang Daoling during the latter days of the second century C.E. The lineage of the Celestial

Masters has become associated with Mount Longhu in Jiangxi, and although their successive heirs never constituted any central authority, or even any orthodoxy, to receive an ordination certificate from the reigning Celestial Master on Mount Longhu was considered by many to be a prestigious honor. Nowadays, most Daoist lineages recognize Zhang Daoling as their founder, but he plays only a minor role in the daily practice of Daoism.

Inspired largely by the example of the Buddhist *Sangha,* the medieval period witnessed the new phenomena of Daoist monasteries. The tradition that has come to be the predominant school of monastic Daoism is the tradition of Complete Perfection (*Quanzhen*). Although the monks of Complete Perfection were typically associated with the practice of inner alchemy (*neidan*), a type of self-cultivation by meditative alchemical processes, they also engaged in ritual services to lay communities. Moreover, the practice of inner alchemy was a standard aspect of almost all Daoist lineages by the late imperial period, and probably much earlier.

The story that explains an important part of Daoism and its symbolical language is the story of Lao Zi's birth. It narrates how the nameless mother of Lao Zi was pregnant for an unusually long time, namely eighty-one years, and how inside her womb the unborn Lao Zi devoted himself to cultivation of the Dao during all that time. When he was born, he was thus a "transformed" human being of eighty-one years old. His mother called him "Old Child," which is indeed the other way in which the ambiguous name Lao Zi can be translated. She died after she had given birth to him. This story explains the meaning of Daoist cultivation, namely the possibility that one could realize the growth of a perfected self by spiritual exercises within one's body. This perfected self, literally imagined as an embryo that could "transform" into a "Perfected Person" (*zhenren*), could transcend the world and attain union with the Dao. The story posits human life as part of a cyclical process in which death leads to new life. A similar story, that of the primordial being Pan Gu ("Coiled Antiquity"), even states that the entire world is born out of Pan Gu's body. Both stories emphasize the fact that each human body carries an entire universe within—one that can be "realized" or "perfected" through proper cultivation.

What is the way of life of the community of the faithful?
What are the rules of conduct and the rites of passage? What
is the notion of sacred time and space? How does the way of
life embody the story that this religion tells about itself?

Although there is thus no Daoist "community of faithful" that
would parallel the Abrahamic context from which such a notion is
derived, the mere fact that most Daoists lived among the lay members of the communities in which they served as ritual specialists
does imply that they shared some common way of life.

Sacred Time

In this respect the notion of sacred time and space is crucial, as it
is the calendar that dictates the rhythm of the life of the community,
of both Daoists and laypersons. The traditional Chinese calendar is
based on the lunar cycle and as such embodies the same alternation
of *yin* and *yang* that forms the basis of all cosmic processes. On a
small scale, every day is a new cycle of *yin* (night) and *yang* (day).
On a large scale, the year is one long cyclical oscillation between *yin*
(winter) and *yang* (summer), a process that begins anew every year.
Each of these time cycles (day, year) is classified on the basis of the
waxing or waning of yin and *yang,* and thus expresses a particular
modality of cosmic energy. This scheme of cosmic energies has been
worked out in great detail so that every time cycle is subdivided into
multiple energy nodes. Each of the stages represents a type of cosmic
condition that has an impact on earthly life. For example, when the
first thunder sounds during early spring, the myriad creatures are
awakened. Or, the peak of *yin* during winter also marks its decline
because it includes the first beginning of a new cycle of *yang.*
Moments such as these have to be celebrated, propitiated, or otherwise ritually responded to. Thus, the calendar offers many occasions
for Daoists and laypersons to interact by means of ritual activities.

Sacred Space

The space for sacred activities depends on the occasion. Public celebrations that are occasioned by the calendar tend to be celebrated
in the more widely respected temples, whether the temples are Daoist
or devoted to some local divinity. The festivities range from the lunar
New Year or the Festival of Ghost Month on the fifteenth day of the
seventh month to the anniversaries of gods or the temples in which
they reside. Furthermore, in cases where the local populace builds

new temples for their divinities, Daoists are most commonly called upon to consecrate these new buildings with a ritual called "opening the temple doors." However, any space can be transformed into a sacred space, so most minor rituals that are performed for private individuals are performed in the intimacy of the client's home, which is temporarily consecrated, and where a Daoist altar is temporarily set up. The Daoist priest also has an altar at his own home, where he performs small ritual services such as the appeasement of frightened children.

Initiation

Initiation into the ranks of Daoists is complex and takes many years. Those Daoists who live among lay communities have to undergo several stages of initiation, a process that starts when young acolytes accompany their masters on ritual performances. Step-by-step they acquire the necessary knowledge to become priests, starting with the layout of the altar and the most basic rhythms of the gong and drum, and moving on to more complicated melodies, songs, hymns, and ultimately complex ritual sequences. The entire process is rooted in practice, in social interaction, and in the endless repetition of the same procedures. Memorization occurs in the act of participating rather than in a classroom, although monastic training is nowadays more heavily slanted toward classroom learning.

Rules of Conduct

As expressed in Daoist classics such as *Daode Jing* or *Zhuang Zi,* the need for the imposition of rules is precisely the kind of human preoccupation that shows how far a society has deviated from the natural order of the Dao. The *Daode Jing* of Lao Zi states in chapter 18 that only "when the great Way falls into disuse, there will be benevolence and rectitude," thus suggesting that only in a society that is afraid of collapsing is there any need for stipulating detailed moral precepts or legal codes of behavior. Another core Daoist notion, "nonaction," or "nonintervention" (*wuwei*), also seems to imply that Daoists would not issue codified rules to impose on others, nor would they obey such rules. Although these notions are still upheld as religious ideals, in reality, of course, there are certain ways of behavior in Daoism that are associated with taboos.

The earliest regulations of the Daoist *ecclesia* include a text called the *One Hundred and Eighty Precepts*. The gist of these rules is apparently geared toward instilling a sense of responsibility in human beings rather than fear of punishment. For example, precepts state that Daoists should refrain from wantonly felling trees or digging holes in the ground and thereby destroying the earth. Codes such as these are indeed related to the specific Daoist ideal of "non-intervention" in the world, but also correspond with the more general notion that all natural being is sacred: as products of the Dao, trees or pieces of earth should also be treated with respect. Indeed, it still is common for modern people to hire a Daoist for the performance of a ritual to propitiate the spirits of the local soil when a new house is built. Sometimes, indeed, particular sites are subsequently deemed inappropriate for the construction of buildings.

There are strands of Daoism that adhere to a vegetarian diet, especially the monastic traditions. More generally, the majority of Daoists will try to refrain from eating beef because tradition has it that Lao Zi rode an ox to the western lands where he departed from worldly life. Other animals are often associated with dietary taboos as well: the goose (bird of the Daoist immortals), the snake (equated with the majestic dragon), and the turtle (associated with the Black Emperor, ruler of the spirits of the dead). These taboos are more or less flexible. For example, many Daoist monks are required to eat a strictly vegetarian diet only for as long as they reside in the monastery; or, during the two or three days before an important ritual, they do not eat meat for reasons of purity. The decision to adopt a vegetarian diet is also a common phenomenon among laypeople, but usually is not a decision for life or a strict dogma. For example, the fulfillment of a vow to not eat meat for several years is more common than the ideological decision in favor of exclusive vegetarianism for a lifetime.

The Story of Daoism

The story that Daoism tells about itself—Lao Zi's birth as a "transformed" body of cultivation—has been embodied in the most literal sense of that word. The earliest known Daoist community, that of the Celestial Masters, founded a sacred empire on earth that sought to integrate the mortal bodies of its members into the cosmic body of the universe by establishing twenty-four dioceses that were based upon the positions of stellar lodges projected on earth. The members of these dioceses would unite during festivals—a dynamic that integrated the social body in a way similar to the ritual celebrations that bring Daoists together with their respective local communities nowadays. United as one body, they could "transform" toward reunion with the Dao.

What is the worldview of the community, the story that it tells about itself in the context of history, the conception of divinity and the relationship of the divinity (or divinities) to the believers, and its principal ethical teachings? How do women fit into the system in its classical formulation? What are the attitude and behaviors toward persons outside the faith community?

The worldview of the community is based on the concept of *qi*, "pneuma," "breath," or "energy-matter." According to this worldview, *qi* is the constituent element of the universe for living beings as well as inanimate objects. With *qi* originally being produced by the Dao, there is nothing that is not subjected to the laws of that Dao: *yin* and *yang*—the two basic aspects of the Dao—apply to every aspect of the world as humans know it. Those who understand the intricate dynamics of *qi* are capable of making reasonable predictions of all kinds of natural phenomena ranging from atmospheric disturbances to marital relationships. The more accomplished knowers of the laws of *yin* and *yang*, as well as the Five Phases (*Wuxing*), the Eight Trigrams (*Bagua*), the Ten Celestial Stems (*Tiangan*), the Twelve Earthly Branches (*Dizhi*), and so forth, are also capable of manipulating time, space, and ultimately *qi*.

Divinity—if such a term could find a proper equivalent in the Chinese context—is an intricate notion. Whereas Daoists theoretically view the gods worshiped by local communities of laypeople less as "gods" than as coagulations of *qi* that are in need of purification, they still will treat local gods with great respect. In principle, however, Daoists themselves predominantly worship the three abstract and perfectly pure *qi* that the Dao emanates; in practice these three *qi* are represented in personified manifestations of divinity called the Three Pure Ones (*San Qing*). Other divinities worshiped by Daoists include stellar gods.

Chinese theology is largely related to notions of the family. A natural death of old age will allow the soul to be fully absorbed in the ancestral cult that each family maintains, and most deceased family members will gradually fade away into increasing anonymity. But the souls of some family members may not be included in the ancestral cult, namely those who are prematurely deceased in illness, war, or other accidents, as well as those who simply have no offspring. These souls become "orphan souls" (*guhun*) and will roam restlessly in order to find food and lodging. Some become dangerous and start harassing the living so that they need to be given a small shrine. If the shrine becomes associated with miracles, the spirit may receive a larger shrine, and if it is thought to have become very efficacious, a temple may be built to honor the spirit. The local population will offer sacrifices and expect divine retribution in return. Thus a process starts by which an "orphan soul" could ultimately end up as a god. The hagiographies of many of the most famous gods of China include exactly this crucial detail. From a Daoist perspective, such souls can be saved only by including them in the community via ritual festivities and the accompanying rites of purification.

Gender is an issue in social interaction, but not in religious doctrine itself. As far as the sources allow us to look back in time, women have always played a prominent role in Daoism as priestesses no less than as divinities (or, in the Daoist case, as female immortals). Even nowadays the gender of the gods is equally spread between male and female divinities. Nevertheless, in a society that for the last several centuries has divided its gender roles in public offices for men and household tasks for women, the profession of Daoists has come to reflect social standards: to the extent that the performance of ritual services is a social event where priests and local dignitaries interact as official representatives of their community, female presences would lead to somewhat uncomfortable social situations. For that reason, few women are trained as Daoist priests nowadays—at least, outside of monasteries. In monastic settings, this situation is entirely different, and many women have contributed to the revival of monastic Daoism since the 1980s by becoming nuns (*kundao*).

Attitudes toward outsiders are not especially developed in any ideological sense. Some Daoists are secretive about the ritual knowledge they have received from their patriarchs or forefathers and may be reluctant to answer questions about Daoism. While such an attitude helps in the mystification of their own trade, it certainly is equally important as a means of protecting their livelihood as religious professionals. As a general rule, however, outsiders are treated well and without any missionary zeal to convert them.

How does this religion function in the world today? What are its relationships with culture?

The relationships Daoism has had with Chinese culture are as profound as they are elusive. On a public or official level, Daoism was not always very prominent, although the choice to withdraw from public life and pursue cultivation of the Dao was as much an honorable cultural stereotype as was the decision to pursue an official career. Certain areas of Chinese culture were more obviously associated with Daoism than others, especially artistic aspects such as the poetry of the Tang dynasty (618–907) or the landscape painting of the Song (960–127) and Yuan (1271–1368) dynasties. On an ideological level, while the Daoist lore of Lao Zi and Zhuang Zi has appealed to many of the greatest minds throughout Chinese history, the medieval formation of Chan Buddhism (Zen) has structurally taken place within the language and epistemology of Daoism. Furthermore, the new Confucianism of Zhu Xi (1120–1200) and his contemporaries was particularly heavily influenced by Daoist cosmology.

The tight relationship that Daoists have had with the culture of their local communities has allowed them to survive many of the religious persecutions to which various governments have subjected them. By virtue of their interaction with local societies and their local divinities, Daoists have been the keepers of local knowledge. Newly ordained priests receive registers that include the sacred geography of their region, explaining the local history through the eyes of its sacred presences: the "orphan souls" that have become gods, the spirits of mountains and lakes, as well as the legions of divine warriors their lineage has recruited throughout the ages. Because Daoists predominantly lived outside monasteries, woven into the fabric of society, they could easily escape the attention of republicans or revolutionaries who wanted to reeducate or eradicate them.

This local character of Daoism, however, seems to be leading to its gradual disappearance. Wherever the traditional structures of local society are destroyed, such as in modern cities or newly developed areas, Daoists are no longer as prominent as before. Although even in cities that have been completely reinvented, such as Beijing, some people may still visit a Daoist temple to pray for success with their business, most people in the capital would visit the Daoist White Cloud Temple only for tourist purposes—if they have heard of it at all. Certainly, the old neighborhood Daoist is long gone. Although at this point the Daoists in local communities still outnumber monastic Daoists by far, it seems likely that Daoist monasteries will ultimately be the prime social structure where Daoism may survive.

Therefore, the future of Daoism looks somewhat bleak, especially when compared to Buddhism. Throughout East Asia Buddhist organizations have been able to ensure a steady flow of donations that allows them to play an increasingly significant role in modern society. The Buddhist message of salvation certainly sells better than the quiet and noninterventionist strategies Daoism has chosen to integrate the different elements of Chinese society into one body. The local knowledge of Daoists is at this moment relegated to museums, folklorists, and peasants. Modern urbanites could not care less about Daoist warnings that their building has disrupted the local flow of *qi* or other such unscientific observations.

Daoism and its cosmological lore are increasingly claimed by enthusiasts from Western cultures who take it out of their religious context (which they reject as "superstition") and who are not interested in—or simply have no knowledge of—the ritual dimensions that are part and parcel of what it means to be Daoist.

At a Glance

Classic Texts

Daode Jing ("Classic of the Way and Its Virtue"): originally named after its putative author Lao Zi ("Old Master" or "Old Child"), who may have lived around the sixth century B.C.E. Considered to be the foundational text of Daoism.

Huainan Zi ("Prince of Huainan"): encyclopedic work compiled in the second century B.C.E.

Huangting Neijing ("Inner Scripture of the Yellow Court"): poetic visions of the inner landscape from the second century C.E.

Laojun shuo Yibaibashi jie ("The One-hundred-and-eighty Precepts Propounded by the Old Ruler"): admonitions and precepts from the early Celestial Masters, second to third century C.E.

Zhuang Zi ("Master Zhuang"): book named after the author of its oldest chapters, roughly fourth century B.C.E.

Important Figures

Kong Zi ("Confucius"): eminent transmitter of the Way of the Ancient Kings. He is said to have asked Lao Zi for instruction about ritual matters

Lao Zi ("Old Master" or "Old Child"): alleged founder of Daoism. He dictated his insights to a disciple who wrote them down in five thousand words as the *Daode Jing*. Lao Zi was later regarded as the primordial cosmic being, deified, and venerated as "Most High Old Ruler" (*Taishang Laojun*).

Zhang Daoling: legendary founder of the Way of the Celestial Masters (*Tianshi Dao*). He had a covenant with the "Most High Old Ruler" (the deified Lao Zi) to liberate humans from demonic infiltrations.

Zhuang Zi ("Master Zhuang") or Zhuang Zhou: interpreter of the Way of Lao Zi during the period of the Warring States. His book stands as one of the greatest literary and philosophical works of China and has remained popular until the present day.

Characteristic Beliefs

Oneness (*yi*): the idea that all being is related through the wellspring of existence called Dao

Transformation (*hua*): alignment with the natural oscillation between *yin* and *yang* that can be emulated through Daoist techniques of cultivation

Return (*fan*, or "regression"): the abandonment of worldly existence and return to original oneness via transformation

Brief Time Line

Spring and Autumn	770–476 B.C.E.	(Kong Zi and Lao Zi)
Warring States	475–221 B.C.E.	(Zhuang Zi)
Han	202 B.C.E.–220 C.E.	(Huainan Zi and *Huangting Jing*)
Ming	1368–1644	(printing of *Daozang* in 1445)

Important Symbols

Taiji (the "Great Ultimate"): term used to refer to the symbol of *yin* and *yang*

hulu ("gourd," "calabash"): symbol of an embryo-like object containing the universe

Kunlun: name of the mythical mountain of transcendence, dwelling of immortals

Glossary

guhun ("orphan soul")	spirit of the unquiet dead
Hundun ("Hodgepodge")	onomatopoeia denoting the "primordial soup" of pure and unified potential
Jin Que ("Golden Gate")	portal that grants access to the Great Void

248

neidan ("inner alchemy")	meditative procedures to transform the self by alchemy
qi ("breath," "pneuma," "energy-matter")	term used for the stuff of which the universe is built
yang	the male aspect of the cosmos; also: sun, south, summer, fire, One
yin	the female aspect; also: moon, north, winter, water, Two

Suggestions for Further Reading

Bokenkamp, Stephen. *Early Daoist Scriptures*. Berkeley: University of California Press, 1997.

Kaltenmark, Max. *Lao Tzu and Taoism*. Stanford: Stanford University Press, 1969.

Schipper, Kristofer. *The Taoist Body*. Berkeley: University of California Press, 1993.

CONFUCIANISM

Mark A. Csikszentmihalyi

What is Confucianism's overriding question?

Like many ostensible founders of world religions, the fifth-century teacher and ritual expert Confucius (Chinese: *Kongzi*) may be described as a lens through which a variety of ancient texts and practices were focused and projected out into future traditions. As an editor and interpreter of the archaic order of the Zhou period (beginning in the twelfth century B.C.E.), he revised and reoriented ideas about political legitimacy and social hierarchy to make them relevant to a process of individual moral self-cultivation. Confucius's status in Chinese culture was such that later generations idealized him as exemplary in multiple areas of endeavor—for example, as a statesman, a scholar, and an educator. These ideal images are central to the set of distinct but linked traditions that are called "Confucianism," which share the view that the best performance in a particular area of endeavor is dependent on the cultivation of individual dispositions in the manner of Confucius. Whereas these traditions might be seen to have a slightly different chief concern, each in its own way is concerned with identifying the process by which those dispositions should best be nurtured.

How do we know about this religion? What classics define its norms?

Through a combination of archaeological excavations and a process of continuous textual transmission, a wealth of texts and material culture is available to historians of Confucianism. Since different varieties of Confucianism still thrive in China and especially in the Chinese diaspora, contemporary Confucian ceremonies and teaching may also be experienced firsthand. Modern students of the tradition share with their traditional counterparts a strong emphasis on learning the classical canon, in part according to rules in the canon itself.

The earliest surviving written records composed prior to the time of Confucius were divination records on "oracle bones" (cattle scapulae and tortoise plastrons), commemorative inscriptions on bronze sumptuary vessels, and poems and speeches that appear in the two collections that were canonical for Confucius: the *Classic of Odes* (Chinese: *Shijing*) and *Book of Documents* (Chinese: *Shujing*). From these records, we may recover several key features of religion in China before Confucius.

The oracle bones recorded the ruler's tentative actions, which were accepted or rejected by the "highest ancestors" (Chinese: *Shangdi*) through cracks that developed when the oracle bones were subjected to heat. The idea that a ruler's actions were subject to the response of deceased clan ancestors indicates the way that early religious practice was based on maintaining communication between the living and the dead. It also demonstrates how the clan-based social organization of ancient China provided the structure for ancient Chinese religion—there was no independent religious caste or clergy. This means of communication was certainly complemented by sacrifice to the ancestors, something that is explicit in the earliest written records and in historical references to the early period. Generally, scholars have argued that these records show that humans stood in relation to the ancestors in a *do ut des* relationship, while at the same time the former were anxious lest the exchange at the foundation of that relationship be jeopardized by the sometimes capricious actions of the latter. These early records testify to a developed system of ancestor worship that reinforced the value of intergenerational family loyalty. These records for the most part date to the Shang dynasty, prior to the twelfth century B.C.E.

Bronze vessel inscriptions reinforced alliances between the rulers of the subsequent period, the Zhou period, and their vassals, and commemorated events in the lives of the aristocracy. With their highly formulaic language, the inscriptions appear on elaborately decorated food and liquor containers suitable for sacrificial offerings, the sizes and shapes of which exactly reflected the social rank of the subject of the inscription. The content of the vessels point to an elaborate ceremonial context for their presentation, and later records reveal the Zhou ritual system was complex and all-encompassing. Just as in the case of the oracle bones, social and political hierarchies largely overlapped the religious hierarchy, with the ruler occupying the apex of the ritual order. Yet Zhou period records also indicate a world where sacrifice was carried out by private individuals and freelance diviners using oracle bones and also yarrow stalks. They continue the ancestral focus of the Shang ritual system, but reveal new objects of sacrifice, such as sets of astral deities. Other late Zhou texts indicate a rich world of deities and semidivine beings, from divinized culture heroes to animistic spirits of mountains and rivers. The diversity of the spirit world in the Zhou may not be a change from the Shang picture as much as a result of the survival of a wider variety on nonelite artifacts, but it is safe to say that in the Zhou period from circa 1100 almost through 200 B.C.E., Chinese religion was characterized by a complex sacrificial culture that centered on maintaining the mutually beneficial relationship between individuals or societies and a diverse and populous spirit world.

The centralization of the Zhou in the twelfth century B.C.E. was of profound importance to the development of later religious traditions not just because of value placed on the social institutions the Zhou created, but also because of the importance of its central political narrative. Drawing on the examples of the legendary sage kings Yao, Shun, and Cheng Tang, the founders of the Zhou laid claim to the moral authority of the culture heroes of the past. The moral quality that led to endorsement by the ultimate authority of the corporeal Highest Ancestors (Chinese: *Shangdi*) and the derived abstraction of the heavens or "heaven" (Chinese: *tian*) was the pivot that united politics and cosmology. Epic retellings of successful military conquest centered on the way that heaven conferred the Allotment of Heaven (Chinese: *tianming*) on the founders, and it was these tales that became the authorizing mythology of the Zhou ruling clan.

By extension, the sacred authority of the founders inhered in the body of texts and practices that they were credited with creating. There have been a number of different formulations of the "Confucian canon," but perhaps the most influential one was the

Five Classics (Chinese: *Wujing*). The *Five Classics* are bound by their putative connection to Confucius, but were the object of Confucius's attention because of their status as a repository of the practices of the Zhou. One saying attributed to Confucius in the *Analects* (Chinese: *Lunyu*) describes his goal in serving a ruler that even some of his disciples disdained: "If he were to employ me, could I not perhaps create a Zhou in the East?" (17.5). In addition to the *Odes* and *Documents* mentioned above, the *Five Classics* include the *Classic of Changes* (Chinese: *Yijing*), *Spring and Autumn* (Chinese: *Chunqiu*), and the *Records of Rites* (Chinese: *Liji*). There is a long tradition of connecting the classics to Confucius either as author or as editor, although in truth his connection to most of these works is probably much less direct than most of these works has traditionally been thought.

Although the *Five Classics* have diverse origins, both generically and temporally, they were placed on equal footing during the Han dynasty in the period from 136 to 51 B.C.E. when they became the basis for the civil service curriculum, and government posts were established in interpretation of each one. The classics, and, increasingly, their attached commentaries, became the key to a career in official service, to knowledge of and commitment to the programs associated with Confucius, and to achieving the highest levels of erudition prized by noble society.

An alternative formulation of the canon for understanding the patterns of human society was the work of the Song dynasty synthesizer Zhu Xi (1130–1200), whose *Four Books* (Chinese: *Sishu*) combined two chapters of the *Records of Rites* with the late Zhou period *Analects* and the *Mencius* (Chinese: *Mengzi*), a text that recorded the teachings of a third-century B.C.E. follower of Confucius. With the arrival of Buddhism in China and the development of organized Daoism in the first centuries C.E., alternative models of personal spiritual development and interaction with the spirit world became available and economically viable. Within Confucian traditions, the goal of personal moral development vied with raw careerism as a motive for studying the canon. In response to these developments, the Confucian revival of the Tang (619–907 C.E.) and Song (960–1127 C.E.) dynasties was, on the part of many, an attempt to restore a measure of authentic commitment to the cultivation of virtues as outlined in earlier self-cultivation programs. Yet this revised

Confucianism, with its central concern with metaphysical dualism and the recovery of original nature, also owed quite a bit to Buddhist influence. So-called neo-Confucians like Zhu took part in a version of "quiet sitting" meditation that resembled that of Chan (Japanese, Zen) Buddhism. Both the *Five Classics* and *Four Books* were originally organized as curricula, necessary but not sufficient for mastery of particular Confucian disciplines and ultimately the key to a type of social ordination on the part of Confucius's followers.

What is the community of the faithful called? What story explains its traits?

The several traditions known as "Confucianism" each have their own set of core tenets and ground their practices in different narratives. Despite their diversity, these traditions have shared views such as a theory of history based on a particular model of familial and social relations, an ethic of stewardship, a view of archaic ritual practice, and the importance of a set of texts and interpretations that form the curriculum of the civil service examinations. In addition, the goal of personal moral development through a program of self-cultivation is at the heart of the personal practices of members of the Confucian community.

In the late Zhou period, the training received by the community that grew around the itinerant ritual expert and royal adviser named Confucius had both ethical and political concerns. The first goal of his teaching program, facility in ethical self-cultivation practice, was geared to developing a set of personal dispositions that were useful to students of different backgrounds in acquiring positions as officers of noble families. The second goal, familiarity with the political methods associated with the sage kings of the past, was valuable in that mastery of their rituals and methods had a legitimizing effect for the regional kings who were Confucius's patrons.

Early narratives about Confucius center on his relationship to the cultural forms instituted at the founding of the Zhou dynasty some five centuries prior to his birth. The *Analects* (*Lunyu*) depicts Confucius both teaching and conducting the rites in the same manner that he believed they had been conducted in antiquity. He stressed the knowledge contained in them, and also their ability to transform character. The rites and music of the past were preserved, but their performance was now justified in terms of their effect on the practitioner. Michael Nylan has written that "study of the musical odes, therefore, was credited with power to raise humans to loftier aspirations" (100), a reference to the cornerstone element of the *Classic of Odes*. Expertise in the classics made one a "Classicist" (Chinese: *Ru*), and beginning in the Han dynasty also made one employable by the state. Stories about the classical expertise of Confucius and his academic teaching provided narratives for later Confucians. The *Analects* tells us that one of the goals of the *Odes* is "acquiring wide knowledge of the names of birds, beasts, plants and trees" (17.9), and in many ways the *Five Classics* were seen as playing the same role for later Confucians. The status of classicist exegetes varied over the two thousand years of the imperial state, but the valuation of their expertise was often tied closely to the status of Confucius.

At times, the story of Confucius was altered to emphasize the political aspect of Confucius's life. Early narratives tell of his frustration with the feudal lords who employed him and chronicle his principled self-exile from a lengthening list of states because of the shortsightedness of their rulers. Two examples of the way in which classical knowledge often had political application are medieval readings of the *Spring and Autumn* and the application of the classics to the interpretation of portents.

One narrative about the political Confucius, in a terse account of the composition of the classic *Spring and Autumn,* finds its earliest expression in a late-fourth-century B.C.E. *Mencius*. It relates the composition to Confucius's intention to preserve his plan for governing China through the writing of the terse chronicle: "Kongzi was worried, and wrote the *Spring and Autumn*. The writing of history is a matter for the Son of Heaven, and so Kongzi said: 'Those who understand me will do so on account of the *Spring* and *Autumn,* and those who blame me will also do so on account of the *Spring and Autumn*'" (3B9). In effect, Confucius is portrayed as consciously usurping the prerogative of a king, for which he predicted he would receive both praise and blame. It was only a matter of centuries until Confucius was regularly thought of as someone who had the moral qualities that would have allowed him to receive the Allotment of Heaven, but instead he had been born into the wrong age. In the Han dynasty, the *Gongyang Commentary* to the *Spring and Autumn* explained that differences in writing styles of different sections of

Kongzi's chronicle were a function of their distance in time from him. These styles marked events as arising from the "Three Ages" (Chinese: *sanshi*) of the "seen," "heard," and "transmitted" information. This scheme promises classical scholars a means to recover value judgments embedded in the narrative and decode the hidden plan for governance. He Xiu (129–182 C.E.) developed this view of history that grew out of the *Gongyang Commentary*'s interpretation of the *Spring and Autumn Annals* into a comprehensive moral-historical theory. This view of Confucius made him into a politically potent icon and was adapted by reformists like the late imperial Confucian Kang Youwei (1858–1927) in an attempt to reinvigorate He Xiu's theory and turn it into a dispensationalist scheme that supported his view that China needed to adopt a constitution.

Another narrative about Confucius combines his knowledge of the classical age of the Zhou with the early imperial cosmological view that certain earthly occurrences are the reflection of heavenly patterns. Such knowledge allowed Confucius to identify precedents that allowed him to "read" strange occurrences in the manner of portents. An example is the story of Confucius's expertise in knowledge of peasant songs in the *Garden of Persuasions* (Chinese: *Shuoyuan*) of 17 B.C.E. When a strange object rammed the boat of King Zhao of Chu, the king consulted Confucius, and Confucius identified it as duckweed fruit. He later explained his knowledge to his disciples in this way: "Once I heard a children's song that went like this: 'Crossing the Yangtze River / the king of Chu found duckweed fruit, / large as a fist, red as the sun, / when cut up and eaten, / it was as sweet as honey.' That was [heaven's] response in the state of Chu." It is through knowledge of the regional songs of children that Confucius is able to identify seemingly anomalous phenomena that were in effect a sort of sign from heaven that recalls the ancient concept of the Allotment of Heaven. This narrative also resonates with a passage from the *Analects* where Confucius's mastery of the *Classic of Odes* leads to a similar kind of interpretive knowledge. When a disciple of his spontaneously matches a passage from the *Classic of Odes* to a problem in the present day, Confucius says: "Only with you may I discuss the *Odes*. If I tell you something about what has happened, then you know what has yet to happen" (1.15). This is one reason those who read auguries and portents in the early empire looked back to Confucius as the founder of their art and medieval classicists spent much of their time combing through classical allusions to identify precedents that allowed them to determine the causation of natural disasters and irregular occurrences.

Because they are usually studied in the context of the modern academy, there is a tendency to read the traditional Confucian Classicist as a university-style teacher, complete with humanistic commitments and a disdain for the powers that be. Although classical learning and exegesis are indeed key to the claim to authority of the Classicists, the application of their expertise had ramifications that stretched from politics to omen interpretation to the explanation of natural phenomena. As a result, the link between government and Confucianism was not simply a question of state support for an orthodox educational approach; it existed on multiple levels and comprised multiple kinds of mutual authorization and support.

What is the way of life of the community of the faithful and its rules of conduct? How does the way of life embody the story that this religion tells about itself?

Confucianism is perhaps simpler to summarize than some other traditions in terms of its normative rules of conduct because the category of *li*—ritual—is at the core of its normative vision of life. The semantic range of the word *li* runs from etiquette to the performance of purification rites and sacrifice, and it also includes the normative quality of "ritual propriety" that Confucius wanted his disciples to learn.

The Zhou religious system, at least as it existed in the imagination of early imperial China, was based on an elaborate regimen of sacrificial observances. Traditionally, the reconstruction of the ritual system of the Zhou dynasty has been accomplished on the basis of three texts: the *Records of Ritual,* the *Rituals of Zhou (Zhouli)*, and the *Ceremonies and Rituals (Yili)*. These works relate how the Zhou state had altars for sacrifice to heaven and earth (Chinese: *tan* and *zhe*), temples for sacrifice to the imperial ancestors (Chinese: *zongmiao*), and platforms for sacrifice to the spirits of the soil and grain (Chinese: *she* and *ji*). There were also altars to the seasons, cold and heat, sun and moon, stars, floods and drought, and the four directions. The *Records of Ritual* also enumerates sacrifices to the "hundred spirits." These are the spirits animating the "mountains and forests, rivers and valleys, rises and hills. They can generate clouds, make the wind and rain, and appear as monstrous beings." Official worship of the spirits (*si*) centered on particular demons and spirits, and was conducted "on behalf of the common people." Confucius carried out many of these same sacrificial practices in the *Analects*.

One ritual text that probably dates to the Han dynasty explains that the ten-day rite of "retreat and abstinence" (Chinese: *zhaijie*) is further divided into two parts. The first seven days of abstaining from music, wine, meat, fish, sex, participation in marriage or funeral rites, and other forms of social interaction are the "dispersing" (Chinese: *sanzhai*), and take place outside the retreat. The last three days are the "arriving" (*zhizhai*), and take place in the retreat itself. Another period source identifies this as a means of "communicating with the spirit intelligences" (*jiao yu shenming*), post-mortem continuations of the ancestors. The *Analects* describes Confucius in these terms: "In periods of purification, he invariably changed to a more austere diet and, when at home, did not sit in his usual place" (10.7), and, "After assisting at a sacrifice... [Confucius] did not keep his portion of the sacrificial meat for more than three days" (10.9). The purification and fasting described in the Zhou records is also something Confucius took part in, and consequently it became a normative practice for later Confucians.

Many early ritual texts describe the proper ritual attitude for the participant as that of fear, awe, and reverence. The attitude of reverence (Chinese: *jing*) is optimal in sacrificial contexts, whereas grief (Chinese: *ai*) is appropriate to funerals (see *Analects* 3.26 and 19.1). This deep degree of reverence in the context of ancestral sacrifice is seen in the description of King Wen of the Zhou in the chapter "Significance of Sacrifice" (*Jiyi*) in the *Records of Ritual*:

> In sacrificing, King Wen served the dead in the same way he served the living. He thought of the dead as if he himself did not wish to live. On the day of remembrance of their deaths, he was sad. When he called to his father using his taboo name, he looked as if he saw him. So loyal was he in sacrifice that he acted as if the offering was an object his parents cared about, so his desire for it made him blush—this was King Wen.

Acting *as if* the ancestors were present, King Wen was establishing a precedent that Confucius and his followers continued. The *Analects* records that "Confucius offered sacrifice to his ancestors as if his ancestral spirits were actually present" (3.12). This is not meant to denigrate traditional explanations of the function of sacrifice or imply that the ancestors were not present. Instead, the point to emphasize is the fear and awe that Confucius felt, in many ways recalling the attitude of King Wen of Zhou. The vocabulary that was used in the Zhou to describe the psychological dimension of ancestral sacrifice was adapted into the Confucian program and was specifically used to describe the state of mind in which ritual had to be performed.

In the *Analects,* sacrificial practice was more than action; it was also about the attitude behind the action. This nuance is clear from a quotation of Confucius in the *Analects*: "What is meant by filial piety today may be called 'being able to nourish.' When it comes to dogs and horses, all of them are able to 'nourish.' If [people] are not reverent, on what basis may we distinguish them?" (2.7). Anyone can feed his or her parents, but authentic filial piety is done with a sense of reverence that distinguishes humans from other animals. The idea is that virtues of character are more important than evaluating actions, and the attitude behind the action is what is telling in terms of those virtues. In fact, *Analects* 3.26 describes Confucius raising the possibility of performing ritual "without reverence," something he condemns. Indeed, the rites themselves, he observed, are often hollowed in a way that makes impossible authentic ritual performance with proper feelings: "When one says, 'The rites this, the rites that...' is it really only a matter of jade and silk?" (17.10). The attitude behind the action was so important that one chapter of the *Records of Ritual* refers to the proper way to rule as being able to exhibit the "three absences" (Chinese: *sanwu*), which are described as: "music absent sound, rites absent the body, and mourning absent garments." Although the idea that the essence of music and ritual can be expressed without any outward forms is not an especially common one in the tradition, it does highlight the sense in which the core of ritual action is the proper attitude of reverence, not the outward form of the practice.

Proper performance of ritual is key to the daily life of a traditional Confucian. At times, this dedication to ritual appears to be constraining. For example, the following dialogue between Confucius and a disciple appears in the *Analects* (12.1):

Yan Yuan once asked about benevolence.
The Master said, "Controlling yourself and returning to *li* [i.e., the rites] constitutes benevolence."
Yan Yuan said, "Allow me to ask for a list."
The Master said, "Do not look at what is contrary to the rites, do not listen to what is contrary to the rites, do not speak what is contrary to the rites, and make no move that is contrary to the rites."
Yan Yuan said, "Although I'm not clever, I will try to apply your words."

The restrictions on anything contrary to the rites Confucius described conjure a picture of an exceptionally strict and disciplined life, and historical descriptions of the childhood education of members of the imperial family to some extent bear this out. At the same time, it is important that the question being asked by Confucius's disciple Yan Yuan is about benevolence. Ritual is not an end in itself; it is always seen as the incubator of the personality traits needed by the ruler, and by extension, by the true gentleman. To paraphrase the *Analects,* ritual is much more than a matter of jade and silk.

The connection between ritual and education is grounded in the life story of Confucius himself. His example in the realm of religious practice and his teaching of the virtues were two aspects of the same enterprise. Just as ritual performance for show was not genuine ritual, Confucius also attacked those disciples who studied "with an eye to an official career" (2.18). His emphasis on the texts and methods of the Zhou period signified a return to a time when the motivation for study was purer: "The Master said, 'Men of antiquity studied to improve themselves; men today study to impress others'" (14.24). In the disciple community itself, Confucius replaced money with ritual exchange, on several occasions asking for sacrificial meat for his teaching. At times, Confucius was even critical of disciples who worked for rich families in such a way that he deemed to be socially destructive. In his criticism of the materialism endemic in his time, Confucius was followed by the most influential later commentator on his writings, the Song exegete Zhu Xi. Zhu established an academy called "White Deer Hollow" (Chinese: *Bailu dong*) where moral instruction, commentary on the classics, and ancestral sacrifice were all part of the curriculum. Zhu Xi was deeply critical of the way study was undertaken in order to attain office and sought to revive the study of the classics in order to "improve oneself."

A constant and deeply felt commitment to ritual and to the study of the classics not only describes the daily life of the traditional Confucian, but also points to the self-discipline that is the key to the formation of virtuous dispositions. Just as heaven recognized the sage kings because of their virtue, so too Confucians more generally sought to demonstrate their dedication to a set of ideals through the performance of service that told about their level of spiritual achievement. Whereas the core of the teachings of Confucius are based on the texts and practices of the Zhou, this fundamental reorientation to facilitate a regimen of self-cultivation is the central way in which Confucius sought to "rewarm old knowledge so as to understand the new, [which is what] allows one to be a teacher of others" (*Analects* 2.11).

At a Glance

Classic Texts

Chan Wing-Tsit. *A Source Book in Chinese Philosophy.* Princeton: Princeton University Press, 1963.

Lau, D. C. *Mencius.* Harmondsworth: Penguin Books, 1970.

———. *The Analects.* Harmondsworth: Penguin Books, 1979.

Legge, James. *The Chinese Classics.* 5 vols. Oxford: Clarendon Press, 1895. Reprint, Hong Kong: Hong Kong University Press, 1970.

Lynn, Richard John. *The Classic of Changes: A New Translation of the I Ching as Interpreted by Wang Bi.* New York: Columbia University Press, 1994.

Waley, Arthur. *The Book of Songs.* London: Allen & Unwin, 1937.

Important Figures

Confucius: Latinization of Kongzi's name

Kang Youwei (1858–1927): Qing dynasty reformer and author of *Confucius as Reformer*

Kongzi (trad. 551–479 B.C.E.: ritual teacher and founder of Confucianism

Mencius: Latinization of Mengzi's name

Mengzi (385–ca. 290 B.C.E.): major Confucian thinker

Shun (trad. ca. 2300 B.C.E.): legendary sage king whose filial behavior caused Yao to tranfer the empire to him over Yao's own son

Yao (trad. ca. 2300 B.C.E.): legendary sage king

Zhu Xi (1130–1200): Song dynasty reinterpreter of the canon and of Confucianism (also romanized as Chu Hsi)

Characteristic Beliefs
de: virtue of a ruler that causes him to receive *tian ming*
li: ritual or ritual propriety, a cardinal disposition that Confucians seek to cultivate
ren: benevolence or humanity, a cardinal disposition Confucians promote
tian ming: Allotment of Heaven, heaven's support for a virtuous ruler

Brief Time Line

ca. 1150 B.C.E.	Zhou Dynasty is founded by Kings Wen and Wu.
ca. 450 B.C.E.	Confucius teaches disciples and advises kings.
ca. 300 B.C.E.	Mencius revises Confucius's message.
124 B.C.E.	Emperor Wu establishes an imperial academy with experts in the *Five Classics*.
ca. 100 B.C.E.	Sima Qian compiles the first biographical treatment of Confucius.
241 C.E.	First sacrifices to Confucius are carried out at the imperial capital.
651	Emperor Taizong of the Tang sponsors the *Corrected Meanings of the Five Classics* (*Wujing zhengyi*).
ca. 1200 C.E.	Zhu Xi establishes the Four Books and produces his own commentaries to the classics.
1897	Kang Youwei publishes *Confucius as a Reformer* (*Kongzi gaizhi kao*), portraying Confucius as a religious founder.

Suggestions for Further Reading
Allan, Sarah. *The Heir and the Sage: Dynastic Legend in Early China.* San Francisco: Chinese Materials Center, 1981.
Berthrong, John H. *Transformations of the Confucian Way.* Boulder, Colo.: Westview Press, 1998.
Csikszentmihalyi, Mark. *Readings in Han Chinese Thought.* Indianapolis: Hackett, 2006.
Fingarette, Herbert. *Confucius: The Secular as Sacred.* New York: Harper & Row, 1972.
Goldin, Paul. *Rituals of the Way: The Philosophy of Xunzi.* Chicago: Open Court, 1999.
Ivanhoe, Philip J. *Confucian Moral Self Cultivation.* Indianapolis: Hackett, 2000.
Nylan, Michael. *The Five "Confucian" Classics.* New Haven: Yale University Press, 2001.
Schwartz, Benjamin. *The World of Thought in Ancient China.* Cambridge: Belknap Press, 1985.
Tu, Wei-ming. *Confucian Thought: Selfhood as Creative Transformation.* Albany: State University of New York Press, 1985.

SHINTO

James L. Ford

A comprehensive survey of the religions of Japan would include Shinto, Buddhism, Daoism, Confucianism, Christianity, and numerous new religions that have sprouted since the nineteenth century. Given the limitations of space, this chapter will focus exclusively on Shinto or what is often, but erroneously, labeled the "indigenous" religion of Japan—erroneous because there is little evidence to suggest that Shinto represents an original, self-contained, and continuous tradition preexisting the influx of Chinese and Buddhist culture. Nevertheless, evidence does suggest that there was a tradition of customs and practices distinguished by devotion to divine beings known as *kami,* reverence for nature, and ritual emphasis on purity and fertility. It is this tradition that we will provisionally label "Shinto." Before addressing the questions at hand, a brief historical overview of Japan will be helpful.

Prominent Eras of Japanese History	
Nara	710–794
Heian	794–1185
Kamakura	1185–1333
Muromachi	1336–1573
Edo	1600–1868
Meiji	1868–1912
Showa	1926–1989

Historical Overview

Prehistory to ninth century. The early inhabitants of the Japanese archipelago migrated from various parts of Asia including Polynesia, the Korean peninsula, mainland China, and parts of Russia. Thus, many of the practices and beliefs that come to be labeled "Shinto" have their origins in cultures beyond the shores of Japan. Archaeological evidence suggests that, over time, these first peoples formed clans around an agrarian lifestyle. The introduction of wet-rice agriculture from the mainland around 300 B.C.E. contributed to a gradual process of urbanization.

The first recorded source we have of these early inhabitants is actually from the Chinese Wei Chronicles, produced by a bureaucrat of the Western Chin dynasty (265–317 C.E.). Based on reports from Chinese emissaries who visited the Japanese islands, it states that Japan was divided into thirty or so political provinces (*kuni*) headed by chieftains, all of whom paid allegiance to Himiko, a female ruler of a kingdom named Yamatai. The people of the land of "Wa," as it is called, lived in grass huts, practiced forms of divination, performed rituals of purity related to death, and were socially stratified. Perhaps as early as the fourth century, but certainly by the sixth, the Yamato clan, which controlled what is now known as the Yamato plains around present-day Nara, attained a position of dominance over competing clans (*uji*). Buddhism, along with many other elements of Chinese culture, was officially introduced from the mainland in the sixth century as well. By the early eighth century, a permanent capital was established in Nara and a Chinese-style administrative structure was fully in place headed by the emperor and an aristocratic court. It is difficult to overstate the attraction to and influence of Chinese culture on the emerging Japanese state. China, with its much longer history of development, was significantly more advanced technologically and culturally in terms of language, political structure, architecture, literature, and so forth. Japanese leaders, in particular, were anxious to import many of these advances and Buddhism became a central conduit.

Medieval Japan (tenth to seventeenth centuries). The power and authority of the imperial family and aristocratic court gradually waned, culminating in the victory of the military elite (*samurai*) in the late twelfth century. At this point (1185), while the capital and emperor remained in Kyoto, the true seat of power moved to Kamakura, just south of present-day Tokyo. During this period, Buddhism essentially assimilated *kami* worship into its system through a process known as the "amalgamation of *kami* and Buddhas" (*shinbutsu shugo*). For example, virtually all Buddhist temples included a Shinto shrine and most well-known *kami* were perceived to be foundational entities or temporary forms of buddhas and bodhisattvas worshiped in India and China. In short, Buddhism and Shinto virtually became a unified system of religion.

Edo period (1600–1868). Military commander (*Shogun*) Tokugawa Ieyasu finally unified the country after a long period of intense internal warfare known as the Warring States period. The regime established its seat of power in Edo (present-day Tokyo), adopted neo-Confucianism as its central ideology, and required all citizens to register at Buddhist temples. Based on fears of foreign and indeed Christian missionary influence, the *Shogun* evicted all foreigners and strictly controlled trade beginning around 1635. Japan remained largely isolated for the next two hundred years. During the latter part of the eighteenth century and the early nineteenth, leading intellectuals such as Motoori Norinaga (1730–1801) and Hirata Atsutane (1776–1843) turned to ancient Japanese literature in search of an authentic Japanese spirit. This led to what became known as the National Learning (*Kokugaku*) movement and demands to separate "Shinto" *kami* worship, the true form of Japanese spirituality, from Buddhist (i.e., "foreign") influence. It is, with the emergence of this movement, that we can truly talk about a self-identified tradition of Shinto that, retroactively, traces its origins to an ancient devotion to *kami*.

Meiji Restoration to World War II (1868–1945). Stimulated by pressure from the Americans, Japan opened its ports for trade to begin an astonishingly swift transition from a feudal society to a powerful and industrialized modern power. The military leader fell from power and imperial authority was ostensibly restored with the help and considerable influence of powerful oligarchs. As we shall see, Shinto became the cornerstone of ideological legitimation for this change in political structure and authority.

World War II to the present. After Japan's defeat, occupying American authorities compelled the emperor to renounce his "divine" status and supervised a process of rewriting the constitution to ensure separation of religion from state authority. Various other political, economic, and social reforms were introduced as well, including a democratically elected legislature (diet).

What is this religion's overriding question? What makes the system self-evidently valid to the community of the faithful?

Shinto has no founder, no sacred canon, no explicit ethical code, no ecclesiastical structure prior to the nineteenth century, and, indeed, no identifying name as a religious tradition until, at the earliest, Buddhism was transmitted from the Korean peninsula in the mid-sixth century C.E. *Shinto*, made up of two Chinese/Japanese characters for *kami/spirit* and *path/way*, is generally rendered in English as "the way of the *kami*."[1] This mirrors the Chinese conventions for Daoism (the way of the Dao), Buddhism (the way or teachings of the Buddha), and Confucianism (the way or teachings of Confucius). The precise meaning of *kami* is both ambiguous and decidedly malleable over the history of the tradition. The oft-used translation of "god" or "deity" can be somewhat misleading, for it suggests a personified being. There are many such deities within Shinto, to be sure. There were, for example, numerous clan ancestral figures deified as *kami*. However, there are also many features of nature—including auspicious rocks, trees, rivers, the sun, the moon, and even Mount Fuji—that are believed to be endowed with or manifestations of *kami* or a spiritual essence, much like the ancient Roman concept of *numen*.[2] The link between *kami* and nature is particularly instructive for understanding many of the persistent themes in this tradition.

The central question that appears to inform Shinto practice for most of its history is this: how can humans, individually and as a group, maintain and foster a relationship with these mysterious forces (*kami*), particularly as they are manifest in nature, to yield prosperity, fecundity, and social harmony? Thus, the emphasis in this tradition is clearly on what are often labeled "this-worldly" benefits and not so much on "otherworldly" issues of afterlife and salvation, for example. The self-evidence of the tradition is to be found less in sacred texts or doctrinal claims, but rather in the traditions and practices that are perceived to be efficacious in securing the various "this-worldly" benefits sought (e.g., fertile crops, infrequent natural disasters, fertility, and communal harmony).

How do we know about this religion? What classics define the norms?

As noted above, Shinto claims no sacred canon. However, several texts are mythologically and ritually important in defining the parameters of the tradition. The most oft-cited texts are the *Kojiki* (712 C.E.) and the *Nihon shoki* (720 C.E.; also known as the *Nihongi*), early chronicles sponsored by the reigning emperors to record the origins of Japan and trace the imperial line. These are not sacred texts in the sense that they are regularly studied, recited, or ritually enacted. Indeed, they are perhaps most significant within the history of Japan for their role in legitimating the political authority of the emperor. When read with a critical eye, however, they offer a glimpse into beliefs about *kami* and related ritual protocol during the seventh and eighth centuries. As in many premodern cultures, the distinction between religion and politics is virtually nonexistent.

Although these texts are often paired together, they differ in emphasis. The *Kojiki* (*Records of Ancient Matters*) provides a rich description of the mythical origins of Japan up to the imperial rulers of the sixth century. The *Nihon shoki* (*Chronicles of Japan*), a bit more elaborate and detailed in its presentation, also begins with a section on the "age of the *kami*," and goes on to trace the imperial line and exploits from the sixth century up to the date of its writing (720).

Read in totality, a number of important themes emerge that can be illustrated by highlighting scenes from the creation narrative. Both texts describe gods residing in the high plain of heaven above an ill-formed watery mass. A pair of deities, Izanagi (male) and Izanami (female), are instructed by their divine elders to create a land below, which they do by stirring a heavenly jeweled spear in the briny liquid. Islands form and the pair descend, erecting a heavenly pillar and a spacious palace. Through the process of procreation, these two beget other islands and gods. Eventually, Izanami is severely burned and dies giving birth to the god of fire. Izanagi makes a valiant attempt to save her from the underworld of the dead, but he is too late because she has already consumed food in the polluted realm. He flees to the earthly surface whereupon he quickly purifies himself in the sacred ocean. In the process, he creates another generation of gods. Cleansing his left eye, for example, he creates the critically important sun goddess Amaterasu. Washing his right eye produces the moon god Tsukiyomi. From his nostrils comes the god of wind, Susano-o, and so forth. Amaterasu's descendants eventually give birth to the first emperor of Japan, Jimmu.

First among the important themes evident in this summary is the fact that the Japanese archipelago is of divine origin. It was created by the gods and inhabited by an assortment of spiritual beings. Second, the imperial line traces its lineage directly to the goddess Amaterasu. Indeed, we can surmise that one major purpose of this account was to sanction the divine origin of emperors and empresses whose reigns are listed in the rest of each text. Third, the theme of pollution related to death, and the necessity for purification, is also illustrated in this account. Finally, the proliferation of *kami* populating the land speaks to the close, almost symbiotic relationship between the sacred and profane realms. This also relates to the Japanese veneration of and often overlooked fear of nature.

Another significant textual resource for knowledge of ritual practices within the early tradition is a tenth-century (927 C.E.) collection known as the *Codes of the Engi Era* (*Engishiki*). This text, portions of which derived from a previously existing oral tradition, details a set of laws and procedures governing various government departments and ministries. The first ten volumes of the fifty-volume collection deal specifically with the Council of *Kami* Affairs (*Jingikan*) and provide detailed descriptions of calendrical and special rituals, including almost thirty liturgies or *norito* prayers recited by priests on various occasions, as well as a list of more than six thousand shrines identified in connection with annual offerings from the court. This text is critically important for understanding the institutional development of early Shinto and the degree to which the tradition had adapted to and even emulated many Buddhist and Chinese precedents.

What is the community of the faithful called? What story explains its traits?

To speak of Shinto as an autonomous tradition with a community of followers who self-identify as "Shintoists" raises immediate issues and should compel us to reflect on presuppositions that may inform the very questions we ask of other religious people. Just as relatively few Chinese, with the exception of religious specialists or members of exclusive sects, would have traditionally identified themselves as

"Daoist," "Confucian," or even "Buddhist," so also few Japanese identify themselves exclusively with Shinto or Buddhism, the predominant religious traditions of Japan, or even with Confucianism or Daoism, two traditions that also contributed to the religious ethos of Japan at different times in history. At various times in their lives, most Japanese participate in all of these traditions in one way or another.

The defining attributes of Shinto, in particular, relate far more to praxis (traditional practice or custom), or a way of life, than to belief. Put simply, to be Japanese is to be Shinto. As asserted in the creation account summarized above, the imperial family and, by extension, the Japanese people are descendants of the *kami*. Metaphorically speaking, it is in their blood—not their minds—to follow the "way of the *kami*." For this reason, Shinto is not and never has been a proselytizing religion. It offers no missionaries seeking to convert others to the tradition.

What is the way of life of the community of the faithful? How does the way of life embody the story that this religion tells about itself?

Several recognized themes characterize the Shinto way of life. The first is *naturalness and simplicity*. On the one hand, nature is inherently good. It should be honored. Sacred sites, the dwelling places of *kami*, are demarcated, revered, and appropriately cared for. On the other hand, nature is untamed and threatening. Efforts are required to control the potentially chaotic forces of nature. Thus, there is within Shinto a perceived and necessary symbiotic relationship between nature and humanity. The ideal is not to pursue a primitive, wholly natural existence. Rather, *human culture*—in the form of ritual practice, architecture, language (e.g., poetry) and so forth—is a necessary and harmonizing ingredient. The ideal balance is particularly evident in the architecture of Shinto shrines, where naturalness and simplicity are the overriding features. At the ancient shrine of Ise, dedicated to the sun goddess Amaterasu, a traditional form of woodworking using only raw Japanese cypress and thatched reed with virtually no man-made nails, hardware, or ornamentation, is maintained to this day.

A second theme relates to *purity and pollution*. There is no concept of sin within Shinto. Ritual purity, however, is critically important.

Impurities and pollution related to death (contact with a corpse), blood (e.g., menstruation), and disease, not uncommon in many premodern cultures, are thought to be an offense to the *kami* and may even result in natural disasters or social calamities such as famine or war. Generally speaking, such pollution, known as *tsumi,* carries no moral connotation and thus does not require repentance. Rather, it necessitates specific purification rites, with water often playing a central role.

Finally, *communal solidarity* is a third prominent theme within Shinto. The earliest clans or tribal groups that inhabited Japan were the fundamental basis of each member's individual identity. Allegiance to a particular *kami,* sometimes a quasi-historical ancestral figure, came to symbolize the group's identity. Thus, ritual practices and beliefs, as well as sacred sites, played a crucial role in defining and authorizing the clan's identity. Over time, the Yamato clan emerged as the dominant group. Not surprisingly, its patron *kami,* the sun goddess Amaterasu, eventually became the ranking deity of the sacred hierarchy. At all levels of society—from the smallest villages and city neighborhoods to the nation as a whole—Shinto beliefs and practices play an important role in nurturing communal solidarity and social harmony.

Another side to this, however, is the role these beliefs and practices play in validating a particular structure of society and legitimating religious and political authority. Shrine priests benefit from the status and income generated by performing sacred rites. The imperial and other aristocratic families certainly profited as inheritors of a sacred lineage. And over time, the subordinate status of women was increasingly legitimated by Shinto norms as it was by all of the religious and cultural traditions in Japan. In short, while communal solidarity and social harmony may be virtues, we should not gloss over the fact that they can often conceal some degree of coercion and subjugation that privilege one segment of society over others.

Primacy of Ritual

Ritual customs and practices constitute the core of the Shinto tradition. It may be helpful to examine the way of life within Shinto through various types of rituals, including rites of passage, calendrical rites, and rites for special circumstances (e.g., healing, purification, and so forth).

For anyone who visits Japan for an extended period, the seemingly unbroken succession of local festivals (*matsuri*) will not go unnoticed. As the saying goes, you can always find a festival *somewhere* in Japan. Today these may be Shinto, Buddhist, or even secular in nature. The oldest of these predate the arrival of Buddhism and pay homage to local *kami*; they petition for good fortune, protection from misfortune, and, in particular, successful harvests. Indeed, within agricultural communities, every phase of growing rice occasions a ritual of blessing or thanksgiving (see *Niiname sai* under "Important Rituals"). A typical Shinto festival, held annually and common to virtually every town, village, and even neighborhood in larger urban settings, centers on the local shrine. A portable shrine (*mikoshi*) is constructed and the local *kami* is paraded around, essentially sanctifying the community for another year. Participants offer (and consume) food and sacred rice wine to the honored *kami*. Such festivals, it should be noted, require considerable planning, resources, and communal cooperation. Thus, in addition to honoring the *kami,* these annual performances play an important role in maintaining social cohesion and nurturing group identity.

In addition to these annual regional festivals are other rites that take place at virtually every Shinto shrine at the same time each year. For example, it is customary for families to visit the local shrine (or a Buddhist temple) during the first three days of the year to make an offering and petition for a healthy and prosperous new year. In mid-November, there is the well-known *Shichigosan*—literally "seven, five, three"—*matsuri,* a rite of passage of sorts. On this occasion, five-year-old boys and seven- and three-year-old girls dress up (girls in traditional kimono) to visit the shrine and pray for a healthy and secure future. Other rites of passage include a birth ritual when an infant is welcomed into the community, a blessing ceremony one hundred days after a child has been born, and, of course, marriage ceremonies. In each case, the shrine priest ritually purifies participants.

Beyond such recognized occasions, many Japanese visit shrines periodically for a variety of personal and spiritual reasons. For example, students may petition for success prior to taking exams, mothers may appeal for a healthy child and safe childbirth, businessmen may pray for a successful commercial venture, or devotees may make an offering of thanksgiving. On such occasions, the ritual is fairly standardized and, once again, reflects the Shinto emphasis on purity and "this-worldly" benefits.

The entrance to all shrines is marked by a *torii* (gate), the recognizable Japanese cultural symbol of two slanting upright poles connected at the top by two crossbars that extend beyond the vertical poles. This gate demarcates the sacred shrine from the profane everyday world. Traditionally, one who is considered unclean—a menstruating woman or someone who has recently experienced a death in the family, for example—should not enter the sacred grounds of the shrine so as not to offend the *kami* within. Before the main hall, the devotee must ritually purify (*oharai*) himself or herself at the purification fountain by washing his or her hands and mouth using the ladles provided. Before the altar, the devotee will clap twice and perhaps even pull on the large rope that rings a gong. This ensures that the *kami* pays attention to the devotee's prayers. After making an offering, usually a few coins, the devotee devoutly offers a prayer in silence and quietly leaves the hall.

There are occasions of more formal worship, led by a priest, such as the *kami's* observance day (i.e., day of descent) or the shrine's founding day. The priest chants prayers that praise the *kami* and make specific reference to the ritual being performed and its purpose. Rich offerings—rice, vegetables, fruit, fish, and salt—are presented, and at the conclusion of the ritual the priest or his attendant serve this sacred feast, along with rice wine, to participants as an act of communion with the *kami*.

Shinto's ritual influence on the broader Japanese culture is evident in a number of ways. For example, the notable importance of cleanliness in Japanese culture, remarked upon often in the diaries of Western missionaries first arriving in the sixteenth century, is no doubt rooted in the Shinto emphasis on purification. The national sport of sumo wrestling, as another example, derives from a Shinto contest honoring the *kami*. The ring is decorated like a shrine; the referee dresses much like a Shinto priest; and the contestants ritually throw salt to purify the ring before a bout. In these and other ways, the themes highlighted above pervade Japanese culture well beyond the parameters of Shinto shrines.

Shinto Ethics

It may strike some readers as unusual that Shinto does not provide a set of ethical guidelines or moral imperatives, as most religions seem to offer. We can say that Shinto generally views the world and humans as inherently good. Benign harmony (*wa*) is inherent in nature and human relationships. Put another way, as Hirata Atsutane asserted, to follow the "way of the *kami*" is good; to deviate, evil. Thus, anything that disrupts the natural harmony—whether it is behavior, desires, emotions, and so forth—is considered bad. Beyond this, Shinto does not offer a list of commandments for one to follow. Here it is important to remember that Shinto has never operated as an isolated tradition but, rather, in concert with the traditions of Buddhism and Confucianism, in particular. These traditions offer extensive ethical constructs that have had considerable influence on Japanese culture (e.g., filial piety, karmic causality, and transmigration). Thus, we should always be mindful of the syncretistic and nonexclusive nature of religious traditions in Japan that has yielded, past and present, a complex, intertraditional web of meaning and action that is quite different from Western monotheistic traditions.

What is the worldview of the community, the story that it tells about itself in the context of history?

As we have seen, Shinto is rooted in practice—not speculation—and a strong affirmation of life and this world. The centrality of Amaterasu, the sun goddess, is emblematic in many ways. The sun is vital to life, (agricultural) fertility, and prosperity—in opposition to death, sterility, and misfortune. It is not surprising, then, that Buddhism, with its stress on the reality of suffering and impermanence, assumed responsibility for all things related to death in Japan. As the popular saying goes, the Japanese are born Shinto and die Buddhists—a reflection of the symbiotic relationship between these two traditions. But this clear distinction between Shinto and Buddhism is a relatively new one; so the story told is highly dependent on *when* it is being told.

To speak of community as in the "Shinto community of believers" is, as we have seen, awkward if not misleading. Generally speaking, one can say that to be Japanese is to be a follower of Shinto. But even this link between Shinto and national identity is a relatively recent phenomenon, first evident in the National Learning (*Kokugaku*) movement of the seventeenth and eighteenth centuries. This movement, led by Motoori Norinaga (1730–1801) and Hirata Atsutane (1776–1843), among others, sought, and presumably found, a pure and golden age of Japan that preceded the influx of "foreign" Chinese and Buddhist influences. Educational emphasis during the Meiji era shifted from the ancient Chinese, particularly neo-Confucian, curriculum to classical Japanese poetry and mythology as found in the *Man'yoshu*, a mid-eighth-century poetry collection, and the ancient texts of the *Kojiki* and the *Nihon shoki*. The leaders of this religio-political movement touted Shinto as the pure, uncontaminated, and "indigenous" religious tradition of Japan. Soon after the restoration of imperial power in 1868, officials initiated a campaign to separate Shinto from Buddhism, which for centuries had become virtually indistinguishable. For a period of time, nationalists incited by government propaganda destroyed many Buddhist temples and treasured artifacts. Shrines were forced to destroy any evidence of Buddhist worship on their grounds and ecclesiastical order was imposed on all shrines. In essence, Shinto became the state religion and an ideological tool to promote the divinity of the emperor and the uniqueness of Japan. In State Shinto, all shrines were declared the property of the state and administered by the restored *Jingikan* (Ministry of *Kami* Affairs), which established a twelve-tiered hierarchy of shrines with Ise, home of Amaterasu, naturally at the top. Moreover, all Japanese citizens were required to register as a member of their local shrine. This nationalization of Shinto culminated in the events leading up to World War II.

The point here is that the story the community tells about itself depends on the historical context in which that story is being told. Prior to the eighteenth century, the story would be almost inseparable from Buddhism. *Kami*, buddhas, and bodhisattvas were part of one divine realm, with elaborate relationships drawn between the two traditions. The nationalistic story noted above has, by and large, been left behind, with the exception of lingering controversies surrounding the Yasukuni Shrine in Tokyo that is devoted to the spirits of the war dead. But the Meiji efforts to separate Buddhism and Shinto have clearly survived. The correspondences between the Shinto *kami* and Buddhist divinities are all but forgotten by most Japanese. So again, we return to the common saying, that the Japanese people are born Shinto and die Buddhist. Both traditions place a heavy emphasis on various "this-worldly" benefits, while issues related to death and the afterlife are left almost exclusively to the purview of Buddhism.

Shinto is rooted, as we noted above, in its emphasis on purity, fertility, and social harmony through ritualized relations with the *kami*.

How does this religion function in the world today?

Subsequent to World War II, under the auspices of the American occupation, a new constitution was drafted that officially separated religion from the state. Shinto continued to be practiced, but emphasis on ancient mythology and the divine origins of the imperial family, elements of State Shinto, clearly waned. Approximately 75 percent of the more than one hundred thousand shrines in Japan today belong to the *Jinja Honcho,* a nonprofit organization based in Tokyo. Most of the remainder are dedicated to the rice deity Inari and are affiliated with Kyoto's Fushimi Inari Shrine. Two institutions, Kokugakuin University in Tokyo and Kogakkan University in Ise, train men and women for priesthood. So despite the general lack of institutional structure and theological consistency for most of the tradition's history, contemporary Shinto is decidedly more coherent.

Scholars now distinguish between three forms of Shinto according to institutional structure and practice. It should be noted that this categorization is based on scholarly observation and analysis, not official distinctions. What all of these forms have in common, however, is a definitive focus on *kami* devotion. The first, "Shrine Shinto," includes forms of practice performed at shrines, both national and local. At various times of the year, pilgrims and devotees visit these in the fashion described above. A second form has come to be known as "Sect Shinto," which includes thirteen recognized sects founded in the late nineteenth and early twentieth centuries that function much like a congregational church or temple. In place of a shrine, there is a congregational meeting hall where members gather on a regular basis and perform rituals unique, in some cases, to the particular sect. For example, certain water purification rites (*misogi*) involving standing under a cold waterfall for an extended time are unique to certain sects. Others practice special forms of faith healing, often centered on the revered founder of the sect. And another sect grew out of a cult devoted almost exclusively to Mount Fuji. Finally, a third category has come to be labeled "Folk Shinto" and tends to be a catchall for a variety of practices that are widespread but may not be officially sanctioned by shrine officials or priests. These include practices—some heavily influenced by

Buddhism, Daoism, and Confucianism—such as divination, shamanic healing, and spirit possession. Often these involve devotion to local village or even household deities.

In conclusion, the meaning of the term *Shinto*, from its mention in the *Kojiki* to State Shinto of the Meiji era, has undergone considerable change over the course of Japan's history. "*Kami* worship" is perhaps the generic meaning that would embrace all of the variations covered. It is only in the last half century that Shinto has developed as a distinct and separate "religious" tradition, separate from Buddhism and free of state political authority. Nevertheless, contemporary Shinto still lacks a clear sense of identity and purpose. With the increasing fragmentation of communities and trends toward individualism, evident in most modern societies, many are concerned that shrines will gradually fade away. It remains to be seen whether Shinto leadership can offer moral guidelines, social reforms, and a coherent theology relevant to the demands of contemporary Japanese society.

At a Glance

Classic Texts

Kojiki (*Records of Ancient Matters*): details the mythological origins of the islands of Japan and traces the imperial lineage up to the sixth century

Man'yoshu: an anthology of almost forty-five hundred poems that offers critical insight into the lived beliefs (perceptions of *kami* and spirits) and ritual activities (ceremonies, divination, spells, and so forth) of the ancient inhabitants of Japan

Nihon shoki (*Chronicles of Japan*, 720 C.E.): covers the "age of the *kami*" and events of the rulers up to the forty-first emperor, Jito (r. 686–697)

Important Figures

Amaterasu: the sun goddess and mythological ancestor of the imperial household

Emperor Jimmu: the mythical founder and first emperor of Japan

Hirata Atsutane (1776–1843): influential *Kokugaku* (National Learning) scholar who played a significant role in popularizing the movement

Motoori Norinaga (1730–1801): leading intellectual in the *Kokugaku* movement of the Edo period

Characteristic Beliefs

Shinto places far more emphasis on practice, as opposed to belief or doctrine. As a result, most Japanese (approximately 85 percent) participate in both Shinto and Buddhist rituals on a regular basis.

Shinto devotion is directed toward *kami,* which includes spiritual realities ranging from animistic forces of nature (sun, moon, wind, and so forth) to clan ancestral deities.

Brief Time Line

652	Official introduction of Buddhism to Japan
645–710	Taika Reform: adoption of Chinese legal and institutional structures in an effort to centralize imperial authority
710	Establishment of the first permanent capital in Nara; the formal transmission of six schools of Buddhism from China soon follow
794	Capital moves to present-day Kyoto; hegemony of Buddhism firmly established
1185	Military dictator (Minamoto Yoritomo) takes power and the seat of government moves to Kamakura
1600	Tokugawa Ieyasu restores peace and stability after a destructive period of warring and civil strife. Neo-Confucianism is adopted as the official ideology of the state.
1868	Meiji Restoration and the adoption of Shinto as the state religion (State Shinto)
1945	End of World War II and beginning of Allied Occupation (1945–52); Shinto disestablished as the official state religion

Important Symbols

Sakaki: a type of flowering evergreen tree or bush that is considered sacred within the Shinto tradition. Sakaki branches are often decorated with paper streamers (*shide*) as offerings to the *kami.*

Shimenawa: a braided rice-straw rope that demarcates the sacred presence of a *kami*

Torii: gate that marks the sacred entrance to a shrine

Important Rituals

En'nichi (occasion varies by shrine): founding day or the day the enshrined kami is believed to have descended

Hatsumiyamode: "first shrine visit" after the birth of a child

Hatsumode (January 1–3): first and most important visit to a shrine by families in order to offer thanksgiving and petition for good fortune in the coming year. At national shrines, such as the Meiji Shrine in Tokyo, an estimated 3.5 million people will visit over three days.

Niiname sai (November): "celebrations of the first taste" or harvest festivals carried out at the imperial palace and shrines throughout the country when new rice is offered to the *kami* in thanksgiving

Setsubun (first day of spring): Literally "season division," this now refers to the day before spring (also known as *Haru matsuri*) when petitions for a successful planting season are offered.

Shichigosan (November 15): "seven-five-three" ritual when children of seven, five, and three years old visit the shrine with their parents

Glossary

jinja	the most general name for shrine
matsuri	annual shrine festival
mikoshi	portable shrine paraded during a festival
misogi	water purification rite
norito	ritual prayers or liturgy
oharai	ritual purification before worshiping the *kami*
shinbutsu shugo	"amalgamation of *kami* and Buddhas"; a process in which Buddhism essentially absorbed *kami* belief into its system by interpreting *kami* as temporary manifestations of Buddhist deities (buddhas and bodhisattvas)
tsumi	state of defilement or impurity generally because of association with death, blood, or disease

Sacred Spaces and Times

Inari Shrine: a Shinto shrine dedicated to the rice god Inari

Ise Shrine: abode of Amaterasu, the sun goddess, which is located on the Ise peninsula

Meiji Shrine: Dedicated to the emperor Meiji, this is the most visited shrine in Japan.

Yasukuni Shrine: Located in Tokyo, this national shrine dedicated to the war dead remains controversial within Japan and among Japan's neighbors because of semiofficial visits by state dignitaries that appear to violate postwar sanctions against state patronization of Shinto.

Suggestions for Further Reading

Aston, W. G. *Nihon shoki: Chronicles of Japan from the Earliest Times to A.D. 697.* Rutland, Vt.: C. E. Tuttle Co., 1972.

Bock, Felicia Gressitt. *Engishiki: Procedures of the Engi Era.* Tokyo: Sophia University, 1970.

Breen, John, and Mark Teeuwen. *Shinto in History: Ways of the Kami.* Honolulu: University of Hawaii Press, 2000.

Chamberlain, Basil Hall. *Kojiki: Records of Ancient Matters.* Rutland, Vt.: C. E. Tuttle Co., 1982.

Ellwood, Robert S. *Introducing Japanese Religion.* New York: Routledge, 2008.

Hardacre, Helen. *Shinto and the State, 1868–1988.* Princeton, N.J.: Princeton University Press, 1989.

Havens, Norman. "Shinto." In *Nanzan Guide to Japanese Religions* (14–37). Edited by Paul L. Swanson and Clark Chilson. Honolulu: University of Hawaii Press, 2006.

Kasulis, Thomas P. *Shinto: The Way Home.* Honolulu: University of Hawaii Press, 2004.

Kuroda, Toshio. "Shinto in the History of Japanese History." *Journal of Japanese Studies* 7, no. 1 (1981): 1–21.

Littleton, C. Scott. *Shinto: Origins, Rituals, Festivals, Spirits, Sacred Places.* New York: Oxford University Press, 2002.

Nelson, John K. *A Year in the Life of a Shinto Shrine.* Seattle: University of Washington Press, 1996.

———. *Enduring Identities: The Guise of Shinto in Contemporary Japan.* Honolulu: University of Hawaii Press, 2000.

Teeuwen, Mark, et al., eds. *Shinto, A Short History.* New York: RoutledgeCurzon, 2003.

INDIGENOUS RELIGIOUS TRADITION

Jualynne E. Dodson and Sonya Maria Johnson

Overriding Understanding(s) about Indigenous Religious Tradition

When most if not all of us consider the word *indigenous,* we normally associate the term with people who occupied a land space before contact with post-Enlightenment Europeans and their influence. Before those encounters, original or autochthonous people were the people of the land. Members of these cultural communities were not native people, primitive people, indigenous people, or any other comparative hierarchal notation; *they were the people of the land.* This means that there continue to be communities throughout the world that are made up of descendants of original human occupants of a land space. Life ways practiced by such descendants living in intimate association with a land space, with one another, and with the universe, while sustaining aspects of their sacred practices through time, might be considered indigenous religions.

However, the fact of European cultural insertion and expansion throughout the globe, coupled with the usurpation and annihilation of several original cultural communities, propositions that there are locations without descendants of the initial inhabitants. Our question is: do the intensive efforts to eradicate cohesive cultural and sacred customs of original people of a land space equal the absence of their sacred practices in contemporary times? Nowhere are the potentials about such continuations more possible than in the Americas, specifically in the Caribbean.

The purpose of this chapter is to explore the reality that despite and because of contact between cultural communities in the Americas, there are sacred cultural practices that were stimulated by the contact. We are interested in those ritual practices that are based upon customs of descendants of autochthonous communities even as they continue today. Our exemplary case is the eastern, Oriente region of Cuba, but in conducting the exploration we wish to avoid, to the best of our abilities, European language significations. This is not easy because Western civilization in the Americas has imposed such terms and concepts as *religion, indigenous, cult, magic, primitive, tribal,* and more on people of the land. The language was inflicted to distinguish these "others" from arriving Europeans and their perceived higher state of evolution. In reality, the inflicted articulations about other communities' traditions merely dismiss core meanings of the sacred and affirm or reaffirm Western civilization's hierarchal definitions.

How do we know about indigenous religious tradition?

Aside from films and other media that ridicule if not demonize original people and their sacred practices, too much of what academic and colloquial arenas claim to know about behavioral activities of these communities has come from outsiders' transporting their conceptual and methodological frameworks into communities presumed to be less "developed." These disclosures of presumed academic credence have produced our contemporary understanding and misunderstanding about original people, not to mention informed a colloquial vision—or we might say "tele-vision"—of distanced understanding about the same. Volumes of ethnographic literature on cultural people of sub-Saharan Africa, India, Pacific Islands, Southeast Asia, Asia, and the Americas have become the basis of what we think we know.

A time-consuming yet not impossible challenge might be to clarify values, beliefs, and ritual practices used by global cultural communities whose origins are intimately embedded within and associated with particular land spaces, and some students of humanity have tried to produce such a compilation. However, human migration—voluntary, semivoluntary, and involuntary—has brought about changes and adaptations. Some changes stem from amalgamations of practices of the people of the land and practices of the newcomers to the site. Most existing attempts at collecting data about first inhabitants' cultural priorities, behavioral patterns, and uses of the land's flora and fauna fall short for no other reason than human migration adds social, political, and cultural dynamics that complicate what were original realities, particularly realities about sacred matters.

We want to expand this whole process further by reviewing the contact of Africans and Indians in Cuba in the sixteenth century. This contact was before Spain had fully colonized Cuba and there were yet remaining autochthonous people on the island. We know that by 1550 nearly all the coherent communities of Cuban Indians had been eliminated but the contact with Africans had already occurred. Therefore, our proposition about indigenous religion is that, based on particular overlapping sacred understandings, the two cultural peoples sharing the Caribbean island land space developed ritual practices that they merged and transmitted to descendants, and aspects of those ritual practices continue as part of contemporary customs. To companion this type of meditation about the development, production, and building of sacred life ways, we suggest a closer consideration of the intersecting cosmic orientations of the Caribbean original people and the African newcomers. Our interest in the Cuban phenomena has heightened as many sacred practices, including cohesive sets of customs distinct to the island, also have migrated to an international presence. Given this contemporary excitement and appeal, we propose to envision at least some contemporary Cuban sacred rituals as indigenous.

Forgotten Indigenous Religious Tradition

Land appears to be a common denominator for sacred practices that have emanated among cultural groups of people who were original inhabitants. The land possesses the bodily remains and spirits of ancestors of a human cultural group. Physical remains of those who have gone before current generations have been interred in the land. The moral authority of a community's traditions is known to dwell with ancestors, and a logical nexus is that the land of ancestors' interment is sacred. Newcomers to the lands of original inhabitant communities must demonstrate a comparable respect for the land in order to be taken seriously or, most important, to be accepted.

Native American cultural communities have identified or reified the concept of indigenousness and protect it as an exclusive conceptual and practical territory for their historical experiences. Appropriately, it does belong to Native American histories, to Australian Aboriginal experiences, and to other First Nation people of the world as well. However, that may not preclude indigenous sacred practices from evolving, within these histories, from specialized contact with newcomers. We suggest that the cultural contact of Native People in Cuba and imported enslaved Africans was just such a specialized encounter that matured to produce at least one set of indigenous sacred practices.

Overlaps in Cosmic Orientation

The eastern region of Oriente, Cuba, known as "land of the dead," was the first landscape of sixteenth-century newcomers to the island. This historical encounter was not merely with Europeans. The meeting also was between enslaved descendants from Africa's west-central Kongo Kingdom ethnic groups and early-sixteenth-century island inhabitants the Taínos of the Arawak family.

The Kongo Kingdom of Bantu families was the largest number of persons from a single ethnic group imported to Cuba between the first decades of the 1500s and the close of the seventeenth century. This Kongo-Cuba relationship was not coincidental, as the Spanish purchased Africans from the Portuguese whose trade had been established with Africa's Kongo people since the mid-fifteenth century (1400s). The Portuguese's human cargo of the period was imported to Cuba as cheap substitute labor for the decimated Indian population and was used for work in copper and other ore mining as well as for the development of small agricultural enterprises.

Initial encounters between Indians and Africans did not resemble that of contact between Europeans and Indians. The two communities of people of color shared oppressive social status and were subjects of the conquering and colonizing Europeans. More important, enslaved Africans found that many of their comprehensions about being human and how to effectively actualize that humanity were shared with remaining Indians they encountered. For example, both Indian and Kongo descendants understood the significance of ancestors, the interconnection of ancestors and the land, and the necessity to revere these ancestors and communicate with spirits; and they both understood that spirits could and did inhabit the world of humans. These commonalities of cosmic orientation became part of the region's spiritual foundation, part of the inhabitants' cultural memory, as the two sixteenth-century cultural groups continued to interact and develop new united ritual activities.

A legendary musical chant is embedded in that memory and continues as part of contemporary religious life in Oriente. It signifies this historical, intercultural, and creative colonial exchange and identifies the sustainability of human intangible cultural traditions. The chant was passed from generation to generation with one component of its lyrics saying, "Indian met African; now the Indian is African." Legends contend further that Indians shared with early Africans the ritual use of tobacco, and Kongo Kingdom descendants introduced Indians to the use of drum rhythms to invoke a spiritual atmosphere. Hence the use of tobacco and Africa-derived drum rhythms, as well as the common cosmic orientation and shared phenomenological principles or rules about spirits, took root in Oriente.

Spiritual affinity, sociopolitical status, and mutually constructed rituals linked the two groups of early-enslaved people. In 1533, the linkage expanded as together Africans and Indians attacked the colonial town of Baracoa. The rebellious act was designed to raid the small town and take food and other consumer resources. Significantly, enslaved Africans had begun arriving in notable numbers only in 1522 and the Baracoa settlement had begun only in 1514. In less than a decade of sharing, the two bonded groups worked sufficiently well together to implement the joint attack. This suggests that the creation of new behavioral forms began immediately and focus on sacred activities was not omitted.

For example, practitioners of Oriente's sacred tradition of Palo Monte Mayombe inherited from these early ancestors the sacred emphasis on those who have died and the emphasis on working with spirits—spirits of the dead, spirits of ancestors, and divine spirits. This sacred priority of spirits became a cultural marker for the region, giving it the identification as "the land of the dead," even though most original Cuban inhabitants and their descendants would not survive as a distinguishable cultural group.

The combination of these early colonial social, political, and cultural circumstances signal an indigenous people of Cuba and their sacred practices as those descended from inhabitants who respectfully joined their behaviors and beings. As the early colonials designed combined sacred ritual behaviors, and used those behavioral patterns to inter their dead, a new indigenous sacred tradition was emerging. The landscape now held the remains of Indians and Africans, and, over generations of new descendants, those so interred became ancestors of and in Cuba, thereby becoming the moral authority for practitioners who continued to practice the sacred tradition. Such is the nature of Palo Monte Mayombe in Oriente.

Way of Life

In Oriente, the early-twentieth-century association with coherent practices that migrated from western Cuba has influenced Palo Monte Mayombe life ways. At the same time, the way of life for practitioners in the east continues to incorporate and reflect behavior patterns inherited from their early colonial ancestors. The tradition is one of Cuba's several *reglas conga,* "rules of conga," and is similarly derived from a region in west-central Africa that was associated with Kongo Kingdom ethnic groups. Linguists have found that much of the ritual language of this tradition in Oriente continues from Kikongo colonial speakers.

Practice of Palo Monte Mayombe emphasizes contact with elements of nature and with spirits as well as with remains of the recently departed. Practitioners refer to the full collectivity of spirits as *muertos,* "the dead," though they distinguish within this larger group *mfundi/nfumbe,* generalized spirits of the dead; *mpongo/npungo,* specialty spirits of nature; and the living dead. The importance of spirits is a signifier for Palo, and most Cubans consider traditions that work with spirits and remains of the dead as being the most complex, the most powerful—and the most effective. Many also acknowledge fear, hesitancy, and respect for Palo Monte Mayombe.

Like their colonial ancestors, today's practitioners understand that spirits are active in humans' material world. There is a reciprocal relationship between spirits and humans; *muertos* can be called on to help humans accomplish goals, and humans are obligated to maintain active communication with spirits. Spirits can contact as well as occupy a human devotee's body in order to transmit knowledge and wisdom to help guide life in the present world. Spirits of all categories have no gender-specific designations and neither are receivers of spirit communications gender specific. Women are eligible and do receive spirit wisdom, just as the female aspect or avatar of spirits can be called upon for assistance.

A fundamental component of Palo Monte Mayombe sacred work is the *nganga*. This is the iron cauldron, usually with three legs, that holds consecrated elements from a variety of land locations of the world. Only initiated practitioners—men and women called *paleros*—can possess this ritual instrument. Cuban legend contends that an enslaved colonial woman, Carlota of Matanzas, was the first woman to possess a *nganga*. She was one of three leaders of the 1844 Triunvirato uprising of enslaved persons in that western region of Cuba.

Family is another fundamental component of the Palo Monte Mayombe lifestyle, and it too is intertwined with sacred understandings. Blood relationships, initiated members of a practicing community, and spirits associated with the tradition are all considered active members of a single practicing "family." *Ñsambe,* "divine Creator," is at the apex or head of all family in the universal world, including the families of human beings. The human mother of a practicing community is the *Yayi*, and her presence is mandatory as a guide for the spiritual affairs of an entire worship community. There also is a human father, the *TaTa Nganga,* with whom the Yayi works. The Yayi is the "confidante" to the TaTa but cannot be his wife. There can be as many Yayi as there are TaTa in a given community.

The *nganga* is the ultimate sacred object that the Yayi and TaTa use to conduct spiritual work, as it contains consecrated objects that possess the sacred essence imparted by the Creator to all created things of the universe. Some objects in the *nganga* also hold the presence of ancestral or other powerful spirits. This means that a four-way collaboration is needed to unite in order to direct and instruct human Palo practitioners toward effective living. This collaboration includes: (1) the two human family leaders, (2) the sacred cauldron instrument, (3) material objects within that *nganga,* and (4) spirits within each of these.

All potential members of Palo Mayombe are required to experience symbolic, spiritual "rebirth through the *nganga*" by way of an *embele*—a scratching rite of initiation. Although the *embele* can be a scarification, usually of the arm, in Oriente the slight body scratches disappear within a week or two. The TaTa and Yayi ritualistically accomplish this event and are then "godparents" to all initiated members of a given community. They also are the leaders to be consulted for assistance in resolving personal as well as spiritual problems, as the tradition understands that everything is spiritual because problems of life are regularly interconnected to spiritual matters.

At a Glance

Brief Time Line

1503	Spanish rulers authorize importation of Africans to replace depleting Native Indian population
1533	Enslaved Native Indians and Africans jointly attack the settlement of Baracoa
1565	Govenor of Santiago de Cuba acknowledges continued harassment by African and Indians living in *palenques* surrounding the capital city

Glossary

palenques   settlements of runaway enslaved workers that were considered liberated or free zone

Suggestions for Further Reading

Harvey, Graham, ed. *Indigenous Religions: A Companion.* London: Cassell, 2000.

Olupona, Jacob K., ed. *Beyond Primitivism: Indigenous Religious Traditions and Modernity.* New York: Routledge, 2004.

Padgett, Doug. "Anthropology of Religion." http://www.indiana.edu/~wan thro/religion.htm. May 1998.

AFRICAN INDIGENOUS RELIGIONS

Jacob Olupona

Arican religious traditions have their roots in a variety of religious practices, beliefs, ideas, and institutions pertaining to the African people. This chapter will present an overview of African indigenous religious traditions and will be concerned with the following issues: religious worldview and cosmology; views about gods, deities, ancestors, and the spirit world; ritual ceremonies and practices; and the relationship between African indigenous religions and the environment. Further, this chapter will examine the sources for understanding African indigenous tradition, including sacred scriptures, myths, songs, proverbs, and so forth, and, finally, will consider the role of African indigenous religions in the contemporary world. Because of their diversity, however, generalizations about traditional African religions are inherently problematic. In an effort to recognize the complexity of these traditions, scholars typically emphasize the common elements found across the continent as well as the unique practices, experiences, and worldviews that characterize ethnic, regional, and national African communities.

Of course, the problem of generalization is not confined to African traditional religions; it also plagues other spiritual and religious traditions across the globe, including Islam, Christianity, Hinduism, and Buddhism. Although "African indigenous religion" refers to the autochthonous traditions of the African people before the advent of Christianity at the time of the early church in the fifth century and Islam in the seventh century, these two world religions have made significant inroads into the religious worldview and practices of the African people to the extent that one might argue that there are uniquely African forms of both these religions. Indigenous African religion has not been—and is not now—static. Migration and conversion to world religions have shaped and altered the beliefs, ideas, and practices of indigenous traditions. For example, it is common to find elements of Islam and Christianity in some of the oldest oral narratives belonging to indigenous traditions such as the Ifa divination texts of the Yoruba people of Nigeria or the scriptures of the Anlo people of Ghana, oral narratives that now constitute indigenous "scriptures" in West Africa. It is also important to note that following the transatlantic slave trade that occurred between the fifteenth and the nineteenth centuries, African religious traditions were carried to the New World. Through this contact with Old World traditions, especially Christianity, new forms of African traditions emerged such as Candomble, an Afro-Brazilian tradition; Santeria, an Afro-Cuban tradition; and Vodou, an Afro-Haitian tradition, as well as other forms in Trinidad and elsewhere. While these traditions continue to flourish in the Americas, their devotees have also developed transnational linkages with African traditions in their places of origin. All these factors help explain the dynamic character of African indigenous traditions today.

How do we know about African indigenous religion?

Principles of African Indigenous Religion

African indigenous traditions exist in multiple forms, reflecting the diversity of the continent: its regions, ethnic groups, cultures, and traditions. Membership in the African indigenous religious communities varies from tradition to tradition and from place to place. It is often assumed that one belongs to the community of the faithful of one's birth, whether Yoruba, Efik, Ibo, Masai, or another. Although a sizable number of Africans have converted to Christianity and Islam, many continue to participate—albeit indirectly—in indigenous traditions when they participate in the life of their clan, family, lineage, and ancestral heritage. The unifying ethos is an affirmation of a temporal, "this-worldly" essence and enjoins a quest for the creative engendering of multiple blessings, particularly children, prosperity, long life, and peaceful coexistence with neighbors and the community. Indigenous African religions emphasize and celebrate the goodness of life and daily living. The focus is communal rather than individual, and although they encourage selfhood, they discourage individualistic behavior. The wants and needs of the individual cannot override the good of the community. African indigenous religions are premised on the human quest for meaningful existence in the world. This is achieved through a relationship to and bonding with both the visible and the invisible world of spirits, ancestors, and gods. The human quest for the manifold blessings is anchored on the maintenance of harmony between the living and the invisible realm. There is an unwritten contract between human beings and the supernatural world in which both are expected to fulfill their obligations to the other. In addition to leading a good life of peaceful coexistence, humans are enjoined to labor for the common good and maintain justice, keep the taboos, respect the ancestors' totemic subjects, and make sacrifices to the spirit world. Though the quest for the afterlife is encouraged, this quest is one for the realm of the ancestors and not for a paradise such as that found in Islam and Christianity and later imposed on the indigenous African worldview. The realm of the ancestors guarantees the continuity of the clan, the lineage, and the ethnic group, and offers protection to the living in exchange for their remembrance through regular festivities and sacrifices.

In the African indigenous religious imagination the three spheres of the cosmos—the sky, the world, and the earth—are linked. Though human activity occurs primarily in the second sphere, it also impinges upon the activities of the gods in the sky and the ancestors who occupy Mother Earth. Human existence in the world assumes a strong relationship with the beings that occupy all three spheres of existence. African religion espouses the existence of various forms and hierarchies of spirits who maintain, through human propitiation, their own identity and concern for the humans in the sphere of the world. It is, therefore, difficult in African religious traditions to separate the visible and the invisible.

Implicit in the cosmology of African indigenous religions are notions of multiple deities that resemble the polytheistic beliefs present in other religious traditions. Yet, within the myriad of deities and spirit forces, there is a strong notion of a supreme god such as is found in monotheistic traditions. The relationship between the many gods and the supreme god varies from place to place and region to region. In some areas, the supreme god is perceived of as the highest and most powerful among the hierarchy of beings. In other places, the supreme god is universally acknowledged as superior but also as of near-equal status with other deities. Indeed, in some traditional communities the supreme god is almost completely extinct and is seen as an import from Christianity and Islam. Although the supreme god is not the object of worship in some places, in others the supreme god shares in the attributes of humans and lesser spirits and may be approached through these figures who are regarded as the supreme god's messengers or subordinates. The manifestation of both monotheistic and polytheistic characteristics in African traditions has made them difficult to classify among other religions that have more distinct labels. Perhaps one could say that monotheism and polytheism, meaningful terms in the history of religions, are totally irrelevant in the African context.

Ancestral tradition is a central feature in African indigenous religions, primarily relating to ritual practices pertaining to the veneration of deceased parents and forebears. The core of ancestral tradition varies widely. Some regard the ancestors as supernatural beings equal if not superior to the gods, deities, and spirits of the African pantheon. As such, they are treated as objects of veneration. For those for whom ancestral tradition relates primarily to the social structure of the lineage, clan, and family, the ancestors are understood as deceased elders whose commemoration is important for human survival. Whichever notion of ancestral tradition we retain, ancestral veneration is linked to the idea of death and immortality in African religion. Ancestors, by virtue of their transition to a new life, occupy a higher realm of existence and are equipped to bestow honor and blessings on the living members of their lineage. As in other aspects of African religion, the relationship between the ancestors and the living is reciprocal. That is, in exchange for the blessings bestowed on the living, the living make ritual sacrifices to the ancestors. Although the spirits and deities are not visible entities, except when they are represented in images found in shrines and temples dedicated to them, ancestors are largely made visible during their annual celebrations.

In the West African Egungun festival, the festival of masks, ancestral spirits are represented in a celebration during which lineages and clans collectively present their deceased ancestors in dance and ritual practice. The masqueraders wear the emblems and symbols of their lineages and parade them around the towns and villages. Ancestral traditions, then, reflect an element of indigenous tradition as "this-worldly," proximate and immanent. The ancestral masks, guided by members of the lineage, are moved through the streets and family houses to exchange greetings with living kith and kin, the wealthy and the peasantry. On these occasions, gifts of food and drink are given to the residents of the ancestral world who reside above. The occasion of the ancestral festival may coincide with the agricultural harvest or with the dry season when the fruits of their annual labor are harvested and blessed by the ancestors in order to sanctify the quest of the living for continuity, prosperity, fertility, and riches. On such occasions the stories of the lineages are recalled and celebrated by members of the group. Thus the recitation of familial songs, the playing of music, and the performance of dance help perpetuate the lineage and its traditions.

The vulnerability of humans in the ancestral world is portrayed in a large number of African proverbs. For example, the Yoruba of Nigeria will describe the visits of the ancestors in physical terms and portray their interaction with the living in a concrete way. One proverb says, "If the land of the ancestors is full of gold and diamonds, they will not return to the human community to solicit gifts." This proverb relates to the reciprocal relationship between the living and their ancestors and also projects a human face onto a spiritual entity. Another proverb enjoins the living, who express weariness over the ancestral masquerade, to exercise patience because the people of the ancestral world are also capable of becoming weary. This proverb confirms that the ancestral world is both human as well as divine.

Gender relations and the role of women in African indigenous religion are germane to the discussion. It has been long assumed that because African societies are patriarchal women play a minimal role in religious tradition. Recent research has proved this assumption untrue. First, in the creation narratives of several communities such as the Dogon, the supreme god is androgynous, whereas other traditions characterize the supreme god as female. Many deities and spirits from a variety of groups are also female. Second, women participate actively in religious practices. Women perform forms of divination such as that of the sixteen cowries, and there are certain sacred societies such as the Sande in Sierra Leone and Liberia that belong to women. There are cults, shrines, and temples that are controlled by priestesses, and women often function as heads of lineages and clans. It is difficult to translate traditional Western feminist concerns about the invisibility of women in religion to the African context. Though African women are subject to oppression, gender dynamics in African religion are more fluid than is the case in many Western traditions.

What is the way of life of the community of the faithful? What are the rules of conduct and the rites of passage? What is the notion of sacred time and space?

The African Religious Worldview

African religion espouses a worldview and cosmology that has been developed and shaped by African environment, geography, culture, and society in general. This religious worldview, pertaining to specific clans and ethnic groups, defines the people's identity and forms the basis of their communal relationship and their ways of life. It circumscribes their ethos, ethical practices, and knowledge of their environment and defines who they are. Indeed, African indigenous religion is so much a way of life that many scholars, most notably anthropologists, argue that it is not a religion per se but an entire worldview that encompasses religion, politics, and economic relations.

Africans place a strong emphasis on the moral and social order, so much so that it is difficult to conceive of transcendence and sacred order that is not anchored in the social and moral formation of the African people. Religion permeates the regular daily affairs and conduct of human society. The guidance of this moral social order as conceptualized by the African people may derive from spirits, gods, and ancestors. In mundane life, this moral social order is maintained through observance of taboos and ritual practices that rulers and custodians of customs, such as kings, chiefs, and priests, carefully guide. Although the objective of religion is the advancement of a peaceful coexistence among people, there is a significant emphasis on the attainment of blessings such as human prosperity, long life, and riches and fertility—both human and agricultural. It is assumed that the world contains both good and evil elements controlled by supernatural forces. Through the agency of humans, however, these elements are regulated and humans are guided as they navigate their cosmos. Thus Africans accept the reality of both natural and supernatural forces. As such, practices such as witchcraft, sorcery, and magic are recognized as important forces that human beings can manipulate to regulate human existence within the moral and social order that the spirits and deities ordain. This is one of the central reasons medicine men and women play a very important role in the maintenance of the social moral order. Because of their training in the healing arts and their deep spiritual experiences and knowledge of tradition, they are qualified to navigate the complex and intricate universe of humankind. Through acts of divination and dreams, diviners and priests are able to decipher hidden secrets and revelations that are ordained by gods and the spirit world. As an Ifa poem says, "What today brings may be different from what yesterday brought." Consequently, the diviner is enjoined to make daily divinatory investigations of events in order to ensure continued peace. This proverb also points to a significant idea in African religion, namely the link between the past, the present, and the future. Even though time is cyclical in the African worldview, there is a temporality that recognizes both the significance of the past as well as the possibilities of the future.

African religious identity is defined according to ethnic, clan, and lineage histories and traditions. Those in the traditional setting—members of specific ethnic, linguistic, and religious groups such as the Yoruba, Ibo, Efik, Buganda, and Mandingo—would be described as belonging to the religious traditions of their people. Because they participate in the rituals and practices of their group, they derive their spiritual sustenance through their relationship to their cosmology and religious expressions. The various cosmogonic narratives describing the origin of the universe also refer to their existence as members of a collective group. The common language spoken by the group provides the bond of unity and their connection to the ancestral and spirit world, which is conceived of as an extension of the temporal human world.

Gods, Spirits, and Deities

African cosmology, the description of the cosmos itself, is described in numerous cosmogonic myths and narratives. Among African ethnic groups, communities present various narratives that

297

are at times mutually exclusive. However, four hierarchies of deities and spirits are present in all cosmogonic myths: gods, spirits, ancestors, and cultural heroes. All these supernatural beings are integrated into narratives that spell out the structure of both the human and the spiritual realms and the place humans occupy in the universe. While the supreme god appears in several stories of many African people, his or her status and gender vary from place to place. In some places, the supreme god is male, in others female, and in yet still others androgynous. While there is no doubt that the advent of Islam and Christianity influenced and hastened African indigenous conceptions of the supreme god, it is also the case that among autochthonous African people, long before the arrival of Christianity and Islam, ample references were made to the supreme god. Robin Horton, for example, in his well-known articles on African conversion, has argued that while the presence of the supreme god in a number of cosmologies was remote and the spirit world guided the daily affairs of humans, conversion to Islam and Christianity spearheaded the elevated status that the supreme god later assumed. The expansion of scale from microcosm to macrocosm introduced by Islam and Christianity brought the once remote—but still present—idea of the supreme god to the fore. God is also often described in anthropomorphic terms and images in language that points to the African physical and social environment.

The world contains both good and bad principles, and their configuration will vary from place to place. The world of the *orisa* is both malevolent and benevolent, depending on the orisa's reactions to certain conditions and situations. Thus the gods serve a dual function as forces that both protect and avenge.

The gods, deities, and spirits, and the myths, legends, and proverbs told about them in African indigenous religion, illuminate a code of conduct that is intended to regulate the activities of individuals and group members and ultimately guarantee peaceful living. Though these moral values and ethical principles do not take the form of canonical injunctions as they do in other world religions, the community takes them very seriously. Indeed, a breach of the rules can lead to disaster and tragedy. Although African religions have a plenitude of deities, many traditions assign responsibility for the propagation of moral and ethical principles to one or two gods or goddesses. For example, for the Igbo of Nigeria, the goddess Ala and the god of thunder and lightning, Amadioha, are the primary deities overseeing the community's moral universe. To offend Ala is to commit a great "sin" against Mother Earth and the collective community. Such an offense may spur the deity to extreme violence manifested as famine, drought, or the inexplicable death of the members of the community. Incest, adultery, and murder are regarded as grave sins against the earth goddess, and if they do occur, special sacrifices are required not only to cleanse the community but also to appease the goddess. African religion is based on communal welfare and the belief that individual actions affect the collective survival of the group. Communal moral values govern the lineages and clans, and individual rights and privileges are restrained, especially when they clash with communal values, obligations, and principles.

As a result, African notions of communal justice and fairness are strong. Certain deities are assigned to oversee the daily conduct of individuals, particularly as it relates to care for the poor, the disabled, children, and widows. In the Yoruba cosmology, Ogun is the god of justice who supervises oath taking, which in turn guarantees fairness, profession of truth, honesty, and good character. To break an oath that has been taken with an iron implement, considered the symbol of Ogun, is to court great disaster. The continued power of this belief is reflected in the refusal of some Yoruba Christians and Muslims to take oaths on iron implements for fear of arousing the displeasure of Ogun.

Rituals and Ceremonial Practices

Ritual and ceremonial practices are the core of African religion. Indeed, to assess and understand African cosmology and beliefs, rituals are the necessary entry point. Rituals entail propitiation, prayer, libations, and formal sacrifices. Sacrifices are the highest form of ritual practice and are always preceded by propitiation, prayer, and libation. There are various forms of rituals in contemporary African practice relating to personal, communal, and group occasions and events.

Sacrifice is essential to African religious practices. Not only does it establish the bond between humans and the gods, but it also highlights the importance of gift-giving in African religious and social life. Various domestic animals, including goats, sheep, cows, roosters, and, in the past, even human beings, are victims of sacrifice. They are ritually killed according to the tastes of the spirits and ancestors being propitiated. The pivotal essence of animal sacrifice is the shedding of the victim's blood, since blood symbolizes life offered in exchange for the gift of life the deity provides the individual and the group. Sacrifices are offered to ensure that the forces of the cosmos are kept in order. The fascinating research of E. E. Evans-Pritchard among the Nuer people of southern Sudan revealed the importance of cattle as objects of sacrifice. For the Nuer people, cattle, regarded as their most highly prized possessions, are the ultimate substitution for human life and possessions. The Nuer regard cattle as very nearly human, so the sacrifice of cattle is akin to human sacrifice. Whereas this example illustrates the importance of pastoralism in African ritual, most African rituals relate to the agricultural life of communities. Planting and harvesting seasons are important occasions for sacrifices to ensure success in the field, including seasonal rainfall. In times of drought and famine, similar sacrifices are made to appease the deities and ancestors and to ensure the continuity of life despite hardships.

Rituals of sacred kingship often relate to the celebration of the communal life as represented by the reigning king or chief. Indeed, in several African communities these sacred kingship festivals have become a form of civil religion, helping to define the identity of the group and unifying what has come to be a pluralistic community. In modern Africa, though many people have converted to Islam and Christianity and, among these converts, many abhor the practice of traditional religion, they nevertheless participate in the rituals of sacred kingship. In this context, kingship rituals represent a sacred canopy under which a diverse group of people with divergent belief systems, including Islam and Christianity, can make a claim to a common source and origin. These festival spectacles are thus not viewed as "pagan" practices but are instead seen as comprising important symbols of group identity.

Among the most celebrated rituals in African indigenous religions are the rites of passage that accompany the life passages from birth to death: naming, puberty, marriage, elderhood, and death. These rituals and ceremonies not only bestow a new status on those who accomplish them; they also ensure smooth transition from one stage of life to the next. In the naming rite, a new child is officially welcomed to the world of the living and severed from its connection with the other world, or the world of the ancestors. This rite ensures that the child is fully accepted into the community of the living and is identified with his or her parents and clan. In West Africa, the naming rite is also an occasion for consulting a diviner who will describe not only the circumstances surrounding the birth but the destiny of the child in its new abode, the world of the living. Name-taking and naming ceremonies are replete with the history and customs of the child's people. From the names given to a child, much can be determined about the circumstances surrounding his or her birth, the lineage, and the family history. For example, among the Yoruba people, children who are born with the umbilical cord tied around their neck, breech births, and twins or children born with locked hair are all given generic names to reflect the personalities and kinds of children. Indeed, in Yoruba society even one and two siblings born after the twins will be given names reflecting their position as members of the twin cult. Taboos and totems that accompany these named individuals mark their bearers out as unique. Prescribed rituals are then performed to guarantee a smooth passage throughout all the stages of life until death. Puberty rites celebrate the coming of age of the child. In several places, these rites mark the beginning of adulthood and its attendant social responsibilities, including, for the Masai and Igbo, joining the warrior class. For girls among the Efik of Nigeria, puberty rites are intended to prepare them for a life of marriage and motherhood. Transition to honored elder status comes after a fairly long period of service to one's community. In places where this rite is practiced, such as among the Owo Yoruba people of Nigeria, the individual celebrates with his peers in what is called the Ero festival, retires from politics, and is regarded as a senior citizen and an elder statesperson. The elder becomes a consultant whose years of wisdom and experience are offered to the youth for the benefit of the community. The last rite of passage, death, marks the transition from the world of the living to the world of the ancestors. The rite not only guarantees this new status but also, in most West African traditions, ensures the possibility of a reincarnation.

African Religion and the Environment

The ways of life of African people are vividly reflected in the religious expressions and practices of the group. These practices situate the African people in their various social and physical environments from which they derive sustenance. People do not have dominion over natural phenomena, but rather are given the courage to live with nature and to treat nature as a living reality with which it is important to maintain a reciprocal relationship. Certain animals such as monkeys, for example, are endowed with human qualities. Religious practices are often ways of sacralizing the environment and negotiating human existence with invisible beings considered greater than the individual or even greater than the group as a whole. African religion functions in ways that enable individuals and group members to cope with the unpredictable forces of life and the taken-for-granted realities of the cosmos. As modes of expression of the sacred, environmental and physical features such as vegetation, forests, the wilderness, hills, mountains, and rivers maintain special relationships with human beings and are considered living subjects akin to humans. Unlike in those cultures and societies where the environment and natural world have lost their sacred qualities, modern Africans continue to imbue their natural world with transcendent and numinous qualities. Not only is the natural world a physical and social space where the gods and ancestors manifest their agency, it is also a hierophany, to use Mircea Eliade's term, by which spirits and invisible beings interpenetrate the world of humans.

In order to maintain a proper relationship with this physical and social environment, Africans must follow established customs and traditions of taboos and prohibitions and abide by ancestral moral codes of conduct. In several African communities, such customs prohibit theft, lying, murder, and incest, and encourage respect for elders, children, ancestors, and the spirit world. The spirit world must also be regularly propitiated to ensure the reciprocal benefits it bestows on the living. Through this relationship, Africans obtain the blessings of long life, material wealth, fertility, and peace. African converts to Christianity and Islam have brought some of these traditional principles to their new faith. In the midst of poverty, churches and mosques continue to beseech poor Africans to donate their final pennies to the collection plate or to give the Muslim *zakat*. The reciprocal relationship between humans and the representatives of the divine continues. However, as an African proverb suggests, if one continues to propitiate a deity without receiving something in return, one is enjoined to set aside the divinity and seek one's salvation elsewhere. This indigenous religious pragmatism penetrates the African sense of life and relationship to the spirit world.

Sources of African Indigenous Religion

African religion is conveyed to us through various sources, primarily oral narratives, visual images, and performance. Oral narratives refer to the numerous genres of sacred stories, proverbs, and legends that describe the activities of the gods, ancestors, and spirits and their relationship with human society. These narratives form the basis for constructing the history of African religion because they are regarded as indications of the truth contained in the tradition. The narratives define the cosmology, the activities of the gods and the ethical beliefs and value systems, and explain the creation of the world. The telling of these narratives also constitutes part of the tradition, as these become the oral scriptures and serve as sources for constructing indigenous theologies. Examples include the Ifa divination practices of the Yoruba people of West Africa, the scripture of the Anlo people of Ghana, and the oral musical narratives of the griots and griottes of Mali, Niger, Senegal, and Gambia. Among these, perhaps the best-studied sources of indigenous religion are the epics and oral narratives that arise from divination processes such as the Ifa among the Yoruba of Nigeria.

The Ifa divination corpus is a large body of poetic oral narratives that diviners memorize and recite during divination sessions. Through a highly complex process of divination, poems taken from the 256 *odu* that contain detailed information relating to the customs, traditions, epistemology, and metaphysics of the West African Yoruba and Fon people are consulted. In recent years, scholars have begun collecting, translating, and interpreting these texts in an effort to address issues surrounding environment, health, and justice, among others. The divination process is a vehicle for revelation, as is the related practice of spirit possession. This mode of revelation differs from divination in that during possession a spirit who claims to convey a message from the spirit realm bodily possesses the priest or priestess. Through the priest or priestess, messages are revealed and interpreted for the client. Revelation through possession is central to the diagnosis of illness and the prescription of the correct ritual sacrifice and medicine for the ailment. While the shamanic pilgrimage and return is uncommon in the African setting, possession remains a significant avenue for revelation.

In addition to oral narratives such as proverbs, legends, myths, and folktales, other forms such as songs, music, and ritual arts such as sculpture, drawings, and paintings are also important sources for learning about these traditions. These verbal and visual materials, including songs, music, and wood and stone sculptures, make references to the African spiritual practices from which Africans derive significant lessons of daily life. The carved images of the ancestors and deities provide symbolic expression of the power of the invisible entities such as deities, spirits, sacred kings, and chiefs, numinous realities that are normally too abstract to grasp without iconographic references. Through the dance and drumming that accompany festivals and ceremonies in honor of the ancestors and deities, and in celebration of the rites of passage of human beings, individuals and the community facilitate contact with the invisible world. On such occasions, it is not uncommon to witness humans' encounters with the divine in mystical contexts such as spirit possession during which visiting spirits manifest their presence by mounting the human hosts and devotees. These are also occasions when powerful messages from the spirit world are conveyed to the living and when answers to difficult questions of existence are sought from the spirit world.

The literature on African indigenous religion is vast. Among these sources are oral and written texts in both European and African languages. African writers such as D. O. Fagunwa, Chinua Achebe, Wole Soyinka, and Ngugi wa Thiongu vividly capture the religious worldview of the African peoples, particularly at the dawn of colonialism. Since African historians began to take oral histories seriously, especially since the pioneering work of Jan Vansina, oral narratives that were once discarded and condemned as worthless by European scholars have gained respectability as valued sources for the construction of the African religious past. In the precolonial period, before the advent of archival sources upon which African historians now base their work, African oral narratives were limited to myths and legends and were of limited use to intellectual historians. For the Yoruba, for example, *itan* means story, legend, history, and folktale, highlighting the importance of these texts in teaching people about their past—a past in which the world of human beings and the world of the gods, deities, and spirits intersect. Archaeological findings shed much light on the religious life and ceremonies of ancient times. In addition, in the contemporary period, when technology has advanced communication, the production of home videos accessible to the general populace has become an important medium for reflecting on African religious culture and worldview. For Africans born in the postcolonial era who are no longer exposed to the traditional practices, video has become a powerful means for exploring the magical and spiritual world of the African past.

How does African indigenous religion function in the world today? What are its relationships with culture?

African indigenous religion has succumbed to significant changes spurred not only by the advent of Christianity and Islam but also by the forces of globalization and influence from Europe and America. However, it has also in its own way resisted change, transforming itself in some places from a primarily ethnic or national faith to a global faith. An excellent example is the global spread of the Yoruba traditions. Further, though many Africans are converting to Islam and Christianity, African indigenous traditions continue to be the primary definers of the African worldview. Thus, the worlds of the spirits, ancestors, and gods, as well as notions of magic, witchcraft, and sorcery, are still much alive in the African society. African indigenous religions have responded both internally and externally to pluralism of belief, so much so that the African identity is best described as a plurality.

The African-derived religions of the New World—Candomble, Vodou, and so forth—continue to shape the religious contours of the Americas. Indeed, some of these traditions are reimagining themselves as world religions and are reconnecting with the traditions of their mother countries. Thus, today these New World traditions are being brought back to Africa through the agency of the devotees in America, Cuba, Brazil, and Haiti who after pilgrimages are returning to the New World to create local shrines and communities like the Oyotunji village in South Carolina and African American Yoruba communities and centers in New York, Los Angeles, Miami, and San Francisco. Indigenous African religious traditions thus continue to influence religious communities across the world, either directly through conversion or indirectly through the power of African modes of music, dance, songs, drama, and literature. Thus, despite the predictions of some scholars of African indigenous religions that with the onset of modernization and globalization indigenous traditions would suffer, we have witnessed a resurgence of traditional practices, some of which can be read as critiques of modernity. For instance, the use of traditional oaths and shrines for secret oath-taking ceremonies, such as the Okija shrine in the eastern part of Nigeria, has reemerged.

There has also been a marked increase in witchcraft accusations, ritual killings, and certain cults. In Cameroon, Nigeria, Tanzania, and South Africa reports on the reemergence of witchcraft have doubled over the past few years. Perhaps unsurprisingly, witchcraft and exorcism have also emerged, especially in Pentecostal charismatic churches and Muslim mosques. The discourse between indigenous religion and Islam and Christianity, between tradition and modernity, continues to be a live dialogue.

Indigenous religious traditions continue to experience intolerance and cultural assault from the monotheistic traditions of Islam and Christianity. Since these two traditions began to exert a significant influence on African culture in the nineteenth century, African religions have never before undergone such violent attack. This development may be traced in part to the growth of evangelical Christianity and radical Islam. The peaceful relations that existed between religions at the time of African independence in the 1960s were partly the result of religious indigenization projects. In preparation for independence, Africans began to take seriously African culture and tradition. On one hand, the African Christian churches encouraged the cultivation of African cultures, arguing that understanding and practicing African culture was essential for the propagation of the Christian gospel. On the other hand, Islam, through African Sufism, promoted indigenized Muslim traditions. Indeed, African cultural traditions properly domesticated both Islam and Christianity. Today, evangelical Pentecostalism and fundamentalist Islam have supported serious clashes with indigenous African traditions and continue to influence the state, which had historically remained neutral on the question of religion. More important, the worldview of the monotheistic traditions runs counter to the traditional African worldview. While the traditional worldview supports a communitarian outlook that emphasizes group solidarity, the emphasis of the new religious movements on personal salvation and their concern for the quest for paradise runs contrary to the traditional ethos. It is not unusual today to witness aggressive assaults during indigenous religious ceremonies in West African cities. Born-again evangelical Christians and radical Muslims are discarding ancestral lineage traditions such as naming practices that bear the hallmark of indigenous tradition. For example, a family name that bears signs of the importance of Ifa tradition, such as *Fayose* ("Ifa is capable of doing it all"), has been changed to a

Christian name, *Oluwayose* ("the Lord is capable of doing it all"). The implication is that markers of lineage identity are exorcised to make room for a new Christian identity. In addition, indigenous religious traditions that have for centuries provided the resources for African popular culture such as singing, drumming, dance, and artistic performances are being rapidly replaced by Christian and Islamic traditions. In the past it was fashionable for the African state to recognize in state functions the African triple heritage of indigenous religion, Christianity, and Islam. For example, during state ceremonies, priests from all three traditions were called upon to provide invocations and benedictions. Today, such activities are often assigned to representatives of Islam and Christianity alone, as the case of Nigeria vividly shows.

In conclusion, although it is difficult to predict the future of African indigenous traditions, one may speculate that they will continue to exist and to influence African culture and society despite the rapid social and religious changes sweeping the continent. But, given the influence and impact of the African diasporic communities and their strong interest in their African cultural heritage, they may continue to play an increasingly important role in renewing and reinvigorating African traditional religion.

At a Glance

Important Figures
Chinua Achebe
Mircea Eliade
D. O. Fagunwa
Wole Soyinka
Ngugi wa Thiongu

Characteristic Beliefs
Monotheism, polytheism, ancestors, deities, Ifa divination, arts, witchcraft, sculpture, music, dance, taboos, totems, spirit possession

Sacred Spaces and Times
Cameroon
Egungun festival
Ero festival
Gambia
Ile-Ife

Mali
Niger
Nigeria
Okija shrine
Osun
Senegal
Sierra Leone
South Africa
Tanzania
Uganda

Suggestions for Further Reading

Abimbola, Wande. *Ifa: An Expositions of Ifa Literary Corpus.* Ibadan: Oxford University Press Nigeria; New York: Oxford University Press, 1976.

Achebe, Chinua. *Things Fall Apart.* London: Heinenmann, 1958.

Bascom, William Russell. *Ifa Divination: Communication between Gods and Men in West Africa.* Bloomington: Indiana University Press, 1991.

Eliade, Mircea. *The Sacred and the Profane.* New York: 1959.

Evans-Pritchard, E. E. *Nuer Religion.* Oxford: Clarendon Press, 1962.

Fagunwa, D. O. *Ogboju Ode Ninu Igbo.* Irunmole, Ibadan: Heinenmann, 1957.

Horton, Robin. "On the Reality of Conversion in Africa." *Africa* 7, no. 2 (1975): 132–64.

Idowu, E. Bolaji. *African Traditional Religion: A Definition.* London: S.C.M. Press, 1973.

Kenyatta, Jomo. *Facing Mount Kenya: The Tribal Life of the Gikuyu.* London: Secker and Warburgh, 1938.

Mbiti, John S. *African Religions and Philosophy.* Portsmouth, N.H.: Heinenmann, 1990.

Olupona, Jacob K., ed. *African Spirituality: Forms, Meanings, and Expressions.* New York: Crossroad, 2000.

———. *Kingship, Religion, and Rituals in a Nigerian Community: A Phenomenological Study of Ondo Yoruba Festivals.* Stockholm, Sweden: Almqvist & Wiksell International, 1991.

Some, Malidoma P. *The Healing Wisdom of Africa.* New York: J. P. Tarcher/Putnam, 1999.

Soyinka, Wole. *Myth, Literature and the African World.* New York: Cambridge University Press, 1978.

Turner, Victor W. *The Ritual Process: Structure and Anti-structure.* Ithaca, N.Y.: Cornell University Press, 1977.

Van Binsbergen, Wim, and Matthew Schoffeleers. *Theoretical Exploration in African Religion.* Berkeley: University of California Press, 1985.

Zuesse, Evan M. *Ritual Cosmos: The Sanctification of Life in African Religions.* Athens: Ohio University Press, 1979.

NEW NINETEENTH-CENTURY AMERICAN RELIGIONS

Danny L. Jorgensen

A huge number and bewildering variety of religious groups existed in the United States by the nineteenth century. Most of them were European imports adapted to the new social and cultural circumstances encountered during the conquest, settlement, and development of the Americas. A few of them originated in the United States as products of the Americanization of European cultures. This chapter focuses attention generally on Christian "Restorationism" (also sometimes called "Primitivism"), a broad-based new religious movement of nineteenth-century America. It is one of the most significant of several prominent variations on the ways in which European religious traditions shaped the American experience and were transformed by it.

Christian Restorationism generally was a negative social reaction to the cultural and religious pluralism of the United States, particularly the perplexing variety of religious options and organizations. Less than six generations earlier many of the Restorationists' Puritan ancestors had found religious refuge in the New World. They envisioned it as the land promised to them by God for the purpose of building the utopian kingdom of God and eventually establishing its sovereignty over the entire earth. Most Americans appreciated the Constitution's guarantee of freedom to practice any religion or none at all. Yet, for the Restorationists and some other Americans, the decision of the republic's founders to prohibit the establishment of an official state religion or religions was not an altogether pleasing compromise to religious pluralism and diversity. The Restorationists yearned for one correct religion, most commonly envisioned as the one true Christian church. Restorationism in one form or another provided the answer for many Americans to the question of how to achieve eternal salvation and its corollary, the one true church—Christianity in pure and original form.

The diffuse American Restorationist movement spawned the Churches of Christ and Christian Church (also known as the Disciples of Christ), as well as the Christadelphians, Jehovah's Witnesses, Seventh-day Adventists, and Latter Day Saints (also known by the nickname "Mormon"; the spelling, *Latter Day Saints,* serves to distinguish between this religion generally and one of its many, albeit the largest and best known, forms). Most of them became substantial religious communities, contributing further to the tremendous diversity of American religion.

The Latter Day Saint religion is one of the largest, most successful, and more exceptional expressions of Restorationism. The Church of Jesus Christ of Latter-day Saints (or LDS), headquartered in Salt Lake City, Utah, is the largest and best-known organization of more than a hundred variations of this religion. It, specifically, will be used here to illustrate exactly how this question about salvation and the proper form of Christianity was resolved and its consequences for the community of believers in the United States and around the world today.

American Religion and Restorationism

Religion was a central matter and the most important feature of culture, society, and identity for European immigrants to the Americas, not just the Puritans. It provided the reasons or justifications for the conquest of the Americas and their native inhabitants, settlement, importation of African slaves, and most all other aspects of the European cultures and societies the European immigrants envisioned, re-created, and enacted in the New World. It provided the model for the normative order and moral values they endeavored to create and reenact. It fostered and supported a more pluralistic, egalitarian, and democratic culture and society, and it eased the transition of successive generations of Europeans to the New World. Religion, even more specifically, assisted them in preserving familiar and socially identifying elements of their ethnic European heritage while adjusting to a new world composed of a multitude of different immigrants. Religion, in short, was the principal ingredient in fashioning a new culture, a new society, a new country, and a comprehensive set of new social institutions as well as new identities as Americans.

The imported European religions were biblical. Protestant Christianity in one form or another predominated in the upper regions of North America. Roman Catholicism prevailed from the lower regions of North America to farther south. In spite of a relatively small Jewish minority, Judaism was recognized and influential, although mostly by way of the Old Testament of the Christian Bible. Russian, Greek, and other ethnic minorities represented Orthodox Christianity regionally (Alaska, California, Florida, and elsewhere). A fundamental commitment to the exclusive legitimacy (or absolute truth) of biblical religion prevented European Americans from acknowledging the religions of Native Americans, Africans (including Islam), or most any other form of religion as authentic until later.

Yet, perhaps ironically, European Americans also imported a wide assortment of magic, folklore, and Western syncreticisms of paganism and Christianity as well as heterodox and syncretic varieties of Christianity. Many colonial Americans, for instance, believed in a vast array of hidden and mysterious entities and forces. They used occult arts like alchemy, astrology, and magic for healing, divination, agriculture, and a wide variety of other purposes. They organized and joined secretive societies, such as Freemasonry, based on the Renaissance synthesis of Hermeticism (an esoteric or Gnostic Christianity) and the Christianized Kabbalah (a mystical Jewish text). Elements of these informal but popular religions were influential and practiced with little apparent tension or contradiction alongside the orthodox varieties of Catholic and especially Protestant Christianity. Sometimes they were mixed with new American religions.

Protestant Anglicanism—the Church of England and its schismatic variations or close relatives—greatly influenced the re-creation of European culture and society in North America. By the nineteenth century successive religious revivals had produced Americanized versions of Episcopalians and Methodists, particularly in the middle and southern states. In New England the dissenting English Puritans resulted in the Americanized forms of Congregationalists, Baptists, and Presbyterians, along with even less-orthodox Universalists and Unitarians. The elite social, economic, and political classes of the United States were closely aligned with these religions. These

Americanized varieties, especially the evangelical Methodists and Baptists, were sources of upward social mobility and a means for achieving or maintaining a middle-class identity and respectability as modern Americans.

Other religions supported alternative identities and images of what it meant to be an American. German and Scandinavian immigrants imported and Americanized Lutheranism along with other ethnic varieties of European Protestantism. Quakers, Shakers, and Anabaptists, as well as Hutterites, Brethren, Amish, and Mennonites, became substantially American religions and thrived after being imported from Europe. Many smaller yet distinctively American innovations resulted in still greater religious variety in the United States during the nineteenth century. Besides the Restorationist movement, significant American originals were Transcendentalism as well as Spiritualism and, before the end of the century, New Thought, Christian Science, Unity, and Theosophy. Many other even smaller and less-well-known religious prophets, communes, groups, and movements—such as Christian Perfectionism as represented by John Humphrey Noyes's Oneida Community—were a part of the tremendous variety of nineteenth-century American culture.

Restorationism emerged out of the fiery religious revivalism that repeatedly swept through and revitalized American Protestantism during the eighteenth century. These "awakenings" produced America's predominant evangelical forms, especially the Baptists and Methodists. For the Restorationists, however, the Protestant Reformation in general and its Americanized variations did not go far enough in correcting and purifying Christianity. They maintained that the existing teachings of Christianity and all of its forms—Protestant as well as Catholic—were corrupted, beyond remediation, and in apostasy. The Restorationists rejected all Christian creeds and historically derived doctrines as divisive. They, for instance, abandoned orthodox Christian trinitarianism—the principle that God, Christ, and the Holy Ghost are manifestations of and unified in one monotheistic deity. They also repudiated the predominant Calvinist theology of salvation—the teaching that humanity is totally depraved (sinful because of the fall), God has selected very few people (the elect) to be saved (unconditional election), Christ's atonement for original sin is limited to the elect, and God's grace for the elect is irresistible (they must obey the gospel).

Christianity, the Restorationists maintained, must be rediscovered and restored in terms of the principles and structures exemplified by Jesus Christ and the first-century disciplines. They ultimately aimed to reunite or unify all of Christianity on the basis of the Bible, especially the New Testament Scripture. They shared this general sentiment with others such as the Quakers, many Baptists, Unitarians, Universalists, and the Anabaptists. Their Restoration was envisioned as a "new dispensation" (a new historical dispersing) of the Christian gospel to humanity. It reinforced their sense that the United States was divinely sanctioned as well as their American identity as God's chosen people. The Restorationists, more specifically, taught a primitive New Testament gospel based on four major tenets.

Faith in Jesus Christ as the Son of God was the first and most important principle. The second precept was the requirement for repentance of one's sins, but not original sin (the sin of Adam and Eve). Adult baptism by immersion for the remission of sins—those of the individual, not original sin—was the third basic gospel principle. The fourth tenet was possession of the gift of the Holy Ghost bestowing grace for Christian living on human beings as children of God. They believed that human salvation and eternal life followed from conforming with and embracing these basic principles of the Christian gospel. The Restorationists, like many other Christians, commonly emphasized Adventism and Millennialism. They, in other words, believed in the more or less imminent second coming of Jesus Christ to earth (Adventism), and that Christ would reign for a thousand years on earth at the end of time (Millennialism).

For the rest of this chapter, we will look at the Latter-day Saint restoration.

What is this religion's overriding question? What makes this system self-evidently valid to the community of the faithful?

The overriding question for the Latter-day Saint religion is: what exactly is required for human beings to be saved and to live eternally in the glory of the heavenly kingdom of God? It is answered by conformity to the gospel of Jesus Christ, God's Son, as comprehensively restored by the authority of the priesthood of Christ through continuing revelation and a modern-day prophet of God. The Latter-day

Saint religion teaches that God's plan for humanity's earthly existence presents the opportunity for human beings to perfect themselves by way of the gospel of Jesus Christ. By complying with the Christian gospel, as restored in its purity and fullness by the Latter-day Saint religion, human beings may become godlike and obtain eternal life to reign as kings and priests or queens and priestesses with the supreme God, the Father, and his Son, Jesus Christ (as well as other godlike beings, such as Adam and Eve, the prophets and other saintly Old Testament figures, and other Latter-day Saints), in the glory of the celestial world (heaven). The belief that God restored priesthood authority for the gospel of Jesus Christ in all of its purity and fullness through a modern-day prophet and continuing revelation to humanity in this dispensation makes the Latter-day Saint religion self-evidently valid for the community of the faithful.

How do we know about this religion?

The Latter-day Saint religion is known through the revelations of God in the form of scriptures and the gift of the Spirit (Holy Ghost). The scriptures specifically are (a) the Christian Bible, King James version, insofar as it is translated correctly and is modified by revelations to Joseph Smith Jr., the founding Latter-day Saint prophet; (b) the Book of Mormon, a record of the ancient Americas as translated by Joseph Smith, understood as a second testament to the gospel of Jesus Christ; (c) the Doctrine and Covenants, containing the revelations of God to Joseph Smith and subsequent Latter-day Saint prophets; and (d) the Pearl of Great Price, comprising additional translations of scripture and revelations of God to Joseph Smith. This religion also teaches that God reveals himself to all of humanity who accept and believe in the gospel of Jesus Christ, not just the church's prophet, through the gift of the spirit of God. The blessings of the Holy Ghost (spirit of God) include prophecy, speaking in tongues, interpretation of tongues, discerning spirits, wisdom, knowledge, faith, healing, and other miracles.

What is the community of the faithful called? What story explains its traits?

The Latter-day Saint religion envisions the community of the faithful as a continuation of Israel, God's chosen people of the Old

Testament. In this view the gospel of Jesus Christ and the disciples, the New Testament, perpetuates and extends God's ancient covenant with Israel. The Latter-day Saint religion, by restoring the purity of the fullness of the gospel of Jesus Christ (including the ancient covenant), is an extension of the Old and New Testament covenants and dispensations. This religion thereby has responsibility and authority for these covenants, as contained in the fullness of the gospel of Jesus Christ, for the dispensation of this gospel in the last or latter days, meaning from this religion's restoration of the gospel to the end of time.

The Latter-day Saint story tells how Joseph Smith restored authority for the gospel of Jesus Christ following centuries of apostasy. Multiple versions and variations of this story and debates about them notwithstanding, the narratives quoted here are from the canonized *History of the Church of Jesus Christ of Latter-day Saints* ([HC], edited by B. H. Roberts, 7 vols. [Salt Lake City, Utah: Deseret News, 1902–12]). This story narrates how the youthful Joseph Smith, like many other Americans, found the multitude of religious options available to nineteenth-century Americans, all of them offering salvation, to be confusing. Smith later recorded: "My mind at times was greatly excited, the cry and tumult were so great and incessant" (HC 1:3). He explained further:

> The Presbyterians were most decided against the Baptists and Methodists, and used all the powers of both reason and sophistry to prove their errors, or, at least, to make the people think they were in error. On the other hand, the Baptists and Methodists in their turn were equally zealous in endeavoring to establish their own tenets and disprove all others. (HC 1:3)

Joseph, implicitly risking his very salvation, consequently found it difficult to choose among them.

The story of the Latter-day Saint restoration begins with Joseph Smith's "First Vision" at fifteen years of age in 1820. He recounted being especially impressed with the statement "If any of you lack wisdom, let him ask of God, that giveth to all men liberally, and upbraideth not: and it shall be given to him," found in the Epistle of James of the Christian New Testament (HC 1:4). With this justification Joseph tells of going to a remote grove of trees in upstate New

York near Palmyra to seek God's counsel. In response to his prayer, he reported:

> I saw a pillar of light exactly over my head, above the brightness of the sun, which descended gradually until it fell upon me. . . . I saw two personages, whose brightness and glory defy all descriptions, standing above me in the air. One of them spake unto me, calling me by name, and said—pointing to the other—"THIS IS MY BELOVED SON, HEAR HIM." I asked the personages who stood above me in the light, which of all the sects was right—and which I should join. I was answered that I must join none of them, for they were all wrong, and the personage who addressed me said that all their creeds were an abomination in His sight: that those professors were all corrupt; that "they draw near to me with their lips, but their hearts are far from me; they teach for doctrines the commandments of men: having a form of godliness, but they deny the power thereof." He again forbade me to join with any of them. (HC 1:5)

The Latter-day Saint story reports that the prophet Joseph Smith subsequently received many other revelations from God.

In September 1823, after going to bed, Joseph tells of the appearance of an angel in response to his prayer for additional guidance. He later elaborated:

> He called me by name, and said unto me that he was a messenger sent from the presence of God to me and that his name was Moroni; that God had a work for me to do. . . . He said there was a book deposited, written upon gold plates, giving an account of the former inhabitants of this continent, and the sources from whence they sprang. He also said that the fullness of the everlasting Gospel was contained in it, as delivered by the Savior to the ancient inhabitants; also that there were two stones in silver bows and these stones, fastened to a breastplate, constituted what is called the Urim and Thummim deposited with the plates; and the possession and use of these stones were what constituted "Seers" in ancient or former times; and that God had prepared them for the purpose of translating the book. (HC 1:11-12)

In this vision Joseph describes a series of biblical prophecies (from Malachi 3 and 4; Acts 3:22 and 23; Joel 2:28-32; and Isaiah 11) that Moroni quoted, indicating to him that God was using him in preparation for the return of Christ to earth.

The story of the Latter-day Saints narrates how Joseph Smith received the ancient plates, compiled by Mormon, from Mormon's son, the angel Moroni. After a series of ordeals, Smith eventually completed the translation and published it as the Book of Mormon in 1830. During the translation in 1829, Joseph Smith and Oliver Cowdery, Smith's scribe and associate, recount praying for specific instructions on baptism for the remission of sins. They reported that John the Baptist, acting as a messenger of God, appeared to them saying: "Upon you my fellow servants, in the name of Messiah I confer the Priesthood of Aaron, which holds the keys of the ministering of angels, and of the Gospel of repentance, and of baptism by immersion for the remission of sins; and this shall never be taken again from the earth" (HC 1:39). With this priesthood authority, they describe baptizing each other and shortly thereafter other believers. Some unspecified time later Smith and Cowdery reportedly received the keys to the higher "Melchizedek" priesthood with the keys to the eternal salvation of humanity by the authority of the Christ's apostles Peter, James, and John. Shortly thereafter, on 6 April 1830, Smith describes the formal organization of the Latter-day Saint religion by about forty or fifty converts at Fayette (or Manchester) in upstate New York under God's direction.

The Latter-day Saint story consequently locates itself comprehensively within the larger narrative of the Christian Bible. The Book of Mormon incorporates the Americas into the biblical account. Its abridged translation by Joseph Smith, from the record of Mormon, chronicles the migration of two groups of people from the Old World to the New. The "Jaredites" are the first of the immigrants at the time of the Tower of Babel. After building a great civilization, they become disobedient to God and disappear. The second group leaves the Middle Eastern world shortly before the fall of Jerusalem to the Babylonians (about 586 B.C.E.). In the Americas they divide into warring factions of "Nephites" and "Lamanites." Jesus Christ enters the Book of Mormon story after the Resurrection and teaches these people the biblical gospel, resulting in several generations of peace and prosperity. Eventually, however, the disobedient Lamanites, who are understood to be the ancestors of the later Native Americans, destroy the Christian Nephites. The Book of Mormon consequently is an entirely new scripture, integrating the

Americas into the biblical narrative, explaining Native Americans, and providing another testament to the gospel of Jesus Christ.

What is the way of life of the community of the faithful?

The way of life of the Latter-day Saint community is defined by obedience to the basic principles of the restored Christian gospel. Many of these requirements are specified by thirteen "articles of faith" (HC: 540–42). The "first principles and ordinances" are faith in Jesus Christ, repentance for one's own sins, baptism by immersion for the remission of sin, and the laying on of hands for receiving the gifts of the Holy Ghost. All of the Saints are responsible for sharing the restored gospel with others and significantly contributing to the realization of Zion, the kingdom of God on earth.

The Saints also are expected to observe and obey all of God's commandments, as defined by the scriptures, such as the biblical Ten Commandments; pray frequently to God for guidance and direction; study the scriptures; observe the Sabbath day (Sunday) and keep it holy; sustain the prophet and priesthood of the church; live the law of tithing (defined as 10 percent of annual income as well as other offerings); engage in fasting and prayer once a month; honor and obey the laws of the state; and observe the "Word of Wisdom." The Word of Wisdom generally urges prudence, thankfulness, and moderation in all things (Doctrine and Covenants 89). It advises eating grain, herbs, vegetables, and fruit, eating meat only sparingly, and avoiding strong drinks. As this scripture is understood today, the use of alcohol, tobacco, coffee, tea, and illegal drugs is prohibited. The Saints also are expected to be honest, true, chaste, benevolent, and virtuous, and are expected to do good to everyone.

Observant Latter-day Saints, but no one else, are permitted access to the temple—the most sacred "House of the Lord"—for performing special salvation ordinances. The basic temple rite is the "endowment," whereby the Saints reenact the basic covenant with God and receive God's blessings, including the promise of eternal life. They also receive and thereafter wear a special undergarment symbolizing their covenant with God. The ritual of "baptism for the dead" enables the Saints to serve as proxies for the baptism of their ancestors and relatives who lived before or who did not receive the fullness of the restored gospel. In addition to being married for time only, male and female couples can have their relationships "sealed" eternally in the temple and their children sealed eternally to them, thereby creating eternal family relationships extending back to Adam and Eve. Last, a priesthood member and his spouse may enter into a special covenant with God whereby they receive the promise of reigning as a king and priest or queen and priestess with God (along with other godlike beings) in the celestial world.

Joseph Smith, the founding prophet, introduced the Latter-day Saints to the Old Testament practice of patriarchal marriage, the possibility of a man's having more than one wife, based on a revelation from God (Doctrine and Covenants 132). The practice of plural marriage—technically polygyny, a form of polygamy—was abandoned and prohibited in 1890 out of deference to the laws of the United States. Monogamy, exclusively defined as marriage between a man and a woman, is the only form of marriage sanctioned by the Church of Jesus Christ of Latter-day Saints today, although some other organizations of this religion continue the practice of patriarchal marriage. The LDS Church also prohibits the practice of homosexuality, all sexual relationship outside of marriage, and sexual relationship with anyone but a marriage partner.

Families are defined as the basic social unit of the Latter Day Saint religion. Fathers are responsible for spiritually directing the family unit and economically providing for it, while mothers have primary responsibility for the welfare of the home and children. Families are encouraged to be mutually supporting, to work and worship together, and to reserve at least one evening a week exclusively for their activities. They also are encouraged to put aside a year's supply of food and other necessities in the event of an emergency. Males are eligible for ordination to the priesthood and other special callings by prophetic revelation—and most are called by age to successive ranks of the hierarchal priesthood. Females also are expected to perform special duties and callings, including the possibility of serving as full-time missionaries. The Latter-day Saint community is organized further by congregations, known as "wards," and collections of wards forming "stakes" of the larger tent of Zion, with the Latter-day Saint church representing the kingdom of God on earth.

What is the worldview of the community?

The worldview of the Latter-day Saint religion is that it exclusively has the authority and responsibility for taking the restored gospel of

Jesus Christ to "all nations, kindreds, tongues, and people" (Doctrine and Covenants 42:58). The restored gospel of Jesus Christ offers human beings the opportunity to perfect themselves, achieve eternal salvation, and reign with God, Christ, and other godlike beings eternally in the celestial world (the kingdom of God in heaven). This religion sees its mission as building Zion, the kingdom of God on earth, in preparation for the second coming of Jesus Christ, and the Millennium. It is a comprehensive biblical worldview, beginning with Adam and Eve and their covenant with God in the Garden of Eden, continuing the gospel of Jesus Christ as restored in its fullness by a modern-day prophet of God, and concluding with the Advent and millennial reign of Christ on earth at the end of time.

How does this religion function in the world today?

All members of the community share in the responsibility for spreading the restored gospel of Jesus Christ among all peoples of the world. The membership is strongly encouraged to share the restored gospel with their friends, acquaintances, and anyone else willing to listen. Young men are urged to devote two years of full-time missionary service, supported by their families, following graduation from high school and their ordination as "elders" in the higher or Melchizedek priesthood. Young women over twenty-one years of age also may serve missions, along with married couples, many of whom are retirement age. Latter-day Saint missions worldwide are supervised by older adult priesthood members under the direction of the current prophet and president, the Quorum of the Twelve Apostles, and the Seventies, supported by a full-time staff of church employees. There are about 129 temples (with nine more under construction and eight more planned) located worldwide today for the Saints to perform the ordinances necessary for eternal salvation.

During much of the nineteenth century the Latter-day Saints experienced considerable tension and conflict with other Americans. They eventually fled the then United States, likening themselves to the Old Testament Israelites, under the leadership of Brigham Young, the second LDS president, for what eventually became the state of Utah. Even in the remote Utah Territory, however, the Saints became embattled with federal authorities through much of the nineteenth century. Many of their beliefs were viewed as heretical from the standpoint of more orthodox forms of American Christianity. The

Saints' economic and political activities sometimes were seen as over-stepping the American division of church-state functions, and the practice of plural marriage was especially offensive to other Americans. These sources of tension were moderated greatly, however, during the late nineteenth and early twentieth centuries.

The Church of Jesus Christ of Latter-day Saints today has substantial economic assets—many of them temples, wards, stakes, and other buildings devoted to religious functions—but it is not different in this regard from other successful American religious denominations. The Saints tend to be associated with conservative American politics and the Republican Party, but some of them are more liberal and Democrats. They have served under Republican and Democratic administrations and at all levels of American government, including the United States Congress and presidential cabinets. In the United States today Latter-day Saints are prominent in federal and military service, amateur and professional athletics, entertainment, education, medicine, agriculture, and many other walks of life. Latter-day Saint families generally embody highly traditional and idealized American values, and the Saints otherwise have embraced and reflect quintessentially mainstream American norms and values.

Today the Church of Jesus Christ of Latter-day Saints reports a worldwide membership of more than thirteen million (and there are at least another half million people who belong to other Latter Day Saint organizations, such as the Community of Christ). The Latter-day Saints are active in more than 167 countries worldwide and on all continents, although the largest concentration of membership outside North America is in Central and South America. Slightly less than one-half of the church's membership (about six million) is located in the United States. The Saints comprise about 2 percent of the population of the United States, making it a highly significant religious minority. The Church of Jesus Christ of Latter-day Saints is one of the largest religious organizations in the United States, ranking below only the Roman Catholic, Southern Baptist, and United Methodist denominations.

Conclusion

Restorationism, which was born out of a concern for the multiplicity of nineteenth-century forms of American Christianity, now is a highly diffuse worldwide movement with more than forty million adherents, a majority of whom are North Americans. The Latter Day Saint religion, as represented by the Church of Jesus Christ of Latter-day Saints as well as many other distinctive but smaller organizations, is one of the largest and most distinctive manifestations of American Restorationism. There are other important variations on Restorationism, not reviewed here, that merit brief mention in conclusion. For example, the Christadelphians (or Brothers of Christ), who emphasize the basic truths of a restored New Testament Christianity, with about fifty thousand members in 120 countries worldwide, is one of the smallest forms of American Restorationism.

The multiorganizational Adventists, known best in the form of Seventh-day Adventists, emphasize the second coming of Christ and, like other Sabbatarians, the sanctity of the seventh-day Sabbath, defined as Saturday. There are about fourteen million Seventh-day Adventists worldwide today, well known through their medical and educational institutions, with a presence in two hundred or more countries, and with especially large populations in the United States, India, the Philippines, Brazil, and other portions of South America. They, like the Jehovah's Witnesses, derived historically from the mid-nineteen-century Millerite movement. It splintered and reorganized in an assortment of different organizations after William Miller's prophecy of the Advent failed to transpire in 1844—an event known as the Great Disappointment.

The Jehovah's Witnesses emerged under the direction of Charles Russell and became well known through active proselytizing and conscientious objection to military service and nationality pledges as well as the refusal of blood transfusions. The Witnesses stress the exclusive authority of and a literal understanding of the Christian Bible, and the immediacy of the Advent and the Millennium. Based in the United States, there are more than seven million Jehovah's Witnesses active around the world today, except in countries prohibiting them.

Finally, the autonomous Churches of Christ form one of the organizational bases of the original American Restorationist movement. There are about 1.3 million American members and more than five million members worldwide. The Christian Church (also known as the Disciples of Christ) is the other large portion of the original Restorationist movement. There are about seven hundred thousand disciples in North America.

At a Glance

Classic Texts
Christian Bible, King James Version: a record of God's revelations, including the Old and New Testaments

Book of Mormon: a record of the ancient Americas translated by Joseph Smith and understood as a second testament to the gospel of Jesus Christ

Doctrine and Covenants (LDS version): revelations of God to Joseph Smith and subsequent Latter-day Saint prophets

Pearl of Great Price: other revelations of God to Joseph Smith and his translations of additional scriptures

Important Figures
Joseph Smith Jr.: founding prophet of the Latter Day Saint religion

Mormon: ancient American historian

Moroni: son of Mormon and the angel who delivered the Book of Mormon plates to Joseph Smith

Brigham Young: second LDS president who led the Saints to Utah

Characteristic Beliefs
Faith in Jesus Christ

Repentance for one's sins

Baptism by immersion for the remission of sin

Laying on of hands for the gifts of the Holy Spirit

Obedience to all of God's commandments, resulting in eternal life

Essential Creeds or Codes of Conduct
The commandments and revelations of God contained in scripture

Articles of Faith (HC 1:540-42)

Word of Wisdom (Doctrine and Covenants 89)

Brief Time Line
December 23, 1805	Birth of Joseph Smith Jr.
1820	Joseph Smith's "First Vision"
April 6, 1830	Organization of the Latter Day Saint religion
June 27, 1844	Martyrdom of Joseph Smith
1847	LDS establish headquarters at Salt Lake City
1890	Manifesto renouncing plural marriage in the United States

Important Symbols
The temple: symbolic of God's covenant with humanity and promise of eternal life through obedience to the restored gospel of Jesus Christ

Important Rituals

Baptism for the remission of sin, and Confirmation conveying the gift of the Holy Spirit

Holy Sacrament of the Lord's Supper (a form of the Christian Eucharist): the partaking of bread and wine (water) performed every Sunday in remembrance of the atoning sacrifice of Jesus Christ, baptism, and the commitment to obey the gospel

Ordination to the offices of the Aaronic and Melchizedek priesthoods (open to all worthy male members only)

Patriarchal Bless: a fatherly blessing on the life of the individual

Endowment: initiatory temple rite and covenant with God, offering the blessing of eternal life

Sealings for eternal life: temple rites sealing marriage partners together and children to parents eternally

Second Anointing: temple rite and covenant with God of a priesthood member and his wife conveying the blessing of eternal life as king and priest or queen and priestess to reign with God in the celestial world eternally

Baptism for the Dead and other salvation ordinances for the deceased: temple rituals (baptism, ordination, seals) performed by proxy for people who lived before the Latter-day Saint restoration

Glossary

Aaronic priesthood	lower priesthood formed by the offices of deacon, teacher, and priest
Advent	second coming of Jesus Christ to earth
Endowment	temple covenant with God promising eternal life
Lamanites	ancestors of Native Americans
Melchizedek priesthood	higher priesthood formed by the offices of elder and high priest
Millennium	thousand-year reign of Christ on earth at the end of time
Restorationism	nineteenth-century American belief that all existing forms of Christianity were apostate and that the true form of Christianity must be rediscovered on the basis of the primitive New Testament disciples of Christ
Zion	kingdom of God on earth

Sacred Spaces and Times

Palmyra, New York: the Sacred Grove and site of Joseph Smith's First Vision in 1820

Hill Cumorah (near Manchester, New York): where Mormon's record of the ancient Americas was buried and Joseph Smith received the golden plates from the angel Moroni in 1823

Formal organization of the Latter Day Saint religion on 6 April 1830 at Fayette or Manchester, New York (Doctrine and Covenants 21)

Independence, Jackson County, Missouri: site designated by Joseph Smith in 1831 as the location of Zion, the kingdom of God on earth (Doctrine and Covenants 57)

Kirtland Temple: the location of the first House of the Lord (temple) at Kirtland, Ohio, dedicated in 1836 (Doctrine and Covenants 95)

Adam-ondi-Ahman: site designated by Joseph Smith in 1838 as the residence of Adam and Eve after being expelled from the Garden of Eden (a site for a temple and the gathering of the priesthood prior to the Advent), located above the east bluffs of the Grand River near Gallatin, Daviess County, Missouri (Doctrine and Covenants 116)

Nauvoo Temple: the location of the second temple constructed by the Latter-day Saints at Nauvoo, Illinois, dedicated in 1845 (Doctrine and Covenants 124)

The martyrdom of the prophets, Joseph Smith and his brother Hyrum, on 27 June 1844 at Carthage, Illinois

Temple, Salt Lake City, Utah: This temple site was selected by Brigham Young, the second Latter-day Saint president, in 1847, shortly after the Mormons migrated to the Salt Lake Valley. It was dedicated in 1853 and the temple was completed and dedicated in 1893.

Suggestions for Further Reading
(a) History of American Religion

Butler, John. *Awash in a Sea of Faith: Christianizing the American People.* Cambridge, Mass.: Harvard University Press, 1990.

————. *New World Faiths: Religion in Colonial America.* New York: Oxford University Press, 2008.

Butler, John, Grant Wacker, and Randall Balmer. *Religion in American Life: A Short History.* New York: Oxford University Press, 2008.

Hatch, Nathan O. *The Democratization of American Christianity.* New Haven: Yale University Press, 1989.

(b) New Religions

Clarke, Peter B., ed. *Encyclopedia of New Religious Movements.* New York: Routledge, 2006.

Ellwood, Robert S., and Harry B. Partin. *Religious and Spiritual Groups in Modern America.* Englewood Cliffs, N.J.: Prentice Hall, 1988.

Jenkins, Philip. *Mystics and Messiahs: Cults and New Religions in American History.* New York: Oxford University Press, 2000.

Lewis, James R. *Cults: A Reference Handbook.* Santa Barbara, Calif.: ABC-CLIO, 2005.

———, ed. *The Encyclopedia of Cults, Sects, and New Religions*. Amherst, N.Y.: Prometheus Books, 2002.

Melton, J. Gordon. *Encyclopedic Handbook of Cults in America*. New York: Garland, 1992.

Miller, Timothy. *America's Alternative Religions*. Albany: State University of New York Press, 1995.

(c) Restorationism and Churches of Christ

Hughes, Richard T., ed. *The American Quest for the Primitive Church*. Urbana: University of Illinois Press, 1995.

Hughes, Richard T., Nathan O. Hatch, and David Edwin Harrell Jr., with an introduction by Douglas A. Foster. *American Origins of Churches of Christ: Three Essays on Restoration History*. Abilene, Tex.: ACU Press, 2000.

(d) The Latter Day Saint Religion

Allen, James B., and Glen M. Leonard. *The Story of the Latter-day Saints*. Salt Lake City, Utah: Deseret Book Company, 1992.

Brodie, Fawn McKay. *No Man Knows My History: The Life of Joseph Smith, the Mormon Prophet*. New York: Alfred A. Knopf, 1845.

Bushman, Richard Lyman, with the assistance of Jed Woodworth. *Joseph Smith: Rough Stone Rolling*. New York: Alfred A. Knopf, 2005.

Davies, Douglas J. *An Introduction to Mormonism*. New York: Cambridge University Press, 2003.

Rust, Val D. *Radical Origins: Early Mormon Converts and Their Colonial Ancestors*. Urbana: University of Illinois Press, 2004.

Shields, Steven L. *Divergent Paths of the Restoration: A History of the Latter Day Saint Movement*. Los Angeles: Restoration Research, 1990.

NEW TWENTIETH-CENTURY AMERICAN RELIGIONS

Dell deChant

As the nineteenth century drew to a close and the twentieth century dawned, America's already densely populated religious landscape was also becoming increasingly diverse. Joining the nation's long-established religious communities and the new religions of the nineteenth century (presented in the previous chapter) were a host of even newer and in many cases strikingly original religious groups. In short, the bewildering variety of religions in nineteenth-century America became even more bewildering in the twentieth century. It was not simply a question of numbers, although the numbers are considerable, but also a question of public awareness. In 1900, if an American belonged to a religion, it was most likely some form of Christianity, or perhaps Judaism. By 2000, however, the options had expanded exponentially, and America had become home to a kaleidoscopic array of faiths. Christianity was still unquestionably the dominant religion, and its historic forms still claimed vast numbers of followers, but many Americans were now committed to religions that were quite different from those of the previous century; and many of these newer groups were becoming quite well known in American popular culture. Among the more recognized of these groups that came on the scene between 1900 and 2000 were Pentecostalism, Wicca, Jehovah's Witnesses, Scientology, the Unification Church, Transcendental Meditation (TM), and the International Society for Krishna Consciousness, to name a few. With the dramatic proliferation of new religions during the course of the twentieth century, the United States became the most religiously pluralistic society on earth, and the most religiously diverse culture in the history of the world.

Perhaps the single most notable feature of the vast majority of twentieth-century new religions is their remarkable difference from the religions (even the new religions) that had dominated American culture prior to 1900. As the chapter on nineteenth-century new religions revealed, prior to the twentieth century the overwhelming majority of Americans and American religious groups were accurately identified as Christian. Even the new religions of the nineteenth century, with a few notable exceptions, were largely derived from rather traditional, European forms of Christianity. By the 1950s, however, conditions had changed, and by the latter decades of the twentieth century the change was evident throughout society. Not only had many new, distinctly American forms of Christianity become firmly established, but also a vast multitude of non-Christian religions were successfully attracting converts from all segments of society. These groups included ones directly associated with or derived from larger global religions previously marginalized in America, others that were popular repackaging of long-suppressed traditions (such as Western esotericism, paganism, and Wicca), and still others that were highly original syncretistic religions that melded together beliefs from two or more otherwise distinct traditions.

This chapter will focus on the Metaphysical Movement, a collection of new religions that took root and flourished throughout the twentieth century in America (and certainly into the twenty-first century). Although the movement is by no means representative of *all* new religions from this period, its various groups reveal features characteristic of many others while also presenting us with issues in understanding relevant to our grasp of twentieth-century new religions as whole.

The American Context of the Metaphysical Movement

The American Metaphysical Movement is a broad, diverse, and ever-expanding collection of religious groups and individual spiritual seekers. It was first identified and analyzed by J. Stillson Judah in the 1960s, and more recently and in much more detail by Catherine Albanese.[1] The movement (or collection of movements) has received relatively little scholarly attention despite its significant impact on

American culture—although Albanese's recent book may help rectify this situation.

The movement emerged in the late nineteenth century from a variety of different strands of religious thought and practice, chiefly the mental healing (or Mind Cure) movement, Spiritualism, the Western esoteric tradition, New England Transcendentalism, popular religious idealism, and export forms of Hinduism and Buddhism. These diverse strands came together with varying degrees of emphasis in the first metaphysical religions, and these same strands can still be seen in the newest metaphysical communities of today. Indeed, metaphysical religions have historically revealed pronounced syncretistic tendencies, comfortably bringing together beliefs and teachings from various traditions, generally endorsing the good in all religions, and rejecting beliefs and practices seen as exclusivistic or condemnatory.

In this regard, the movement as a whole developed as a reaction against and a rejection of nineteenth-century forms of Euro-American Christianity—especially its stricter forms. It took particular issue with a number of specific features typical of mainstream Christianity: the anthropomorphic concept of deity, the belief in human sinfulness, claims of exclusivity and authority in matters of human destiny and religious truth, and beliefs about the nature and role of Jesus. In each instance, the metaphysical religions found these long-established beliefs and teachings antiquated and inadequate to meet the needs of contemporary culture. Had this been an earlier time, the first metaphysical religions would have been declared heretical, their leaders prosecuted, and their followers persecuted. Cultural conditions in late-nineteenth-century America were different, however. Powerful forces of change were sweeping through American society, remaking the nation, and reordering the sensibilities of its citizens. Secularization, industrialization, urbanization, and the rise of the middle class created a cultural environment that was hospitable to new ideas of all sorts—including new religious ideas.

In this new American culture, still very much in the throes of its own self-creation, the Metaphysical Movement had space to make its case. It did so with confidence and enthusiasm, entering American society and the awareness of average Americans through periodicals, pamphlets, books, public lectures, opening religious centers, and establishing schools. The movement also was a trendsetter in its empowerment of women as religious leaders, sanctioning them as teachers, religious practitioners, and ministers. In fact, women founded many of the metaphysical groups, the most notable being Theosophy (Helena Petrovna Blavatsky), Christian Science (Mary Baker Eddy), and New Thought (Emma Curtis Hopkins).

Rooted in the socially volatile world of America's late-nineteenth-century urban culture, its earliest manifestations were groups such as Theosophy and Christian Science. Later manifestations include Divine Science, Religious Science, Unity, the International New Thought Alliance, the I AM Movement, Church Universal and Triumphant, Homes of Truth, Alice Bailey's Arcane School, the Church of Truth, and numerous other groups. There was also, from the outset, a desire in the metaphysical groups to make religion relevant to the contemporary world, to have it meet the needs of everyday life. This was very much in the spirit of the American philosophic tradition known as "pragmatism," which evaluated the meaning and truth of beliefs on the basis of the results they produced. In practice, this meant that the metaphysical religions tended to have a highly optimistic worldview and understood their beliefs to be in harmony with the ideals of the modern world—ideals predicated on science, technology, and the capitalist economic system. As a result, the Metaphysical Movement was and continues to be attractive to a wide cross section of the population, although the majority has always been from the economic middle class. Typically, its participants are also dissatisfied with traditional forms of religion and willing to pursue new religious horizons, generally accepting of religious diversity, and extremely self-confident.

Of all the various communities in the Metaphysical Movement, those associated with New Thought proved to be the most successful in terms of membership and cultural penetration. Emerging at the turn of twentieth century, by its close New Thought had become the largest and most widespread embodiment of the Metaphysical Movement. In addition to New Thought, today the movement includes religious traditions such as the Raelians, the World Metaphysical Association, *Course in Miracles* Study Groups, the Movement for Spiritual Inner Awareness, the American Gnostic Church, and numerous others, including the broad assembly of groups and teachings classified under the heading of the New Age. A good case could also be made for the inclusion of a Seicho-no-Ie within the movement.

Although many different religions came to comprise the Metaphysical Movement, the movement as a whole developed around four central beliefs. These can be contrasted with features of traditional Christianity, noted previously. First, the Supreme Reality is universally present, wholly good, and not localized in a singular deity. This characterizes the movement as monistic rather than monotheistic. A wide variety of terms are used to refer to the Supreme Reality, God being one. Others, more illustrative of the movement, are: *Divine Mind, Infinite Reality, Spirit, Principle,* and *Truth.* The material universe is understood as an expression of the Supreme Reality. The recognition of the Supreme Reality as Mind identifies groups within the Metaphysical Movement as forms of religious idealism, a system that recognizes the highest reality to be mental or spiritual, with the material-physical world being subordinate to the higher spiritual reality of Divine Mind.

Second, the movement recognizes humans as spiritual beings, one with the divine, and innately good. As such, humans are understood to possess spiritual powers and abilities, which generally are unrecognized. The Metaphysical Movement seeks to educate persons to their true divine nature and allow them to develop their latent spiritual powers. Third, because the Supreme Reality is omnipresent and omnibenevolent, and because of the divine nature of humankind, the destiny for all humanity is positive, and for individuals this positive destiny can begin to be expressed immediately in their present life experience. Fourth, although Jesus is a central figure in most metaphysical groups (in some more than others), he is identified as an advanced spiritual being but not the sole offspring of divinity. In this regard, his primary role is that of a teacher and a guide to humanity in its spiritual development. Often Jesus is presented as one among many such beings who have appeared throughout history to aid humanity as it seeks to realize its spiritual destiny. While these core beliefs are present in all branches of the Metaphysical Movement, New Thought, which will be the focus of the rest of the chapter, has been particularly successful in developing enduring religious communities that embody them—both in the United States and, today, throughout the world.

What is this religion's overriding question? What makes this system self-evidently valid to the community of the faithful?

The overriding question for New Thought is: how do we discover and bring into expression the reality of our innate divinity, to live in accord with the principles of Truth and demonstrate the reality of that Truth in experiences of health, prosperity, love, peace of mind, and other positive conditions? New Thought proposes that the answer to this question is given to each individual according to her or his receptivity and her or his willingness to follow principles and specific practices (e.g., prayer, meditation, spiritual treatment, and other specific rituals) suggested by the tradition. New Thought believes that everyone can discover and express their divine nature and overcome any seeming challenge, from disease and illness to poverty, depression, and abuse. In discovering one's innate divinity, the New Thought participant comes to realize that she or he is an individualized expression of Supreme Reality (referred to variously as *Divine Mind, God, Ultimate Reality, Truth, Spirit, the Good,* and other terms). Because Divine Mind is both omnipresent and omnibenevolent, New Thought affirms that the realization of one's divinity puts one in touch with the reality of Divine Mind, which brings with it power over material conditions and the elimination of undesirable circumstances. The validity of the system is reflected in the experiences of individuals who find that through following the principles and practices they experience spiritual growth and associated improvement in their personal lives. Such improvement is often referred to as a "demonstration." New Thought understands that its principles and practices were taught and demonstrated by Jesus, but their ultimate validity rests with each individual's specific demonstrations.

How do we know about this religion? What classics define the norms?

Unlike other major religious traditions, New Thought does not have a single authoritative scripture or a canon of sacred texts. There are no formal doctrines or creeds in the movement or its various groups. Instead, the various New Thought communities emphasize certain works as primary sources for religious development. They also publish brief statements summarizing their beliefs and principles. The largest single religious community in New Thought is the Unity movement, which identifies itself as an expression of Christianity and puts great emphasis on the Bible as "a valuable spiritual resource."[2] Other New Thought groups generally affirm the importance of the Bible as a religious text, although none claim it as the singular source of revelation. When the Bible is used in the movement, it is engaged as a symbolic text and explicated using what the movement calls a "metaphysical" (or allegorical) method of interpretation. Using this method, Christian Scripture is revealed to be illustrative of New Thought principles and practices.

From the vast library of New Thought texts that present the religious norms of the movement, several texts can be specified as classics. These are *The Science of Mind* by the founder of Religious Science, Ernest Holmes; *Christian Healing* by the cofounder of Unity, Charles Fillmore; and *Lessons in Truth* by H. Emilie Cady. Besides being among the best-known works within New Thought, these texts present the idealistic worldview of the movement, its primary theological claims, and specific religious instructions for participants to follow. The classic source for interpreting the Bible is Fillmore's *Metaphysical Bible Dictionary,* and perhaps the best brief summary of New Thought beliefs is the "Declaration of Principles" of the International New Thought Alliance.

What is the community of the faithful called? What story explains its traits?

New Thought is most broadly and accurately understood as a community of spiritual seekers. As such, there are many diverse expressions of religious and cultural identity within the movement. Common terms of self-identification for participants are *metaphysician,* meaning one who understands that the spiritual meaning of life transcends the physical realm; *Truth student,* meaning one who sees life as an ongoing study of idealistic religious teachings; and *New Thoughter,* meaning one who identifies with the movement in a denominational sense. More often than not, participants will identify themselves with their particular New Thought community, such as Religious Science, Unity, or Universal Foundation for Better Living. Under these and many other categories of identification, the community is made up of persons who have dedicated themselves to a religious way of life premised on the quest to discover the reality of Divine Mind and bring that reality into expression in their lives here and now.

The story that explains this religion of spiritual seeking is the story of overcoming difficulties through idealistic religious practices. As other religious traditions tell a story of religious growth and transcendence through narratives of time and space, history and geography, New Thought tells its story in narratives of individual healing and personal success. This master story has been told and retold in the personal narratives of countless New Thought followers over many generations and in numerous texts. Notably, biographies of founders of several New Thought groups include a version of the master story as it applies to their own lives.

There are three common features in the story. First is the realization that material conditions have no power over the individual, and through discovery of one's inner spiritual identity (which is one with the Supreme Reality) some specific difficulty can be eliminated. Second is the commitment to seek and discover this inner reality through the practice of idealistic religious rituals. Third, and finally, is the actual discovery itself, and with it elimination of the difficulty—the "demonstration," as it is often called. Early in the movement's history, demonstrations primarily concerned healing of bodily ills, but over the course of the twentieth century they came to include a host of other areas—professional achievement, personal relationships, financial well-being, improved living conditions, and so on. Above all, the New Thought participant aspires to a fuller and deeper experience of divinity. The demonstrations are secondary; it is divinity that is the goal for these spiritual seekers.

What is the way of life of the community of the faithful?

For many participants, New Thought is understood as a way of life rather than a religion. They also prefer "spirituality" to religion in characterizing their religious beliefs and practices. This is entirely acceptable in New Thought, since the community is predicated on the freedom of individuals in matters of belief. As noted previously, New Thought is a nondoctrinal movement. There are no creeds, no formal doctrines, and no canon of approved scriptures. Participants understand themselves as spiritual seekers, and the movement allows them the opportunity to pursue their quest for Truth without formal guidelines and strictures. As stated in the "Declaration of Principles" of the International New Thought Alliance: "We affirm the freedom of all persons as to beliefs, and we honor the diversity of humanity by being open and affirming of all persons, affirming the dignity of human beings as founded on the presence of God within them, and therefore, the principle of democracy."[3] It further states: "We affirm our evolving awareness of the nature of reality and our willingness to refine our beliefs accordingly."[4]

These statements are representative of the general stance of the movement in matters of personal religious practice. In short, the primary doctrine of New Thought is the denial of doctrine. Everyone is welcome since we are all spiritual beings, and beliefs are subject to change because we are all still evolving. Such a stance has led to loosely structured religious communities, with a fairly high turnover in membership, and a relatively weak commitment to the movement and its individual groups.

This being said, the various communities within New Thought are structured to allow for a high degree of personal freedom. Members are not obliged to attend religious services, participate in community events, share financial support, or recruit new members. The door is open to everyone: come if you like but do not feel that you must. Those who attend do so as a matter of personal commitment and very much in the spirit of spiritual seeking. It is very clear to them that they are not required to attend and there is no religious penalty for absences.

Although this concept of community may seem strange to those familiar with more traditional religions, it is not uncommon in the Metaphysical Movement as a whole, and it is a feature of many other new religions of the twentieth century. It is for good reason that Wade Clark Roof's study of religious tendencies of the baby-boom generation was titled *A Generation of Seekers*.[5] New Thought has particular appeal to this generation, but it has had such appeal to seekers of all generations from the dawn of the twentieth century.

This does not mean that New Thought communities are restless, anomic gatherings of uncommitted individuals—hardly. In fact, New Thought communities are organized very much like those in other traditions, most closely resembling those of Protestant Christianity, and the interest and commitment of participants is typically quite intense and focused. The key here is that those who do participate do so by free choice—not out of a sense of obligation, but from an abiding desire for spiritual growth.

New Thought congregations meet together on Sundays for religious services. Their meeting places are typically called "churches" and their services appear virtually the same as those of mainstream Protestant Christianity. Persons of all walks of life attend, and all are welcome. Families attend together, with adult and youth education programs being offered. A sermon is offered, congregational rituals are performed (prayer, meditation, and spiritual treatment), hymns are sung, an offering is received, and a benediction or closing statement is affirmed; and after the service attendees enjoy coffee and pastries, and perhaps a visit to the church bookstore. Of course, the theological content of the service is different from what one would find in a Protestant church, but often not too different, especially in the case of theologically liberal forms of Protestantism.

Secular holidays, such as New Year's, Fourth of July, and Martin Luther King Jr. Day, are recognized in most New Thought communities, often with Sunday services addressing themes related to the holiday in the context of New Thought beliefs. The movement generally follows mainstream Christianity with special services on Easter and Christmas-themed services through the month of December. Many New Thought groups have unique rituals reserved for Easter, Christmas, and New Year's Eve.

Familiar rituals of transition—marriages, funerals, and christenings—are a normal part of the New Thought community. Again, the theological language of the services will be reflective of New Thought beliefs, but the organizational structure of the services is quite similar to those of mainstream Protestantism. It is not uncommon for New Thought clerics to preside at transition services for individuals who have no religious affiliation or in situations where conflicting religious beliefs within families have made a more traditional service impossible.

In addition to congregational services, members of the New Thought community routinely engage in personal rituals to facilitate spiritual growth. Again, this is not a requirement, but a personal choice by the believer. The degree of commitment to such personal rituals varies, of course, just as it would in any other religious community. Some participants are extremely devout, others less so, and some hardly at all. Ritual practices typically involve transactions done in the mind of the believer, leading to a higher understanding of Divine Mind or the divine nature of the individual. The most common terms for such rituals are *prayer, meditation,* and *treatment* (e.g., prayer treatment, mental treatment, spiritual treatment). Rituals are often done to eliminate an undesired condition by realizing the reality of Divine Mind (the Good) and thus replace it with a more positive (more spiritual) condition. They can also be done to simply reacquaint oneself with the reality of Divine Mind.

Although no one is required to engage in personal rituals, most members of the community do so. Devout participants may engage in personal rituals on a daily basis, and even several times a day. Others may do so less frequently but on a routine schedule. Still others may do so only as a part of Sunday religious services or in times of crisis. In all instances, the purpose of the ritual is spiritual growth, even though a desire for a tangible improvement in life may be a precipitating cause.

What is the worldview of the community?

New Thought is an expression of *religious idealism,* a term mentioned briefly earlier in this chapter. As an idealistic system, New Thought's worldview is premised on the belief that the material-physical world is derived from and related to a higher spiritual realm. This spiritual realm is identified with various terms, most commonly *Mind* or *Divine Mind, Spirit,* and *Principle.* God is also used, but the understanding at work here is that the highest reality and ultimate power of the universe is an omnipresent mental-spiritual substance. New Thought specifically affirms that the physical-material world is an expression of this Divine Mind, which is ever active, ever creative, and the source of all good. Further, and perhaps most important, human beings participate in the creative expression of Divine Mind in and through their thoughts and mental states.

There is thus a direct relationship between one's consciousness (thoughts and mental states) and one's physical-material experiences. As a result, physical-material limitations (e.g., illness, poverty, aging, death) are attributed to thoughts of limitation or states of consciousness that accept the reality of such limitations. The source of these "error thoughts" or limited consciousness is "mortal mind." In contrast, constructive and healthy thoughts, or a positive consciousness, bring about positive conditions. The source of good thoughts and a positive consciousness is Divine Mind. Scripturally inclined New Thought clerics find support for this basic worldview in the Christian Bible, "metaphysically" interpreted, of course. A particularly apt passage is Romans 12:2: "Do not be conformed to this world, but be transformed by the renewing of your minds, so that

you may discern what is the will of God—what is good and acceptable and perfect."

For New Thought, this is how the world works, the foundational
basis of life itself. In short, all human experiences transpire through
a process of cause and effect (mental cause, physical effect). Mind is
primary and causative; negative (mortal) thoughts create negative
conditions, and positive (spiritual) thoughts create positive conditions. The mechanics through which this creative process transpires
is believed to be as precise as the laws of nature, and mastery of the
process is understood as a scientific undertaking. In a technical sense,
the movement refers to the process with terms such as "the Law of
Mind Action" or "Mind in Action."

Although New Thought actively promotes its idealistic worldview
as the truth, it also celebrates the freedom of all persons in matters
of belief. Its doors are open to everyone, and individuals are free to
accept or reject its teachings. Members are under no obligation to
personally promote the movement's beliefs. In point of fact, most do
not. Remember, this is a religion for spiritual seekers, predicated on
healing; it is a system designed to assist and inspire people in their
religious quest. Rather than advancing its beliefs as an ultimate revelation of religious truth or claiming singular access to divinity, New
Thought is more commonly presented as a practical system for living a fuller, richer life. Its teachings are essentially conditional in
nature, "if . . . then" propositions. If you desire a better job, then try
this spiritual exercise. If you seek healing, then this prayer technique
may be effective. If you are unhappy, then make an effort to establish these divine ideas in your consciousness. The goal is always to
come to a higher, clearer awareness of Divine Mind and one's own
spiritual identity, but this is never a demand.

In this regard, the movement is generally accepting of other religious traditions, affirming that Truth can be found in all religions
and rejecting only religious activities that are condemnatory or
aggressive in word or deed. In time, all people will discover the reality of Divine Mind and the idealistic basis of the universe. Ultimately,
there is no competition between religions, only a process of spiritual
evolution.

Consistent with its nondogmatic, idealistic religious posture, the
movement as a whole is best characterized as egalitarian. From its
origins to the present, women have played a prominent role in New

Thought. Its founder, Emma Curtis Hopkins, was the first woman to ordain women into the Christian ministry, and since that time New Thought's various subgroups have always offered leadership opportunities to women, sanctioning them as ecclesiastical officials of every rank—from ministers, teachers, and practitioners to regional and national leadership offices. Hopkins was also a social activist, but this dimension of New Thought never fully developed, and over time New Thought groups have become progressively less involved in debates about major social and political issues. Rather than taking public stands on such issues, New Thought groups typically support individual choice, allowing participants to reach their own conclusions and take whatever action they deem appropriate. Of course, individuals would be encouraged to seek inner guidance and act in harmony with Divine Mind.

How does this religion function in the world today?

When New Thought emerged, Theosophy and Christian Science largely defined the Metaphysical Movement. Today, it contains a vast and exceptionally diverse array of religious beliefs and practices. It has also gained a high degree of cultural acceptance. Once considered mysterious and marginal, today metaphysical religion has become defined in the popular imagination by best-selling spiritual self-help books; blockbuster movies based on its worldview; and, perhaps most prominently, New Age teachings, celebrity representatives, and numerous religious communities. In the midst of this now crowded religious terrain, New Thought remains significant in terms of both its success and its longevity. Theosophy and Christian Science are still around, but they are not as large or as well known as they once were. New Thought, however, continues to grow in both size and cultural awareness.

Despite its unquestionable success, New Thought faces a number of significant challenges. The challenges are both internal and external, but both types are predicated on the movement's relationship with culture. The external challenges and New Thought's response are the most illustrative of the movement's general cultural stance and the ways in which religion and culture have changed since the early twentieth century.

As noted above, when New Thought came on the scene, it was a new addition to the Metaphysical Movement, which at the time was defined largely by Theosophy and Christian Science. It was bold, fresh, and very much in tune with the changing culture of the times. By midcentury it was expanding rather briskly while the earlier groups were beginning to contract. Around this same time, however, American culture again began undergoing significant changes. Notably, these changes brought with them another wave of new religions, religions that challenged the status quo of American religious culture just as New Thought had done half a century before. Fueled by the countercultural inclinations of the baby-boom generation, the last half of the twentieth century witnessed an eruption of religious enthusiasm that William McLoughlin characterized as America's "Fourth Great Awakening."[6] Earlier new religions that had been largely dormant suddenly began to grow, perhaps most notably Pentecostalism. With the rescission of the Oriental Exclusion Act (in 1965), new religions from other parts of the world entered American culture, with the International Society for Krishna Consciousness becoming one of the better-known groups. Finally, the Metaphysical Movement experienced a revival of its own under the banner of "New Age."

Today, American seekers enthusiastically embrace these and many other new religions. New Thought, one of the original seeker religions, has also continued to attract new followers, but it now has considerably more competition than it had prior to the 1950s. It is certainly less socially dynamic than some of its newer rivals and clearly less doctrinally coherent than others. Moreover, a number of the teachings and principles it had long promoted (the innate divinity of humanity, spiritual healing, and so on) have been appropriated by the newer religions—many of which are decidedly evangelical, which New Thought most certainly is not.

New Thought has not formally and systematically addressed the external challenges posed by other new religions. Instead, it has continued in its traditional practice of affirming the good in all religious traditions while embracing the notion of personal freedom in matters of religious belief. This approach has proved to be successful, and the movement has continued to flourish. There is, after all, an abundance of spiritual seekers in contemporary culture and plenty who find in New Thought's practical religious idealism and commitment to spiritual freedom just what they are seeking. As with all new religions, the future success of New Thought is by no means certain. What is certain, however, is that as it enters its second century of life, New Thought stands as the largest and most identifiable branch of the Metaphysical Movement and the most successful form of religious idealism in the contemporary world, if not in the history of the world.

At a Glance

Classic Texts

The Science of Mind: the foundational text of Religious Science, written by its founder, Ernest Holmes

Christian Healing: the first book by the cofounder of Unity, Charles Fillmore, presenting the movement's idealistic worldview and instructions on religious practices

Lessons in Truth: the longest continually published New Thought text; offers systematic instruction on the idealistic healing methods

The Metaphysical Bible Dictionary: a lexicon of biblical words and terms and their "metaphysical" (symbolic) meanings

"Declaration of Principles" (International New Thought Alliance): perhaps the best brief summary of New Thought beliefs

Important Figures

Mary Baker Eddy: founder of Christian Science

Helena Petrovana Blavatsky: most important of the founders of Theosophy

Emma Curtis Hopkins: founder of New Thought

Ernest Holmes: founder of Religious Science

Charles Fillmore: cofounder (with his wife, Myrtle Fillmore) of Unity

Characteristic Beliefs

Divine Mind

The divinity of humanity and the causative nature of consciousness

Freedom of individuals in matters of religious belief and practice

Idealism

Law of Mind Action

Monism

Essential Creeds or Codes of Conduct

"What We Believe: Declaration of Principles"(International New Thought Alliance)

"What We Believe" (Unity)

"What We Believe" (United Centers for Spiritual Living/Religious Science)

Brief Time Line

1889	First ministers ordained by Emma Curtis Hopkins; Unity movement begins
1898	Divine Science incorporated
1899	First New Thought convention
1903	Unity (Society for Practical Christianity) incorporated
1914	International New Thought Alliance founded
1926	*Science of Mind* published
1927	Institute of Religious Science incorporated
1930	Seicho-no-Ie founded
1954	Religious Science International separates from United Church of Religious Science
1966	Association of Unity Churches formed
1974	Universal Foundation for Better Living incorporated
1980s	Emergence of the New Age movement

Important Symbols

New Thought has no distinctive symbols, although for most of the twentieth century Unity's winged globe (similar to the Steak 'n Shake logo) was widely reproduced by that movement. It is no longer used today.

Important Rituals

Meditation: mental focus on a religious concept, "divine idea," or desired outcome; practiced individually or collectively; a common ritual during congregational church services, when religious professionals often lead "guided meditations"; often a preface to prayer

Prayer: conscious engagement with Divine Mind; the realization of one's inner divinity; full appropriation of divine ideas and recognition that they are being carried forward into physical manifestation; may be done individually or collectively; standard prayers are spoken aloud collectively in congregational settings

Reading: reading spiritual texts and even short statements with keen focus, dwelling on the words and ideas, and seeking to understand the spiritual reality they disclose; often a preface to meditation and prayer

Spiritual Treatment: a specific mental-spiritual transaction carried out for a particular end; often performed by a religious professional at request of others, it typically seeks to overcome a specific limitation or achieve a specific demonstration; also called "Prayer Treatment" or "Spiritual Mind Treatment"

Glossary

demonstration	Achieving a desired result through the right use of idealistic religious principles, often

	including the elimination of an undesired condition or situation.
Divine Mind	Commonly used term for Supreme Reality in New Thought, believed to be the omnipresent creative principle. Numerous other terms for Supreme Reality are used, including *Truth, Principle, Universal Mind, Spirit, the Good,* and *God.*
idealism	Worldview in which Supreme Reality is believed to be nonmaterial (mental or spiritual), with the material-physical world being a subordinate reality.
Law of Mind Action	General term for the process through which human consciousness directly influences the physical-material world.
Monism	Concept of Supreme Reality that affirms the sacred is a universally present principle or substance.
Metaphysical Movement	Widely diverse collection of twentieth-century religious groups, which share a monistic worldview, belief in the divinity of humanity, and seek to guide seekers in their spiritual development.
New Thought	Idealistic religious movement, and largest and most representative branch of the Metaphysical Movement.
omnipresent	Everywhere present; used in reference to Supreme Reality (God).
omnibenevolent	All-good or all-loving; used in reference to Supreme Reality (God).

Sacred Spaces and Times

As with symbols, New Thought is largely bereft of sacred spaces and times. As an idealistic movement, specific physical locales, dates, and times tend not to be imbued with heightened religious significance. This being said, locations of historical significance to branches of the movement may possess special religious meaning for some followers. Two notable locations are the First Divine Science Church in Denver, Colorado, and Unity Village, just outside of Kansas City, Missouri. The distinctive tower (often mistakenly referred to as a "prayer tower") at Unity Village is the most well-known structure in the movement. Annual conventions or conferences of the various groups may be treated as times of greater religious importance than others but not sacralized as would be holy days in more traditional religions. A cultural holiday that may come closest to functioning as a sacred time in New Thought is New Year's Eve, when many New Thought communities engage in collective rituals of renewal.

Suggestions for Further Reading
(a) Religion in America
Albanese, Catherine. *America Religions and Religion*. 4th ed. Belmont, Calif.: Thomson/Wadsworth, 2007.

Butler, Jon. *Awash in a Sea of Faith*. Cambridge, Mass.: Harvard University Press, 1990.

Eck, Diana L. *A New Religious America*. New York: HarperCollins, 2001.

McLoughlin, William G. *Revivals, Awakenings, and Reform*. Chicago: University of Chicago Press, 1978.

(b) New Religions
Clarke, Peter B., ed. *Encyclopedia of New Religious Movements*. New York: Routledge, 2006.

Ellwood, Robert S., and Harry B. Partin. *Religious and Spiritual Groups in Modern America*. Englewood Cliffs, N.J.: Prentice Hall, 1988.

Hunt, Stephen J. *Alternative Religions: A Sociological Introduction*. Burlington, Vt.: Ashgate, 2003.

Lewis, James R., ed. *The Encyclopedia of Cults, Sects, and New Religions*. Amherst, N.Y.: Prometheus Books, 2002.

(c) The Metaphysical Movement
Albanese, Catherine L. *A Republic of Mind and Spirit*. New Haven, Conn.: Yale University Press, 2007.

Judah, J. Stillson. *The History and Philosophy of the Metaphysical Movements in America*. Philadelphia: Westminster Press, 1967.

(d) New Thought
Braden, Charles S. *Spirits in Rebellion: The Rise and Development of New Thought*. Dallas: Southern Methodist University Press, 1963.

Harley, Gail M. *Emma Curtis Hopkins: Forgotten Founder of New Thought*. Syracuse, N.Y.: Syracuse University Press, 2002.

Satter, Beryl. *Each Mind a Kingdom: American Women, Sexual Purity, and the New Thought Movement, 1875–1920*. Berkeley: University of California Press, 1999.

CONTRIBUTORS

Mark L. Blum is Assistant Professor at the University of Albany in Albany, New York.

Douglas Brooks is Professor of Religion at the University of Rochester in Rochester, New York.

Bruce Chilton is Bernard Iddings Bell Professor of Religion, Chaplain of the College, and Executive Director of the Institute of Advanced Theology at Bard College in Annandale-on-Hudson, New York.

Mark A. Csikszentmihalyi is Professor at the University of California in Berkeley, California.

Lawrence S. Cunningham is Professor, The Rev. John A. O'Brien Chair in Theology, at Notre Dame University in Notre Dame, Indiana.

Dell deChant is Instructor and Director of Undergraduate Studies, Department of Religious Studies, at the University of South Florida in Tampa, Florida.

Jualynne E. Dodson is Professor at Michigan State University in East Lansing, Michigan.

James L. Ford is Associate Professor, East Asian Religions, at Wake Forest University, Winston Salem, North Carolina.

William Scott Green is Senior Vice Provost and Dean of Undergraduate Education, and Professor in the George Feldenkreis Program in Judaic Studies at the University of Miami in Coral Gables, Florida.

Th. Emil Homerin is Professor of Religion at the University of Rochester in Rochester, New York.

Sonya Maria Johnson is a dual PhD candidate in the Department of Anthropology and African American and African Studies at Michigan State University in East Lansing, Michigan.

Danny L. Jorgensen is Professor at the University of South Florida in Tampa, Florida.

Baruch A. Levine is Professor Emeritus at New York University in New York.

Martin E. Marty is Fairfax M. Cone Distinguished Service Professor Emeritus of the History of Modern Christianity in the Divinity School, the Committee on the History of Culture, at the University of Chicago in Chicago, Illinois.

J. A. McGuckin is Nielsen Professor of Late Antique and Byzantine Christian History at Union Theological Seminary in New York.

Mark Meulenbeld is Assistant Professor at the University of Wisconsin, Madison, in Madison, Wisconsin.

Jacob Neusner is Distinguished Service Professor of the History and Theology of Judaism, and Senior Fellow, Institute of Advanced Theology, at Bard College in Annandale-on-Hudson, New York.

Jacob Olupona is Professor of African and African American Studies and Professor of African Religious Traditions, Chair of Committee on African Studies, at Harvard University, Cambridge, Massachusetts.

Mario Poceski is Associate Professor at the University of Florida in Gainesville, Florida.

Kristin Scheible is Assistant Professor of Religion at Bard College in Annandale-on-Hudson, New York.

Liyakat Takim is Associate Professor at the University of Denver in Denver, Colorado.

NOTES

Introduction

1. Richard Dawkins, *The God Delusion* (Boston: Houghton Mifflin, 2006).
2. David Sloan Wilson, *Darwin's Cathedral: Evolution, Religion, and the Nature of Society* (Chicago: University of Chicago Press, 2002).
3. Timothy Samuel Shah and Monica Duffy Toft, "God Is Winning: Religion in Global Politics," in *Blind Spot: When Journalists Don't Get Religion,* ed. Paul Marshall, Lela Gilbert, and Roberta Green Ahmanson (New York: Oxford University Press, 2009), 11–28.
4. Ibid., 14.
5. Ibid., 15.
6. Ibid.
7. Ibid.
8. Ibid., 19.
9. Ibid.
10. Ibid., 22–23.
11. Ibid., 24.
12. Ibid., 25.
13. Ibid., 14.
14. For an earlier discussion of religion as a native category, see William Scott Green, "Religion and Society in America," in *World Religions in America,* ed. Jacob Neusner (Louisville: Westminster John Knox Press, 2000), 246–53.
15. Melford E. Spiro, "Religion: Problems of Definition and Explanation," in *Culture and Human Nature: Theoretical Papers of Melford E. Spiro,* ed. Benjamin Kilborne and L. L. Langness (Chicago: University of Chicago Press, 1987), 187–222.
16. Ibid., 197.
17. Ibid.
18. Professor Rahuldeep Singh Gill.
19. Professor Karen Ruffle notes that this applies particularly among the Sunni sect of Islam where male head-covering during worship is regarded as an imitation of the behavior of Muhammad himself.
20. I am grateful to Professor Karen Ruffle for this reference.
21. The examples are not distributed equally among these traditions. Their purpose is to be suggestive rather than definitive.
22. *The Holy Qur'an,* trans. Abdullah Yusuf Ali (Miami: AMANA, 2003), 417.
23. Raimundo Panikkar, *The Vedic Experience: Mantramanjari: An Anthology of the Vedas for Modern Man and Contemporary Celebration* (Berkeley: University of California Press, 1977).
24. See Jacob Neusner and Bruce Chilton, eds., *Altruism in World Religions* (Washington, D.C.: Georgetown University Press, 2005).
25. I owe this illustration to my colleague Karen Ruffle.

347

26. For an elegant discussion of religion as a "unifying system" from an evolutionary perspective, see Wilson, *Darwin's Cathedral,* chapter 7.

27. What is here called "system" also could be called "structure." See Jeppe Sinding Jensen, "Structure," in *Guide to the Study of Religion,* ed. Willi Braun and Russell T. McCutcheon (New York: Cassell, 2000), 314–33.

28. I thank my colleague Michelle Gonzalez Maldonado for suggesting this reference.

29. As Spiro notes, "Although the differentiating characteristic of religion is the belief in superhuman beings, it does not follow...that these beings are necessarily objects of ultimate concern." Spiro, "Religion: Problems of Definition and Explanation," 196.

30. Peter L. Berger, *The Sacred Canopy: Elements of a Sociological Theory of Religion* (New York: Anchor Books, 1967), 28.

31. The study of religion is by nature a collaborative exercise. I have benefited from the help of Natania Widensky, Emily Packard, Alex Kurtz, and Ethan Green, who read the chapter from a student's perspective and offered many useful comments. My colleagues Michelle Gonzalez Maldonado, Karen Ruffle, Douglas Brooks, and Rahuldeep Singh Gill advised me on the use of materials from Christianity, Islam, Hinduism and Buddhism, and Sikhism, respectively, and Glenn Starkman set me straight about science and empiricism. As ever, Jacob Neusner was a supportive, understanding, and most patient editor.

Judaism: The Formation

1. The fringes are today attached to the prayer shawl worn at morning services by Conservative and some Reform Jews, and perpetually worn on a separate undergarment for that purpose by Orthodox Jews. The fringes remind the Jew of all the commandments of the Lord.

2. Italics signify Aramaic in the original. The Talmud is a bilingual document, in Hebrew and in Aramaic. The Golden Rule is formulated in Aramaic for its ethical version and in Hebrew for its theological statement.

Judaism in Modern Times

1. The Pittsburgh Platform (November 16–19, 1885). http://www.jewishvirtual library.org/jsource/Judaism/pittsburgh_program.html.

2. Arthur Hertzberg, "Conservative Judaism," *Encyclopedia Judaica* (Philadelphia: Coronet, 1994): 5:901–6.

Islam: Beginnings

1. Al-Bukhari, *Sahih al-Bukhari,* ed. Muhammad Muhsin Khan (Mecca: Dar al-Fikr, n.d.), 2:187 (al-Jana'iz: 2:331), my translation.

Buddhism: The Theravada Tradition

1. All Buddhist terms herein appear in their Pali form, the language of the canon—the commentarial, monastic, and historical texts of Theravada Buddhism. In Sanskrit he is known as Siddhartha Gautama. Likewise kamma/karma, dhamma/dharma, nibbana/nirvana, and so forth.

Shinto

1. The Chinese/Japanese character for *kami* is also alternatively pronounced "shin," thus the rendering *Shinto* instead of *Kamito*.

2. *Numen,* meaning "presence," is a Latin term for a divine power or spirit that is believed to inhabit a particular object or place in Roman religion.

New Twentieth-century American Religions

1. J. Stillson Judah, *The History and Philosophy of the Metaphysical Movements in America* (Philadelphia: Westminster Press, 1967), and Catherine L. Albanese, *A Republic of Mind and Spirit* (New Haven, Conn.: Yale University Press, 2007).

2. See statement on the Bible in document "What We Believe," at website *What Is Unity?* http://www.unity.org/aboutunity/index.html.

3. Fifth Declaration in "What We Believe: INTA's Declaration of Principles, Revised 2000," *New Thought* 92, no. 1 (spring 2008): 19.

4. Tenth Declaration, ibid.

5. Wade Clark Roof, *A Generation of Seekers: The Religion of the Baby Boom Generation* (San Francisco: HarperSanFrancisco, 1993).

6. McLoughlin specifies four "Great Awakenings," with the fourth beginning in 1960. See William G. McLoughlin, *Revivals, Awakenings, and Reform* (Chicago: University of Chicago Press, 1978).